Masters of
Meditation and Miracles

CVG

Masters of Meditation and Miracles

Lives of the Great Buddhist Masters of India and Tibet

TULKU THONDUP

Edited by Harold Talbott

SHAMBHALA
Boston & London
1999

SHAMBHALA PUBLICATIONS, INC.
HORTICULTURAL HALL
300 MASSACHUSETTS AVENUE
BOSTON, MASSACHUSETTS 02115
WWW.SHAMBHALA.COM

BUDDHAYANA SERIES: VI

9 8 7 6 5 4 3 2 1

FIRST PAPERBACK EDITION

PRINTED IN THE UNITED STATES OF AMERICA

♾ THIS EDITION IS PRINTED ON ACID-FREE PAPER THAT MEETS THE AMERICAN NATIONAL STANDARDS INSTITUTE Z39.48 STANDARD.

DISTRIBUTED IN THE UNITED STATES BY RANDOM HOUSE, INC., AND IN CANADA BY RANDOM HOUSE OF CANADA LTD

THE LIBRARY OF CONGRESS CATALOGS THE HARDCOVER EDITION OF THIS BOOK AS FOLLOWS:

THONDUP, TULKU.
MASTERS OF MEDITATION AND MIRACLES:
LIVES OF THE GREAT BUDDHIST MASTERS OF INDIA AND TIBET /
TULKU THONDUP: EDITED BY HAROLD TALBOTT.
— 1ST ED. P. CM. ISBN 1-57062-113-6 (ALK. PAPER)
ISBN 1-57062-509-3 (PBK.)
1. RÑIṄ-MA-PA LAMAS—CHINA—TIBET—BIOGRAPHY.
2. MEDITATION—RÑIṄ-MA-PA (SECT)
I. TALBOTT, HAROLD. II. TITLE.
BQ7662.A23T48 1995 95-15854
294.3′923′092—DC20 [B] CIP

Contents

ACKNOWLEDGMENTS ix
AUTHOR'S NOTE xi
PREFACE xiii

Part One
INTRODUCTION

SHĀKYAMUNI BUDDHA 4
After the Buddha 11
BUDDHISM IN TIBET 13
THREE MODES OF LINEAL TRANSMISSION OF THE GENERAL NYINGMA INNER TANTRAS 18
Mind Transmission of the Buddhas 18
Symbolic Transmission of the Knowledge-holders 19
Oral Transmission of the Ascetics 22
LINEAGES OF THREE MAJOR NYINGMA INNER TANTRAS 23
Mahāyoga 23
Anuyoga 28
Atiyoga (Dzogpa Chenpo) 29
Semde 30
Longde 31
Me-ngagde 32

Part Two
THE LINEAGE OF LONGCHEN NYINGTHIG

LONGCHEN NYINGTHIG TEACHINGS 43
THE LINEAGE MASTERS OF LONGCHEN NYINGTHIG 46
1. Dharmakāya 48
2. Sambhogakāya 51

3. Nirmāṇakāya 53
4. Prahevajra (Garab Dorje) 55
5. Mañjushrīmitra 59
6. Shrīsiṃha 62
7. Jñānasūtra 65
8. Vimalamitra 68
9. Guru Rinpoche, Padmasambhava 74
Guru Rinpoche's Visit to Tibet 83
The Five Principal Consorts of Guru Rinpoche 92
The Chief Disciples of Guru Rinpoche in Tibet 96
10. Künkhyen Longchen Rabjam (1308–1363) 109
11. Rigdzin Jigme Lingpa (1730–1798) 118
12. First Dodrupchen Jigme Thrinle Özer (1745–1821) 136
13. Jigme Gyalwe Nyuku (1765–1843) 163
14. Dola Jigme Kalzang (nineteenth century) 173
15. Fourth Dzogchen Mingyur Namkhe Dorje (1793–?) 175
16. Do Khyentse Yeshe Dorje (1800–1866) 179
17. Gyalse Zhenphen Thaye (1800–?) 198
18. Dzogchen Khenpo Pema Dorje (nineteenth century) 200
19. Paltrül Jigme Chökyi Wangpo (1808–1887) 201
20. Second Dodrupchen Jigme Phüntsok Jungne (1824–1863) 211
21. Jamyang Khyentse Wangpo (1820–1892) 215
22. Nyoshül Lungtok Tenpe Nyima (1829–1901/2) 222
23. Önpo Tendzin Norbu (nineteenth century) 226
24. Adzom Drukpa Drodül Pawo Dorje (1842–1924) 228
25. Lushül Khenpo Könchok Drönme (1859–1936) 230
26. Third Dodrupchen Jigme Tenpe Nyima (1865–1926) 237
27. Shuksep Lochen Chönyi Zangmo (1865–1953) 251
28. Fifth Dzogchen Thupten Chökyi Dorje (1872–1935) 256
29. Gekong Khenpo Künzang Palden (1872–1943) 258
30. Yukhok Chatralwa Chöying Rangtröl (1872–1952) 260
31. Kathok Khenpo Ngawang Palzang (1879–1941) 266
32. Alak Zenkar Pema Ngödrup Rölwe Dorje (1881–1943) 275
33. Dzongsar Khyentse Chökyi Lodrö (1893–1959) 278

34. Kyala Khenpo Chechok Thöndrup (1893–1957) 283
35. Dilgo Khyentse Tashi Paljor (1910–1991) 292
36. Chatral Sangye Dorje (b. 1913) 296
37. Fourth Dodrupchen Rigdzin Tenpe Gyaltsen (1927–1961) 298
38. Fourth Dodrupchen Thupten Thrinle Palzang (b. 1927) 314

LINEAGE TREE 333
WORKS CITED 351
NOTES 359
INDEX 379
CREDITS 384

Acknowledgments

MY gratitude is due to Harold Talbott for his wisdom and patience in editing this book with great care and appreciation; Michael Baldwin for his never ceasing support and guidance of my Dharma projects for over one and a half decades; Lydia Segal for inspiring me to put this book together and checking many parts of the book; the patrons of Buddhayana, under whose sponsorship I have been able to spend the days of my life writing and translating the precious Buddhist teachings since 1975; David Dvore for computering assistance; Jonathan and Joan Miller for taking care of my health; the private Library of Kyabje Dodrupchen Rinpoche at the Mahasiddha Nyingmapa Temple, Hawley, Massachusetts, and the Lehman Library at Columbia University, New York City, for their precious resources; Victor and Ruby Lam for allowing me to use their easeful apartment.

I am grateful to Steven Goodman for his many insightful contributions and for preparing the index. I am also thankful to Zenkar Thupten Nyima Rinpoche, Khenpo Chöyag, Gelong Konchog Tendzin, Ani Ngawang Chödron, Ani Lodrö Palmo, and many others who provided much valuable information.

I am grateful to master Samuel Bercholz and the staff of Shambhala Publications for providing the perfect channel for the lives of the Masters to reach the readers, to Larry Mermelstein for refining the book with his great editorial mastery, to Kendra Crossen for infusing the book with her literary insight, and to Brian Boland for designing the book with artistic talent.

Author's Note

I HAVE capitalized the root letters (Ming gZhi) of each word in the transliterated Tibetan in order to ensure a correct and easy reading. For the phonetic transcription of Tibetan, I mainly followed the Nālandā Translation Committee guidelines provided by Larry Mermelstein.

Throughout the book I have added words in parentheses to make the meaning of the quoted texts clear or to provide their Sanskrit, Tibetan, or English equivalents. I have also provided a number of alternative translations or synonyms in square brackets.

In the bibliography, *f* stands for "folio," the Tibetan style of pagination; and *p* for "page" according to the Western style.

In the notes, the titles of texts quoted are indicated by abbreviations, such as BC for *sNying Thig Gi brGyud 'Debs Byin rLabs Ch'ar rGyun* discovered by Jigme Lingpa. The full titles are alphabetically listed in "Works Cited" at the end of this book. When a text in the Tibetan pagination style is quoted, the letters signifying the title are followed by the folio number, which is followed by the letter *a* or *b* to designate the front or back side of the folio. This is then followed by the line number. For example, "BC 1a/1." Page and line numbers without the letter *a* or *b* indicate the Western style of pagination.

Preface

Masters of Meditation and Miracles is a collection of biographies of realized teachers whose lives were full of peace, enlightenment, and amazing miracles. They flourished in Tibet, the Roof of the World, in its golden days. These teachers belong to the *Longchen Nyingthig* lineage of the Nyingma school of Tibetan Buddhism.

Longchen Nyingthig (the heart-essence of infinite expanse, or the ultimate truth of the universal openness) is a cycle of mystical teachings that represent the innermost meditation of Dzogpa Chenpo, revealed by the great scholar and adept Jigme Lingpa (1730–1798). Jigme Lingpa discovered them as a "mind ter" (or "mind treasure"), teachings that were discovered from the enlightened nature of the mind. To Jigme Lingpa and then from him to the present, the transmission of *Longchen Nyingthig* was passed through the lineage of many enlightened masters, the most outstanding being the ones whose lives are presented in this book.

In the past, when I read the biographies that I have epitomized here, I saw them as most inspiring and amazing lives. But this time, as I was retelling them in my own words with my own feelings, I myself frequently underwent the experiences of pain, hardship, or excitement as well as peace, joy, light, or openness that the masters were going through. So the lives were no longer just stories to read or objects "out there" to think about. They were glimpses of the inner light of the masters, which is the "true nature" of the enlightened lives. In that "true nature," all the different phases and expressions of lives are in communion, like rivers flowing into the ocean, a single body of water. If these biographies are read as stories with intellectual and emotional perceptions, the best possible benefit that could come is inspiration. If the lives are read in order to feel and unite with the experiences of the masters, the stories will certainly arouse spiritual realization, love, peace, openness, light, and healing in the reader's heart.

It was improper and indeed impossible for me to try to avoid the typical characteristic of Tibetan biographies, namely the inclusion of endless lists of teachers, teachings, and disciples of the masters, even though those lists might be boring for readers who are not Tibetan. But I tried not to let these details diminish the vividness of the narrative. Wherever possible, I attempted to bring out the inner feelings of the spiritual lives, and at the same time the external daily lives, of the masters: how they faced and healed their physical pain, how they dealt with their emotional turmoil, how they overcame their spiritual or meditative illusions, and, more important, what kind of experiences they had when they awakened their own inner Buddha Mind and Buddha qualities.

This book has two parts. The first is an introduction providing a short life of the Buddha and a list of major lineages of Buddhism in Tibet. While basing the Buddha's life on traditional scriptures, I have tried to present it in terms of its meaning and his teachings rather than as a historical narrative. For the list of lineages of Buddhism in Tibet, I have given a structural outline of some of the major ones, but few details of them or their teachings.

The second part is the main body of the book. It presents the principle of the three Buddha bodies and the biographies of thirty-five masters of the Longchen Nyingthig lineage.

The three Buddha bodies are Dharmakāya, the ultimate body, which is the total openness, the absolute nature of the Buddha; Sambhogakāya, the enjoyment body, which designates all the true Buddha forms that appear without subject-object duality; and Nirmāṇakāya, the manifested body, which is the forms of the Buddha perceived by ordinary beings. The three Buddha bodies are the sources of the ultimate teachings, such as Longchen Nyingthig.

The first master of the Longchen Nyingthig lineage in human form is Prahevajra (also known as Garab Dorje). The lives of the early human masters from Prahevajra down to Guru Rinpoche (9th century CE) have a unique quality. They were manifested as a higher power of discipline and attainments, possessing superhuman endowments and power. From Longchen Rabjam on, although the lives of these later masters reflect a path, dedication, and power different from our own, still they had many experiences that are similar to our own hardships, pain, and emotions, and we can imagine ourselves reaching the point when we would possess their capacity for dedication, healing, and realizations. Thus, the lives of the early masters are the most important ones, but for many readers the lives of the later masters might be easier to understand and empathize with.

It seems that there are two reasons for having these two types of biographies. Changes in the art of writing account for some of the differences between the accounts of early and later masters. But the main reason is the change of circumstances and gifts of the audience and their level of openness and appreciation.

Among the lives of the later masters, too, there are many, such as Do Khyentse, who were born with amazing wisdom and power, while others, such as the First Dodrupchen and Jigme Gyalwe Nyuku, accomplished the highest spiritual attainments through disciplines of austerity and dedication. Many masters often faced harsh obstructions in their spiritual journey, but the power of their understanding, commitment, and inspiration not only kept them on the path, but led them to their goals.

The Longchen Nyingthig transmission flowed through many masters of various lineages. In this book I was able to include only the main masters of the Longchen Nyingthig lineage itself and those masters who were directly involved in bringing the Longchen Nyingthig transmission to my teachers and then on to me.

Concerning the lives of many masters there is a vast literature, but for some important masters, Dola Jigme Kalzang, Gyalse Zhenphen Thaye, Khenpo Pema Dorje, the Second Dodrupchen, and Önpo Tendzin Norbu, I could find very little material. Also, I focused more on those masters about whom there is little material in English rather than on masters whose lives are already available in English.

The masters whose lives are chronicled in this book are some of the many rare individuals whom we had in Tibet during its more than ten-century-long history of Buddhism. One should not, however, get the impression that most of the Tibetans were great meditators and accomplished adepts displaying miraculous powers, as the novel *Lost Horizon* might portray! Such accomplished masters were very rare in Tibet in comparison with the population as a whole. At the same time, there is no reason to doubt that they were people of great spiritual power and realization. Where the circumstances were right and there was total dedication to the advancement of the spiritual quality of the mind rather than to material progress, such spiritual attainments were witnessed not just in Tibetan civilization, but in many cultures throughout the history of the world during the golden times of their spiritual wealth.

For me the material in this book was the most inspiring that I have ever worked on. Each master is totally different, yet they are very similar. Each great master has his or her own unique character to manifest, role to play, and place to fill in this golden lineage of Longchen Nyingthig. Most of these great masters have gone, disappeared into the distant past. But their presence in the golden lineage, their words of enlightening teachings, and their power of liberating blessings are still with us.

Part One

Introduction

BUDDHA is the universal truth, and Buddhism is the path to realize it. Buddha is the true nature, the openness, and the enlightened state of the universe, "as it is." All the phenomenal appearances are just the manifestative power of that true nature itself, "as they appear." If we realize our own true nature, the ultimate peace, openness, oneness, and enlightenment, we are all Buddhas. Then all phenomena will spontaneously arise as the Buddha pure land, the power of the true nature.

Buddhism is the stages of the path to realize Buddhahood, and it is the teachings that inspire us to that realization.

Shākyamuni Buddha (fifth–fourth century BCE)[1] is one of the many beings who became Buddha through the path of Buddhism in this age of ours. He is the master who propagated the path popularly known as Buddhism. But he is not the only Buddha, and Buddhism is not limited to his words alone.

Tantras are the original esoteric scriptures of Buddhism. They include many Nyingma tantras, such as the tantras of the *Longchen Nyingthig* cycle. These are not necessarily the written records of words uttered by the Shākyamuni Buddha. However, they are Buddhist teachings since they came from the Buddha bodies, and they provide the methods that lead us to Buddhahood. Furthermore, they were discovered by the realized followers of Shākyamuni Buddha and are in harmony with his teachings.

Shākyamuni Buddha

SHĀKYAMUNI Buddha, the Fully Awakened One, was born amid wondrous signs over twenty-five centuries ago, in the Lumbinī garden, now in Nepal, to King Shuddhodana and Queen Māyādevī of the Shākya lineage. He was named Siddhārtha, and he soon became versed in various kinds of knowledge and skilled in different arts in order to become the future ruler of his kingdom. In time, his consort Princess Yashodharā conceived their son, Prince Rāhula.

Prince Siddhārtha lived amid the supreme enjoyments of worldly pleasures and luxuries that could be provided in his time. His father even tried to prevent him from seeing or learning about people's miseries. But Siddhārtha realized that in this mundane world no one has any true joy and there is nothing but suffering, the overwhelming suffering of old age, sickness, death, and endless woes. Whatever is born ends in death, whatever is brought together ends in separation, and whatever is full of joy ends in pain. All the mundane activities, directly or indirectly, cause only suffering of dissatisfaction. All these sufferings are rooted in the wrong mental approach of grasping at "self,"[2] burning with negative emotions of hatred and desire, and craving for painful joy, as when yearning for the sensation of scratching an itch. Siddhārtha was determined to find the way to freedom from the life cycle of suffering and to lead others, the mother beings, to the realization of freedom and enlightenment.

When he was twenty-nine, after his father reluctantly gave him permission to renounce his mundane life, he became a homeless ascetic wanderer. He went to a number of famous sages of India and meditated according to their teachings. He contemplated while observing severe austerities for six years on the banks of the Nairajñanā River. These pursuits generated high stages of absorption, peace, and joy, but none led him to the ultimate goal he was seeking: total freedom from grasping at self, for all those attainments retained some degree of residue of grasping at self.

At the age of thirty-five, after realizing that physical austerity was not an effective means of reaching the truth, Siddhārtha drank some refined milk. Having nourished himself, he went to Vajrāsana, now known as Bodhgayā in the state of Bihar, India. There, on the eve of the full moon of the Vaishākha month (April/May), he sat in the meditation posture beneath a pipal *(ashvattha)* tree (known since then as the Bodhi Tree) and entered into absorption.

After dusk, demonic forces massed before him with threats and temptations to prevent him from entering enlightenment. Clouds of demonic forces thundering threats and raining of weapons appeared. Celestial virgins came dancing to him to arouse his senses. But none moved his mind, and he remained in the contemplation of loving-kindness. The rain of weapons became the rain of flowers, and all the apparitions faded away like a mirage.

Then, in the early part of the night,[3] he entered into the four stages of absorption (bSam gTan bZhi). The first stage is a one-pointed absorption with joy (dGa') and bliss (bDe), detached from the sensations of the desire realm, reached by thinking about (rTog) and analyzing (dPyod) those sensations as gross and negative. The second stage is a one-pointed absorption in clear mind with joy and bliss, detached from thoughts and analysis of the sensations as in the first stage. The third is a one-pointed absorption with bliss, detached from taking joy in the sensations as in the second stage through equanimity (evenness), recollection, and awareness. The fourth is a one-pointed absorption with equanimity, detached from the feelings of bliss of the third stage by seeing it as too gross by means of pure mindfulness.

Then, with that total calm, collected, luminous, applicable, and clear mind created by the four stages of absorption, he focused on developing the three states of awareness (Rig Pa gSum). (1) He acquired the "awareness of realizing the wisdom with divine eyes"[4] which sees the infinite details of the vicissitudes of all beings with their karma, the cause behind them. (2) He acquired the "awareness of realizing the wisdom of past lives,"[5] which sees infinite numbers of past lives of oneself and others and their various happenings and experiences in complete detail. (3) Then, in the early part of the full-moon day, he acquired the "awareness of realizing the wisdom of exhausting the contamination"[6] by thinking about and realizing the nature of the "twelve-links of interdependent causation" (rTen 'Brel bChu gNyis), the law of life.

In this stage, he realized that because of (1) ignorance (unenlightenment) there arises the (2) formation of karma (volitional action), because of the formation arises (3) consciousness, because of consciousness arise (4) designation and form (mental and physical objective phenomena), because of designation and form arise the (5) six sense faculties, because of the sense faculties arises (6) contact (of objects, senses, and their application), because of contact arises (7) sensation, because of sensation arises (8) craving, because of craving arises (9) clinging, because of clinging arises (10) becoming [existence], and because of becoming arise (11) birth, sickness, (12) aging, pain, and death. Then also he realized the law of the reversed process of the twelve-link interdependent causation. Because of the cessation of ignorance formation ceases, and so on.

He realized the four noble truths ('Phags Pa'i bDen Pa bZhi) of each twelve-link interdependent causation. He saw what is ignorance, what is the cause of ignorance, what is the cessation of ignorance, and what is the path of the cessation of ignorance, and so on.

He realized the four noble truths. (1) He realized the truth of suffering, that the whole of mundane existence in its totality is nothing but a cycle of suffering. (2) He realized the truth of the cause of suffering, the karma with emotional forces rooted in craving and grasping at self. (3) He realized the truth of the cessation of suffering, the attainment of nirvāṇa, enlightenment. (4) He realized the truth of the path of the cessation of suffering, the training in the eightfold noble path, namely right view, right thought, right speech, right action, right livelihood, right effort, right mindfulness, and right concentration.

Then, in the early dawn, he entered a vajralike absorption, solid, as no obstruction can destroy it; stable, as it cannot be moved by concepts; of the nature of oneness, as all things are of one taste in it; and all-pervading, as it is the true nature of all existents. In a single instant he exhausted even the most subtle traces of obscurations that he had harbored in himself, perfected the realization of the three states of awareness, and became the fully enlightened one, the Buddha. He leaped into the air to a height of seven *tal* (palm) trees and, sitting there, proclaimed:

> Today, all the rebirths [for me] have ceased.
> The path is completed.
> There is nothing more to pursue.

And:

> I have realized an ambrosia-like Dharma.
> It is a clear light: uncreated, profound, peaceful, and free from elaborations.

During the remaining forty-five years of his life, tirelessly traveling on foot and living on alms of one meal a day, with love and wisdom Buddha taught the way to Buddhahood and served his saṅgha, the community of monks, nuns, and devotees and all those whom he met and who came to him. During that period, the Buddha taught various paths for people of different temperaments.[7]

According to the Mahāyāna and Vajrayāna traditions of Buddhism, Buddha taught not only Hīnayāna, the common or orthodox Buddhism, but also Mahāyāna, advanced Buddhism, and Vajrayāna, esoteric Buddhism.

Hīnayāna (or Theravādin) teachings of the Buddha are known as the Tripiṭaka, the three baskets. They are the Vinaya, on the moral discipline of the monastic community and lay devotees; Abhidharma, on the wisdom of Buddhist psychology and metaphysics; and Sūtra, on contemplations and various discourses.

His first sermon was on the four noble truths. It explains the whole evolution of the mental and physical cycle of the mundane world and the cycle in reverse. He taught it to his first five monk-disciples at the Deer Park, now known as Sārnāth, near Vārāṇasī in India. The Buddha said:

> O monks, there are four noble truths. They are suffering, the cause of suffering, the cessation of suffering, and the path of the cessation of suffering. (1) What is the noble truth of suffering? It is the suffering of birth, old age, sickness, death, separation from desirable things, facing the unwanted, and not getting what one is seeking. In short, the five aggregates of attachment are suffering. This is called suffering. (2) What is the noble truth of the cause of suffering? It is the craving [which produces] re-existence (or re-becoming as beings) and which is accompanied by passionate desire, and which finds total delight in [or attachment to] this and that. This is called the cause of suffering. (3) What is the noble truth of the cessation of suffering? The cessation of suffering is the total cessa-

tion of and total freedom from the desire, the craving, which produces re-existence and which is accompanied by passionate desire, and which finds, creates, and takes total delight in this and that. (4) What is the path that leads to the cessation of suffering? It is the noble eightfold path, which consists of right view, right thought, right speech, right action, right livelihood, right effort, right mindfulness, and right concentration.[8]

The achievement of the fruits of Buddhism is dependent on the efforts of the individual practitioners themselves, and the Buddha's part is only to teach and inspire them. The Buddha said:

I have shown you the path of liberation.
You should understand that your liberation depends on yourself.[9]

The essence of Buddhist training is to act only with the proper discipline and to tame one's own mind through the eightfold noble path. The Buddha said:

Commit no evil deeds. Perform all the virtuous deeds.
Tame your own mind. That is the Buddha's teaching.[10]

If we could tame our mind, all our physical actions would naturally become well disciplined, for the mind leads all. Buddha said:

Mind is the main factor, and it leads all the actions.
With a pure mind, whatever you say or do
Will cause only happiness.
It is like a shadow that follows.[11]

When we understand and realize the truth of life and nature with our mind, we will attain freedom from all the sufferings. The Buddha said:

When you see with your wisdom that all the compound things
Are impermanent, . . . suffering . . . [and] selflessness, . . .
You will never be hurt by any suffering.
That is the right path![12]

For Mahāyāna disciples, both human and nonhuman beings, the Buddha delivered the Mahāyāna teachings such as "transcendental wisdom" and "Buddha essence" on Mount Gṛidhrakūṭa (Vulture Peak) in Rajgir (Rājagṛiha) in India and in many other places. Mahāyāna teachings were given to limited audiences, for the time of Mahāyāna teachings was not yet ripe. Centuries later, they were revealed to the public by masters who were keeping them and also by many who brought them back from different lands and world systems.

Most of the Mahāyāna disciplines are based on Hīnayāna, or common Buddhist teachings, but the attitude and view are different. Compassion is an important practice in common Buddhism also, but the intention to take total responsibility for others or to remain until every mother being is liberated is called bodhichitta, the mind of enlightenment. To train in the six perfections[13] with that bodhichitta is the unique approach of Mahāyāna.

In respect to view, the concept of emptiness is the central core of Mahāyāna doctrine. In absolute meaning or ultimate truth all phenomena are emptiness, and on the relative level or in conventional truth all are arising through interdependent causation, like a dream, mirage, or reflection. Thus the two truths are in union, and they are the nature of everything, with no contradictions. Emptiness is not a negative or nil, but it is total openness and freedom from dualistic mentality, conceptual designations, and notions of any extremes, either of existence or nonexistence, neither or both. Primordial wisdom, which is emptiness and the realization of emptiness, clearly sees everything simultaneously without any limits. This wisdom is also symbolized as the mother, the source or dwelling place of all the Buddhas.

In respect to training,[14] the followers of Mahāyāna first employ their mundane mind and mental events as the means of attaining Buddhahood, and by progressing through that process, they finally attain Buddhahood. The Buddha said:

> Those bodhisattvas who have attained the wisdom of realizing the
> [union of] interdependent arising and the unborn and
> unceasing [nature of emptiness],
> Like the rays of the unclouded sun dispelling the darkness,
> Destroy the ignorance and attain the naturally present
> [Buddhahood].[15]

And:

> I bow to the great mother of the Buddhas of the three times,
> [The emptiness, which is] the domain of self-awareness wisdom,

Freedom from designations, thoughts, and expressions,
And, unborn and unceasing, like space.[16]

And:

Form is emptiness. Emptiness is form.
Emptiness is not separate from form.
Form is not separate from emptiness.[17]

To Vajrayāna disciples, the exceptionally matured human and nonhuman audience, the Buddha gave the empowerments or initiation (abhiṣheka) and teachings of tantras,[18] the esoteric teaching of Guhyasamāja and Kālachakra and so on at Dhānyakaṭaka in Oḍḍiyāṇa, and other places, by transforming himself into the Sambhogakāya form, the true Buddha manifestation. Centuries later, when the time had come, those teachings were brought back from different lands and revealed to the public. In addition, many tantras were revealed by the Buddha(s) to numerous great realized adepts.

The teachings of tantra are not just teachings but also convey a transmission of the esoteric power, the realization of primordial wisdom. This transmission takes place during the empowerment of the disciple into the learning and realization of tantra. Then the disciple maintains the continuity of that transmission, and that is called observing the samaya, the esoteric vow. With unbroken samaya, the disciple trains in the two stages.[19] The development stage cleanses attachment to phenomena, body, and mind. In it, with mental efforts, one visualizes the world, body, and mind as the maṇḍala of the deity, appearing but empty, in order to purify birth, death, and the intermediate state. The perfection stage fulfills the attainments of power, blessing, and realization. In it, by admitting the air/energy and mind into the central channel, one realizes and perfects the wisdom, which is innate presence, free from thoughts and all-pervading. Tantric trainings[20] embody an extraordinary skill of perfecting. For example, they perfect one's mind as the union of the realization of emptiness and the arising of all as the wisdom of great bliss (or compassion) and as the three Buddha bodies. Tantric training brings about the attainment of Buddhahood in this very lifetime. The Buddha said:

The teachings of the vajra-holder [trantra]
Are based on the two stages.

> They are the development stage
> And the perfection stage.[21]

And:

> The inseparability [union] of emptiness and compassion
> Is called the Enlightened Mind.[22]

At the age of eighty,[23] on the full-moon day of the Vaishākha month (April/May), sitting beneath *shāla (Shorea robusta)* trees at Kushinagara in northern India, the Buddha proclaimed to his followers:

> Monks, I am about to enter into nirvāṇa. Don't torment yourselves by sorrow over it. If you have any question, ask me, so that no one will have to feel remorse over missing such an opportunity.

He repeated this three times, but all kept silent. Then the Buddha took off his upper robes and, showing his bare golden chest, repeatedly asked the audience to see the body of the Buddha, which is rare to witness. All felt the peace of an absorption by watching, without blinking, the purified goldlike body of the Buddha. Then once again he put on the robes, and, lying on his right side, he entered into mahāparinirvāṇa, the great cessation of sorrow, the ultimate peace, Buddhahood. He left his body as the source of blessing and recollection of the teachings and the presence of the Buddha.

AFTER THE BUDDHA

After the Buddha, the seven patriarchs, notably Mahākāshyapa and Ānanda; the two excellents and six ornaments of Mahāyāna, notably Nāgārjuna and Asaṅga; the eighty-four mahāsiddhas of Vajrayāna, notably Saraha and Nāropa; and the eight knowledge-holders, notably Prahevajra and Mañjushrīmitra, maintained and propagated the Buddha's teachings, both sūtras and tantras, in India and brought them to almost every corner of the Asian continent.

About five centuries after the Buddha, Mahāyāna teachings began to be widely propagated. Then, ten centuries after the Buddha, Vajrayāna teachings began to be widely propagated in India, under the umbrella of Mahāyāna. So Buddhism gradually developed into two major schools:

Hīnayāna, orthodox Buddhism, and Mahāyāna, advanced Buddhism. The Hīnayāna spread to the southern countries and the Mahāyāna into northern countries of Asia. This development has undergone various changes throughout the ages, but from the beginning of the twentieth century the distribution has been roughly as follows: Mahāyāna Buddhism, following the Sanskrit texts, has been propagated in Nepal, Central Asia, China, Korea, Java, Sumatra, Japan, Tibet, Bhutan, and Mongolia. Hīnayāna, or Theravādin, Buddhism, following the Pāli texts, has been propagated in Sri Lanka, Burma, Thailand, Cambodia, and Laos. In Vietnam both Hīnayāna and Mahāyāna were practiced.

Unfortunately, in the twelfth century CE, the nonviolent nature of Buddhism caused it to disappear from the land of its birth, India, in the face of Hindu domination and, later, the Muslim invasions. However, it remained flourishing in Sri Lanka, Thailand, Burma, Nepal, Indochina, China, Korea, Japan, Tibet, Bhutan, Mongolia, and other countries in Asia. Today, in the twentieth century, Buddhism has been brought back to India and has spread to many places around the globe.

One of the unique skills of Buddhism is the presence of multiple approaches in view and training. The *Laṅkāvatāra-sūtra* says, "To the extent that thoughts go on occurring to beings, there is no limit to the yānas or approaches of Dharma." In the world there are innumerable beings, each of whom has a different nature and capacity. Therefore, it is necessary for there to be different paths for them to practice according to their natures. But it is impossible to teach as many yānas as there are sentient beings. However, the Buddha did give many different kinds of teachings of sūtras and tantras for people of lesser, middle, and higher intelligence, all of which lead to the same goal. Depending on the different methods followed, the goal can be reached swiftly or after lengthier practice.

In distinguishing the character of the three main yānas, the example is given of a poisonous plant, which represents the defilements of ignorance, lust, and anger. In Hīnayāna a trainee avoids the danger of the poison. In Mahāyāna the trainee destroys the poison by its antidotes. In Vajrayāna, the trainee transmutes the poison into supreme wisdom.

Buddhism in Tibet

Buddhism in Tibet originated in the seventh century CE, during the reign of King Songtsen Gampo (617–698 CE).[24] In the ninth century, in the time of King Trisong Detsen (790–858 CE),[25] Shāntarakṣhita, Guru Rinpoche (Padmasambhava), Vimalamitra, and many of the greatest scholars and sages of their time in India were invited to Tibet. With hundreds of translators they translated the Hīnayāna, Mahāyāna, and Vajrayāna teachings into Tibetan. Tibet became a flourishing center for the entire range of Buddhist teachings. From the ninth until the middle of the twentieth century Tibet preserved the teachings of the three yānas in an unbroken transmission.

All Tibetans are Buddhists, following the Mahāyāna and Vajrayāna. There are many distinctions in philosophy, discipline, and aspirations between Hīnayāna and Mahāyāna, but the main point that distinguishes them is said to be attitude. One who practices Buddhism mainly for the happiness and liberation of himself is a Hīnayānist. One who practices with bodhi-mind, the attitude of taking responsibility for the happiness and liberation of others, is a Mahāyānist, a bodhisattva. In Tibet, at least at the start of a session of practice, if one begins with the development of bodhichitta, one is trying to be a follower of the path of Mahāyāna.

Not only among the lamas and monks, but also among the laity, there is no one in Tibet who does not receive empowerments for tantric training; thus, all Tibetans are followers of tantra too. In ancient India the tantra was practiced in secret, but in Tibet most of the tantras are practiced without much restriction. Teachers observe that the practice of tantra depends on devotion to the teachings, so that devotion qualifies a person to receive the instructions. India was never totally devoted to Buddhism, but Tibet was an entirely Buddhist country; hence there was not the same need for secrecy and discrimination in authorizing the study of the tantras.

In addition to Mahāyāna and Vajrayāna teachings, many Hīnayāna scriptures, such as the four divisions of vinaya texts and many sūtras, form the basis of Buddhist practice in Tibet. So Tibet is a country in which the entire scope of Buddhist teachings is kept alive and practiced thoroughly.

Various schools—four major and many minor traditions—of Buddhism emerged in Tibet. Interpretations of sutric teachings varied with different Tibetan scholars, but the main distinctions were in the interpretations and practice of tantras. The tantras that were translated from Sanskrit before the eleventh century are called Ngak Nyingma, the "old tantras," and the tantras translated during and after the eleventh century are called the Ngak Sarma, the "new tantras." There are tantras that were translated in both the early and later periods, but many were translated in the earlier period but were not retranslated in the later period. Some tantras translated in the earlier period were lost, so that only the translations of the later period exist. And some earlier translations were revised during the later period and exist as the tantras of both the earlier and later schools. The tantras unique to the Nyingma are the three inner tantras, namely the tantras of Mahāyoga, Anuyoga, and Atiyoga.

As the result, four major lineages or schools developed in Tibet. The school of the original Buddhist tantric tradition of Tibet is called the Nyingma, the Old One. The followers of the new tantras developed into three different schools:

1. Kagyü, founded by Marpa Lotsāwa (1012–1099)
2. Sakya, founded by Khön Könchok Gyalpo (1034–1102)
3. Geluk, founded by Je Tsongkhapa (1357–1419)

In the sūtra tradition there is no division of old and new translations. But the division that does apply to the sūtras in Tibet is that of the early and later disseminations. The early dissemination (bsTan Pa sNga Dar) refers to the teachings propagated before the reign of King Lang Darma, who is credited with the destruction of the foreign religion, Buddhism, in Tibet. The later dissemination (Phyi Dar) begins with the reestablishment of sūtra Buddhism after the assassination of Lang Darma in 906 CE. The historical claim of the Nyingma in relation to the interim period occasioned by royal apostasy is that while sūtra Buddhism was forbidden, the practice of tantric Buddhism could not be destroyed by persecution, because it did not depend upon a visible monastic and hierarchical structure, and also because of the fear of the power of the great tāntrika Nupchen Sangye Yeshe, who threatened the king with a display of miracles.

Many sūtras and tantras translated during the period of early dissemination were retranslated or edited in the later dissemination, so that, despite some textual variations, they are common to both phases. For example, early and later translations exist for the following scriptures: most of the thirteen volumes of the *Vinayapiṭaka;* the entire *Prajñāpāramitā* corpus; all six volumes of the *Ratnakūṭa;* six volumes of the *Avataṃsaka;* many sūtras and *Mantrasaṃgraha;* and the *Mahāparinirvāṇa-sūtra,* all belonging to the *Kanjur* (bKa' 'Gyur), the collection of canonical teachings of the Buddha (in 104 volumes containing about 1,046 treatises). Many texts of the *Tenjur* (bsTan 'Gyur), the collection of writings by Indian scholars (in 185 volumes containing about 3,786 treatises) translated into Tibetan, are also preserved in both new and old translations. The followers of both disseminations agree in accepting all the sūtras as authentic and in practicing them. The differences arose because of the different interpretations of the texts by Tibetan scholars as well as the differences in defining which texts are of "absolute meaning" (Nges Don) and which are of "interpretable meaning" (Drang Don).

Concerning the revelation of the tantras, the major ones of the new tantras were taught by the Shākyamuni Buddha while manifesting himself as Sambhogakāya deities. Buddhism is classified by the followers of the new tantras as follows:

THE THREE YĀNAS OF CAUSE:
- Shrāvakayāna
- Pratyekabuddhayāna
- Bodhisattvayāna

THE FOUR MANTRAYĀNAS OF RESULT:
- Kriyāyoga
- Charyāyoga
- Yogatantra

ANUTTARATANTRA:
- father tantra
- mother tantra
- nondual tantra

According to the Nyingmapas, the followers of the Old Tantras, most of the Nyingma tantras were given by the wisdom bodies of Buddhas to the great Buddhist adepts. The Nyingma classifies the entire Buddhist teachings into nine yānas, or vehicles:

THE THREE EXOTERIC YĀNAS:

1. Shrāvakayāna [Hīnayāna]
2. Pratyekabuddhayāna [Hīnayāna]
3. Bodhisattvayāna [Mahāyāna]

The Six Tantric Yānas [Vajrayāna]:

THE THREE OUTER TANTRAS:

4. Kriyāyoga
5. Charyāyoga
6. Yogatantra

THE THREE INNER TANTRAS:

7. Mahāyoga
8. Anuyoga
9. Atiyoga

The three inner tantras are the special tantras of the Nyingma. In particular, Atiyoga, or Dzogpa Chenpo (Skt. Mahāsandhi[26] or Ati), is the summit of Buddhist teachings. A person of high intelligence who practices this path with diligence will attain the absolute state within three years; a person of middle intelligence in six years; and one of lesser intelligence in twelve years.

Some of the tantras of the three inner tantras are included in the *Kanjur* collection, but there is a separate collection of the three inner tantras known as the *Nyingma Gyübum* in twenty-five (or thirty-one) volumes. There are also many tantras of this tradition that spontaneously occurred to the minds of realized masters. There are numerous texts of sādhana and tantra transmitted by Guru Rinpoche which he and his consort concealed and which were recovered as Ter (gTer) by hundreds of tertöns at different times, from the eleventh century till today.

Atiyoga itself has three divisions: Semde, Longde, and Me-ngagde. Master Shrīsiṃha further divided Me-ngagde into four cycles, namely the Outer, Inner, Esoteric, and Innermost Esoteric Cycles. The Me-ngagde teachings in general, and especially the Innermost Esoteric Cycle, became known as the Nyingthig (the Innermost Essence).

Through the Trekchö (Khreg Ch'od, cutting through) practice of Atiyoga in general, and especially of Nyingthig, many meditators realize the intrinsic nature of their minds and swiftly merge their minds into the ultimate nature, Buddhahood, in this very lifetime. At the time of death, with beams, auras, and circles of light, many dissolve their mortal bodies, leaving behind only their hair and fingernails and toenails. It is called the attainment of rainbow body or rainbow-light bodies ('Ja' Lus), for lights appear during the dissolution process and the wisdom-light body of the Sambhogakāya is attained.

Through the Thögal (Thod rGal, direct approach) practice of Nyingthig, great meditators also attain Buddhahood, and at the time of death many transform their mortal bodies into light-bodies, and remain in them, visible only to realized beings, as long as they wish. This is called the rainbow body of great transformation ('Ja' Lus 'Pho Ba Ch'en Po).

In addition to the seventeen tantras (rGyud bChu bDun), Nyingthig includes many other tantras and teachings discovered by tertöns. For example, Chetsün Nyingthig, discovered by Chetsün (and rediscovered by Khyentse Wangpo); Khandro Nyingthig, discovered by Pema Ledreltsal; Karma Nyingthig, discovered by the Third Karmapa, Rangchung Dorje; Dorsem Nyingthig of Vairochana tradition, discovered by Künkyong Lingpa; Longchen Nyingthig, discovered by Jigme Lingpa; Bairö Nyingthig, discovered by Chögyur Lingpa, and Tsasum Ösal Nyingthig, discovered by Khyentse Wangpo. The same teachings are also found in many cycles of Nyingma teachings without being designated as Nyingthig, for example, Gongpa Zangthal, discovered by Rigdzin Gödem; Dorje Nyingpo, discovered by Longsal Nyingpo; and Sangye Lakchang, discovered by Namchö Mingyur Dorje.

Of all these Nyingthig teachings, the Vima Nyingthig, transmitted in Tibet by Vimalamitra, and the Khandro Nyingthig, transmitted by Guru Rinpoche, which were later propagated through the revelations and writings of Longchen Rabjam (1308–1363), are the most profound and elaborated teachings on Nyingthig.

In the eighteenth century Jigme Lingpa (1730–1798) revealed the Longchen Nyingthig cycle together with some original Nyingthig tantras as ter. This revelation carried the Nyingthig teachings to their highest popularity. Nowadays, Vima Nyingthig and Khandro Nyingthig are known as the Early Nyingthig and Longchen Nyingthig as the Later Nyingthig.

Three Modes of Lineal Transmission of the General Nyingma Inner Tantras

THE inner tantric, absolute esoteric teachings of Nyingma came from the primordial Buddha and reached our teachers through three modes of transmission. They are the mind transmission of the Buddhas, symbolic transmission of the knowledge-holders, and oral transmission of the ascetics.

MIND TRANSMISSION OF THE BUDDHAS

Mind transmission of the Buddhas (rGyal Ba dGongs brGyud) is the unique transmission that exists between the Buddhas. Just by the realization of the meaning of the tantras by the teacher (the Buddha), the retinue of disciples (the Buddhas who are manifestations of himself) also has the same realization. This is the transmission of the nature of the mind of teacher and disciples. There is also a secondary or similar type of mind transmission in which the disciples who are not one with the teacher become inseparable in mind from the teacher by means of the teacher's blessing.

The Dharmakāya dwells without change throughout the three phases of time (past, present, and future) in the luminescent vision of inseparable Dharma space and primordial wisdom, being the primordial Buddha and the absolute nature of all phenomena.

By the power of display of immeasurable compassion and the spontaneous clarity of vision of the Dharmakāya, the nature of primordial wisdom which can neither be indicated nor described, the five prosperous circumstances of Sambhogakāya are present. Thus it is called the teaching of the Dharmakāya, although no direct teaching actually takes place. The five prosperous circumstances are:

PLACE: The unexcelled pure land, appearing spontaneously as the very pure perception of primordial wisdom.

TEACHER: Vajradhara, who is fully adorned with the excellent signs and marks.

DISCIPLES: The Buddhas of the five classes and the oceanlike maṇḍalas of peaceful and wrathful deities, who are inseparable from the teacher himself.

TEACHING: The expressionless teaching of the deep and sacred Vajrayāna; the absolute nature of phenomena.

TIME: The three phases of time without change.

SYMBOLIC TRANSMISSION OF THE KNOWLEDGE-HOLDERS

The symbolic transmission of the knowledge-holders (Rig 'Dzin brDa brGyud) is the transmission from a knowledge-holding teacher who has realized and perfected the primordial wisdom of tantra to bodhisattva disciples whose minds are fully ripened to receive the teachings. The teacher focuses his mind, the primordial awareness wisdom, and merely gives the indication or symbolic gesture (mudrā) and utters sacred syllables, phrases or hymns (mantra), whereupon the disciple instantaneously comprehends the perfect meaning of the tantra. It is also known as the awareness transmission of the bodhisattvas.

Thus, the tantras came to the human world through two stages of symbolic transmission:

1. *Transmission to the Nonhuman knowledge-holders.* Vajradhara, the tantric teacher, manifested himself as the bodhisattvas of the three classes of beings (Rigs gSum)—Mañjushrī of wisdom, Avalokiteshvara of compassion, and Vajrapāṇi of power—and transmitted the tantras to the realms of gods, nāgas, and yakṣhas through the symbolic transmission.

In the Trayatriṃsha Heaven, the Heaven of the Thirty-three Gods, the god Zangkyong had five hundred mind-born sons. The eldest, Künga Nyingpo, was superior to the others in knowledge and athletic prowess. He liked to stay alone in a house of meditation and do vajra recitations. He was known as Adhichitta (Extraordinary-Minded One). In his dreams he saw four kinds of signs:

> Rays projecting from the Buddhas of the ten directions encircled all sentient beings and dissolved into the crown of his head.

He swallowed Brahmā, Viṣhṇu, and Maheshvara.
He held the sun and moon in his hand, and the rays spread all over the world.
A rain of nectar fell from jewel-colored clouds in the sky and produced a great spread of trees, flowers, and fruit.

The following morning he recounted his dream to Kaushika [Indra], one of the lords of the gods, who then praised him in the following verses:

Marvelous! Now is the time that the doctrine of the effortless essence will arrive.
You are the manifestation of the Buddhas and bodhisattvas of the three times.
You are the master of the tenth stage and the excellent light of the world.
You are the ornament of the realm of the gods. It is wonderful!

Then Kaushika explained the significance of the dreams. The first dream indicated that Adhichitta would attain the understanding of all the Buddhas and become their regent. The second indicated that he would cut off at the root the māras (negative forces) and the three poisons: hatred, greed, and ignorance. The third dream indicated that he would dispel the darkness from the minds of disciples and become the lamp of the doctrine. The fourth dream indicated that he would pacify the sufferings of the heat of the defilements by the nectar of the self-arisen Atiyoga teachings and would spontaneously attain the effortless result of the Atiyoga.

Then all the Buddhas assembled and urged Vajrasattva with the following verses:

You who possess the skillful means of precious miraculous power,
Open the door to the fulfillment of whatever a disciple wishes.
Give him the wealth of effortlessness [teachings of Dzogpa Chenpo].

Then from the heart of Vajrasattva a radiant jeweled wheel appeared, and he handed it to Sattvavajra,[27] urging him with these verses:

The path of nondual primordial wisdom, the secret meaning,
Actionless, effortless, enlightened from the beginning,

Known as the Great Middle Way:
Please show it to the disciples.

Sattvavajra made the promise to teach in the following verses:

Vajrasattva, the great space,
Is not the object of verbal expression;
It is very difficult for me to expound.
But for unrealized beings, through the indication of words,
In order to bring them to realization,
By all appropriate means I shall liberate the trainees.

Then Sattvavajra received the complete teachings of Atiyoga from the Buddhas of the five classes. Sattvavajra appeared before the Devaputra Adhichitta in the victorious palace of the Trayatriṃsha realm of the gods and gave him the complete initiations through the indication transmission. He gave all the numerous tantras and instructions in a single moment and empowered him as his regent. Then he spoke the following verses:

May the essence of the wonderful teaching,
After being spread throughout the three realms of the gods
By the manifested heart-son,
Be propagated in the center of the Jambu continent.

Thereupon, Adhichitta expounded the Dzogpa Chenpo teachings and spread them in the realm of the gods.

2. *Transmission of the Tantras to Both Nonhuman and Human Knowledge-holders.* According to scriptures, twenty-eight years after the passing away of Shākyamuni Buddha, the five excellent beings (Dam Pa'i Rigs Chan Dra-Ma lNga)—namely, the god Yashasvī Varapāla, the nāga Takṣhaka, the yakṣha Ulkāmukha, the rākṣhasa Matyaupāyika, and the human being Licchavi Vimalakīrti—arose from their contemplation. They knew by the power of foreknowledge that the Buddha had already attained mahāparinirvāṇa. By their miraculous power they gathered on the summit of Mount Malaya in the country of Laṅkā. They sang twenty-three songs of lamentation, including these lines:

Alas, alas, alack! O Vast Expanse!
If the light of the teacher's lamp sets,
Who will dispel the darkness of the world?

Urged by the Buddhas, Bodhisattva Vajrapāṇi appeared before them and gave the teachings of the sacred yāna, the tantra, which was renowned in the three realms of the gods, the Akaniṣhṭha, Tuṣhita, and Trayatriṃsha realms.

The rākṣhasa Matyanpāyika wrote the tantras on golden sheets with malachite ink and concealed them in the sky.

Mount Malaya, where Vajrapāṇi revealed the tantras to the five excellent beings, is identified as Adam's Peak (or Shrīpāda) in Sri Lanka by Kathok Getse Mahāpaṇḍita, and Kyabje Dudjom Rinpoche[28] agrees with it.

ORAL TRANSMISSION OF THE ASCETICS

Oral transmission of the ascetics (rNal 'Byor sNyan brGyud) is a transmission not by divinities or Buddhas, but through a person in ordinary form. However, this refers mainly to their appearance to disciples rather than the actual nature of the transmitters, who include Buddhas and bodhisattvas such as Prahevajra (dGa' Rab rDo rJe) and Guru Rinpoche.

In *Künzang Lame Zhalung,*[29] Paltrul Rinpoche designated the succession from King Ja and Prahevajra down to Guru Rinpoche and Vimalamitra, etc., as "symbolic transmission." This division was mainly made on a basis of the actual nature of these transmissions. But in the present account the divisions are made on the basis of general Nyingma tradition.

Shākyamuni Buddha himself gave tantric teachings by manifesting as various deities of the tantra. Many adepts also brought tantras of the outer yānas from different lands and practiced them in strict secrecy. But the inner tantras of Nyingma, which were received by great adepts from Buddhas in pure visions and were preserved in India under the strictest secrecy, reached Tibet, where they flourished and became the most sacred teachings of Nyingma. The inner tantras have three categories: Mahāyoga, Anuyoga, and Atiyoga.

Lineages of Three Major Nyingma Inner Tantras

MAHĀYOGA[30]

In all the inner tantras, the initiates practice both stages or the union of the two stages, the development stage and the perfection stage. But sometimes the three inner tantras are also characterized as being of the development stage, perfection stage, and great perfection. However, there are differences in emphasis in view and meditation and the swiftness of results.

In Mahāyoga,[31] the initiates emphasize mainly the development stage, the visualization of the deity maṇḍala. By visualizing phenomenal existents as the deities and their pure lands, bodies, elements, and faculties, and so on, as the deities, they purify the five energies (or airs) of the five elements and transform the delusory phenomena into the Buddha Land. As the result, they attain the wisdom of bliss, clarity, and freedom from concepts. They achieve liberation for themselves in this very lifetime and are able to fulfill the needs of others.

In Mahāyoga there are two categories of teachings: tantra and sādhana.

TANTRA

As the Buddha prophesied, because of the power of blessing of the tantric discourses of Vajrapāṇi to the five excellent beings, King Ja, Vyākaraṇavajra, who was practicing the outer tantras, had seven dreams. Thereafter, many tantric texts written on gold paper in malachite ink and an image of Vajrapāṇi two feet high and fashioned out of precious jewels descended from the sky onto the roof of his palace. He made offerings and prayers to the sacred objects. This awakened his karma of previous experience of tantra, and he understood the meaning of the chapter entitled *Dorje Sempa Zhalthong* (Seeing the Face of Vajrasattva).

Using the chapter and the image of Vajrapāṇi, he practiced for six months. He beheld the pure vision of Vajrasattva and received from him a prophetic instruction, in accordance with which he performed the physical purification through the development stage. He beheld Vajrapāṇi, received teachings and blessings, and understood all the tantric texts that he received. Then Vajrapāṇi gave him the empowerment of the absolute meaning of the teachings, and he advised the king to receive the verbal teachings from Licchavi Vimalakīrti. Then the king went to Vimalakīrti and received the eighteen tantras[32] of Mahāyoga, and he transmitted them to the great siddha Kukkurāja.

King Ja is identified differently by various historians. Some say that he is the same person as the great King Indrabhūti, and some say that he is the son of that king. Others say that he is the middle one of three Indrabhūtis, an identification that Dudjom Rinpoche in his *History of the Nyingma School of Tibetan Buddhism* says might be the correct one.

Sādhana

The sādhana category also has two divisions: *kama,* the canonical scriptures, and *terma,* the revealed hidden treasures.

Kama, Canonical Sādhanas

The five *kama* (bKa' Ma), the canonical sādhanas, are the sādhanas of body, speech, mind, virtues, and action. They were received by the five great teachers, who attained accomplishment by practicing them.

The sādhana of body, *Jampal Tröwo Sang-gyü,* and other tantras of Wrathful Mañjushrī (Yamāntaka) of the Vairochana Buddha family, were received by master Mañjushrīmitra. The tantra of speech, *Hayagrīvalīlā,* and other tantras of Hayagrīva of the Amitābha Buddha family were received by Nāgārjuna. The tantra of mind, *Herukakalpo,* and other tantras of Vajraheruka (Shrīheruka or Yang Dag) of the Akṣhobya Buddha family were received by master Hūṃkara. The tantra of virtues, *Vajrāmṛita* of the Ratnasambhava Buddha family, was received by Vimalamitra. The tantra of action, *Vajrakīla* of the Amoghasiddhi Buddha family, was received by master Prabhāhasti. Guru Rinpoche received all the tantras from those masters[33] and achieved attainments, especially of Vajraheruka and Vajrakīla, and brought them to Tibet.

Terma, the Sādhanas of Hidden Treasures

The terma (gTer Ma) category of the sādhana section of the Mahāyoga tantras originated as follows:[34]

PLACE: In the sacred unexcelled pure land.

TEACHER: Samantabhadra manifested in peaceful form as Vajrasattva and in wrathful form as Mahottaraheruka.

DISCIPLES: His self-awareness appears as the assembly of disciples.

TIME: The state of equality without beginning or end.

TEACHING: The general tantras of Vajrayāna are taught by the natural vajra-sound of dharmatā.

Guhyapati Vajradharma compiled the five general, ten special, and numerous branch tantras and arranged them in the form of written texts.[35] He entrusted them to the ḍākinī Mahākarmendrāṇī (Las Kyi dBang Mo Ch'e). She placed them in caskets and concealed them in the Shaṅkarakūṭa chaitya (bDe Byed brTsegs Pa) in the Shītavana charnel ground.

In later times the eight great masters of India knew about the concealment through their visionary power, and they assembled at Shītavana charnel ground. The Ḍākinī Mahākarmendrāṇī appeared and handed over to the eight masters the eight caskets containing the eight particular tantras. The casket of the tantra of *Yamāntaka* was entrusted to Mañjushrīmitra; *Hayagrīva* to Nāgārjuna; *Shrīherukā* (Yang Dag) to Hūṃkara; *Mahottara* (Ch'e mCh'og) to Vimalamitra; *Vajrakīla* to Prabhāhasti, *Mātaraḥ* (Ma Mo) to Dhanasaṃskṛita, *Lokastotrapūja* ('Jigs rTen mCh'od bsTod) to Rambuguhya, and *Vajramantrabhīru* (Drag sNgags) to Shāntigarbha. Each master practiced his designated tantra and attained accomplishments through it. The casket of *Deshek Düpa* was entrusted to Guru Rinpoche. Guru Rinpoche also received all the tantras, sādhanas, and instructions from each master and accomplished the attainments of all of them. Later, he transmitted them to his nine chief disciples and twenty-five main disciples in Tibet.

The following is the lineage of the major kama and terma teachings of Mahāyoga from the primordial Buddha to my teacher:[36]

1. Samantabhadra, the Dharmakāya.
2. Vajrasattva, the Sambhogakāya.
3. The bodhisattvas of the three classes, the Nirmāṇakāya.
4. Licchavi Vimalakīrti along with the four other excellent beings.
5. King Ja, Vyākaraṇavajra (or Middle Indrabhūti).

6. Kukkurāja, along with an assembly of one hundred thousand disciples.
7. The Shakraputra, the younger Indrabhūti with an assembly of ten thousand disciples.
8. Siṃharāja with an assembly of one thousand disciples.
9. Uparāja with an assembly of five hundred disciples.
10. Princess Gomadevī with an assembly of one hundred disciples.
11. Kikkurāja.
12. Līlāvajra, Vetālasukhasiddhi, Ṛiṣhi Bhāṣhita, and Nāgārjuna.
13. Līlāvajra transmitted the teachings to Buddhaguhya; Sukhasiddhi to Vajrahāsya and Hūṃkara.
14. Both Līlāvajra and Buddhaguhya transmitted to Vimalamitra, and Buddhaguhya also transmitted to Guru Rinpoche. Both Ṛiṣhi Bhāṣhita and Vajrahāsya transmitted to Prabhāhasti. Vajrahāsya also transmitted to Shrīshiṃha, and Prabhāhasti to Guru Rinpoche. Guru Rinpoche also received Mahāyoga teachings from King Ja himself.

In Tibet:

15. Ma Rinchen Chok and Nyak Jñānakumāra received the transmission from Vimalamitra. Nyak received the transmission from Guru Rinpoche also.
16. Ma transmitted to Tsuk-ru Rinchen Zhönu and Kyere Chokyong. Nyak to Sokpo Palkyi Yeshe and both Ma and Nyak to Khu Changchup Ö.
17. Khu, Tsuk-ru, and Kyere all transmitted to Zhang Gyalwe Yönten.
18. Both Sokpo and Zhang transmitted to Nupchen Sangye Yeshe. Nupchen became the holder of all the major lineages of Mahāyoga teachings.
19. Nupchen to Nup Yönten Gyatso and So Yeshe Wangchuk.
20. Both to Nyang Sherap Chok.
21. Nyang Sherap Jungne and Yeshe Jungne.
22. Yeshe to the great Zurpoche Shākya Jungne.
23. Zurchung Sherap Trakpa (1014–1074).
24. The four Thukse Kawas (four chief disciples of Zurchung).

25. Zur Shākya Senge (aka Dro-phukpa Chenpo, 1074–?).
26. Tsaktsa Shakdor.
27. Tsak Shākya Jungne.
28. Lantön Dorje Ö.
29. Lan Sönam Gyaltsen.
30. Palden Chökyi Senge.
31. Lan Sangye Pal.
32. Lan Sönam Gönpo.
33. Drölchen Samdrup Dorje (1295–1376).
34. Zur Gendün Bum.
35. Zur Shākya She-nyen.
36. Trao Chöbum.
37. Könchok Zangpo.
38. Lama Dorje Zangpo.
39. Trülzhik Dorje Namgyal.
40. Chatang Matishrī.
41. Karmaguru.
42. Künzang Paljor.
43. Rigdzin Thrinle Lhündrup (1611–1662).
44. Lochen Chögyal Tendzin.
45. Minling Terchen Gyurme Dorje (1646–1714).
46. Minling Gyalse Rinchen Namgyal.
47. Minling Drubwang Shrīnatha.
48. Künkhyen Jigme Lingpa (1730–1798).
49. First Dodrupchen Jigme Thrinle Özer (1745–1821).
50. Dola Jigme Kalzang (or Chökyi Lodrö).
51. Dzogchen Gyalse Zhenphen Thaye (1800–?).
52. Dzogchen Khenpo Pema Vajra (aka Damchö Özer).
53. Jamyang Khyentse Wangpo (1820–1892).

Or after Minling Terchen:

46. Minling Lochen Dharmashrī.
47. Minling Jetsün Mingyur Paldrön.
48. Minling Gyalse Rinchen Namgyal.
49. Minling Pema Tendzin.
50. Minling Thrinle Namgyal.
51. Minling Jetsün Thrinle Chödrön.
52. Minling Trichen Sangye Künga.
53. Jamyang Khyentse Wangpo.

The lineage of kama after Khyentse Wangpo:

54. Kathok Situ Chökyi Gyatso (1880–1925).
55. Jamyang Khyentse Chökyi Lodrö (1893–1959).
55. Fourth Dodrupchen Thupten Thrinle Palzangpo (b. 1927).

The lineage of terma after Khyentse Wangpo:

54. Third Zhechen Gyaltsap Gyurme Pema Namgyal (1871–1926).
55. Zhechen Kongtrül Pema Tri-me Lodrö (1901–1960?).
56. Fourth Dodrupchen Thupten Thrinle Palzangpo (b. 1927).

Or:

54. Kongtrül Yönten Gyatso (1813–1899) of Palpung.
55. Fifth Dzogchen Rinpoche Thupten Chökyi Dorje (1872–1935).
56. Gyarong Namtrül Drodül Karkyi Dorje.
57. Fourth Dodrupchen Thupten Thrinle Palzangpo (b. 1927).

ANUYOGA

In Anuyoga,[37] the whole universe is seen as the Buddha in its true nature, the ultimate sphere, but not much emphasis is put on the development stage. Anuyoga concentrates on the perfection stages of generating the wisdom of bliss, clarity, and freedom from concepts by the training of channels, energy (air), and essence of one's vajra body. After preparing one's body as a skillful means, the great bliss of fourfold joy (dGa' Ba bZhi) is also generated with the support of the maṇḍala of the mudrā. As the result enlightenment is attained.[38]

In reality King Ja learned the meaning of the entire tantra from Vajrapāṇi. But he acted out the receiving from Licchavi Vimalakīrti of the tantras of Anu, which had been revealed to the five excellent beings by Vajrapāṇi and were later written down by Rākṣhasa Matyaupāyika.

The Lineage of the Anuyoga Tantra[39]

1. Samantabhadra, the Dharmakāya.
2. The Buddhas of the five classes, the Sambhogakāya.

3. The bodhisattvas of the three classes, the Nirmāṇakāya.
4. Licchavi Vimalakīrti, the first human master.
5. King Ja, Vyākaraṇavajra (aka Middle Indrabhūti).
6. Uparāja and King Ja's three sons, Shakraputra, Nāgaputra, and Guhyaputra. Shakraputra is also known as the Younger Indrabhūti and Kambalapāda (Lva Ba Pa, the Ragged One).
7. The later Kukkurāja received them from the younger Indrabhūti.
8. Vetālasukha, the Blissful Zombie.
9. Vajrahāsya.
10. Prabhāhasti (aka Shākyaprabha).
11. Shākya Senge.
12. Dhanarakṣhita.
13. Master Hūṃkara.
14. Sukhoddyotaka (bDe Ba gSal Byed).
15. Dharmabodhi of Magadha, Dharmarājapāla of Nālandā, King Vasudhara of Nepal, and Tusklak Palge.
16. Chetsen Kye of the country of Trusha (Bru Sha, Gilgit?) received the tantras and teachings from the four preceding teachers.
17. Nupchen Sangye Yeshe of Tibet received them from Dharmabodhi and Vasudhara, and in particular from Chetsen Kye.

The lineal transmission of the tantras of Anuyoga, after Nupchen Sangye Yeshe, is more or less identical with the lineal transmission of Mahāyoga.

ATIYOGA (Dzogpa Chenpo)

Atiyoga[40] emphasizes the realization and perfection of the spontaneously present clear primordial wisdom, the ultimate nature of one's mind and of the universe, free from any concepts, partiality, dimensions, and designations of plurality or singularity. As a result, not only does one's mind unite with Buddhahood, the ultimate nature, but even one's mortal body dissolves into a wisdom light body.

The teachings of Dzogpa Chenpo, the summit of the yānas, in 6,400,000 verses, were revealed by Vajrasattva to Prahevajra, the first human teacher of Dzogpa Chenpo. Prahevajra compiled them into written texts and disseminated them.

The Lineal Transmission of Ati Yoga

1. Samantabhadra, the Dharmakāya.
2. Vajrasattva, the Sambhogakāya.
3. Prahevajra (Garab Dorje), the Nirmāṇakāya, the first human master.
4. Mañjushrīmitra. He divided the 6,400,000 verses of Dzogpa Chenpo into three categories: Semde, Longde, and Me-ngagde. He divided Me-ngagde into the tantras of oral transmission (sNan rGyud) and the expository tantras (bShad rGyud).
5. Shrīsiṃha. He divided Me-ngagde into four cycles: outer, inner, esoteric, and innermost esoteric cycle.
6. Jñānasūtra and Guru Rinpoche. Vairochana received the Semde and Longde teachings of Dzogpa Chenpo from Shrīsiṃha.
7. Jñānasūtra transmitted to Vimalamitra. Vimalamitra also received the transmission from Shrīsiṃha directly and from Garab Dorje in pure vision.

Semde and Longde were mainly brought to Tibet by Vairochana and Vimalamitra, and Me-ngagde was mainly brought to Tibet by Vimalamitra and Guru Rinpoche.

Semde

Semde, the cycle on mind,[41] teaches that all the appearances are mind, that mind is emptiness, emptiness is intrinsic awareness, and emptiness and intrinsic awareness are in union.

For teaching that the appearances are mind, Semde classifies the appearances as three characteristic of the mind: power (rTsal), play (Rol Ba), and attributes (rGyan). The power of mind is the aspect of mere seeing or awareness of things, which for ordinary people has become the basis of delusion into saṃsāra. The play of the mind is the arising of the defiled-mind-consciousness and other consciousnesses. The attributes are the display of phenomenal existents, mountains, houses, bodies, and so on. Both the play and attributes have arisen from or are due to the power of the mind.

Having realized that phenomenal existents are the mere play of one's own mind, Semde meditators have attained freedom from what they have to get free from, but they are not yet free from grasping the means of that freedom, the awareness and clarity of mind.

The awareness presented in Semde is an aspect of clarity and awareness of the mind, but it is not the ultimate spontaneously perfected profound intrinsic awareness of Me-ngagde.[42]

Longde

Longde, the cycle on the ultimate sphere,[43] teaches that the awareness and clarity aspect of mind is emptiness. The meditators of Longde still maintain a trace of grasping at the emptiness. So they are free from both the things from which to get free and the means by which to attain freedom, but are still not beyond holding on to the emptiness; thus Longde does not introduce one to the naked primordial wisdom, which transcends mind.[44]

The Lineal Transmission of Semde and Longde

1. Samantabhadra, the Dharmakāya.
2. Vajrasattva, the Sambhogakāya.
3. Prahevajra (Garab Dorje), the Nirmāṇakāya.
4. Mañjushrīmitra.
5. Shrīsiṃha.
6. Vairochana.
7. Nyak Jñānakumāra, Pang-gen Mipham Gönpo, Yudra Nyingpo, Sangtön Yeshe Lama, and Liza Sherap Drönma.
8. Pang-gen transmitted to Ngenlam Changchup Gyaltsen. Nyak transmitted to Sokpo Palkyi Yeshe.
9. Ngenlam to Zatam Rinchen Yik and Sokpo to Nupchen Sangye Yeshe.
10. Zatam to Khugyur Salwe Chok.
11. Nyang Changchup Trak.
12. Nyang Sherap Jungne.
13. Yölmowa Bagom Yeshe Changchup.
14. Dzeng Dharmabodhi.
15. Dzengkar Chose and Kyetse Yeshe Wangchuk.
16. Kyetse to Zik Yeshe Wangpo.
17. Khenchen Ngurpa.

18. Tutön Vajreshvara.
19. Sönam Gyaltsen.
20. Sherap Gyaltsen.
21. Zhönu Sherap.
22. Zhönu Trakpa.
23. Sangye Zangpo.
24. Tsöndrü Wangchuk.
25. Thazhi Trakpa Rinchen.
26. Shākya Gyalpo.
27. Gölo Zhönu Pal (1392–1481).
28. Chen-ngawa Chökyi Trakpa (1453–1525).
29. Sheltrakpa Chökyi Lodrö.
30. Khyungtsangpa Lodrö Palden.
31. Pangtön, Karmaguru.
32. Pangtön Chöwang Lhündrup.
33. Chöwang Künzang.
34. Pangtön, Künzang Chögyal.
35. Minling Terchen Gyurme Dorje (1646–1714).
36. Minling Lochen Dharmashrī (1654–1717).
37. Minling Jetsün Mingyur Paldrön.
38. Minling Gyalse Rinchen Namgyal.
39. Minling Pema Tendzin.
40. Minling Thrinle Namgyal.
41. Minling Jetsün Thrinle Chödrön.
42. Minling Trichen Sangye Künga.
43. Jamyang Khyentse Wangpo (1820–1892).
44. Kathok Situ Chökyi Gyatso (1880–1925).
45. Dzongsar Khyentse Chökyi Lodrö (1893–1959).
46. Fourth Dodrupchen Thupten Thrinle Palzangpo (b. 1927).

Me-ngagde

Me-ngagde, the cycle on the ultimate instructions,[45] teaches realization of the true nature, as it is, without falling into extremes or creating something new. The true nature is the union of three principles; the essence of emptiness (openness), nature of clarity, and compassion (power) of all pervading presence.

Me-ngagde has four cycles of teachings and trainings: Outer, Inner, Esoteric, and Innermost Esoteric. All these cycles are similar in being the teachings on the primordially pure nature (Ka Dag), which is called "cutting through" (Khregs Ch'od) all the graspings. However, the Innermost Esoteric cycle focuses on the trainings of spontaneous perfection of appearances (Lhun Grub), which is called "direct approach" (Thod rGal).

The Outer cycle teaches the nature of the primordial basis in detail. The Inner cycle teaches the ways of introduction to the nature with symbols, meaning, and significances. The Esoteric cycle teaches the four methods of natural contemplation (Chog bZhag). The Innermost Esoteric cycle teaches all the following: the primordial nature, the explanation of symbols, meaning, and significances for introduction to the true nature, the arising of the four visions of lights (sNang Ba bZhi) in the path, appearances of lights in the intermediate state, and the attainment of liberation in the ultimate sphere of the spontaneous perfection.

While there are many tantras and instructional texts of Me-ngagde, nineteen of these constitute the root texts of the Innermost Secret of Me-ngagde.[46]

There are many Branch or Instructional (Man Ngag) teachings. The instructional teachings are elucidated and condensed in two major traditions of Nyingthig. The first one is the detailed teachings for/of the scholars (rGya Ch'e Ba Paṇḍita), brought to Tibet by Vimalamitra and known as *Vima Nyingthig*. It is mainly based on the Seventeen tantras and Troma tantra. The second one is the profound teachings for/of mendicants (Zab Pa Ku Sa La), brought to Tibet by Guru Padmasambhava and known as *Khandro Nyingthig*. It is mainly based on *Longsal Barma* tantra.

In addition to the original tantras of Nyingthig, the Innermost Esoteric teachings of Me-ngagde translated into Tibetan, many other Nyingthig teachings were brought to Tibet mainly through Vimalamitra and Guru Rinpoche (and also Vairochana). Some were transmitted in pure visions to great realized masters by siddhas who lived centuries before them. Some were discovered by masters in their state of realization of the primordial wisdom. Some were revealed by masters as ters,[47] which had been transmitted to them in their past lives by enlightened masters and awakened in this life to be revealed by others. They include *Vima Nyingthig, Khandro Nyingthig, Chetsün Nyingthig, Gongpa Zangthal, Katak Rangjung Rangshar, Gongpa Yongdü, Yangti Nakpo, Ati Zaptön Nyingpo, Karma Nyingthig, Longchen Nyingthig, Ösal Nyingthig, Dorsem Nyingthig,* and *Tsogyal Nyingthig.*

Of all of them, four teachings are preeminent for the study and practice of Nyingthig. They are known as the two mother and two son teachings. The two mother Nyingthigs are the teachings brought to Tibet by Vimalamitra known as *Vima Nyingthig* and the teachings brought by Guru Rinpoche known as *Khandro Nyingthig*. The two son teachings are the revelations of Longchen Rabjam concerning the two mother teachings. They are *Lama Yangtig* on *Vima Nyingthig*, and *Khandro Yangtig* on *Khandro Nyingthig*, as well as *Zabmo Yangtig* on both the mother Nyingthigs.

However, over the last couple of centuries, *Longchen Nyingthig*, which contains the essence of all the early Nyingthig teachings, has become the most popular and powerful teaching on Nyingthig to study and practice in Tibet.

So, in this book, my main intention is to present a brief but comprehensive set of lives of the Longchen Nyingthig lineage masters. But it is preceded by the names of lineage masters of Vima Nyingthig and Khandro Nyingthig. The lineage masters of these transmissions descend from the primordial Buddha to my crown jewel, the present Dodrupchen Rinpoche.

Lineal Transmission of *Vima Nyingthig*[48]

1. Samantabhadra, the Dharmakāya.
2. Vajrasattva, the Sambhogakāya.
3. Prahevajra (Garab Dorje), the Nirmāṇakāya, the first human master of Dzogpa Chenpo.
4. Mañjushrīmitra.
5. Shrīsiṃha of China.
6. Jñānasūtra.
7. Vimalamitra, who brought the lineage from India to Tibet. He transmitted the first three cycles of Mengagde teachings with texts to Nyang and four others in Tibet. He transmitted the Innermost Esoteric cycle to the king, Prince Mu-ne Tsepo, Kawa Paltsek, Chok-ro Lü'i Gyaltsen, and Nyang, but concealed the texts in Kekung at Samye Chimphu.
8. Nyang Tingdzin Zangpo (9th century), who concealed his texts of the first three cycles and the oral transmission in Zha'i temple in Drikung Valley. He transmitted the oral teachings to Dro Rinchen Bar.
9. Dro Rinchen Bar.

10. Be Lodrö Wangchuk.
11. Neten Dangma Lhüngyal (11th century) discovered the texts concealed by Nyang at Zha'i temple.
12. Chetsün Senge Wangchuk (11th–12th centuries), discovered the texts concealed by Vimalamitra at Kekung at Samye Chimphu.
13. Zhangtön Tashi Dorje (1097–1167).
14. Se Nyima Bum (1158–1213).
15. Guru 'Chober (1196–1255).
16. Trülzhik Senge Gyapa (13 century).
17. Drupchen Melong Dorje (1243–1303).
18. Rigdzin Kumārādza (1266–1343).
19. Künkhyen Longchen Rabjam (1308–1363). He became the most important master of the Nyingthig tradition. The transmission of both *Khandro* and *Vima Nyingthig* flowed into him, and he then disseminated both traditions by revealing his own *Lama Yangtig* on *Vima Nyingthig, Khandro Yangtig* on *Khandro Nyingthig,* and *Zabmo Yangtig* on both *Nyingthigs,* and by putting them all together as the *Nyingthig Yabzhi,* the four volumes on Nyingthig.
20. Khedrup Khyapdal Lhündrup (14th century).
21. Tülku Trakpa Özer.
22. Trülzhik Senge Önpo (14th century).
23. Gyalse Dawa Trakpa.
24. Drupchen Künzang Dorje.
25. Künga Gyaltsen Palzang (1497–1568).
26. Tülku Natsok Rangtröl (1494–1560).
27. Sungtrül Tendzin Trakpa (1536–1597).
28. Tülku Do-ngak Tendzin (1576–1628).
29. Rigdzin Thrinle Lhündrup (1611–1662).
30. Minling Terchen Gyurme Dorje (1646–1714).
31. Minling Gyalse Rinchen Namgyal.
32. Minling Khenchen Ogyen Tendzin Dorje.
33. Fourth Dzogchen Rinpoche Mingyur Namkhe Dorje (1793–?).
34. Gyarong Namtrül Künzang Thekchok Dorje.
35. Third Dodrupchen Jigme Tenpe Nyima (1865–1926).
36. Gekong Khenpo Künzang Palden.
37. Fourth Dodrupchen Thupten Thrinle Palzangpo (b. 1927).

Or:

32. U Chörap?
33. Minling Drubwang Shrīnatha.
34. Rigdzin Jigme Lingpa (1730–1798).
35. First Dodrupchen Jigme Thrinle Özer (1745–1821).
36. Fourth Dzogchen Rinpoche Mingyur Namkhe Dorje and Dola Jigme Kalzang.
37. From both Gyalse Zhenphen Thaye (1800–?).
38. Khenchen Pema Dorje of Dzogchen.
39. Jamyang Khyentse Wangpo (1820–1892).
40. Third Dodrupchen Jigme Tenpe Nyima (1865–1926).
41. Gekong Khenpo Künzang Palden (1872–1943).
42. Fourth Dodrupchen Thupten Thrinle Palsangpo (b. 1927).

The Lineal Transmission of *Khandro Nyingthig*[49]

1. Samantabhadra, the Dharmakāya.
2. Vajrasattva, the Sambhogakāya.
3. Prahevajra (Garab Dorje), the Nirmāṇakāya.
4. Shrīsiṃha.
5. Guru Rinpoche (Padmasambhava), who brought the teachings to Tibet.

6a. Khandro Yeshe Tsogyal, Chögyal Trisong Detsen, and Lhacham Pemasal. Yeshe Tsogyal helped Guru Rinpoche to conceal the *Khandro Nyingthig* teachings, as a ter.

6b. Pema Ledreltsal (1291–1319?), who was the rebirth of Lhacham Pemasal and who discovered the *Khandro Nyingthig* teachings as a ter.

7. Gyalse Lekpa (1290–1366/7).
8. Longchen Rabjam (1308–1363).
9. Yeshe Rabjam.
10. Khedrup Samten.
11. Jinpa Zangpo.
12. Sönam Rinchen.
13. Ngawang Pema.
14. Sönam Wangpo.
15. Rigdzin Chökyi Gyatso.
16. First Dzogchen Rinpoche Pema Rigdzin (1625–1697).

17. Namkha Ösal.
18. Second Dzogchen Gyurme Thekchok Tendzin (1699–?).
19. Nyila Pema Tendzin.
20. Tendzin Dargye.
21. Fourth Dzogchen Rinpoche Mingyur Namkhe Dorje (1793–?).
22. Second Gyarong Namtrül Künzang Thekchok Dorje.
23. Third Dodrupchen Jigme Tenpe Nyima (1865–1926).
24. Gekong Khenpo Künzang Palden.
25. Fourth Dodrupchen Thupten Thrinle Palzang (b. 1927).

Or:

13. Zablung Tülku.
14. Sönam Rinchen.
15. Karmaguru.
16. Künzang Paljor.
17. Tülku Do-ngak Tendzin (1576–1628).
18. Rigdzin Thrinle Lhündrup (1611–1662).
19. Minling Terchen Gyurme Dorje (1646–1714).
20. Minling Gyalse Rinchen Namgyal.
21. Minling Drubwang Shrīnatha.
22. Rigdzin Jigme Lingpa (1730–1798).
23. First Dodrupchen Jigme Thrinle Özer (1745–1821).
24. Dola Jigme Kalzang.
25. Dzogchen Gyalse Zhenphen Thaye (1800–?).
26. Dzogchen Khenpo Pema Dorje.
27. Jamyang Khyentse Wangpo (1820–1892).
28. Third Dodrupchen Jigme Tenpe Nyima (1865–1926).
29. Gekong Khenpo Künzang Palden (1872–1943).
30. Fourth Dodrupchen Thupten Thrinle Palzangpo (b. 1927).

Part Two

The Lineage of Longchen Nyingthig

Longchen Nyingthig is a collection of tantras and sādhanas revealed by Rigdzin Jigme Lingpa (1730–1798) as "mind ter" teachings.

For three principal reasons, this cycle is called *Longchen Nyingthig*. First, they are Nyingthig, the innermost essence teachings of Mengagde, and were discovered by Jigme Lingpa through the blessings he received in a series of pure visions of Longchen Rabjam (1308–1363). Second, they are the teachings that condensed all the Nyingthig teachings that came through Longchen Rabjam. Third, they are the teachings on the subject of Longchen, the "great vastness" or the most profound field, and they are the Nyingthig, the "heart (or innermost) essence" of all the teachings. Jigme Lingpa writes: "It is the sphere of great vastness and it is the heart essence."[50]

Longchen Nyingthig teachings are mainly centered on the Nyingthig, the innermost essence cycle of the Me-ngagde. For example, the development stage of the *Rigdzin Düpa* sādhana arises as the manifestative power (rTsal) of the intrinsic awareness (Rig Pa), and it also merges into the ultimate sphere, the primordial purity in the dissolution (perfection) stage. Kyala Khenpo writes in his commentary on *Rigdzin Düpa:*

> In other Anuttaratantra traditions, the practitioner first ripens his mind by the training on the development stage and then enters into the perfection stage. But in the Mahāyoga meditations of *Longchen Nyingthig,* having been introduced to the luminous intrinsic awareness (the true nature of one's own mind) and having realized the inseparability of one's own intrinsic awareness and the enlightened mind of the lama, the meditator contemplates that realized state and trains on the arisings [of the appearances] as the maṇḍala of the deities [the power of the intrinsic awareness, Rig Pa]. So the

unique method of *Longchen Nyingthig* is to train on the development stage and perfection stage in union. Also, by employing the unification of one's own mind and the enlightened mind of the lama, the realization of wisdom is awakened by force.[51]

Longchen Nyingthig Teachings

Longchen Nyingthig encompasses a few tantras and many sādhanas accompanied by instructions, commentaries, and supplementary texts, in two (or three) root volumes (rTsa Pod). They were discovered by Jigme Lingpa as a mind ter. In addition to the two root volumes, the cycle includes the *Phurpa Gyüluk* on Vajrakīla in one volume, which is recognized as both a mind ter discovery and a compilation of tantras. The main *Longchen Nyingthig* teachings are classified into two categories. They are the original tantras of Nyingthig and the tantric sādhanas and teachings.

The original Nyingthig tantras are the continuum of the absolute nature (Dharmakāya) arisen as the teachings for Jigme Lingpa himself or for his previous incarnations and to which he awakened. While practicing in seclusion for three years at Samye Chimphu, Jigme Lingpa studied the writings of Longchen Rabjam and prayed devotedly, seeing him as a Buddha. He had three pure visions of Longchen Rabjam and received the blessings of his body, speech, and mind. During the third vision, Longchen Rabjam said three times, "May realization of the meaning be communicated to you, and may the transmission of the words be completely accomplished." Thereupon Jigme Lingpa realized the nature of Dzogpa Chenpo free from mental analysis and received the absolute transmission (Don brGyud), and the sacred original tantras of Nyingthig arose in him. These original tantras arose in him as the unified essence of all the three modes of transmission—namely mind, indication, and oral transmissions—of the three Buddha bodies and the masters of all the Dzogpa Chenpo lineage, including Guru Rinpoche, Vimalamitra, and Longchen Rabjam.[52]

The tantric sādhanas and teachings of *Longchen Nyingthig* are the teachings that came to Jigme Lingpa through Guru Rinpoche as a ter.[53]

While Guru Rinpoche was visiting Tibet, on the second floor of the main temple of Samye Monastery he conferred the *Longchen Nyingthig* teachings on King Trisong Detsen, Khandro Yeshe Tsogyal, and Vairochana. Then he entrusted the teachings to them through the means of the naturally arisen ḍākiṇī, the wisdom, the feminine principle of the three bodies of the Buddha. He gave prophetic empowerments by saying that these teachings would be discovered by Jigme Lingpa, an incarnation (tülku) of King Trisong Detsen. Yeshe Tsogyal arranged the teachings in symbolic scripts of unforgetting memory on the yellow scrolls of naturally arisen five colors. With aspirational empowerments, they concealed the teachings in the casket of luminous heart treasure (or mind treasure) of the disciples. They entrusted the concealed teachings to the ḍākinīs, the ultimate sphere wisdoms, for preservation until the right time came to awaken the teachings from the luminous intrinsic nature of the mind of the discoverer.

So, centuries later, when the prophetic empowerments of Guru Rinpoche ripened and the favorable circumstances came to fruition, the concealed *Longchen Nyingthig* teachings were accordingly awakened in the enlightened mind of Jigme Lingpa as a mind ter.

Jigme Lingpa was a reincarnation of both Vimalamitra himself and King Trisong Detsen,[54] who was the recipient of Nyingthig teachings from Guru Rinpoche and Vimalamitra. So the Nyingthig teachings of two major lineages flowed together in Jigme Lingpa. *Longchen Nyingthig* is the essence or embodiment of the two Nyingthig traditions, *Vima Nyingthig* and *Khandro Nyingthig*.[55] The scope, language, meaning, clarity and power of *Longchen Nyingthig* make the teachings easy to comprehend and powerful to practice, so that in recent centuries the study and practice of *Longchen Nyingthig* has become popular among a great number of Nyingmapas in Tibet.

The major texts of *Longchen Nyingthig* are as follows:[56]

ORIGINAL TANTRAS (RGYUD) OF *Longchen Nyingthig*[57]

1. The root tantra (rTsa rGyud): *Küntu Zangpo Yeshe Longki Gyü* (Kun Tu bZang Po Ye Shes Klong Gi rGyud)
2. The subsequent tantra: *Gyü Chima* (rGyud Phyi Ma)
3. Teachings (Lung): *Küntu Zangpö Gong-ńyam* (Kun Tu bZang Po'i dGongs Nyams)
4. Instructions (Me-ngag)
   a. Instructions: *Nesum Shenje* and *Neluk Dorje Tsigang* (gNad gSum Shan 'Byed and gNas Lug rDo rJe'i Tshigs rKang)

b. Their commentaries: *Yeshe Lama* (Ye Shes Bla Ma) with its supporting texts (rGyab Ch'os)

TANTRIC SĀDHANAS AND TEACHINGS OF *Longchen Nyingthig*[58]

1. Male Knowledge-holders
   a. Peaceful: outer: *La-me Naljor* (Bla Ma'i rNal 'Byor)
      inner: *Rigdzin Düpa* (Rig 'Dzin 'Dus Pa)
      secret: *Dug-ngal Rangtröl* (sDug bsNgal Rang Grol)
      ultimate secret: *Ladrup Thigle Gyachen* (Bla sGrub Thig Le'i rGya Chan)
   b. Wrathful: blue: *Palchen Düpa* (dPal Ch'en 'Dus Pa)
      red: *Takhyung Barwa* (rTa Khyung 'Bar Ba)
2. Female knowledge-holders
   a. Peaceful: root sādhana: *Yumka Dechen Gyalmo* (Yum Ka bDe Ch'en rGyal Mo)
   b. Wrathful: secret sādhana: *Senge Dongchen* (Seng Ge'i gDong Chan)

The Lineage Masters of Longchen Nyingthig

THE lineage of Longchen Nyingthig begins with the primordial Buddha, or the ultimate Buddha essence, and comes down to the contemporary masters through an unbroken line of transmission.

This lineage starts from the three Buddha bodies, Dharmakāya, Sambhogakāya, and Nirmāṇakāya, the principle of Buddhahood. Dharmakāya is the formless ultimate nature. Sambhogakāya and Nirmāṇakāya are the manifesting form-bodies of the Buddha. The three Buddha bodies are the ultimate source of all the absolute teachings, such as *Longchen Nyingthig*. From the three Buddha bodies the teachings were received by human masters, as in the case of Dzogpa Chenpo by Prahevajra.

Prahevajra, the first human master, transmitted the teachings to Mañjushrīmitra, who transmitted them to Shrīsiṃha. Shrīsiṃha in turn transmitted them to Jñānasūtra, Vimalamitra, Guru Rinpoche, and Vairochana. Vimalamitra also received them from Jñānasūtra.

Both Vimalamitra and Guru Rinpoche transmitted them to King Trisong Detsen and a few others in Tibet. Guru Rinpoche concealed many of them as ter. He also transmitted *Khandro Nyingthig* to Lhacham Pemasal, the previous incarnation of Longchen Rabjam.

Almost eight centuries after the concealment of *Longchen Nyingthig,* the essence of the Nyingthig teachings, as a ter by Guru Rinpoche, Jigme Lingpa discovered them as a mind ter. Jigme Lingpa was able to discover them because he had had the transmissions and entrustments in his past life and received the blessings of Longchen Rabjam in three pure visions in his current life.

In the lineage prayer of *Longchen Nyingthig,* Jigme Lingpa mentions the lineage of the following masters, through which the *Longchen Nyingthig* was transmitted and revealed:[59]

From the land that is free from dimensions and partialities,
Samantabhadra, the Dharmakāya primordial Buddha,
Vajrasattva, the manifestative power of Sambhogakāya, [appearing]
like a reflection in water,
And Prahevajra in fully perfected attributes of Nirmāṇakāya,
To you I pray. Please bestow [upon us] the blessing
empowerments.

Shrīsiṃha,[60] the treasure of the ultimate Dharma,
Mañjushrīmitra, the master of the chariot of the nine yānas,
Jñānasūtra, and Vimalamitra,
To you I pray. Please show me the path to liberation.

Padmasambhava, the sole ornament of Jambu continent,
With the Lord, the Subjects, and the Support,[61] your supreme
mind-offsprings,
Longchen [Rabjam], who decoded oceans of mind treasures,
Jigme Lingpa, who was entrusted with the ultimate treasure of the
Ḍākinīs,
To you I pray. Please let me obtain the fruition and attain
liberation.

I

Dharmakāya

The Dharmakāya, the ultimate body, constitutes the basis of all the qualities of the Buddha, and of their capacity to function. The nature of the Dharmakāya is pure from its primordial state and pure from any adventitious defilements. Transcending thought and verbal expression, it dwells in freedom from characteristics, like space. Never moving from the state of Dharmakāya, it fulfills the needs of all living beings through the spontaneous presence of two form bodies.

In Nyingma icons, Dharmakāya is symbolized by a naked, sky-colored (light blue) male and female Buddha in union, called Samantabhadra.

Samantabhadra signifies the aspect of realizing the Dharmakāya, the ultimate nature of all the good and bad qualities of saṃsāra and nirvāṇa. He realizes the primordial wisdom of the ultimate sphere, free from conceptualization, from the beginning. Because of this realization he remains neither in the extremes of saṃsāra nor in the peace of nirvāṇa. He is empowered with the knowledge of the ultimate truth, and this knowledge is the all-equalizing primordial wisdom. It is not a mere emptiness brought about by cessation. Instead, the object of the discriminating primordial wisdom of all the Buddhas, which is the essence of subtle primordial wisdom, dwells as the pure land of inner clarity, the "body of the youth within a vase." The inner clarity of the relationship between primordial wisdom and its object may be likened to the way a crystal projects a spectrum of colors, yet the rays are actually inherent in the crystal itself. Because of that sacred power, the inner clarity, the five teachers of the five classes of the Sambhogakāya maṇḍala dwell, through manifestative inherence, in the great display of indivisible forms and wisdom.

The Dharmakāya dwells without change, discrimination, distinction, in a fivefold manner:

PLACE: The ultimate sphere, the pure land of the "body of the youth within a vase"

TEACHER: Samantabhadra, great self-awareness, the primordial wisdom of evenness-suchness

DISCIPLES: The oceanlike assembly of primordial wisdoms

TIME: Changeless time, suchness

TEACHING: The absolute Dzogpa Chenpo, the doctrine of the uncreated body, speech, and mind

Dharmakāya, pure from the beginning, has one taste, like space. It dwells with threefold primordial wisdom, transcending the conceptualization of the extremes, substantialism, and nihilism. The three primordial wisdoms are as follows:

1. The primordial wisdom of the intrinsic essence, pure from the beginning, transcending the extremes of conceptualization and verbal expression, like a transparent crystal.
2. The primordial wisdom of the spontaneously accomplished nature; it is a subtle, deep clarity, which serves as the ground for the arising of the attributes of the manifestative aspect, and it does not exist as a mode of phenomenal particularity.
3. The primordial wisdom of all-pervading compassion (power); it dwells just as the nonobstructiveness of the ground for the arising which occurs through the manifestative power of the intrinsic essence; but this awareness does not analyze its object.

If there were any grossness, then the Dharmakāya would be phenomenal and it would have characteristics, in which case it would not be qualifiable as that which has peace and freedom from conceptualization as its very significance. If there were not the subtle aspect of deep clarity as the ground of arising, then the Dharmakāya would be a mere absence, like a blank. So it is a primordial wisdom of subtle, open clarity, which dwells as the ground of arising, transcending the two extremes of substantialism and nihilism.

The Dharmakāya possesses three great qualities:

1. Great purity (sPang Pa Ch'en Po): The two sudden and illusory obscurations with their habituations, which do not exist in actuality, are fully purified.
2. Great realization (rTogs Pa Ch'en Po): By the great primordial wisdom of the nonduality, the Dharmakāya sees all saṃsāra and nirvāṇa without falling into partiality.
3. Great mind (Sems Ch'en Po): Because of those two previous qualities, the manifestations of the Dharmakāya for the benefit of all beings are spontaneously and naturally accomplished without any conception.

2

Sambhogakāya

The Dharmakāya dwells in the state of inner clarity and the absolute nature of phenomena. Without any modification of its own nature by the Dharmakāya, the self-appearing Sambhogakāya, the enjoyment body, manifests spontaneously. From the essence of the Dharmakāya, the manifestative aspect of primordial wisdom, the myriad Buddha bodies and pure lands, arises as self-perception, just as the rays of five colors appear from a crystal because of the rays of the sun. In the Sambhogakāya the teacher and disciples are united in the sphere of the same realization. The teacher does not give teachings; rather, they are self-arisen in the sameness state. They arise spontaneously as self-perception in a fivefold manner:

PLACE: The self-perceptive "unexcelled pure land of beautiful array"

TEACHER: The Buddhas of the five classes, such as Vajrasattva (Akṣhobhya), adorned with the thirty-two marks and eighty signs of excellence

DISCIPLES: The Buddhas, infinite as the ocean, who appear as the self-manifestation of the primordial wisdom, which is not other than the teacher himself

TEACHING: Great luminescent vision, ineffable and free from the conceptualizations of indications and words

TIME: Changeless; the ever-continuing cycle of time

There are two types of transmission within the Sambhogakāya:

1. In the unexcelled pure land, teachings of tantra are given by Samantabhadra to the self-perceptive Sambhogakāya Buddhas, who are none other than Samantabhadra himself, while the teacher and disciple dwell in the state of undifferentiated realization. This is called the transmission of the same mind of teacher and disciple.[62]

2. The disciples whose minds differ from the mind of the teacher become, by the teacher's blessing, of one mind with the teacher. This is called the transmission of the becoming inseparable of the mind of teacher and disciple.[63]

The five primordial wisdoms of the Sambhogakāya are as follows:[64]

1. Primordial wisdom of ultimate-sphere (dharmadhātujñāna): It is the inseparable union of three aspects: the great emptiness (openness), which is the basis of liberation, pure from the beginning; the basis of self-clarity, natural light of primordial wisdom; and the ultimate sphere of awareness wisdom.

2. Mirrorlike primordial wisdom (ādarshajñāna): The appearances appear in the empty-clarity awareness in the mode of unobstructedness, like the arising of reflections in a mirror. This primordial wisdom is the aspect of the basis for the arising of the two form bodies, Sambhogakāya and Nirmāṇakāya. In response to disciples capable of seeing and training, the two form bodies of the Buddha and the three following primordial wisdoms naturally arise as a reflection.

3. Primordial wisdom of evenness (samantājñāna): It is the primordially liberated great evenness wisdom, in which all the appearances of the form bodies of the Buddha arise according to the perceptions of disciples, without falling or remaining in any of the extremes.

4. Discriminating primordial wisdom (pratyavekṣhaṇajñāna): it is the primordial wisdom that clearly sees all knowable phenomena simultaneously without any confusion.

5. Primordial wisdom of accomplishment (kṛityānuṣhṭhānajñāna): It is the primordial wisdom that accomplishes one's own goals in the state of intrinsic awareness, and spontaneously serves all the needs of others, without any effort, like a wish-fulfilling jewel.

Dharmadhātu primordial wisdom sees what is, the absolute truth; and the four other primordial wisdoms see how things appear, the relative truth.

3

Nirmāṇakāya

WHILE the Dharmakāya remains without moving from the great oneness of saṃsāra and nirvāṇa, the form bodies of the Buddha, the manifestations of effortless compassion, appear in a variety of ceaseless displays like the play of magical apparitions.

The Nirmāṇakāya, the manifested body, will appear in response to the needs of ordinary beings for as long as saṃsāra exists. It is as when the moon is reflected in buckets of water, there will be as many moons as there are buckets to reproduce its reflection. The Nirmāṇakāya can be divided into three classes:

1. The Natural Nirmāṇakāya (Rang bZhin sPrul sKu): For the disciples having pure perception, and who have attained any of the ten stages, the great Sambhogakāya manifestation appears as the unexcelled pure land and the pure lands of the Five Classes of Buddhas, such as Vajrasattva, and of the Three Classes of Buddhas, such as Vajrapāṇi, like a reflection in a mirror. Here the disciples are not of one mind with the teacher, the Buddha, but in actuality these pure lands are Sambhogakāya pure lands, so they are called semi-Sambhogakāya and semi-Nirmāṇakāya pure lands.

2. The Nirmāṇakāya subduer of beings ('Gro 'Dul sPrul sKu): This is the manifestation of the excellent Nirmāṇakāyas, endowed with the thirty-two marks and eighty signs of excellence. They appear in each of the six realms of the countless world systems. By the twelve deeds and

skillful methods they serve the needs and liberation of all beings. The excellent Nirmāṇakāya of the human realm of our world system of the present time is Shākyamuni Buddha.

The twelve deeds of Shākyamuni Buddha are (1) descent from the Tuṣhita heaven, (2) entry into the mother's womb, (3) taking birth, (4) learning the arts, (5) marriage, (6) renunciation of the worldly household life, (7) ascetic practice, (8) journey to the Bodhi Tree, (9) defeat of the hosts of māras, (10) attainment of Buddhahood, (11) turning the wheel of Dharma, Buddhism, and (12) passing into nirvāṇa.

3. Nirmāṇakāya of Various Forms (sNa Tshogs sPrul sKu): In this Nirmāṇakāya expression there is no certainty of the place, form, or duration of the manifestation. It appears in any form that is appropriate for beings, such as living beings; as images, scriptures, houses, gardens, medicine, bridges, roads, and so on.

The primordial wisdom of Nirmāṇakāya is the realization that whatever forms of Nirmāṇakāya appear before beings are not inanimate forms or mere reflections. They are endowed with twofold primordial wisdoms, and those wisdoms are appearing spontaneously for the benefit of beings.

The primordial wisdom of "knowing as it is" is the realization of the nature of absolute truth of all phenomenal existents, without any error. It reveals to others the meaning of the ultimate truth, which is free from conceptualizations of birth and cessation, like space.

The primordial wisdom of "knowing all" phenomenal existents simultaneously is the realization of the relative truth without confusing the different characteristics of phenomenal existents.

The unique transmission of Dzogpa Chenpo was received by Prahevajra (Garab Dorje) from Vajrasattva or Vajrapāṇi. Vajrasattva and Vajrapāṇi are the Buddha appearing in the form of Sambhogakāya or semi-Sambhogakāya, and Prahevajra is the Buddha appearing in the form of Nirmāṇakāya.

4

Prahevajra (Garab Dorje)

Prahevajra (dGa' Rab rDo rJe)[65] is a Nirmāṇakāya, manifested body of the Buddha appearing as the first human master of Dzogpa Chenpo. According to Dzogpa Chenpo sources, Prahevajra was born to a daughter of the king of Oḍḍiyāṇa, which was located, according to some scholars, somewhere around the Swat Valley in present-day Pakistan. Oḍḍiyāṇa was the most important source of esoteric Buddhist teachings, or tantras. It was a place of power and a land of ḍākinīs, rich in natural treasures, forests, and wild animals. In Oḍḍiyāṇa there was also a magnificent temple called Deche Tsekpa (Heap of Joy) surrounded by 6,108 small temples. All were endowed with great prosperity.

Not far off, on an island covered by golden sand, a nun named Sudharmā,[67] the daughter of King Uparāja[68] and Queen Ālokabhāsvati (One with Lights)[69] of Oḍḍiyāṇa was in absorption in a simple grass hut with an attendant named Sukhasāravati (Joyous Heart). One night, the nun had a dream in which an immaculate man with a white complexion came and placed three times on her head a crystal vase adorned with five syllables symbolizing the five Buddhas. The vase emanated beams of light, and she was able to see the three worlds clearly.

In the tenth month after the dream, a son adorned with many auspicious signs was born to the nun. This child was the rebirth of Adhichitta, a manifestation of Vajrasattva who appeared in the god's realm to propagate Dzogpa Chenpo there. The nun was frightened and ashamed. "This fatherless son will be none other than an evil spirit!" she exclaimed, and she threw him into a pit of ashes, although the attendant, who was herself adorned with auspicious qualities, warned the nun that the child was an enlightened manifestation. At that moment wondrous sounds were heard and rays appeared. Three nights later the nun recovered the infant, who was unharmed.[70] She realized that he was an enlightened manifestation, and she brought him home, wrapped him in a white silk cloth, and gave him a bath. At that moment, the ḍākinīs and sages showered praise and offerings on the infant, and from the sky the gods proclaimed:

> O Protector, Teacher, Blessed One,
> The lord of the world, who reveals the true nature,
> Be our powerful protector.
> Vajra of the Sky, we pray to you.

When the child was seven years old, bursting with the energies of wisdom, he insisted that his mother allow him to go see the scholars so that he could debate them about religious doctrine. When he had permission, he rushed to his father, King Uparāja, and requested to meet the scholars. He debated with five hundred scholars, none of whom could defeat him. Unanimously they accepted him as an enlightened incarnation and took his feet upon their heads in the gesture of highest reverence. They gave the boy the name Prajñābhava (Wisdom Nature). The king was very happy and gave the child the name Prahevajra (Vajra of Supreme Joy). He was also called Vetālasukha and Rolang Thaldok (Blissful Zombie and Ash-colored Zombie), as he had been recovered from the ashes where he had been buried.

Then in the north, on the precipice of Mount Sūryaprakāsha (Very Sunny Mountain), in a grass hut, he remained in contemplation until he reached the age of thirty-two. He received the empowerments, instructions, and entrustment of the tantras of Dzogpa Chenpo in an instant from Vajrasattva[71] and attained the stage of "no more training," Buddhahood. The earth shook seven times, various sounds were heard from the sky, and a rain of flowers fell.

When those victorious sounds were heard, a heretical king sent assassins to murder Prahevajra, but they could not harm him, for his body was immaterial like the rays of the sun. Thereupon Prahevajra rose up into the sky, and the king and his subjects developed faith in him and became Buddhists.

At thirty-two, he went to Mount Malaya. He stayed at the submit of the mountain for three years and transcribed the teachings of the Buddhas of the past and especially the 6,400,000 verses of Dzogpa Chenpo, which were present in Prahevajra's memory, with the help of Ḍākinīs Vajradhātu and Aṇantaguṇā. Then he placed the teachings in the care of Khandro Ngönpar Jungwa and charged Ḍākinī Semden to make offerings to the sacred scriptures.

With miraculous display, Prahevajra went to the great stūpa situated in the Shītavana, the mysterious charnel ground.[72] There he gave teachings to numerous disciples including the Ḍākinī Sūryakiraṇā. During that time, in accordance with Mañjushrī's prophetic advice, master Mañjushrīmitra came to the Shītavana charnel ground and received the Nyingthig teachings from Prahevajra for seventy-five years.

According to *Khandro Nyingthig*[73] and other sources, Shrīsiṃha also came to Shītavana charnel ground and received *Khandro Nyingthig* and other teachings from Prahevajra, and later he transmitted them to Guru Padamasambhava and Vairochana.[74]

At the end, at the source of the river Danatika, the mortal body of Prahevajra dissolved into immaculate space, amid wondrous signs of earth tremors, a great mass of rainbow light, and various sounds.

When Mañjushrīmitra offered the prayers of elegy, from the midst of a mass of light in the sky, Prahevajra appeared, and a golden casket the size of a fingernail descended into Mañjushrīmitra's hand. That casket contained the testament of Prahevajra, known as *Three Words That Penetrate the Essence.*[75] It includes the following lines:

> Homage to the realization of confidence in the self-awareness!
> The [nature of] awareness is free from existence,
> And various arisings of self-appearances are ceaseless.
> So all the phenomenal existents are arising as the pure land of
>   Dharmakāya,
> And all the arisings are liberated in the nature [of awareness] itself.
> [View:] Introduction to the nature [one's own awareness] itself.
> [Path:] Becoming certain of the single point [of maintaining the
>   nature itself].

[Result:] Having confidence in the liberation [of all into the primordial nature].

Just by reading the testament, Mañjushrīmitra attained a realization equal to that of Prahevajra.

5

Mañjushrīmitra

Mañjushrīmitra ('Jam dPal bShes gNyen)[76] was born in a brahman family in the city of Dvikrama to the west of Bodhgayā in India. His father was Sādhushāstrī, and his mother was Pradīpālokā.[77] He became a scholar of all the five scholarly fields.

In a pure vision, Mañjushrī gave him this prophetic advice: "O son of good family, if you want to attain the result of Buddhahood in this very life, go to the Shītavana charnel ground." Mañjushrīmitra went there and received teachings from Prahevajra for seventy-five years. Prahevajra told him:

> The nature of the mind is Buddha from the beginning.
> Mind, like space, has no birth or cessation.
> Having perfectly realized the meaning of the oneness of all phenomena,
> to remain in it, without seeking, is the meditation.[78]

Mañjushrīmitra realized the meaning of Prahevajra's teaching and expressed his realization to him:

> I am Mañjushrīmitra.
> I have attained the accomplishment of Yamāntaka.
> I have realized the great equalness of saṃsāra and nirvāṇa.
> All-knowing primordial wisdom is arisen in me.

When Prahevajra attained nirvāṇa in the midst of wondrous signs, Mañjushrīmitra beheld Prahevajra in the sky in the midst of a mass of light, and he uttered this lament:

Alas, alack, alas! O Vast Expanse!
If the light of the teacher's lamp is obscured,
Who will dispel the darkness of the world?

From the mass of light with the sound of a thunderclap came a golden casket the size of a thumbnail. In the air the casket circumambulated Mañjushrīmitra thrice. Then it descended into the palm of his right hand. Upon opening it, he found the testament of Prahevajra, *Three Words That Penetrate the Essence,* written in blue malachite liquid on a leaf made of five precious substances. Just by seeing it he attained a realization equal to that of Prahevajra. Then Mañjushrīmitra classified the 6,400,000 verses of Dzogpa Chenpo into three categories (sDe):

1. The teachings that emphasize the way the mind "dwells" he categorized as Semde
2. The teachings that emphasize freedom from efforts he categorized as Longde
3. The teachings that emphasize the essential points he categorized as Me-ngagde

Mañjushrīmitra divided Nyingthig, the most extraordinary teachings of Me-ngagde into two groups:

1. The teachings of the oral transmission (sNyan rGyud)
2. The expository tantras (bShad rGyud)

He noted down in writing the teachings of the oral transmission. But for the expository tantras, he found no worthy disciple to whom he could pass them on, so he concealed them in a boulder marked with a crossed dorje (vajra) to the northeast of Bodhgayā.

He spent one hundred and nine years[79] at the Sosadvīpa charnel ground west of Bodhgayā, remaining in contemplation, practicing esoteric disciplines with countless ḍākinīs, and giving them teachings. There he transmitted Dzogpa Chenpo teachings to Shrīsiṃha.

At the end of his life, amid wondrous signs, sounds, rays, and lights, he dissolved into the radiant body. Because of the devotional prayers of Shrīsiṃha, the testament of Mañjushrīmitra, *Gom-nyam Trukpa* (The Six

Experiences of Meditation)[80] descended into the hands of Shrīsiṃha. It includes these lines:

> O son of good family! If you wish to see the continuity of the
> naked absolute awareness,
> [a] seek the object of awareness [clear sky]
> [b] press the points of the body [by posture],
> [c] close the way of going and coming [breathing],
> [d] focus on the target [ultimate sphere],
> [e] rely on the unmoving [of body, eyes, and awareness], and
> [f] hold the vast space [the nature of awareness itself].

Masters Shrīsiṃha and Buddhajñāna are the disciples of Mañjushrīmitra and some even think that they may be the same person.[81]

Later on, Mañjushrīmitra was reborn by lotus birth at a place called Serkyi Metok Ki Gyenpe Ling (Island Arrayed with Golden Flowers) in western India and became known as "the later Mañjushrīmitra." He gave the teachings of Dzogpa Chenpo to Guru Padmasambhava and master Āryadeva.

6

Shrīsiṃha

Master Shrīsiṃha (dPal Gyi Seng Ge)[82] was born in a city called Shokyam on Sosha Island in China. His father was Gewe Denpa (Virtuous One) and his mother was Nangwa Salwa Raptu Khyenma (Clear and Wise One). At the age of fifteen, he went to the Bodhi Tree of China and studied with master Haribhala[83] for three years, and he became well versed in the five subjects. Then, while he was traveling westward by camel toward the city called Suvarṇadvīpa (Golden Island), in the sky he beheld the pure vision of Avalokiteshvara, who said, "O fortunate son of good family, if you really wish to attain the result, there is a city in India named Sosadvīpa: go there." Shrīsiṃha was pleased with the prophecy, but he thought to himself, "Still, I ought to learn the complete outer and inner tantras first, so that it will be easier for me to understand the extraordinary teachings." So he went to the Five Peaks (Wu t'ai shan) sacred to Mañjushrī, and there he studied the complete outer and inner tantras with master Bhelakīrti[84] for seven years. He took ordination as a monk (bhikṣhu) and maintained the discipline for thirty years. Again Avalokiteshvara repeated his earlier prophetic advice. Thereupon Shrīsiṃha thought, "It will be better to travel to Sosadvīpa miraculously so that there won't be any obstructions along the way." So he practiced a sādhana for three years and attained power. Then he went like the wind, about two feet above the ground. He reached Sosadvīpa and met Mañjushrīmitra. There he received teachings for twenty-five years and practiced them.

According to *Khandro Nyingthig*[85] and other sources, Shrīsiṃha also went to Shītavana and received Nyingthig teachings from Prahevajra directly, and later he transmitted them to Guru Padamasambhava and Vairochana.[86]

Then master Mañjushrīmitra attained nirvāṇa and his mortal body disappeared at the top of the stūpa in a charnel ground in the center of Sosadvīpa. The atmosphere was full of music and the sky was radiant with lights. Shrīsiṃha uttered a prayer of lamentation, saying,

> Alas, alack, alas! O Vast Expanse!
> If the light of the Vajra Master is obscured,
> Who will dispel the darkness of the world?

Suddenly Mañjushrīmitra appeared in the sky and, stretching out his right hand, placed in Shrīsiṃha's palm a jeweled casket the size of a fingernail. In it Shrīsiṃha found the testament of Mañjushrīmitra, *Gom-nyam Trukpa* (The Six Experiences of Meditation), written on a leaf of five precious metals with the ink of a hundred precious substances.

Shrīsiṃha gained total confidence in his realization and understood the extraordinary tantras, both words and meaning, without any errors. He withdrew the texts that had been concealed at Bodhgayā by Mañju-shrīmitra and returned to China.

In China he arranged the Me-ngagde teachings into four cycles (sKor): Outer, Inner, Esoteric, and Innermost Esoteric. He designated the first three cycles as the "elaborate teachings" and concealed them in the balcony of the temple near the Bodhi Tree in China. The Innermost Esoteric teachings, the Nyingthig, he kept with him without separation, but then, as instructed by a ḍākinī, he concealed them in a pillar of Tashi Trigo (Auspicious Myriad Gate) temple and entrusted them to Ekajaṭī. Then, enjoying esoteric exercises, he stayed at Siljin (Provider of Coolness) charnel ground in China as the master of the hosts of ḍākas and ḍākinīs.

He conferred the oral transmissions of the Outer, Inner, and Esoteric cycles of Me-ngagde on Vimalamitra. He conferred the oral transmission of the four cycles of Me-ngagde with their texts on Jñānasūtra. He also conferred on him the teachings and empowerments of Me-ngagde known as elaborate empowerment, simple empowerment, very simple empowerment, and utmost simple empowerment.

Then Shrīsimha dissolved in radiant body, and his testament, *Zerwu*

Dünpa (The Seven Nails),[87] descended into the hands of Jñānasūtra. It includes these lines:

> Homage to the perfection of primordial wisdom, [the union of]
> clarity and emptiness.
> The awareness wisdom, which pervades all and appears in all,
> Is open and impartial.
> For nailing [the awareness] on the changeless ground,
> By putting the seven great nails on the narrow paths of
> saṃsāra and nirvāṇa,
> Changeless great bliss arises in my mind. . . .
> [a] Strike the nail of unhindered wisdom of clarity at the juncture of saṃsāra and nirvāṇa [in order to unite them as oneness].
> [b] Strike the nail of self-appearing light at the juncture of mind and objects.
> [c] Strike the nail of natural-pure essence at the juncture of mind and matter.
> [d] Strike the nail of freedom from views at the juncture of nil and eternity.
> [e] Strike the nail of awareness, which is beyond phenomena, at the juncture of phenomena and the nature of phenomena.
> [f] Strike the nail of totally liberated five-doors [sense faculties] at the juncture of excitement and torpor.
> [g] Strike the nail of primordially perfect Dharmakāya at the juncture of appearances and emptiness.

7

Jñānasūtra

Jñānasūtra (Ye Shes mDo)[88] was born in the eastern city of Kamalashīla in eastern India. His father was Shāntihasta (Hand of Peace), and his mother was Kalyāṇachitta (Virtuous Minded),[89] in a shūdra (lowest-caste) family. He became learned and went to Bodhgayā, where he lived with five hundred scholars. Among them was Vimalamitra, with whom his relations were very close because of their previous lives.

One day Jñānasūtra and Vimalamitra walked about two miles to the west of Bodhgayā. At that time, from the sky Vajrasattva Buddha appeared and proclaimed, "O sons of good family, you have each taken birth five hundred times as scholars, yet you have not attained Buddhahood. If you would like to attain the enlightenment of the dissolving of the defiled body in this very lifetime, go to the temple near the Bodhi Tree in China."

Vimalamitra went to China, received the oral transmissions of the Outer, Inner, and Esoteric cycles, and returned to India. He and Jñānasūtra met again on the outskirts of the city of Gache Kyi Tsal (Joyful Garden). Vimalamitra told Jñānasūtra about his meeting with the master Shrīsiṃha in China.

Then Jñānasūtra in turn went to China, reaching nine months' distance in a single day through his miraculous power. When he reached the temple near the Bodhi Tree in China, he met a beautiful girl who was carrying a vase filled with water. She instructed him to go to Tashi Trigo.

When he arrived at the giant, magnificent temple, a ḍākinī instructed him to go to Siljin charnel ground. He went there and met the master Shrīsiṃha in person in a temple of skulls. To please the master, he served him for three years. Then with offerings he beseeched him for teachings. Shrīsiṃha taught him the teachings of the oral transmission for nine years. Shrīsiṃha withdrew the hidden texts of these teachings from the temple near the Bodhi Tree and entrusted them to Jñānasūtra.

Then Jñānasūtra was satisfied and prepared to depart. Shrīsiṃha asked him, "Are you satisfied?" Jñānasūtra answered, "Yes, I am satisfied." "The teachings have not yet been entrusted to you," said Shrīsiṃha. Jñānasūtra thought, "There may be still more profound teachings," and he requested Shrīsiṃha to confer them. Shrīsiṃha answered, "It is necessary to have empowerments." In the temple of Tashi Trigo he gave Jñānasūtra the complete elaborate empowerment, followed by the teachings on Innermost Esoteric cycle for three years. But he did not give him the texts, saying, "The texts will appear for you when the time comes." Then, in a deserted town, Shrīsiṃha also conferred on him the simple empowerment. When Jñānasūtra finished one year's training on preparatory exercises on the experiences of saṃsāra and nirvāṇa on the peak of Mount Kosala, Shrīsiṃha conferred on him the very simple empowerment teachings, and an extraordinary confidence was developed in Jñānasūtra. Then, after training for a month, Jñānasūtra was given the utmost simple empowerment, and he realized full control over his mind. Jñānasutra stayed with Shrīsiṃha for sixteen more years, training in meditation and observing the esoteric disciplines of the master. The master kept behaving in mysterious ways, wandering in charnel grounds, transforming himself into various forms, and mingling with ḍākinīs and fearful beings without the slightest timidity.

Then the master was invited by King Paljin (Provider of Glory) of the country of Li[90] and he went there, through the sky, riding a white lion, sitting in a silk tent under three layers of parasols, held up by six powerful young yakṣhas. The morning of the seventh day after his departure, a loud noise was heard in the sky. Jñānasūtra looked in the sky and saw the master seated in the midst of a mass of light. Jñānasūtra realized that the mortal body of the master had dissolved. Jñānasūtra offered prayers, and into his hand fell the testament, *Zerbu Dünma* (The Seven Nails).

Shrīsiṃha also gave him this prophetic instruction: "The texts of the Inner Esoteric teachings, the Nyingthig, are concealed in a pillar of Tashi Trigo. Take them and go to Bhasing[91] charnel ground." Then Jñānasūtra withdrew the texts and went to the most beautiful, fearful, and powerful Bhasing charnel ground, which is situated far to the east of Bodhgayā. While Jñānasūtra was staying there performing esoteric exercises and giving teachings to ḍākinīs, Vimalamitra, who was also doing esoteric practices, received a prophecy from a ḍākinī and came to see Jñānasūtra. Jñāṇasūtra gave him the elaborate, simple, very simple, and utmost simple empowerments and teachings, and he also entrusted him with the texts.

At the end of his life Jñānasūtra attained the dissolution of the mortal body, and when Vimalamitra uttered the prayer of lamentation, Jñānasūtra appeared and conferred on him his testament, *Zhakthap Zhipa* (The Four Methods of Contemplation).[92] It includes these lines:

> Homage to the primordially pure emptiness. . . .
> Wonderful! If you train in these, joy will arise naturally.
> If you wish to attain the state of great equalness, gain experience [in the following contemplations] all the time.
> [a] If you wish to be trained in all the esoteric "activities," maintain all the appearances in the directness (Cher) of natural contemplation.
> [b] If you wish to gain strength in your "meditation," remain in the union of mind and matter through the view of oceanlike natural contemplation.
> [c] If you wish to attain self-liberation from all the "views" [concepts], bring all the existents to their cessation through the mountainlike natural contemplation.
> [d] If you wish to attain all the "results," as they are, liberate all the errors in the training through the mountainlike view.

8

Vimalamitra

Vimalamitra (Dri Med bShes gNyen)[93] was born at the Forest of Elephants (Glang Po'i Tshal) in western India. His father was Deden Khorlo, and his mother was Dak-nyid Salma. He became a scholar of both Hīnayāna and Mahāyāna.

He was one of the five hundred scholars who were residing at Bodhgayā. One day, to ease the heat, Vimalamitra and Jñānasūtra walked about two miles to the west of Bodhgayā to a marsh where many sweet-scented flowers were blooming. From the sky Vajrasattva appeared and said to them, "O sons of good family, you have each taken birth five hundred times as scholars, yet till now you have never achieved the supreme result, nor will you do so in the future. If you would like to attain the enlightenment of the disappearance of the defiled body in this very life, go to the temple near the Bodhi Tree in China."

Vimalamitra was full of diligence. Immediately he took up his begging bowl, which was the only possession he had, and set out for China. He met Shrīsiṃha at the temple near the Bodhi Tree and received the oral transmission of Nyingthig of Me-gagde and the teachings of Outer, Inner, and Esoteric cycles for twenty years. But Shrīsiṃha did not give him their texts. Fully satisfied, Vimalamitra returned to India and recounted his achievements to Jñānasūtra. Jñānasūtra went to China and received the teaching of all the four cycles of Nyingthig from Shrīsiṃha. In addition he was given the texts themselves. Shrīsiṃha also left him his testament when he attained the rainbow body. Then Jñānasūtra returned to India and lived at Bhasing charnel ground, giving discourses to ḍākinīs.

Vimalamitra was practicing esoteric exercises in the charnel ground of Thachung. One day he was wandering through the charnel ground riding on a blue elephant, with his upper robe over his right shoulder and holding a parasol over his head, and the Ḍākinī Palkyi Lodrö appeared in the sky and gave this prophecy: "O fortunate one, if you would like to receive deeper instructions of Nyingthig than before, go to the forest of Bhasing charnel ground." He went at once, and there he met Jñānasūtra, whom he beseeched to give him the deep teachings. In order to show his power of realization, Jñānasūtra emitted a beam of light from his urna (a circle of hair on the forehead) and by a mere glance filled the sky with the display of the Samghogakāya pure land. Vimalamitra developed unshakable faith in him. Immediately Jñānasūtra conferred on him the elaborate empowerment, and the urna of Vimalamitra was opened. He also entrusted Vimalamitra with the texts and instructions of the first three cycles of Nyingthig. One year later at a temple, Jñānasūtra conferred the simple empowerment, and steam[94] emerged from every pore of Vimalamitra's body. He was given the text of the Innermost Esoteric cycle of Nyingthig. After practicing the preparatory exercises on the experiences of saṃsāra and nirvāṇa for six months at the peak of Mount Söche,[95] Vimalamitra received the very simple empowerment, followed by instructions. He achieved uncommon experiences and realizations, and on the tip of his nose there appeared a white letter ĀḤ, which seemed on the verge of falling. Six months later Vimalamitra was given the complete utmost simple empowerment, and he realized the naked nature of the mind. He was also given the complete instructions on the essential points of Nyingthig. Then Vimalamitra stayed with his teacher for fourteen years, perfecting his realization of Nyingthig.

Then Jñānasūtra entered nirvāṇa without bodily remainder. When Vimalamitra prayed with devotion the forearm of the master from the midst of a mass of radiant light in the sky emerged and placed in Vimalamitra's palm a casket studded with five kinds of precious jewels. From it he discovered the testament *The Four Methods of Contemplation,* and instantly he achieved a realization equal to that of his master.

Then, living in a bamboo hut, Vimalamitra spent twenty years as the preceptor of King Haribhadra (Excellent Lion) in the city of Kāmarūpa in eastern India. Then he went to the city of Bhirya[96] in western India and accepted the devotion and services of King Dharmapāla.

Then for seven years, with numerous hosts of ḍākinīs, he practiced Nyingthig in Prabhāskara, a great mysterious charnel ground not very far from Bhirya city. Pursuing esoteric exercises through various forms and methods, he gave teachings to an inconceivable number of disciples. He attained the vision of the perfection of intrinsic awareness (Rig Pa Tshad Phebs), the third of the four stages of high Dzogpa Chenpo, and then achieved the light body of great transformation ('Pho Ba Ch'en Po) and led three thousand people into enlightenment. Then, for thirteen years, he stayed in the same charnel ground in various manifestations.

In this charnel ground he made three copies of the sacred texts of Nyingthig. He concealed one copy in the island covered by golden sand in the ocean of Oḍḍiyāṇa in western India. He concealed another copy in a cave in Suvarṇadvīpa in Kashmir, and the final copy he preserved in Prabhāskara charnel ground as the object of devotion for the ḍākinīs.

Vimalamitra also saw Prahevajra seven times in pure visions and received instructions directly.

At that time, King Trisong Detsen of Tibet had just established the Buddha Dharma in Tibet. A great Tibetan master named Tingdzin Zangpo of the Nyang family gave the king the prophetic advice that he should invite the great esoteric master Vimalamitra from India. Tingdzin Zangpo was able to sustain a period of contemplation for seven years and could see the four continents by the power of his flesh eye, the power of supernormal vision that perceives physical phenomena. Accordingly, King Trisong Detsen sent the translators Kawa Paltsek and Chok-ro Lü'i Gyaltsen to India with presents of gold and a message to the young King Indrabhūti of Serkya city, saying, "Please send a great tantric master from among your five hundred scholar preceptors." Vimalamitra had then attained the body of great transformation ('Pho Ba Ch'en Po) and was staying as one of the five hundred preceptors of the king. King Indrabhūti and his scholars agreed on the choice of Vimalamitra as the one to be sent to Tibet. Realizing that it was the appropriate time to go to Tibet, Vimalamitra accepted the invitation.

Vimalamitra went to Tibet with master Kṣhitigarbha as his attendant, taking along one copy of the sacred texts of Nyingthig. At the time of his departure many people in India had bad dreams, sinister astrological omens occurred, flower and fruit-bearing trees bent to face in the direction of Tibet, and signs appeared indicating the jealousy of the ḍākinīs of the charnel ground. Because of the omens, the Indians realized that the secret teachings had slipped through their fingers, and they sent swift-footed messengers to create doubts in the minds of the Tibetans. The messengers placed posters at the junctures of valleys and the crossroads of cities saying, "Two Tibetan monks have carried off an Indian black magician who is going to destroy Tibet." So when Vimalamitra reached Samye, the Tibetans were in a state of doubt about him. When he paid homage to an image of the Buddha Vairochana, it disintegrated to dust before him. When he blessed the heap of dust, the image restored itself, more magnificent than before. Faith in Vimalamitra slowly developed in the Tibetans, and he was able to give them teachings.

One day, while he was giving sūtric teachings to an assembly of disciples, he returned to the hall after a recess period and found a note on his seat. It said:

> Buddhahood cannot be attained by the babyish Dharma of the shrāvakas;
> the distance cannot be covered by the raven's vajra steps.

Inquiries were made, and the author of the note was discovered. Asked who he was, he replied, "I am Yudra Nyingpo, a disciple of Pakor Vairochana," the great translator. At that time Vairochana was in exile in Gyalmo Rong, in Eastern Tibet. Vimalamitra and Yudra Nyingpo compared their teachings and realizations and found them to be equal.

Thereafter for ten years, Vimalamitra worked together with a team of translators. With Yudra Nyingpo, he translated the thirteen "later translated texts" of Semde, as Vairochana had already translated the five "earlier translated texts" of the eighteen Semde texts. With Nyak Jñānakumāra, he translated the *Guhyagarbha-māyājāla-tantra,* among other texts of Mahāyoga, and some instructional texts of Semde and Longde. He translated the root texts and instructional texts of the Outer, Inner, and Esoteric cycles of Me-ngagde with Nyak Jñānakumāra. The teachings of the Innermost Esoteric cycle, the Nyingthig of Me-ngagde, were kept confidential among the master, the king, and Nyang and were translated in strictest secrecy.[97] The Nyingthig teachings that were brought to Tibet by Vimalamitra are known as *Vima Nyingthig.*

Vimalamitra could find no other disciple to whom it would be appropriate to entrust the texts of the Innermost Esoteric cycle (the four volumes, etc., on Nyingthig). He concealed the Tibetan translations at Trakmar Gekong in Chimphu near Samye Monastery.

After staying in Tibet for thirteen years, Vimalamitra departed for the Five Peaks in China. Because he has attained the rainbow body of great transformation, in fulfillment of his aspiration he shall remain there as long as the Buddha Dharma exists. He has promised to send an incarnation of himself to Tibet every century, to carry out the work of maintaining and disseminating the Nyingthig teachings for as long as the Buddha Dharma exists. When Buddhism ceases to exist, Vimalamitra will dissolve into the ultimate sphere at Bodhgayā.

Believers think that if your spiritual eyes are clear, you can see him in person at the Five Peaks. There are many incidents of seeing and receiving teachings from Vimalamitra at the Five Peaks. I heard many stories from my teacher Kyala Khenpo Rinpoche when I was young. Here is one that I can recall: An important Lama (whose name I have forgotten) went to the Five Peaks on pilgrimage with his disciples. One day when they were going in circumbulation, they saw a Chinese shoemaker sitting under a rock by a footpath. The Lama with respect sat before the shoemaker. The shoemaker without any hesitation put the shoes he was making on the head of the Lama and had him drink the filthy water he kept by his side. All the Lama's disciples were shocked and ashamed, for many pilgrims were watching and laughing at the Lama. Later, the disciples learned from the Lama that the shoemaker was in fact Vimalamitra, and he had been receiving empowerments. The disciples rushed back to the rock but could find no trace that anybody had ever stayed there. Unless you are an accomplished person, the best you can see of Vimalamitra is as a bird, a rainbow light, or an ordinary person and the like.

Fifty-five years after Vimalamitra's departure for the Five Peaks, Nyang built the Zha Temple in Drikung Valley of Uru Province. In that temple he concealed the texts of the expository tantras of the first three cycles as well as the texts that belong to the oral transmission and some Innermost texts. The words of the oral transmission were transmitted to Dro Rinchen Bar. Finally, Nyak dissolved his mortal body into the rainbow body.

Dro Rinchen Bar transmitted the oral transmissions to Be Lodrö Wangchuk, who in turn transmitted them to Neten Dangma Lhüngyal (11th century). Neten also discovered the texts concealed by Nyang and entrusted the transmission to Chetsün Senge Wangchuk (11th–12th centuries). Chetsün also discovered the Nyingthig texts along with Vimalamitra's testament, concealed at Gekong at Chimphu by Vimalamitra and transmitted to Zhangtön Tashi Dorje (1097–1167).

The name of the lineage teachers of *Vima Nyingthig* from the Dharmakāya down to the present masters are as given earlier.

9

Guru Rinpoche, Padmasambhava

Guru Rinpoche,[98] one of the greatest adepts of Buddhist India, is the founder of Buddhism in Tibet. He is known as Padmasambhava (Padma 'Byung gNas), the Lotus-Born, and Guru of Oḍḍiyāṇa. In Tibet he is popularly known as Guru Rinpoche, the Precious Master. The Nyingmapas respect him as the second Buddha.

Before going into the life of Guru Rinpoche, I would like to discuss some of the problems we might have in understanding such a powerful, esoteric, mystical, and enlightened life as that of Guru Rinpoche.

How can an adept perform miracles and attain the light body? Prahevajra, Mañjushrīmitra, Shrīsiṃha, Jñanasūtra, Vimalamitra, and Guru Rinpoche and his consorts, as well as many of his disciples, were manifestations of Buddhas or highly enlightened beings. Their lives and life spans were not limited like the life of an ordinary person. Manifestations of the Buddhas in the form of great adepts appear now and then in the history of the world, but very rarely. Prahevajra, Mañjushrīmitra, Shrīsiṃha, and Jñānasūtra dissolved their manifested bodies into Dharmakāya, without leaving any mortal remains behind at the end of their lives. Because they achieved control over their life span, they lived for centuries. Vimalamitra, as the result of his scholarship and dedication to Nyingthig meditation, achieved the body of great transformation, and he is still in this light body and will remain in the same form for thousands of years. And Guru Rinpoche, although he was a manifestation of

Amitābha Buddha, the Buddha of Infinite Light, manifested as a powerful being who was in pursuit of esoteric trainings to accomplish the results for the benefit of beings. He too is believed to be in the light body of great transformation.

The accomplishments of these adepts lie not in the mere longevity of their mortal bodies or the acquisition of an astral body, but in attainment of the enlightened body, the self-arisen light of the intrinsic awareness, the Buddha nature. Although for us ordinary people it is impossible to see the light body as it is, when there is the possibility of receiving benefits, we will see it in forms that are suited to our nature.

When we hear the stories of adepts living for centuries or exhibiting miracles, most of us are hesitant, at best, to accept them. Also there are people who read about adepts and enjoy stories of longevity and miracles but are unable to accept them because they are not in accord with what they are experiencing now. Yet most ancient cultures and religions have recorded events involving superhuman beings, and supernatural attainments such as longevity and the display of miraculous powers, as the result of inner spiritual strength and meditative power, but not because of material power.

Today we are witnessing material miracles, which would never have been believed in ancient times, but we have lost or are losing touch with our inner power. We have become mere slaves of the external material world. So the problem is not whether the esoteric powers are unfounded, but rather that we are turning ourselves into strangers to the true power of our own inner truth, like a person who keeps riches hidden at home and goes begging for alms in the street.

Why do Buddha manifestations need to study? If masters like Guru Rinpoche are manifestations of the Buddhas, why do they have to go through vigorous training and why do they face obstructions? There are two points. First, the emanations of the Buddhas will appear and will perform their activities strictly in whatever forms and roles they have manifested. If they have manifested as social servants, they will fulfill that role by becoming people who provide food, shelter, and medicine, or they will work to strengthen moral and family values, even if they are Buddha emanations. Therefore, if the adepts have manifested as esoteric masters, they will play the role of learning as students, practicing as meditators, and accomplishing as adepts—just as, if you make a spoon out of gold, it will function as a spoon, and if you make an ornament out of gold, it will function as an ornament; it doesn't matter that the gold is a precious metal that could be preserved as part of the nation's treasures.

Second, various manifestations (Nirmāṇakāya) appear not according to the Buddha's perspective but according to the perspective of ordinary people, for whom they appear in order to serve them. Usually, ordinary people do not have the best karma and temperaments with which to see, feel, and receive the best of the manifestations. According to their karmic and emotional nature, the role of the manifestation will also be limited. Even great adepts like Guru Rinpoche have been seen by most people in ordinary form or similar to ordinary form and not in the light body of great transformation. When Guru Rinpoche was in Tibet, King Trisong Detsen had a hard time believing that he was in the light body. At Guru Rinpoche's insistence, the king hit him with his fist three times, and each time the king could not touch his body and could only touch his seat.[99]

Great adepts such as Prahevajra and Guru Rinpoche not only were manifestations of the Buddhas, but manifested as gifted beings with the qualities of adepts. They are endowed with extraordinary power and enlightened wisdom. Adepts like them have exhibited their power of manifesting many forms at a time, drawing many forms into one, and displaying opposing elements, such as water and fire in harmony, in accordance with the karmic and mental nature and need of the disciples who are their audience. All those miraculous manifestations were possible because of the matured karma of many people of that time and place.

Why are there different versions of the lives of many adepts? The life of Guru Rinpoche in particular is one of the most miraculous lives there could possibly be in any history of the spiritual world, and so it comes with a great number of variants. Variant versions do not imply that one account is true and the others false. The manifestations of the lives of adepts appeared differently to different people in different places and times in order for them to be served in the most appropriate way. On many occasions, a single manifestation in a single instant has been seen differently by different people. This is because of adepts' enlightened power, their ultimate control over the illusory forms, time, and space of ordinary phenomena. That is the very point, which makes the power of the fully accomplished masters extraordinary, and a great source of blessing and positive power for wise, open-minded, and devout people. Also, the whole reason why Buddha manifestations appear before us ordinary people is because of our natures and needs, being various beings, but not because of karmic and habitual pressures of the concepts, emotions, and actions of the manifestations.

Among numerous different versions of the biography of Guru Rinpoche written by great scholars and/or discovered by great tertöns who are his spiritual heirs, there are many that are comprehensible to common people like myself. Relying on those sources, the following is a brief account of Guru Rinpoche's life.

Eight (or, according to some, twelve) years after the passing away of the Buddha, a manifestation of Amitābha Buddha adorned with auspicious physical marks was born not by the womb of a woman, but by immaculate birth[100] in a lotus in the Milk Ocean in the northwestern part of the country of Oḍḍiyāṇa amid wondrous signs.

At that time, there was a great generous king called Indrabhūti[101] in Oḍḍiyāṇa. He had provided for all the material requests of poor people for many years until all his treasure was emptied. Now he had nothing to give, and he also lost his eyesight. He had no child who would succeed him to the throne to take care of his subjects. Still, with his usual courage and enthusiasm in providing for the needs of his people, despite the objections of the ministers, he himself with his loyal minister Kṛishṇadhara and a large crew sailed across the ocean to find the wish-fulfilling gems. On the way back, having obtained the gems and also having restored his eyesight through the power of the gems, the king and his minister saw an amazingly beautiful child of about eight years old sitting in a blossoming lotus in the middle of the Milk Ocean. Astonished, the king asked the child: "Who are your parents? What is your lineage? What is your name? What do you eat? What are you doing here?" In reply the child sang the following verses in an enchanting voice.

> My father is the intrinsic awareness, Samantabhadra.
> My mother is the ultimate sphere, Samantabhadrī.
> My lineage is the union of intrinsic awareness and ultimate sphere.
> My name is the glorious Lotus-Born [Padmasambhava].
> My country is the unborn ultimate sphere.
> I consume dualistic thoughts as food.
> My role is to accomplish the actions of the Buddhas.

When they heard this, faith and joy blossomed in the heart of everyone. The child accepted the king's invitation to join them. The king adopted the child and took him to his palace, where he made him the crown prince. At that time Guru Rinpoche was known as Padmasambhava (or Padmākara), the Lotus-Born.

Once again, the king and his subjects enjoyed great prosperity. The king showered with generous gifts all the needy people of his country. Happiness and peace prevailed in the country. The young prince was schooled in many disciplines and excelled in studies and athletic games. Then he married the Ḍākinī Prabhāvatī (One with Lights) and served the kingdom according to the law of Dharma. At that time he was known as King Shikhin (One with a Turban).

Guru Rinpoche knew that by serving in the role of a king he would not be able to serve the true needs, the spiritual benefits of others. He requested the king to permit him to renounce the kingdom but was refused. Then he saw a skillful means for his escape. By the power of his foreknowledge he saw that the time of death was at hand for the son of the wicked minister Kamata because of the boy's previous karma. So while they were dancing together, Guru Rinpoche let his trident fall from his hand, and it killed the boy. Sorrowfully the king complied with the stern law of the kingdom and banished him to roam in charnel grounds. Taking leave, Guru Padmasambhava sang to his royal parents:

> Although it is rare to find parental [kindness],
> You cared for me as parents and enthroned me.
> Because of his karmic debt, the minister's son was killed by me.
> Even if I am banished, there is no fear, for I have attachment to no one.
> Even if I am executed, there is no fear, for death and birth are the same for me.
> It is excellent that I am being banished, because for the state the law is sacred.
> Father and mother, please stay well.
> Because of our karmic links, we will meet again.

Guru Rinpoche was banished to Shītavana charnel ground. There he practiced esoteric exercises and beheld the peaceful deities. Then he went to the Joyous Grove (Nandanavana; dGa' Ba'i Tshal) charnel ground and received esoteric empowerments from the Ḍākinī Mārajitā (Subduer of Negative Forces). He went to Sosadvīpa charnel ground and was blessed by Ḍākinī Shāntarakṣhitā (Preserver of Peace). Commanding hosts of ḍākinīs, he enjoyed esoteric disciplines in different charnel grounds. He was known then as Shāntarakṣhita (Preserver of Peace).

He went to the island of Dhanakosha, where he spoke to the ḍākinīs in their symbolic language and brought them under his command. At Paruṣhakavana charnel ground, while practicing esoteric exercises, he beheld the pure vision of Vajravārāhī and received her blessings. With his enlightened power, he subdued the nāgas of an ocean and the zas of the sky. Wisdom ḍākas and wisdom ḍākinīs bestowed accomplishments upon him. He was known then as Dorje Trakpo Tsal (the Mighty Vajra-Wrath).

He went to the Vajrāsana, Bodhgayā, and displayed various miracles, acknowledging that he was a self-realized Buddha. With various purposes in mind he went to the country of Sahor and took the ordination of renunciation from master Prabhāhasti. He was known then as Shākyasiṃha (the Lion of the Shākyas).

He received the teachings of Yogatantra eighteen times and beheld the pure vision of the Yogatantra deities. He received empowerment from Ānandā, a wisdom ḍākinī in the form of a nun. She transformed Guru Rinpoche into a letter HŪṂ, which she swallowed. In her body Guru Rinpoche was given the entire Outer, Inner, and Esoteric empowerments, and she passed him out of her body through her padma.

At Deche Tsekpa stūpa, he received the empowerments and instructions of eight maṇḍalas from eight vidyādharas, namely Mañjushrīmitra, Nāgārjuna, Hūṃkara, Vimalamitra, Prabhāhasti, Dhanasaṃskṛita, Rombuguhya, and Shantigarbha. He received the *Guhyagarbha-tantra* from Buddhaguhya, and Dzogpa Chenpo, particularly Nyingthig, from Mañjushrīmitra. In Tsubgyur Tsal charnel ground, he met Shrīsiṃha and studied Me-ngagde tantras and *Khandro Nyingthig* teachings for twenty-five years.[102] He beheld the pure visions of many divinities even without doing any particular practice or meditation on them. He attained the state of Knowledge-holder with karmic residues (rNam sMin Rig 'Dzin). He was known then as Loden Chokse (Wise Supreme Passion).

In the sūtric tradition of Buddhism, the stages of attainments are classified as ten stages and five paths, and they are the steps for reaching Buddhahood. In tantric traditions, the stages are divided or classified in different ways. Most of the Nyingma tantric scriptures have four attainments, called knowledge-holders (vidyādhara).[103]

The knowledge-holder with residues is the first of the four knowledge-holders. He has three characteristics. His mind has been perfected or matured as the deity, but the residues of karmic effect on the gross physical body have not yet been renounced, and immediately after release from the mortal body (death), he will attain the knowledge-holder of great sign (Phyag rGya'i Rig 'Dzin), the third attainment, which I shall discuss later.

He went to the country of Sahor, where he met Princess Mandāravā, the daughter of the king, who was practicing Dharma in solitude as a nun. Because the esoteric meaning of his relationship with the princess was misunderstood, he was burned alive on a huge pyre at the order of the king. Instead of being burned, he transformed the fire into a body of water and the fuel into a lotus. The next day, Guru Rinpoche was seen sitting on the lotus in the middle of the lake. The lake is believed to be the Rewalsar Lake of Mandi District in Himachal Pradesh in northern India.[104] In expiation the king of Sahor offered him his royal crown, robe, and shoes with is whole kingdom, and Princess Mandāravā as his spiritual consort. Guru Rinpoche gave teachings to the king and his subjects, and many attained realization. (In most representations of Guru Rinpoche, he is shown wearing the lotus hat, the brocade cloak, and the shoes offered by the king of Sahor to signify his enlightened power.)

Then he and Mandāravā went to Māratika Cave in Nepal,[105] and for three months they performed the sādhana of long life. Buddha Amitāyus appeared before them and conferred the empowerment of longevity, by which they became inseparable from him. They achieved the state of the knowledge-holder, which has control over life.[106] By this second attainment, not only was his mind perfected as the deity, but even his gross body was perfected. This attainment has the qualities of freedom from four contaminations (Zag Pa). The four contaminations are the afflicted emotions of wrong views, loss of the body (death) without control or choice, no control over the harmony of the elements of the body (health), and taking rebirth according to karma, without control or choice. The first and second knowledge-holders are equivalent to the path of insight, the third path, and the first stage of the ten stage system of sūtric tradition. In this you abandon the obscurations of emotional afflictions (Nyon sGrib), the first of the obscurations, the other being the intellectual obscurations.

Then, with Mandāravā, he returned to the country of Oḍḍiyāṇa. While they were making the rounds in quest of alms, he was recognized as the one who had killed the minister's son. Because he had defied the sentence of banishment, they burned him with his consort in a huge conflagration. But again, the following day they found them both sitting on a lotus in a lake, wearing skull garlands around their necks. He was known then as Pema Thötreng Tsal (the Lotus-Born, Mighty Skull-Garlanded).

With his consort, Guru Rinpoche remained in Oḍḍiyāṇa for thirteen years as the presiding guru of the kingdom, and there he gave the empowerments and instructions of *Kadü Chökyi Gyatso*. The king and many fortunate subjects attained supreme realization and attained the light body. He was then known as Padmarāja (the Lotus-Born King).

Guru Rinpoche manifested himself as Indrasena,[107] an accomplished monk who, with a novice of his, converted Emperor Ashoka (3rd century BCE) to Buddhism. Ashoka, the greatest ruler of Indian history, propagated Buddha's teachings beyond the Indian borders.

Some anti-Buddhists offered poison to Guru Rinpoche, but he remained unharmed. Some threw him into the Ganges, but he was carried upstream rather than down. He was then known as Khyeu Khadeng Tsal (Young Mighty Garuḍa).

At various charnel grounds, including Kula Dzok, he gave the teachings of tantra to ḍākinīs, and he extracted the life essence from powerful spirits, whom he appointed as Dharma protectors. He was known as Sūryarashmi (Rays of the Sun).

At Bodhgayā he defeated five hundred upholders of wrong views in a debate. When they tried to overcome him by magic, he turned it back upon them by the power of the mantras of Ḍākinī Mārajitā, the lion-faced female deity. As the teachers had been silenced, he pacified the villages and converted them to Buddhism. He became known then as Siṃhanāda (Lion's Roar).

Then at Yangle Shö, now known as Pharping in Nepal, with the consort Shākyadevi, the daughter of King Puṇyadhara (Preserver of Virtues) of Nepal, he practiced the sādhana of the Yangdak (Shrīheruka) maṇḍala. At that time there had been no rain for three years because of the obstructions raised by powerful spirits. Disease and famine were widespread. He asked for Vajrakīla texts to be brought to him from India. When just two loads had arrived, the disasters afflicting the country were pacified. Hence there is the saying "Yangdak is rich in attainments, like a merchant. But Vajrakīla is necessary for protection, like a guard." They both achieved the state of the knowledge-holder of great seal (Phyag rGya'i Rig 'Dzin; mahāmudrā Vidyādhara). In this attainment one's base body (or actual body) is in the form of the deity. For the benefit of beings, it appears in various emanated forms. The power of one's foreknowledge and other powers is clearer, purer, and stabler than that of the knowledge-holder with control over life and similar (but not equal) to the qualities of the enjoyment body. This is the equivalent of the realizations up to the ninth stage, and the path of meditation, the fourth path of the common Buddhist tradition.

In Sosadvīpa charnel ground, Guru Rinpoche, who already was a highly accomplished tantric master, received the transmission with the teachings of the three cycles of Dzogpa Chenpo with the tantras and *Khandro Nyingthig* from Shrīsiṃha. He trained in it for three years and attained the light body of great transformation ('Pho Ba Ch'en Po).[108]

The highest accomplished Dzogpa Chenpo meditators exhaust all existents into the true nature and unite their minds into the ultimate enlightened nature, the primordial purity. If they choose, they can also dissolve or transform their physical bodies into purity. There are two major categories of attainment, the rainbow body and the rainbow body of great transformation. Through the perfection of the meditation of cutting through (Khreg Ch'od), at the time of their death (over a period of a couple of days), their bodies dissolve and disappear. They leave no mortal gross form of flesh, bone, or skin behind but only the twenty nails and the hair of the body. Although this is a dissolution of the body and not a transformation of the body into a light body, it is called rainbow body, since during the process of dissolution there always appear tents, arches, and circles of rainbowlike lights of various colors around the body and the dwelling. Through the practice of direct approach (Thod rGal), they transform their mortal body into a subtle light body and remain in that as long as there is a service to perform for the benefit of ordinary beings. For such a person, not only his or her body but all phenomenal appearances have transformed into the form and nature of subtle light. However, ordinary people will not see his or her light body as it is, but will see nothing or will see it in ordinary form, as mentioned earlier in the chapter on Vimalamitra. Also there are many great Dzogpa Chenpo adepts who leave their body, in the form of relics (Ring bSrel), images, and/or letters, as the object of inspiration and the followers.

Guru Rinpoche visited places all over India and many other countries and islands, serving beings by means of his miraculous power and enlightening teachings. He even visited Zhangzhung, manifesting as the Tavihṛicha ('Od Kyi Khyeu), and taught *Dzogchen Nyen-gyü,*[109] now known as one of the main teachings of Dzogpa Chenpo in the Bön religion, to lead many into the attainment of enlightened mind and light bodies.

GURU RINPOCHE'S VISIT TO TIBET

In the ninth century, King Trisong Detsen, the thirty-seventh ruler of the Chögyal dynasty of Tibet, invited Shāntarakṣhita from India with the intention of establishing Buddhism.

Shāntarakṣhita, ordained in the Sarvāstivādin monastic lineage, was one of the celebrated scholars and proponents of the Svātantrika philosophy of Mahāyāna Buddhism. Among his famous writings were *Madhyamakālaṃkāra* on the middle-way philosophy and *Tattvasaṃgraha* on logic. After his arrival in Tibet, for six months he gave discourses on the ten virtuous deeds and interdependent causation, and laid the foundations of Samye Monastery. This agitated the local spirits of Tibet, who were protectors of Bön, the shamanistic native religion that worshiped them with sacrifices. As a result, Phangthang Palace was washed away by flood, and Red Hill Palace, the original structure of the present Potala Palace, was destroyed by lightning. Disease, famine, drought, and hailstorms afflicted the country. Whatever construction of the monastery was done at Samye during the day was dismantled the same night by hostile forces. Anti-Buddhist ministers, who began to oppose the king, demanded that he send Shāntarakṣhita away. Thereupon Shāntarakṣhita said to the king, "You must invite Guru Padmasambhava. He is the most powerful adept living on the earth. There will be no difficulty in getting him to come here, because of the aspirations we made in common during our previous lives." Then he left the country for a while and went to Nepal.

The king dispatched seven emissaries under the leadership of Nanam Dorje Düdjom to invite Guru Rinpoche. Guru Rinpoche knew of their mission by his foreknowledge. He came as far as Mang-yül Kungthang and met them there. He accepted their invitation but advised them to return home, as he would come afterward by himself. He scattered the gold pieces sent to him as presents by the king, saying: "If I need gold, all phenomenal existents are gold for me." He gave a handful of sand to the emissaries, and it all turned into gold.

In the Iron Tiger year (810 CE)[110] Guru Rinpoche came to Tibet. He was then over a thousand years old. With his enlightened power, he traveled all over the three provinces of Tibet: Ngari, the upper or western province; Ü and Tsang, the center province; and Dokham, the lower or eastern province. Displaying his enlightened miracles at many places in Tibet, he bound the powerful nonhuman spirits of Tibet by vow to protect the Dharma and its followers. These included the twelve tenmas, the thirteen gur-lhas, and the twenty-one ge-nyens.

The king received Guru Rinpoche in the garden of Tragmar Ombu. When Guru Rinpoche consecrated the Tragmar Drinzang Temple, the images moved out and in and ate food offerings as if they were people. Then he went to the top of Hepori Hill and brought all the spirits of Tibet under his command by dancing through the sky in fierce vajra steps and proclaiming the song of "overwhelming all the arrogant beings":

> O gods and demons, build the temple!
> With humility and observance, all gather here to do the work!
> Fulfill the wishes of Trisong Detsen!

Thereafter, with the assistance of the spirits, Samye, the Inconceivable One, was built without any hindrances. On the model of Odantapurī Monastery of India, Samye Monastery was built in the design of the traditional Indian cosmos. The main temple in the center had three stories symbolizing Mount Sumeru. The lower story, which represented the Nirmāṇakāya pure land, was built in the style of Indian architecture;[111] the middle story, representing the Sambhogakāya, in the style of Chinese architecture; and the top story, representing the Dharmakāya, in the style of Tibetan architecture. Four large temples were built in the four directions from the main temple representing the four continents; the eight minor temples in between them represented the eight subcontinents. Two temples were built in the east and west representing the sun and moon. At the four corners were built four large stūpas. Bathing, dressing, and residential places were also arranged. All these structures were surrounded by a high wall surmounted by one hundred and eight small stūpas. Outside the wall were three big temples built by the three queens. Within five years the whole structure of the monastery was completed. Guru Rinpoche and Shāntarakṣhita performed the consecration ceremony, which was accompanied by auspicious and miraculous signs. Images of deities in the temples came out and went in, as if they were alive. A rain of flowers showered from the clear sky. Sweet music was heard and continued to be heard now and then. Rainbow beams and tents arched in all directions. The astonished people celebrated in wonder and devotion. Food and entertainments were offered to be enjoyed by all. Guru Rinpoche and Shāntarakṣhita, true Buddhas in human form, were present before the naked eyes of people of every walk of life. The light of Dharma was being established in Tibet for centuries to come. There was nothing but joy and peace.

Samye became the most important place of meditation, worship, teaching, research, and writing. Samye was a great library, museum, and treasury of Buddhist scriptures, religious objects, and invaluable treasures of Tibet along with those brought from India, China, Nepal, and Central Asia. This was the seat where great masters gave discourses, fortunate students became accomplished scholars and adepts, and Indian and Tibetan scholars translated Buddhist scriptures into Tibetan.

Under the patronage of King Trisong Detsen, abbot Shāntarakṣhita, Guru Rinpoche, master Vimalamitra, and other Indian and Tibetan scholars, Buddhism was firmly established in Tibet. The scholars gave teachings of both sūtra and tantra, and many Tibetans emerged as great scholars and adepts. Many great Tibetan translators, such as Vairochana, Kawa Paltsek, Chok-ro Lü'i Gyaltsen, and Zhang Yeshe De, translated many sūtras and tantras into Tibetan with the supervision of great Indian scholars such as Vimalamitra, Shāntarakṣhita, Guru Rinpoche, and Kamalashīla.

Shāntarakṣhita, ordained seven young Tibetans as fully ordained Buddhist monks in the Sarvāstivādin lineage to determine whether or not it was possible for Tibetans to lead the monastic life. They were known as the seven testers. After their success in monastic disciplines, hundreds of others followed them, leading to the formation of one of the greatest monastic communities in the world. In addition to Nyingmapas, many Gelukpa monks are also ordained in the Sarvāstivādin lineage, which was brought to Tibet by master Shāntaraḳshita.

Guru Rinpoche gave the king and his subjects various teachings, empowerments, and entrustments of tantra, especially of the great sādhana of eight maṇḍalas (sGrub Pa bKa' brGyad), which he had received from the eight great masters in India. Among many recipients of this empowerment, eight became the famous accomplished authorities of these eight sādhanas.

During this period two clerical systems were established. The saffron-robed monks, who are celibate, dwell in the monasteries, and the white-robed long-haired ones, who are lay tantric priests, live in temples and villages. The introduction of the system of white-robed clergy brought the benefit of the teachings to the homes of men and women, so that the Dharma reached and was preserved at the grass-roots level. In contrast, during the later period of the Dharma in Tibet, other schools concentrated the learning and practice of Buddhism more among the monks in the monasteries in order to preserve the purity of the discipline.

Guru Rinpoche and his consort Yeshe Tsogyal traveled all over Tibet by miraculous power and worked ceaselessly for the happiness, security, and wisdom of future Tibetans and others. They performed sādhanas, gave blessings, and left imprints of their bodies, hands, and feet. They concealed many ters. Some of the most important sacred places that they visited and blessed are twenty mountains of snow and rock (Gangs Brag) in Ngari, twenty-one sādhana places (sGrub gNas) in Ü and Tsang, twenty-five great pilgrimage places (gNas Ch'en) in Dokham; three (or four) main hidden lands (sBas Yul rGyal Mo), five ravines (Lung lNga), and three valleys (lJongs gSum).

At thirteen different places with the name of Taktsang (Tiger's Lair), such as Mönkha Nering and Senge Dzong (now in Bhutan), Guru Rinpoche manifested in a wrathful form and bound all the high and low nonhuman beings by his command. Then he was known as Dorje Trolö (Wild Wrathful Vajra).

During Guru Rinpoche's visit to Tibet, he fulfilled three major goals. First, as we discussed before, through the display of spiritual power, he pacified the human and nonhuman forces who were obstructing the founding of Dharma in Tibet. Second, he brought Buddhism in general and especially the transmission of the teachings and blessing powers of tantra for his many Tibetan disciples and their followers. Third, in order to prevent the deep teachings and sacred objects from becoming mixed, diluted, or lost in the distant future, and in order to maintain their blessing powers afresh for future followers, Guru Rinpoche and Yeshe Tsogyal concealed them as ter. Because of the ter tradition of Guru Rinpoche, his followers, even today, are receiving his timely teachings and prophesies with fresh blessing powers. In this world there are many systems of mystical discoveries, because of psychic power, spirit power, pure visions, and even minor spiritual power, but the discovery of Guru Rinpoche's ter tradition is totally unique in its process and substance. Drawing on the third Dodrupchen's interpretations,[112] I would like to write a few paragraphs about it.

Guru Rinpoche concealed many teachings as ter, while transmitting esoteric teachings to his realized disciples. It is a concealment of teachings and the esoteric attainments as ter in the pure nature, the intrinsic awareness of the minds of his realized disciples through Guru Rinpoche's enlightened power with aspirations that the ter may be discovered for the sake of beings when the appropriate time comes. By the power of this method, which is called the mind-mandate transmission (gTad rGya), the actual discoveries of the teachings were made possible.

Then, when the time for benefiting beings with a particular teaching arrived, the reincarnations of the realized disciples of Guru Rinpoche discovered the ter, which had been transmitted and concealed in them by the master in one of their past lives.

The transmissions of ter are channeled through six lineages: (1) the enlightened-mind-to-enlightened-mind transmission of the Buddhas, (2) indication transmission of the knowledge-holders, (3) oral transmission of ordinary disciples, (4) the transmission of aspirational empowerment or the mind-mandate transmission, (5) transmission through prophetic authorization, and (6) the entrustment to the ḍākinīs.

In the ters, because of the manner of discovery, there are two major categories. The first is the earth ter (Sa gTer). It involves the discovery of earthly materials such as symbolic scripts (brDa Yig) written on a scroll of paper known as a yellow scroll (Shog Ser). However, the symbolic scripts merely become the key for the discovery; they are neither the real ter of teachings nor the transmission of the attainment, which comes only from the mind of the tertön. When the tertön discovers a symbolic script, he sees or contemplates the symbolic script or unites his naked wisdom with it, and thereby awakens the transmission of the power of Guru Rinpoche's vajra speech wisdom, which has been concealed in him. Contemplation of the symbolic scripts enables him to decode the words of it, and that in turn awakens the concealed transmission of teachings and attainments themselves. In addition to the symbolic scripts, there are the discoveries of thousands of complete texts, medicinal materials, images, and ritual tools discovered from rocks, lakes, earth, or sky as ter or as supporting ter substances (gTer rDzas).

The second category is the mind ter (dGongs gTer). The principles of concealment, transmission, and discovery are similar to those of earth ter, except that mind ter does not rely on any external or earthly support, such as yellow scrolls, as the key to discovery. In many instances of mind ter, seeing or hearing symbolic words or sounds in visions causes the discovery of the ter but usually the discovery does not rely on any external sources and there is no involvement of earthly objects as the means of discovering the ter. A tertön discovers the mind ter by awakening the mind-mandate transmission spontaneously from the expanse of intrinsic awareness of his or her mind, when the circumstances and the time have matured.

There is also a third important system of mystical discovery of teachings known as pure vision (Dag sNang). Pure vision teachings are not terma. They are merely teachings given by Buddhas, deities, and teachers in visions. However, there are cases in which ter teachings have been discovered or designated as pure vision teachings, and when that is the case, they are in fact ter teachings, not an ordinary pure vision discovery.

Now, concerning the Nyingthig teachings, Guru Rinpoche confidentially transmitted the seventeen tantras and *Longsal-tantra* of Megagde of Dzogpa Chenpo, including *Khandro Nyingthig,* to Yeshe Tsogyal at Tidro in Zhotö of Drikung Valley. Later, at Chimphu near Samye, when Princess Pemasal, the daughter of King Trisong Detsen, died at the age of eight, by his power Guru Rinpoche recalled the consciousness to the body. When she regained consciousness, he entrusted to her the instructions and transmission of Nyingthig as her Dharma inheritance, and then she died. Guru Rinpoche instructed Yeshe Tsogyal as follows: "This is the time for *Vima Nyingthig* to benefit the Nyingthig followers. But when *Vima Nyingthig* diminishes, *Khandro Nyingthig* will benefit people. So conceal the *Khandro Nyingthig* teachings as ter." Guru Rinpoche told the king:

> Emaho! Great king, please listen to me:
> There is no essence in worldly affairs.
> Instead of endlessly revolving in the cycle of sufferings again and again,
> Make sure to attain the everlasting reign of the Dharmakāya king.
> Realize the essence of the objects, the unborn ultimate sphere.
> Stay in the essence of place, solitude in the forests.
> Look for the essence of hermitages, the ultimate nature, [the union of] clarity and emptiness.
> Rest in the essence of the house, the innate nature of the mind.
> Set up the essence of the kitchen, mindfulness and awareness.
> Develop the essence of treasure, the twofold mind of enlightenment.
> Have the essence of wealth, dual accumulations.
> Exert yourself in the essence of merits, the ten virtuous deeds.
> Have the essence of fatherhood, compassion toward the beings.
> Sustain the essence of motherhood, emptiness nature.

Have the essence of children, the inseparability of the development and completion stages.
Meditate on the essence of the spouse, the clarity, bliss, and no-thought.
Look at the essence of friends, the teachings of the Sugata.
Observe the essence of the maṇḍala, the changeless clarity.
Obey the essence of teachings, the taming of one's own mind.
See the essence of view, the unchanging clarity and emptiness.
Rest in the essence of meditation, the nature of mind, as it is.
Dismantle the dualistic delusions, the essence of actions.
Accomplish the essence of results, spontaneous perfection with no efforts.
Then you will be happy in both this life and the next,
And swiftly you will attain Buddhahood.[113]

As instructed by Guru Rinpoche, Yeshe Tsogyal concealed the tantras and instructions of Me-ngagde at Senge Trak of Bumthang in Bhutan and the teachings for mendicants *(Khandro Nyingthig)* in Tramo Trak of Takpo Tanglung. Centuries later, Pema Ledreltsal (1291–1319?), who was the rebirth of Princess Pemasal, withdrew the ter of *Khandro Nyingthig* concealed at Tramo Trak. Her next tülku, Longchen Rabjam (1308–1363), was responsible for the wide dissemination of Nyingthig teachings by teaching and writing on them.

On the second floor of the central chapel of Samye Monastery, Guru Rinpoche conferred teachings and mind-mandate transmission of *Longchen Nyingthig* to King Trisong Detsen, Khandro Yeshe Tsogyal, and Vairochana. He gave the prophetic empowerments, saying that these teachings will be discovered by Jigme Lingpa, a tülku of King Trisong Detsen and Vimalamitra.

King Trisong Detsen died at the age of sixty-nine. He was succeeded by prince Mu-ne Tsepo, but he died after only one year and seven (or six) months' reign and was succeeded by his younger brother Prince Mutik Tsepo.[114]

After staying fifty-five years and six months in Tibet, in the Wood Monkey year (864 CE),[115] without heeding the requests of King Mutri Tsepo and his subjects, Guru Rinpoche went with the king and a huge number of followers to the Kungthang Pass in Mang-yül Province in order to leave Tibet for Zangdok Palri (Copper-Colored Mountain), his manifested pure land. On the Kungthang Pass, the king lamented in the following words:

Trisong Detsen has gone to heaven.
Guru of Oḍḍiyāṇa goes to his pure land.
Mutri is left behind in Tibet.
Father's life was too short.
Guru's kindness is too limited.
My merits are too meager.
Now the law of Dharma institutions has diminished.
The joys of Tibetan subjects are exhausted.
While the guru and father were present,
Why didn't I die![116]

Consoling the king and his subjects, Guru Rinpoche said:

While you are young, exert yourself in Dharma practice,
For it is hard to comprehend Dharma in old age.
O lord and subjects, life is momentary.
When you have a gross thought, looking in at the subject [mind],
Relax naturally without discriminations.
O lord and subjects, it is crucial to ascertain the view. . . .
If there is no compassion, the root of your Dharma training is rotten.
Think about the suffering character of saṃsāra again and again.
O lord and subject, do not delay [your dedication in] Dharma.
Devout people accomplish their goal by themselves.
There is no justification in leaving Dharma for others to practice. . . .
Gain the experience of Dharma before you die.
It is too late when you rely on ceremonies after death. . . .
For devout people, Padmasambhava hasn't gone anywhere.
For those who pray to me, I am [always] at their door. . . .
Now Padmasambhava will not stay in Tibet but will go to the land of rākṣhasas,
As birds fly away from the tops of trees.[117]

From the sky in the midst of colorful clouds a divine horse with ornaments appeared, and riding on the horse, Guru Rinpoche rose up and up into the sky and flew toward the west with Yeshe Tsogyal and an ocean of divine beings amid the sweet sound of music and songs of praise. The image of Guru Rinpoche and his party became smaller and smaller as they flew away, and the sound of music slowly faded. Then there was nothing but the quiet, clear, and empty sky of Tibet over the heads of the lord and his assembled subjects. However, different people had different perceptions of his departure. Some saw him leaving by riding a lion and others saw him riding sunbeams.

Then Guru Rinpoche and Yeshe Tsogyal descended to the sacred cave of Tsawa Rong. After giving more teachings and prophecies, he rose to the sky with lights. Taking leave of his consort, with love and kindness Guru Rinpoche said the following to her, and flew away:

> Kyema, Yeshe Tsogyal, please listen!
> Padmasambhava goes to the land of great bliss.
> I remain in the Dharmakāya, the deathless divinity.
> It has nothing in common with the separation of body and mind
> [at death] of ordinary people. . . .
> Meditate on Guru Yoga, which is the quintessence [of the
> trainings].
> Two feet above the crown of your head, on lotus and moon, in
> the midst of lights,
> Visualize Padmasambhava, the Lama of the beings. . . .
> When the visualization becomes clear, receive the empowerments
> and contemplate on it. . . .
> Recite Guru siddhi [mantra], the heart-quintessence [of prayers].
> Finally, unify your three doors with [mine], inseparably.
> Dedicate and make aspiration for the [realization of the mind of
> the] Guru.
> Contemplate in the essence of Dzogchen, effortlessly.
> There are no teachings superior to this.
> The love of Padmasambhava has no rising or setting [but will
> always be there].
> The link of lights of my compassion for Tibet will never be severed
> [even after I have departed].
> For my children who pray to me, I am always in front of them.
> For people who have faith, there is no separation from me.[118]

It is believed that Guru Rinpoche is still present as knowledge-holder of spontaneous accomplishment (Lhun Grub Rig 'Dzin)[119] in Zangdok Palri, a manifested pure land (sPrul Ba'i Zhing), invisible to ordinary beings. The knowledge-holder of spontaneous accomplishment is the fourth and final stage of attainment, before instantly becoming a fully enlightened Buddha. Its realizations and activities are similar to those of the Buddha, and its forms are similar to those of the enjoyment body. This attainment is equal to the tenth stage and the path of meditation, the fourth path of common Buddhism. Also in the third and fourth attainments, one abandons the intellectual obscurations with their traces. So Guru Rinpoche is a Buddha in mind but appears as an adept, who is in the final stages of attainment, without dissolving into Dharmakāya, by taking the form of the light body of great transformation.

Guru Rinpoche will remain in his manifested pure land as long as it is beneficial for many beings, for he has manifested as an adept, who has achieved the attainment of deathless vajra-body and great transformation.

Among the numerous disciples of Guru Rinpoche in Tibet, the great ones are the king and twenty-five subjects, the eighty adepts, who attained the rainbow body at Yerpa, the hundred and eight great meditators of Mount Chuwo, the thirty great tāntrikas of Yangdzong in Drak Valley, the fifty-five realized ones at Sheltrak in Yarlung Valley, the twenty-five ḍākinīs, and the seven yoginīs.

He had numerous highly realized female disciples in Tibet.[120] Tisam of the Dro family flew in the sky as the result of her spiritual power. Rinchentso of the Mago family hung her robes on the rays of the sun. Kargyalpak of the Oche family beheld the visions of deities. Changchup of the Chok-ro family displayed both the opposites, fire and water, in her body simultaneously. Khandro Yeshe Tsogyal of the Kharchen family manifested the presence of various Buddhas in different parts of her body. Lhakarma of the Dzin family flew in the sky and entered into the earth without hindrance. Sherap Phagma of the Shuk family held vast collections of the Buddha's teachings in her memory. Lhamoyang of the Ba family fulfilled various wishes of people through the power of the perfection of her meditative absorption. Dorjetso of the Shelkar family crossed the Tsangpo (Brahmaputra) River standing on a bamboo walking stick.

THE FIVE PRINCIPAL CONSORTS OF GURU RINPOCHE[121]

YESHE TSOGYAL OF TIBET

Yeshe Tsogyal was Vajravārāhī Buddha in human form and also an incarnation of Tārā and Buddhalochanā. She was born amid wondrous signs at Dragda, in the clan of Kharchen. Her father was Namkha Yeshe, the king of Kharchen, an important principality in central Tibet, and her mother was Gewa Bum. At the time of her birth a lake suddenly formed next to the house. It is called the Tsogyal Latso, or Tsogyal's spirit-lake. Even today there is a pond, which is what remains of the lake. When she was a child she stamped the imprint of her foot on a rock near the house, and it was visible till recently.

First she became one of the consorts of Trisong Detsen, the king of Tibet. Later the king offered her to Guru Rinpoche as the maṇḍala-offering before receiving empowerment, and she became Guru Rinpoche's consort. When she was receiving empowerment from Guru Rinpoche, her flower landed on the maṇḍala of Vajrakīla. By practicing the sādhana of Vajrakīla, she beheld the pure vision of Vajrakīla and achieved attainments.

She brought back to life many people who had been killed in fighting. In Nepal she restored a dead boy to life, and then with the gold she was offered in gratitude, she paid the ransom of Āchāraya Sa-le, who was prophesied to be the support of her esoteric training.

She received almost all the teachings that Guru Rinpoche gave in Tibet, and by practicing them she attained the highest realization. With Guru Rinpoche she traveled all over Tibet by their miraculous power, meditated at hundreds of places, and blessed them as power places. As she had achieved the accomplishment of unforgetting memory (Mi brJed Pa'i gZungs), through the power of her memory she collected the inconceivably vast teachings given by Guru Rinpoche in Tibet. And at the command of Guru Rinpoche she concealed the teachings in various places as ter, hidden treasures for the benefit of future followers. Especially, in Tidro of Zhotö in Drikung Valley, she received the *Khandro Nyingthig,* the innermost esoteric teachings of Dzogpa Chenpo, and later concealed them as ter.

Yeshe Tsogyal stayed in Tibet for many years after Guru Rinpoche left Tibet, reconcealing the ters at different places. At the end, from Shang Zabulung she and Kālasiddhi and Tashi Chidren, instead of leaving any mortal bodies behind, flew through the sky to Zangdok Palri, the manifest pure land of Guru Rinpoche.

Yeshe Tsogyal is viewed by the followers of Guru Rinpoche as having the peerless grace and kindness of a mother for them and for the Tibetans.

Princess Mandāravā of Sahor

Mandāravā, an incarnation of Dhātvīshvarī, was born amid wondrous signs in the Ratnapurī Palace of Sahor. Most scholars agree that Sahor is the place now known as Mandi in Himachal Pradesh in northern India. Her father was King Ārṣhadhara and her mother was Hauki.

Her fame and beauty brought many ministers to the court to beg and threaten in order to have her for the consort of their kings. She was made very unhappy by these happenings. She felt a strong disgust for mundane life. As a result, no one could prevent her from renouncing the life of a householder and becoming a nun.

By the power of foreknowledge Guru Rinpoche saw that it was time to meet Mandāravā. He went to the convent where she and her five hundred ladies-in-waiting were living as nuns, and he gave them teachings. At this, malicious reports were given to the king, at whose order Guru Rinpoche was burned on a huge pyre and Mandāravā was thrown into a pit filled with thorns. By his enlightened power Guru Rinpoche transformed the fire into a lake. In the middle of the lake, Guru Rinpoche was found seated on a lotus. The lake is believed to be the Rewalsar Lake of Mandi District and is still a well-known pilgrimage site. Then the king and his ministers, with strong repentance and newfound faith, begging Guru Rinpoche for his forgiveness for their misdeeds, offered him his kingdom and Princess Mandāravā.

In Sahor kingdom, Guru Rinpoche gave tantric teachings and many people, including the king, the princess, and ministers, attained the states of knowlege-holder. Mandāravā became Guru Rinpoche's spiritual consort. They went alone to Māratika Cave, now thought to be the cave of Haileshi in Sagarmatha, in Nepal, and meditated on Amitāyus, the Buddha of Long Life. They beheld the vision of the Buddha of Infinite Life and achieved the knowledge-holder with control over life.

Mandāravā devoted herself to the benefit of others in India, and Guru Rinpoche went to Tibet. Mandāravā also made two visits to Tibet with her miraculous power and lives in the vajra-light body.

Princess Shākyadevī of Nepal

Shākyadevī was an incarnation of Māmakī. Her father was a king called Puṇyadhara in Nepal, but after her mother died in childbirth she was abandoned in a charnel ground with the body of her mother. She was mysteriously brought up under the care of monkeys and was endowed with all the auspicious signs of a ḍākinī.

Later she met Guru Rinpoche and received teachings from him. She became the spiritual support of Guru Rinpoche for the meditation on the Nine Deities of Yangdak (Shrīheruka) at Yangle Shö, now known as Pharping, in the Kathmandu Valley. Guru Rinpoche attained the realization of mahāmudrā, and Shākyadevī achieved the attainments of Māmakī. At the end of her life she attained the vajra-light body.

With the support of Shākyadevī, Guru Rinpoche manifested in many forms in order to fulfill the wishes of devotees, and he became known by twenty different names denoting his various miraculous powers. It was she who first inspired Guru Rinpoche in the tradition of concealing the teachings as ter, so we, the followers of Guru Rinpoche, are especially grateful to her.

Kālasiddhi of India

Kālasiddhi, an incarnation of Pāṇḍaravāsinī, was born as the daughter of weavers in the province of Ngathupchen in India with all the signs of a ḍākinī. Her mother died in childbirth, and she was abandoned with her mother's body in the charnel ground. Princess Mandāravā, who was practicing in forests, transforming herself into a tigress, found the little abandoned infant and brought her up.

When Kālasiddhi had grown up, Guru Rinpoche realized that she was capable of becoming his disciple. Guru Rinpoche manifested as a teacher called Saukhyadeva (Phan bDe'i Lha) and gave her empowerments and teachings. Then, in the Trawachen forest, together they practiced the trainings of the skillful means.

Later, Kālasiddhi blessed a son of a farmer of Ngathupchen and became the master Hūṃkara, who was one of the most famous tantric masters of Buddhist India. At the end of her life she attained the body of the union of bliss and emptiness and went to Zangdok Palri without leaving her mortal body behind.

Tashi Khyidren of Mön

Tashi Khyidren (or Tashi Chidren), an incarnation of Samayatārā, was born at Tsa-ok in Mön. Mön was a name for the Himalayan mountain region south of Tibet, bordering India, including Sikkim and Bhutan. Her faith in Dharma was awakened in childhood. Then, inspired by the prophecy of a ḍākinī, which came to her in a dream, she went to Lhotrak in southern Tibet. There she met Yeshe Tsogyal and received empowerments and teachings from her. Later she met Guru Rinpoche, who gave her the essence of the profound teachings. By practicing she achieved esoteric attainments, and she became the action-consort of Guru Rinpoche.

At Patro Taktsang in Bhutan, Guru Rinpoche practiced the sādhana of Vajrakīla with her. When he manifested as Dorje Trolö, she transformed herself into a tigress and became his mount. Together they bound by vow all the powerful nonhuman spirits of Tibet. She assisted him in concealing many ter. Tashi Khyidren was the most gracious ḍākinī for Tibet apart from Yeshe Tsogyal. Later she went to Zangdok Palri pure land without leaving her mortal body behind.

THE CHIEF DISCIPLES OF GURU RINPOCHE IN TIBET[122]

There are two traditions of counting the twenty-five chief disciples of Guru Rinpoche in Tibet, known as the "king and the twenty-five subjects" (rJe 'Bangs Nyer lNga). According to one tradition, they are the king and the twenty-four subjects, excluding either Yudra Nyingpo or Kharchen Palkyi Wangchuk. The other tradition of counting is the king plus twenty-five subjects, in which both Yudra Nyingpo and Kharchen Palkyi Wangchuk are included. Here the second tradition is followed.

King Trisong Detsen

King Trisong Detsen (790–858 CE)[123] was the thirty-seventh ruler of Tibet in the Chögyal (Dharma King) dynasty, which originated with King Nyatri Tsenpo. Nyatri was believed to be a prince from India, who became the first king of Tibet in 127 BCE. King Trisong was the son of King Me Aktsomchen and Princess Chin Ch'eng Kun Chu, a daughter of King Li Lung Chi of China. At the age of thirteen he was enthroned as the thirty-seventh king of Tibet. He was a wise and powerful ruler who extended his kingdom far beyond the previous borders of Tibet.

He invited Shāntarakṣhita, the celebrated Mahāyāna scholar from India, to establish the Buddha Dharma in Tibet and to build Samye Monastery. But obstructions arose in the form of negative spirits and anti-Buddhist ministers in Tibet, and they were unable to carry out their plans. Shāntarakṣhita then made a prophecy, in accordance with which the king invited to Tibet Guru Padmasambhava, the greatest of the Indian Buddhist tāntrikas of that time. The guru came to Tibet, subdued all the human and nonhuman obstructions by his enlightened power, and bound all the spirits in Tibet to the service of the Dharma.

Since then Guru Padmasambhava has been known in Tibet by the name of Guru Rinpoche, the Precious Master. Thereafter the great Samye Monastery was completed in five years. One hundred and eight Indian scholars, including Guru Rinpoche, Shāntarakṣhita, and Vimalamitra, and Tibetan scholar-translators including Vairochana, Kawa Paltsek, Chok-ro Lü'i Gyaltsen, and Zhang Yeshe De, translated numerous scriptures of Hīnayāna, Mahāyāna, and Vajrayāna into Tibetan from Indian languages, mainly from Sanskrit. In many places institutions were built for study and training in the sūtric and tantric teachings.

At Samye Chimphu Guru Rinpoche conferred the empowerment of the great sādhanas of the eight maṇḍalas (sGrub Pa Ch'en Po bKa' brGyad) of Mahāyoga to his chief disciples, the king and twenty-five subjects. By practicing the sādhanas of the various tutelary deities, they all achieved various siddhis. During the empowerment, the offering flower of the king landed upon the maṇḍala of Chechok Deshek Düpa, one of the eight maṇḍalas. The throwing of a flower on a group of maṇḍalas determines the tutelary deity through whom it will be appropriate for the disciple to practice. By practicing the sādhana of Chechok (Mahottaraheruka/Vajramahāheruka), the king achieved the attainment of unwavering contemplation.

His literary works include *Ka Yangtakpe Tsema* and *Bumtik*. He brought by force the relics of the Buddha from Magadha in central India and built many temples and stūpas to enshrine them.

The king died at the age of fifty-five (or fifty-nine). After his death he took rebirth as many great scholars, saints, and tertöns, in order to preserve and propagate the Dharma for future followers. Among his rebirths were Sangye Lama (1000–1080?), Nyang Nyima Özer (1124–1192), Guru Chöwang (1212–1270), Ogyen Lingpa (1329–1360/7), Pema Wangyal (1487–1542), Tashi Tobgyal (1550–1602), and the fifth Dalai Lama (1617–1682). Jigme Lingpa (1730–1798) and Khyentse Wangpo (1820–1892) were incarnations of both the king and Vimalamitra.

The king had three sons and two daughters.[124] They all became great disciples of Guru Rinpoche and important figures in Dharma lineage. However, in the histories there are differences in the number, names, and seniority of the sons. Some scholars agree that he had three sons and that the eldest was Mu-ne Tsepo, the middle one was Murup(or Murum) Tsepo, and the youngest was Mutik (or Mutri) Tsepo.

When King Trisong Detsen was twenty-one, prince Mu-ne Tsepo was born to Queen Tsepongza. Mu-ne received teachings and empowerments from Guru Rinpoche and practiced them. At the age of forty-seven, he became the thirty-eighth ruler of Tibet, but he died after reigning for less than two years. In addition to the establishment of many Buddhist institutions, he is especially known for his attempts to distribute wealth equally among rich and poor, three times in his short reign. It is interesting to note that Rahula Sankritayana (1893–1963), a great Indian scholar of Buddhism, even dedicated one of his books to Prince Mu-ne Tsepo, saying that he was the first socialist, a socialist king, in the world. Among Mu-ne Tsepo's incarnations were Tülku Zangpo Trakpa (14th century), Drikung Rinchen Phüntsok (1509–1557), and Yonge Mingyur Dorje (1628–?).

When the king was twenty-two, Prince Murup (or Murum) Tsepo, alias Lha-se Tamdzin Yeshe Rölpatsal, was born to Queen Tsepongza.[125] He received the teachings and empowerments from Guru Rinpoche and other teachers. He became a great scholar of the tantras, and by practicing the Vajrakīla sādhana he became a great adept. Also he was entrusted with the *Lama Gongdü* cycle of teachings by Guru Rinpoche. By accident he killed a son of a minister and was banished to the northern Tibetan border with China as military commander for nine years. Later he lived in Kongpo. Under his command the Tibetans defeated the forces of the Chinese and the Turks. At the end of his life, he dissolved into the light body. Among his incarnations were Sangye Lingpa (1340–1396),who discovered *Lama Gongdü,* Zhikpo Lingpa (1464–1523), Pema Norbu (1679–1757), Dodrupchen Jigme Thrinle Özer (1745–1821), and Chogyur Dechen Lingpa (1829–1870).

Princess Nujin Sa-le was born to Queen Tsepongza. I could not find any account of her life.

Princess Pemasal was born to Queen Dromza Changchup. However, she died at the age of eight. Guru Rinpoche wrote a letter NṚI in red at the heart of her dead body, and by his enlightened power he recalled her consciousness to her body. When she had revived and was able to speak, Guru Rinpoche conferred on her the empowerment of *Khandro Nyingthig* and gave her the secret name of Pema Ledreltsal. He placed the casket containing the *Khandro Nyingthig* teachings on her head and spoke the following aspiration: "In future may you find this teaching, and may it be beneficial for many living beings." Then he recorded these events and asked Khandro Yeshe Tsogyal to conceal the *Khandro Nyingthig* teachings for future followers. Then the texts were concealed in two different places. The elaborate teachings were hidden at the lion-like rock in lower Bumthang and the profound condensed teachings of the Nyingthig tantras for mendicants were hidden at Tanglung Tramo Trak in Takpo Valley. Then they were entrusted to the treasure-master ḍākinīs and the protectors Za and Mamo, who were instructed by Guru Rinpoche to hand the teachings over to the appropriate tertön in the future.

Among her incarnations were Pema Ledreltsal (1291–1319?), who discovered the *Khandro Nyingthig* teachings from Tanglung Tramo Trak; Longchen Rabjam (1308–1368), who propagated the teachings by writing and teaching; Pema Lingpa (1450–1521); and Lhatsün Namkha Jigme (1597–?).

When the king was fifty-nine, Prince Mutik (or Mutri) Tsepo, alias Senalek Jing-yön, was born to Queen Droza Changchup. He became the thirty-ninth king of Tibet. He received teachings and transmissions from Guru Rinpoche and achieved high attainments. He was the father of five sons: Tsangma, Gyalse Lhaje (aka Choktrup Gyalpo), Lhündrup, Tri Ralpachen, the fortieth ruler, and Lang Darma, the forty-first and last ruler of the Chögyal dynasty. As mentioned earlier, when Guru Rinpoche took leave of Tibet, Mutri was king.

Among his incarnations were Guru Jotse, Karma Chagme (1613–1678), Zhechen Rabjam Tenpe Gyaltsen (1650–1704), and Apang Tertön (?–1945).

The Twenty-five Subjects (Disciples) of Guru Rinpoche in Tibet[126]

1. Nupchen Sangye Yeshe was born in Drak Valley in the clan of Nup. From the age of seven he studied with Otren Palkyi Zhönu and became a master of the tantras. When he received the empowerment of the great sādhana of eight maṇḍalas from Guru Rinpoche, his flower landed upon the maṇḍala of Yamāntaka, the Wrathful Mañjushrī, which is the maṇḍala of the body of all the Buddhas. After practicing for twenty-one days, he saw the pure vision of the deity. By his miraculous power he destroyed thirty-seven villages of Drak Valley and burned their forces with his magical fire. In the cave of Drak Yangdzong with his wooden phurbu (ritual-magical dagger, kīla), he pierced the rock as if it

were mud. The phurbu was still in the rock in 1956, when I visited the site.

Nupchen visited India, Nepal, and Trusha (in Central Asia) seven times and received teachings from Shrīsiṃha, Vimalamitra, Shāntigarbha, Dhanashīla, Vasudhara, and Chetsen Kye. In Tibet he received various teachings from Nyak Jñānakumāra, Sokpo Palkyi Yeshe, and Zhang Gyalwe Yönten. The tantric transmissions of Mahāyoga, Anuyoga, and Semde of Atiyoga converged in him.

When the evil King Lang Darma began to destroy the Dharma in Tibet, he summoned Nupchen and his disciples, and asked him, "What kind of power do you have?" Nupchen said, "Please observe my power just from reciting a mantra," and he raised his hand above his head in an exhorting gesture. Above the head of Nupchen the king saw nine scorpions the size of yaks. In fear the king exclaimed, "Nupchen, I will not harm the precious tāntrikas." Nupchen said, "Please see this also," and he pointed in an exhorting gesture to a rock, and lightning rained down, splitting the rock into pieces. Fearfully the king said, "I will not harm you and your followers," and he released them. Because of Nupchen, King Lang Darma did not destroy the tantric teachings and its long-haired, white-robed followers.

Nupchen is the second of the three greatest receivers (Babs Sa) of tantra, who transmitted and spread the teachings of Mahāyoga, Anuyoga, and Semde of Atiyoga of the Nyingma tradition of Tibet. The first is Nyak Jñānakumāra, one of Guru Rinpoche's chief disciples. The three masters of the Zur clan together are counted as the third. They are Zurchen Shākya Jungne, his nephew Zurchung Sherap Trakpa, and Zurchung's son Zur Shākya Senge.

Nupchen had many disciples including Khulung Yönten Gyatso, and he wrote many important texts. He lived until the age of 130, although there are other versions saying that he died at the age of 111 or 113. He was alive at the time of Ngadak Palkhortsen, a grandson of King Lang Darma, and he himself has written in one of his works:

> I, Sangye, the young priest from Nup,
> Attained the age of one hundred and thirty.

Among his incarnations were Dumgya Zhingtrom, Tri-me Künga (late 14th century), Tsasum Lingpa (early 15th century), and Sangdak Thrinle Lhündrup (1611–1662).

2. Gyalwa Chok-yang was born in Phen-yul in the clan of Ngenlam. He was made a fully ordained monk by Shāntarakṣhita in the first group of seven Tibetans to receive ordination. He was famous for his disciplined life. When he received the empowerment of the great sādhana of eight maṇḍalas from Guru Rinpoche, his flower landed on the maṇḍala of Hayagrīva. Hayagrīva is the embodiment of the speech of the Buddhas. He practiced the sādhana of Hayagrīva at Wentsa, and he transformed himself as the Hayagrīva deity, and heard the neigh of the horse on the crown of his head. He also attained the power of control over life. It is said that when the grandson of Lang Darma, Ngadak Palkhortsen, was sick, Gyalwa Chok-yang performed Gyalpo Tsedö, and Ngadak recovered.

Among his incarnations were Guru Tseten (13th century), Gyatön Pema Wangchuk (13th century), and Thekchen Lingpa (1700–1775/6). Karma Pakshi (1206–1283), the second Karmapa, acknowledged himself as an incarnation of this adept.

3. Namkhe Nyingpo was born in Lhotrak in the Nup clan. He was also ordained as a monk by Shāntarakṣhita. While receiving the empowerment of the great sādhana of eight maṇḍalas, his flower landed on the maṇḍala of Yangdak (Shrīheruka). This deity is the embodiment of the minds of the Buddhas. As the result of his practice of the sādhana, he moved around by riding on the beams of the sun's rays. He learned Sanskrit and went to India, where he received teachings from Mahāsiddha Hūṃkara among others. When he returned to Tibet the pro-Bön ministers slandered him maliciously, and he was driven into exile to Lhotrak Kharchu in southern Tibet. While he was staying there in a cave called Tragmar near his native village, his brother, who was a poor farmer, came to ask him for some seed to plant. He said to his brother, "You are a farmer, and if you don't have seeds, where can I, a yogi, get them in a cave?" Then he gave him some pebbles and told him, "It is shameful before people if you have nothing to plant; so throw these pebbles in your field and pretend that you are planting." His brother did as he said, and the next summer he got the best crop in the valley.

Once when Namkhe Nyingpo was flying through the sky, his rosary fell down into a valley. When he flew down and picked up the rosary, he created big imprints of his five fingers filled with flowers, and later, ḍākinīs built five stūpas there. Once he gave pebbles to some devotees. They threw them away but one man kept his. Later they became magnificent turquoises.

He practiced mainly at Lhotrak Kharchu and saw the pure vision of the tutelary divinity. He departed for the celestial pure land (mKha' sPyod) without leaving his gross body behind.

Among his incarnations were Changchup Lingpa (14th century), Trati Ngakchang (18th century), and Rigdzin Tsewang Norbu (1698–1755).

4. Jñānakumāra was born in Yarlung Cho in southern Tibet in the Nyak clan. On his throat were moles in the shape of crossed vajras. He is also known by the name of Gyalwe Lodrö. He was ordained as a monk by Shātarakṣhita. He became a great scholar and translated many sūtras and tantras. He received teachings from Guru Rinpoche, Vimalamitra, Vairochana, and Yudra Nyingpo. He became the first of the great receivers of the Mahāyoga, Anuyoga, and Semde of Atiyoga in Tibet. When Guru Rinpoche conferred the empowerment of the great sādhana of eight maṇḍalas, his flower, like the king's, landed upon the maṇḍala of Chechok. He practiced Dütsi Chechok, and as a result at Yarlung Sheltrak he brought forth a stream from a dry rock by piercing the rock with his finger.

He faced many dangers, including danger to his life three times. He practiced the sādhana of Vajrakīla and by the power of his siddhi he eliminated all the negative forces. He could transform himself into different forms. He translated many Buddhist texts into Tibetan.

Among his many disciples he had eight principal ones, who included Sokpo Palkyi Yeshe and Otren Palkyi Zhönu. Among his incarnations were Ramo Shelmen (12th century), Nyi Ösal (13th century), Khedrup Lodrö Gyaltsen, and Kathok Gyurme Tsewang Choktrup (15th century).

5. Khandro Yeshe Tsogyal. A brief note on the life of Khandro Yeshe Tsogyal is given on pages 92–3 among the five consorts of Guru Rinpoche. Among her numerous incarnations were Chomo Menmo, Pema Tsokyi (1248–1283?), Khandroma Künga Bum (14th century), and Rigdzin Thrinle Namgyal.

6. Palkyi Yeshe was born at Yadrok in the Drogmi clan. He became a learned translator of many tantras, notably the tantras of the Mamo Mātaraḥ Bötong deities. In the empowerment of the great sādhana of eight maṇḍalas, his flower landed upon the maṇḍala of La-me Heruka of Mamo Bötong and he became an adept of this maṇḍala. He subdued worldly spirits, especially mamos, and bound them as servants.

Among his incarnations were *Rashak Chöbar* and the Kharak Dechen Lingpa.

7. Palkyi Senge was born into the Lang clan. He went to India and Oḍḍiyāṇa and became a translator. In the empowerment of the great sādhana of eight maṇḍalas, his flower landed upon the Jikten Chötö (Lokastotrapūja) maṇḍala. He attained great esoteric power and was able to bring worldly spirits under his control. At Patro Taktsang in Bhutan, where he did his sādhana practices, he received the vision of the Wrathful Buddha Trakpa Kündü of the Jikten Chötö maṇḍala. He achieved both common and uncommon accomplishments.

Among his incarnations were Ratön Tobden Dorje and Dzogchen Pema Rigdzin (1625–1697).

8. Vairochana[127] was the foremost translator of Buddhist scriptures in Tibetan history. He was responsible for bringing to Tibet and translating many sūtras and tantras, especially two of the three categories of Dzogpa Chenpo teachings, namely Semde and Longde.

He was born at Nyemo Chekhar in Tsang Province as the son of Dorje Gyalpo of the Pakor clan. In his childhood he displayed many miraculous powers such as flying in the sky, making imprints on rocks, and foretelling future events. He was extraordinarily intelligent.

In accordance with the prophetic advice of Guru Rinpoche, King Trisong Detsen brought him to Samye and trained him as a translator. He became one of the first seven Tibetans to take monastic vows from Shāntarakṣhita and was given the name Vairochanarakṣhita. In the empowerment of the great sādhana of eight maṇḍalas, his flower landed on the maṇḍala of Möpa Tra-ngak (Vajramentrabhīru). At the command of the king, Vairochana and the monk Lektrup of Tsang Province went to India in search of Dharma teachings, as two of the first missionaries. On the way they encountered fifty-seven nearly fatal difficulties, but they ignored the obstacles and reached India. They met Shrīsiṃha in secret at the forest of Tsenden Silche in Dhanakosha. One night they received the teachings of Semde in utmost secret. Vairochana wrote down the eighteen tantras of Semde on white cotton with the milk of a white cow in order that people should not see the texts. When he wanted the manuscript to be read, he held it over smoke and the text became visible. The monk Lektrup was satisfied with what they had accomplished and departed for Tibet. On the way back he was killed by road guards.

Vairochana requested more teachings from Shrīsiṃha, and he received the teachings and instructions of all the sixty tantras of Semde. He was also taught the three categories of Longde. Vairochana also received the teachings of the six million four hundred thousand tantras (or verses) of

Dzogpa Chenpo from Prahevajra in pure vision and blessings from master Mañjushrīmitra in his illusory-wisdom-body.

Vairochana reached Tibet by swift-footed power, and there he gave the king common teachings in the daytime and Dzogpa Chenpo at night. Among other works, he translated the first five of the eighteen tantras of Semde. This collection is known as *The Five Early Translations of Semde.*

At that time some jealous Indians sent messengers to spread slander, saying that the teachings brought from India by Vairochana were not Buddhism. Because of the wrong aspirations and influence of Queen Tsepongza and certain wicked ministers, the king was forced regretfully to banish Vairochana to the Gyalmo Tsawe Rong (aka Gyarong), a region on the border of Tibet and China. In exile Vairochana converted the king, his ministers and the population of Gyarong to Buddhism. Prince Yudra Nyingpo, who was the rebirth of the monk Lekrup of Tsang, became one of his principal disciples and a well-known scholar and lineage-holder. Yudra Nyingpo came to Samye and met Vimalamitra. At Vimalamitra's request the king invited Vairochana to return to Tibet. On the way to Tibet, Vairochana met an eighty-five-year-old man named Mipham Gönpo, and he gave him Dzogpa Chenpo teachings. Mipham Gönpo could not sit in meditation postures because of his advanced age, so he had recourse to a meditation cord and support stick in order to sit up straight and remain motionless. The old man attained the rainbow body.

In addition to Yudra Nyingpo and Mipham Gönpo, the principal disciples of Vairochana were Nyak Jñānakumāra and Sherap Dölma from Li. Later on Sherap Dölma invited his master to the country of Li. From there Vairochana went to the Bhashing forest of Nepal, where he vanished into the rainbow body.

Vairochana is the sublime translator of Tibetan Buddhism. He translated many texts of sūtra and tantra, and his scholarship and skill as a translator are far more exalted than those of all the other translators in the history of Tibetan Buddhism. Ngok Loden Sherap (1059–1109), who was one of the greatest translators of the new translation period, said:

> Vairochana is like the clear sky.
> Ka[wa Paltsek] and Chok[ro Lü'i Gyaltsen] are like the sun and moon.

> Rinchen Zangpo [958–1051, the greatest translator of the new period] is like the dawn star.
> And we are merely fireflies.[128]

Among his numerous incarnations were Trapa Ngönshechen (1012–1090?), Dorje Lingpa (1346–1405), Künkyong Lingpa (1396–1477?), Chöden Do-ngak Lingpa (15th century), Trengpo Sherap Özer (1518–1572), Minling Terchen (1646–1714), Rongtön Dechen Lingpa (1663–?), Gyalse Zhenphen Thaye (1800–?) and Kongtrül Yönten Gyatso (1813–1899).

9. Yudra Nyingpo was a prince of Gyalmo Tsawe Rong (aka Gyarong) in Eastern Tibet. When Vairochana was exiled to Gyalmo Tsawe Rong, he received teachings from Vairochana and became a great scholar and translator. Yudra came to Central Tibet and received teachings from Guru Rinpoche, and he translated, among other works, the last thirteen of the eighteen texts of Semde. As a result of his attainments he could take different forms such as a golden vajra. He is notable for his excellent realization of Dzogpa Chenpo. He became one of the greatest masters of the Semde and Longde teachings of Dzogpa Chenpo in Tibet.

Among his incarnations were Minling Lochen Dharmashrī (1654–1717), Tertön Dorje Thogme, and Minling Khenchen Ogyen Tendzin (15th century).

10. Dorje Düdjom was born in Tsang-rong in the Nanam clan. In his youth he became a minister of King Trisong Detsen, and he went to Nepal to invite Guru Rinpoche to Tibet as the king's emissary. He became a disciple of Guru Rinpoche and achieved accomplishments by practicing the Vajrakīla sādhana. Because of his control over mind and air, he traveled through the sky with the speed of the wind and near Samye passed through a mountain unhindered.

Among his incarnations were Palpo Ahung (13th century), Rigdzin Gödem (1337–1408), and Rigdzin Legdenje (15th century).

11. Yeshe Yang was a monk and one of the eight principal calligraphers of the ter texts. He received teachings from Guru Rinpoche and was able to go to the pure lands of the Buddhas and receive teachings from them.

12. Sokpo Lhapal was a blacksmith. Nyak Jñānakumāra discerned in him the appropriate signs for becoming an adept of the Vajrakīla sādhana and took him as a disciple. Both Nyak and Guru Rinpoche gave teachings and empowerments to Lhapal. He achieved esoteric power through

the practice of the Vajrakīla sādhana. As a result, with a gesture he could catch dangerous wild beasts; and on three occasions with his miraculous power he pacified the enemies of his teacher, Nyak.

13. Nanam Yeshe is said to have been the same person as Zhang Yeshe De, who was one of the three translators who rank next to Vairochana in skill and scholarship. The other two were Kawa Paltsek and Chok-ro Lü'i Gyaltsen. He achieved esoteric power through the sādhana of Vajrakīla and became a great master of the Vajrakīla teachings. As a result of his attainment he could fly like a bird.

14. Palkyi Wangchuk of the Kharchen clan was the brother of Yeshe Tsogyal. He was a tantric layman who accompanied Guru Rinpoche when he traveled to different parts of Tibet. He attained esoteric power through the practice of Vajrakīla, as a result of which he could pacify the enemies of the Dharma just by pointing his phurbu at them.

15. Denma Tsemang was born in Den Valley of Kham Province. He was one of the most famous calligraphers, and he transcribed many ter texts and became a great translator. He received many tantric teachings from Guru Rinpoche and possessed the power of "unforgetting memory."

16. Kawa Paltsek was born at Kawa in Phenpo Valley. He was one of the three greatest translators of Tibet, and his role was praised by Guru Rinpoche. He was among the first seven monks to be ordained in Tibet. By practicing he achieved the power of knowing others' thoughts. He translated many sūtras and tantras and was also one of the famous calligraphers and the author of many texts.

Among his incarnations was Trawa Ngönshe (1012–1090?), who rediscovered as a ter the *Gyüzhi* of Tibetan medicine in four volumes. These texts are the main source of Tibetan medicine to this day. Some say that Trawa Ngönshe was an incarnation both of Vairochana and Shüpu Palkyi Senge.

17. Shüpu Palkyi Senge was born in the same clan as the king. In his youth he was a minister at the court of the king, and he was one of the emissaries who went to Nepal to invite Guru Rinpoche to Tibet. He translated many texts of Mamo, Yamāntaka, and Vajrakīla, and he was one of the eight most outstanding minds of Tibet in his time. He achieved esoteric power through the sādhanas of Mamo and Vajrakīla. He demonstrated his esoteric power by reversing the flow of the river Ngamshö, turning the stream of Chimphu upward, and shattering a rock in pieces by pointing his phurbu. At the time of the consecration of

Samye, he distributed clarified butter through pipelines as a sign of his prosperity and dedication.

Among his incarnations was Namchö Mingyur Dorje (1645–1667).

18. Dre Gyalwe Lodrö, in his youth, was a member of the inner circle of the king's court. Later he took ordination and became one of the chief disciples of Guru Rinpoche and a translator. He visited India and received the teachings of Yangdak from Master Hūṃkara. Through his esoteric power he liberated his mother, who had been reborn in an inferior life, and he also transformed a corpse into gold. He attained longevity and was alive at the time of Rongzom Chözang (11th century).

19. Khyechung Lotsā belonged to the Drogmi clan. While still very young he became a translator, hence he got his name, which means "boy translator." He received teachings from Guru Rinpoche and lived as a householder tāntrika. Through his achievement of esoteric power he could summon birds flying in the sky by a gesture of his fingers.

Among his incarnations were Terchen Düdül Dorje (1615–1672), Zhechen Rabjam Tenpe Gyaltsen (1650–1704), Khordong Nüden Dorje (18th–19th century), Düdjom Lingpa (1835–1904) and Kyabje Dudjom Rinpoche (1904–1987).

20. Trenpa Namkha was a great master of Bön and was also known as Kyerpön Chenpo. He was revered by Bön followers as an incarnation of the founder of Bön, whose name was also Trenpa Namkha. He became a disciple of Guru Rinpoche and a translator of Buddhist texts. Through his esoteric power he could summon wild yaks from the northern plains of Tibet with just a gesture.

Among his incarnations were Bönpo Traktsal (11th century) and Rigdzin Lhündrup (1611–1662), who was the incarnation of both Nupchen and Trenpa Namkha.

21. Otren Palkyi Wangchuk was born at Oyugda. He lived as a householder tāntrika and became a heart disciple of Guru Rinpoche and a great scholar of tantra. He achieved esoteric power by practicing the sādhana of the Guru in Wrathful Form. By his miraculous power he could cross big rivers like a fish, although he did not know how to swim.

22. Ma Rinchen Chok was born in Phenpo Valley. He was one of the nine most intelligent people of his time in Tibet. He was among the first seven Tibetans ordained as a monk by Shāntarakṣhita. He was a follower of Nāgārjuna's philosophy and a scholar of the *Guhyagarbha-māyājāla-tantra*. He was next to Kamalashīla among the followers of the

lineage of Shāntarakṣhita, in the famous Samye debate in which they defeated their opponent, the Chinese master Hvashang Mahāyāna. He translated many Buddhist texts and received many teachings from Guru Rinpoche, by practicing which he attained realization. He demonstrated his esoteric power by cutting rocks into pieces as if they were dough and eating them as food. He visited Kham, where Tsuk-ru Rinchen Zhönu became one of his many disciples.

23. Lhalung Palkyi Dorje was born in Kungmo Che. In his youth he was posted on the border of China and Tibet, where he defeated large Chinese forces. With his two brothers he was ordained as a monk by Vimalamitra. He received bodhisattva vows and tantric empowerments from Guru Rinpoche, and as a result of his attainment he could penetrate through mountains without obstruction. When King Lang Darma was destroying Buddhist establishments and executing Buddhists, Lhalung Palkyi Dorje killed the king with an arrow and fled to Kham. At the end of his life his body was absorbed into the rainbow body.

Among his incarnations was Palyül Pema Norbu (1679–1757) and Rigdzin Nyima Trakpa (1647–1710).

24. Langtro Könchok Jungne was born at Chang Tanak in Tsang and became a minister at the king's court. He later became a monk and a translator, and received tantric teachings from Guru Rinpoche. As a result of his practice he became a great tantric adept and could send lightning like shooting arrows wherever he liked.

Among his incarnations were Ratna Lingpa (1403–1471/8), Rigdzin Longsal Nyingpo (1625–1692), and Dzogchen Pema Rigdzin (1625–1697).

25. Lasum Gyalwa Changchup was one of the first group of seven Tibetans to be ordained as the first monks. He was one of the nine most intelligent people of his time. He received teachings and empowerments from Guru Rinpoche, visited India many times, and translated many texts. As a result of his practice he could remain poised in the sky in the meditation posture.

Among his incarnations was Rigdzin Künzang Sherap (1636–1699).

10

Künkhyen Longchen Rabjam
1308–1363

Künkhyen Longchen Rabjam[129] was born at Tötrong in Tra Valley south of the center of Tibet, on the tenth day of the second month of the Earth Monkey year of the fifth Rabjung (1308). His father was Tenpa Sung, a tantric yogī of the Rok clan. His mother was Sönam Gyen of the Drom clan. At his conception his mother dreamed of a sun placed on the head of a lion illuminating the whole world. At his birth the Dharma protectress Namdru Remati appeared in the form of a black woman. Holding the baby in her arms, she said, "I will protect him," and she handed him back to his mother and disappeared.

Longchen Rabjam was an incarnation, or tülku, of Princess Pemasal, a daughter of King Trisong Detsen, to whom Guru Rinpoche had entrusted the transmission of the *Khandro Nyingthig*. In her series of lives, the incarnation directly preceding Longchen Rabjam was Pema Ledrel-tsal, who rediscovered the *Khandro Nyingthig* teachings as a ter.

From childhood Longchen Rabjam was endowed with faith, compassion, and wisdom, the noble qualities of a bodhisattva. When he was five he learned to read and write with no difficulty. At seven, his father conferred on him the empowerments, instructions, and training in the practice of *The Peaceful and Wrathful Aspects of the Guru* and *Kagye Deshek Düpa*. His father also trained him in medicine and astrology.

At twelve, Longchen Rabjam took the ordination of a novice from

Khenpo Samdrup Rinchen at Samye Monastery and was given the name Tsültrim Lodrö. He gained mastery of the Vinaya, the texts on the monastic law of moral conduct, and was able to teach them from the age of fourteen.

At sixteen, with the master Tashi Rinchen and others, he started studying many tantras belonging to the New Tantric lineage, such as the two traditions of the fruit and path (*Lam 'Bras*), two traditions of the six yogas (*Ch'os Drug*), the Wheel of Time (*Kālachakra*), cutting off [the ego] (*gChod*), and the three pacifications (Zhi Byed) traditions.

At nineteen, he went to the famous Sangphu Neuthang[130] Monastery, and studied Buddhist scriptures on philosophy, logic, and meditation for six years. From the masters Lopön Tsen-gönpa and Chöpal Gyaltsen he studied the five mahāyāna texts by Maitreya, the treatises on logic by Dignāga and Dhamakīrti, and many texts on the Middle Way (Madhyamaka) and Transcendental Wisdom (Prajñāpāramitā) philosophies. Also, with the translator Lodrö Tenpa of Pang he studied Sanskrit, poetry, composition, drama, and many sūtras and Prajñāpāramitā texts. Then from the master Zhönu Töndrup, he received the initiations and instructions on the important Nyingma tantras, Do (sūtras) of Anuyoga, *Māyājāla-tantra* of Mahāyoga, and Semde of Atiyoga.

With about twenty teachers, including Master Zhönu Gyalpo, Zhönu Dorje, Lama Tampa Sönam Gyaltsen (1312–1375) of Sakya, and Karmapa Rangjung Dorje (1284–1339) of the Kagyü, he studied teachings and received the transmissions of sūtras and tantras.

While studying, he was also always engaged in meditative training in retreats, and he saw the pure visions of Mañjushrī, Sarasvatī, Achala, Vajravārāhī, and Tārā, and realized various spiritual attainments. His training in studies and meditation opened the door of his speech treasure. By those who knew him he became recognized by the name Master of Infinite Realization (Longchen Rabjam) and Master of Scriptures from Samye (bSam Yas Lung Mang Ba).

At twenty-seven, as prophesied by Tārā, the Buddha in female form, he went to meet master Rigdzin Kumārādza (1266–1343), the holder of the *Vima Nyingthig* teachings, in a retreat camp where about seventy disciples were living in temporary shelters in the highlands of Yartö Kyam Valley. The master received Longchen Rabjam with great joy and gave the prophecy that he would be the transmission-holder of the *Vima Nyingthig* teachings.

He studied with Rigdzin Kumārādza for two years, receiving instructions on all three categories of Dzogpa Chenpo: Semde, the cycle on mind; Longde, the cycle on the ultimate sphere; and Me-ngagde, the cycle on the ultimate instructions. But the main emphasis of his studies was on the texts of the four divisions of Me-ngagde, namely Outer, Inner, Esoteric, and Innermost Esoteric teachings. These texts are the seventeen tantras and the branch or instruction teachings, namely: the four volumes[131] with the one hundred and nineteen treatises of extensive instructions.

Rigdzin Kumārādza conferred all his Nyingthig teachings on Longchen Rabjam and proclaimed him his lineage successor. While he was studying with Rigdzin Kumārādza, Longchen Rabjam lived under circumstances of severe deprivation. In order to combat his attachment to material things, it was Rigdzin Kumārādza's practice to keep moving from place to place instead of settling at one location and getting attached to it. In nine months he and his disciples moved their camp nine times, causing great hardship to Longchen Rabjam and everyone else. Just as soon as he got his simple life settled in a temporary shelter, usually a cave, which would protect him from rain and cold, the time would come to move again. He had very little food and only one ragged bag to use as both mattress and blanket to protect himself from the extremely cold winter. It was under these circumstances that Longchen Rabjam obtained the most rare and precious teachings of the tantras and instructions of the three cycles of Dzogpa Chenpo. Finally the master empowered him as the lineage holder of the Nyingthig transmission.

Then for seven (or six) years he observed meditation retreat, mainly at Chimphu. In addition to Dzogpa Chenpo meditation, he also practiced the forms and rites of various divinities, and he beheld pure visions of the peaceful and wrathful forms of Guru Rinpoche, Vajrasattva, and the peaceful and wrathful deities.

At thirty-two,[132] while still in retreat, Longchen Rabjam for the first time conferred the empowerment and instructions of *Vima Nyingthig* upon his disciples at Nyiphu Shuksep, near Kang-ri Thökar. For a while all the surroundings turned into pure lights, mystical sounds, and divine visions.

Soon his yogī disciple Özer Kocha found the text of *Khandro Nyingthig,* discovered as a ter by Longchen Rabjam's previous incarnation, Pema Ledreltsal (1291–?), and he offered it to Longchen Rabjam. The Dharma protectress Shenpa Sogdrubma also presented him with a copy of the same text. Although he was the reincarnation of the discoverer of the teachings, in order to show the importance of preserving the transmission for future followers, he went to Shö Gyalse, a disciple of Pema Ledreltsal, and received the transmission of *Khandro Nyingthig*.

At thiry-three, he gave the *Khandro Nyingthig* teachings to eight male and female disciples including yogī Özer Kocha at Samye Chimphu. During the empowerments, the Protectress of Tantra (sNgags Srung Ma) entered into one of the yoginīs and gave prophecies and instructions. Some of the disciples beheld Longchen Rabjam transforming into the Sambhogakāya form. A rain of flowers showered down, and arches, beams, and circles of lights of different colors were witnessed all over the mountain. All the assembled people were singing and dancing with overwhelming wisdom energy. Longchen Rabjam saw the vision of Guru Rinpoche and his consort bestowing empowerments and entrusting the transmission of *Khandro Nyingthig* to him. They gave him the names Ogyen Tri-me Özer and Dorje Ziji. Dharma protectors appeared in physical form and accepted the offerings. For a long time, perhaps a month, the minds of the yogī disciples merged into a deep luminous clarity, which transcends designations of sleeping or waking. Longchen Rabjam sang his yogic energies in verses:

> O yogīs, I am very happy and joyous.
> Tonight we are in the Unexcelled Pure Land.
> In our body, the palace of Peaceful and Wrathful Deities,
> Flourishes the assembly of Buddhas, [the union of] clarity and emptiness.
> Buddhahood is not somewhere else, but in us.
>
> O meditators, you who hold your minds one-pointedly,
> Do not hold your mind at one place, but let it go at ease.
> Mind is emptiness [or openness], whether it goes or it stays.
> Whatever arises [in mind] is the [mere] play of the wisdom.

At the request of the Dharma protectress Yudrönma he moved his residence to Ogyen Dzong Özer Trinkyi Kyemö Tsal (the Fortress of Oḍḍiyāṇa in the Joyful Garden of Clouds of Lights) at Kang-ri Thökar, where he composed several famous works and spent a great part of his life. At this place his meditative realization reached the state of perfection of awareness (Rig Pa Tshad Phebs) through the training of the direct approach (Thod rGal) of Nyingthig.

In a pure vision Vimalamitra taught him and entrusted him with the

Vima Nyingthig teachings. Inspired by Vimalamitra, he wrote the *Yangtig Yizhin Norbu* (aka *Lama Yangtig*), a collection of thirty-five treatises on *Vima Nyingthig*.

Longchen Rabjam withdrew the gold concealed in a ter and with it financed the repair of the Uru Zha temple in Drikung, built by Nyang Tingdzin Zangpo, one of the great disciples of both Guru Rinpoche and Vimalamitra. While the repairs were going on, workers inadvertently dug up many objects that had been buried under the temple in order to subdue the power of negative forces, and they flew around in the sky. Longchen Rabjam transformed himself into the wrathful form of Guru Rinpoche and reburied them again with the mystical gesture of power.

At a time when there was great danger of a civil war in central Tibet because of the plot of Kün-rik, the proud leader of Drikung, Longchen Rabjam fulfilled a prophecy concerning an incarnation of Mañjushrī by diverting Kün-rik from his wrongful path of warfare to the path of Dharma and bringing about peace. At first Tai Situ Phagmo Trupa (1302–1364), then the king of Tibet, was suspicious of Longchen Rabjam and sent forces to kill him, because he was the teacher of the Drikung, his sworn enemy. By his mystical power, Longchen Rabjam became invisible when the forces arrived. But the situation forced Longchen Rabjam to move to Bhutan. There he gave teachings and sometimes assembled about one hundred thousand disciples. In Bumthang he established Tharpa Ling Monastery. In Bhutan he had a son named Tülku Trakpa Özer (1356–1409?) by his consort Kyipa of Bhutan, and his son became a lineage holder. Later, Tai Situ understood the impartial position of Longchen Rabjam and became a disciple, and Longchen Rabjam returned to Tibet.

Longchen Rabjam was one of the greatest scholars and realized sages of Tibet, but he devoted his whole life to extremely subtle and strict spiritual discipline of learning, teaching, writing, and meditation to fulfill the purpose of his enlightened manifestation, which was to be an example of a trainee and a teacher of the Dharma. His mind and life were simple and open, natural, spontaneous, pure, and profound. Wherever he lived and whatever he was doing, it was natural for him always to be in the meditative state.

He visited his master Rigdzin Kumārādza again and again to perfect his understanding and realization. Five times he offered all of whatever little he possessed to his master to cleanse his clinging to any material objects. Owing to the fame of his scholarship and realization, he could easily have built huge monasteries or household structures, but he avoided such works because he had no interest in establishing any institutions. Anything offered him with faith he spent strictly for the service of the Dharma and never for other purposes, nor did he ever use it for himself. He never showed reverence to a layperson, however high-ranking in society, saying, "Homage should be paid to the Three Jewels but not to mundane beings. It is not right to reverse the roles of lama and patron." However great the offerings made to him, he never expressed gratitude, saying, "Let the patrons have the chance to accumulate merits instead of repaying it by expressions of gratitude." He was immensely kind to poor and suffering people, and he enjoyed with great pleasure the simple food offered by poor people, and then would say many prayers of aspiration for them.

For most of his life, Longchen Rabjam lived in solitude, in caves in the mountains, first in Chimphu near Samye and then mostly at Kangri Thökar. The peaceful and clear environment of nature inspires peace and clarity in the observers; then the whole merges into one, the union of peace and clarity. Longchen Rabjam summarizes the merits of solitude.[133]

> Far from the towns full of entertainments,
> Being in the forests naturally increases the peaceful absorptions,
> Harmonizes life in Dharma, tames the mind,
> And makes one attain ultimate joy.

He gave teachings in all fields of Buddhism, but his main emphasis was on Dzogpa Chenpo. Summarizing the meditation of Dzogpa Chenpo, he advised in simple words:

> It is important to look straight at [the nature of] the thoughts when they arise.
> It is important to remain [in the nature] when you are certain [about the realization of it].
> It is important to have the meditationless meditation as your meditation.
> With no waverings, maintain it. This is my advice.[134]

And:

> The present mind, which is unhindered—
> No grasping at "this" [or "that"], free from any modifications or dilutions, and

Unstained by [the duality of] grasped and grasper—
Is the nature of ultimate truth. Maintain this state.[135]

At Lhasa, Longchen Rabjam was received with great fanfare, and he spent about two weeks there. Between the Jokhang and Ramoche of Lhasa, sitting on a throne, he gave the vow of bodhichitta and many teachings to a huge gathering from all walks of life. Through his scholarship and realization, Longchen Rabjam tamed the arrogant minds of many scholars and inspired them to attain the pure mind of Dharma. He sowed the seed of inspiration to pure Dharma in the hearts of many people. He became known as Künkhyen Chöje, the Omniscient Lord of Dharma. Then he went to Nyiphu Shuksep and gave Dzogchen teachings to about a thousand disciples. Then at rocky hills near Trok Ogyen, he gave empowerments and teachings of Dzogpa Chenpo to about three thousand people, including forty known as the masters of Dharma.

At the age of fifty-six, in the Water Hare year (1363) of the sixth Rabjung, he suddenly started dictating his spiritual testament, entitled *Trima Mepe Ö* (Immaculate Radiance), which includes the following lines:

As I have long ago realized the nature of saṃsāra,
There is no essence in the worldly existents.
Now, as I am departing from my impermanent illusory body,
I shall tell you what are the beneficial things for you; please listen
to me.

You are taking your life as real, but it will cheat you.
Its nature is changing and it has no reality.
By understanding its untrustworthy character,
Please practice Dharma from this very day.

Changing is the nature of friends, like [a gathering of] guests.
They get together for a while but soon separate forever.
By freeing yourself from attachments to friends,
Please practice Dharma that benefits you forever.

Honeylike wealth drips away even as you collect it.
Although you earned it, others will enjoy it.
Now, while you have the power, invest it for the sustenance of
your future lives,

By earning merits by giving in charity. . . .

People are impermanent like [groups of] earlier and later visitors.
Elder people have gone early. Younger people will go later.
People of the present, none will live for a hundred years.
Please realize it [the nature of impermanence] at this very moment.

Appearances of this life take place like the events of today.
Apearances of bardo will take place like dreams in the night.
Appearances of the next life will come as fast as tomorrow.
Please practice Dharma at this very moment. . . .

Among all the dharmas, the ultimate pith of luminous clarity
Is the Nyingthig, the sacred meaning.
This is the supreme path that leads you to Buddhahood in a single life span.
Please [through this path] accomplish the great blissful universal sublime. . . .

The nature of the mind is the ultimate sphere, like space.
The nature of space is the nature of the mind, the innate nature.
In meaning they are not separate. They are evenness, Great Perfection.
Please realize the nature at this very moment.

Various phenomena are like reflections in a mirror.
They are emptiness while they are appearing, and emptiness is not other than the appearances themselves.
They are joyful [phenomena], free from designations as one or many.
Please realize the nature at this very moment. . . .

My delight at death is much greater than
The joy of traders who have made their fortune at sea,
The lords of the gods who have proclaimed their victory in war,
Or those sages who are abiding in absorption.
Now Pema Ledreltsal [Longchen Rabjam] will not remain here much longer.
I go to secure the blissful and deathless nature.[136]

Then, when he reached Chimphu and was traveling through Samye, he said that he was going to die there, and he started to show the sickness of his body. But he kept teaching a huge gathering of people who were following him or who had assembled to receive teachings from him. On the sixteenth of the twelfth month, with others he performed an elaborate offering ceremony. Then he gave his disciples his last teaching on impermanence and inspired them to practice Trekchö and Thögal with the advice:

> If you have any difficulty understanding my teachings, read the *Yangtig Yizhin Norbu [*aka *Lama Yangtig];* it will be like a wish-fulfilling jewel. You will realize the state of dissolution of all phenomena into dharmatā, the ultimate nature.

On the eighteenth, sitting in the posture of the Dharmakāya, his mind dissolved into absolute Dharma space. Those present experienced the trembling of the earth and heard roaring sounds. While his body was being preserved for twenty-five days, a tent of rainbows arched constantly across the sky. Even in the coldest months in Tibet, the earth became warm, the ice melted, and roses bloomed. At the time of cremation, the earth trembled three times and a loud sound was heard seven times. Many ringsel (relics) and five kinds of dungchens (large ringsels) emerged from the bones as an indication of his attainment of the five bodies and five wisdoms of Buddhahood.[137]

Longchen Rabjam received teachings and transmissions of all the lineages of Buddhist teachings that were present in Tibet. Especially all the streams of Dzogpa Chenpo transmissions converged in him. Among the Nyingthig teachings of Dzogpa Chenpo that came to him were the *Vima Nyingthig* and *Khandro Nyingthig.*

Longchen Rabjam wrote more than two hundred and fifty treatises on history, ethical instructions, sūtric and tantric teachings, and especially on Dzogpa Chenpo in general and Nyingthig in particular.[138] He presented all of his teaching in the form of composed literature. But many scholars affirm that most of his works on the tantras and on Dzogpa Chenpo are actually gongter, mind treasures, discovered through his enlightened power.

11

Rigdzin Jigme Lingpa
1730–1798

Rigdzin Jigme Lingpa[139] was the incarnation (tülku) of both King Trisong Detsen (790–858) and Vimalamitra. He is also known as Khyentse Özer, Rays of Wisdom and Compassion. He discovered the vast and profound *Longchen Nyingthig* cycle of teachings as mind ter.

In *The Secret Prophecy of Lama Gongdü,*[140] discovered by Sangye Lingpa (1340–1396), Guru Rinpoche foretold Jigme Lingpa's coming seven hundred years hence:

> In the south [of Tibet] there will come a tülku named Özer.
> He shall liberate beings through the profound teachings of Nyingthig.
> Whoever is connected to him he will lead to the pure land of the vidhyādharas.

Jigme Lingpa was born in a village in the early morning of the eighteenth of the twelfth month of the Earth Bird year of the twelfth Rabjung (1730) in Chongye Valley in Southern Tibet, not very far from the royal tombs of the Chögyal dynasty, known as "red tombs." Although his parents came from significant families in past history, they were of simple means, which Jigme Lingpa acknowledges as a blessing that allowed him to undertake his religious life without being forced into social obligations or aristocratic pomp.

From childhood he remembered his previous incarnations, such as being the great Tertön Sangye Lama (1000–1080?). One of his teeth was marked with the Buddha's speech syllable ĀḤ, known as the sign of his being the reincarnation of Vimalamitra. Also, as indicated in a prophetic writing, he had thirty small reddish moles in the form of a vajra at his heart, about thirty small reddish moles at his navel in the form of a ritual bell, and lines in the form of a HYA or HRĪḤ letter, the seed letter of the deity Hayagrīva, on his right thumb. From childhood his mind was detached from worldly enjoyments, and he was extraordinarily compassionate, intelligent, and courageous.

He acknowledged being the thirteenth incarnation of Gyalse Lhaje,[141] the receiver of the *Kadü Chökyi Gyatso* teachings from Duru Rinpoche, all of whom were tertöns. Also, in his life lineage prayer, which he wrote for his disciples, Jigme Lingpa mentions many of his past and one of his future lives as he saw them:

> [1] Samantabhadra, all-pervading lord of saṃsāra and nirvāṇa, the continuum of the basis, the very essence of Buddha nature,
> [2] Then [the union of] compassion and emptiness arose as Avalokiteshvara, and
> [3] Prahevajra, to you I pray.
>
> [4] Then manifested as the son of King Kṛikrī in the presence of Buddha Kāshyapa,
> [5] Nanda, the younger brother of the Buddha,
> [6] Ākarma[ti], a manifestation of [King] Songtsen Gampo, and
> [7] [King] Trison Detsen, to you I pray.
>
> [8] [Mahāsiddha] Virvapa [of India], [9] Princess Pemasal,
> [10] Gyalse Lhaje, the lord in person,
> [11] Tri-me Künden [of India], [12] Yarje Ogyen Lingpa [1323–?],
> [13] Daö Zhönu [1079–1153, of Kagyü] and [14] Trakpa Gyaltsen [1147–1216, of Sakya], to you I pray.
>
> [15] Then Longchen Rabjam [1308–1363], the manifestation of the very Mahāpaṇḍita Vimalamitra,
> [16] Ngari Penchen (1487–1542), [17] Chögyal Phüntsok [16th century, son of Drikung Rinchen Phüntsok],

[18] [Changdak] Tashi Tobgyal [1550–1602?], [19] Dzamling Dorje [of Kongpo] and
[20] Jigme Linga [1789–1798], to you I pray.
[21] After this, through manifestation of Yeshe Dorje [1800–66].[142]

At the age of six, as an ordinary novice he entered Palri (Shrīparvata) Monastery in Chongye Valley, the seat of Trangpo Terchen Sherap Özer (1517–1584). Tsogyal Tülku Ngawang Lobzang Pema gave him the name Pema Khyentse Özer.

From the ages of six to thirteen, he spent more time, as he says, "playing dust" with novices of his age than on his studies. He lived the life of a poor novice with little to facilitate learning, and faced very strict disciplinary tutors year after year. However, the intensity of his zeal for the Dharma, his spontaneous devotion to Guru Rinpoche, and his innate compassion for all living beings, especially toward animals, sustained him and made his childhood extremely joyful and meaningful. Although he seemed an insignificant novice, his inner life was full of richness. His days were filled with meditative attainments and inspiring pure visions. His nights merged into dreams of spiritual experiences and visions.

In such circumstances, he mastered grammar, logic, astrology, poetry, history, medicine, and many scriptures of sūtra and tantra. Apart from receiving the transmissions of esoteric empowerments, he felt no need to have a master or study any intellectual subject in detail, as other serious students were doing. He learned various subjects merely by overhearing bits of the classes of other students or glancing at the texts.

Many masters became learned by studying and then realized by meditating. Jigme Lingpa was born learned as the result of awakening the wisdom realization in himself. However, the outward manifestation was that his final and full bursting forth of boundless wisdom took place much later, when he had the visions of Longchen Rabjam, at the age of thirty-one. He writes:

> By nature I felt very happy when I was able to study [any subject, such as] language, secular writings, canonical scriptures and their commentaries, or the Vajra[yāna] teachings on the ultimate nature. I would study them with great respect, both by daylight and lamplight. But I hardly had the opportunity to develop the knowledge by studying with a master, even for a single day. However, at the glorious Samye Chimphu, by beholding the wisdom body of

> Longchenpa three times, and by receiving the blessings through various signs, my karma [of the "learning-wisdom" was] awakened from [the depth of] the Great Perfection.[143]

From Neten Künzang Özer he received his first major transmission, the transmission of *Trölthik Gongpa Rangtröl* teachings discovered by Trengpo Terchen Sherap Özer (aka Drodül Lingpa), the cycle of *Lama Gongdü* discovered by Sangye Lingpa (1340–1396), and the *Seven Treasures* and *Three Chariots* by Longchen Rabjam (1308–1363).

At thirteen, Jigme Lingpa met the great Tertön Rigdzin Thukchok Dorje[144] and instantly experienced a strong devotion that awakened his wisdom mind. From the tertön he received transmissions and instructions on Mahāmudrā and other teachings. Thukchok Dorje became his root teacher, and he received blessings from him in visions even after the master's death. Jigme Lingpa also received transmissions from many other masters, including Thekchen Lingpa Drotön Tharchin (aka Trime Lingpa, 1700–1776), his uncle Dharmakīrti, the seventh Chakzampa Tendzin Yeshe Lhündrup, Thangdrok Tülku Pema Rigdzin Wangpo of Kongpo,[145] Trati Ngakchang Rigpe Dorje (aka Kong-nyön) of Kongpo, and Mön Dzakar Lama Dargye.

At the beginning of his twenty-eighth year, he started a three-year strict retreat at Palri Monastery, with seven vows to be observed for the whole of seven years. These vows show us the importance of perfecting oneself before going out to help others to fulfill the goal of life. His seven vows were as follows:

(1) He would neither enter any layperson's house nor enjoy any entertainment. (2) Even if he were living in the midst of a community, he would abstain from receiving many people (in his cell) or leading any gathering that fostered hatred or attachment. (3) He would not correspond with anyone, neither would any word from outside come in nor any words from inside get out. (4) He would maintain a life of austerity and would refrain from exchanging Dharma teachings for any material gain. (5) He would refrain from any distracting activities, dedicating his efforts only to the ten activities that concern Dharma training.[146] (6) He would live with simple sustenance and not carelessly enjoy any materials offered with faith. (7) He would not perform any of the four actions[147] and would dedicate all activities to liberation from saṃsāra.

He concentrated his meditation on the development stage and the perfection stage, based on *Trölthik Gongpa Rangtröl*. His mindful awareness enabled him to secure his mind from distractions in meditation, even for the duration of the snap of a finger. When he read *The Seven Treasures* by Longchen Rabjam, they answered all the questions he had about his inner meditative experiences.

As he progressed through the stages of realization, he experienced numerous physical and mental signs of attainments. He experienced the visions of many lamas and divinities including Guru Rinpoche, Yeshe Tsogyal, Mañjushrīmitra, and Hūṃkara, which awakened various stages of his inner wisdom. Suddenly, he found that within himself the point of reference of all his mental experiences had been uprooted. He had gained dominion over the process of his karmic energies. All the caves of delusory appearances (i.e., the objects, on which conceptual mind relies to forge the dualistic saṃsāra) had totally collapsed. Through the strength of awakened realization, he could review many past lives clearly. But all those experiences and visions were in the nature of oneness in his realized mind.

Through yogic trainings he achieved control over the channels, energies, and essence of his vajra body. As a result, his throat opened as the "cycle of wealth" of teachings. His physical channels transformed into the "clouds of letters." All the phenomenal appearances turned into the "signs/gestures of Dharma." His speech became the songs of profound realization. His writings became treatises of great wisdom power and scholarship. An inexhaustible ocean of teaching phenomena continued to burst forth for him and from him.

Then he composed his first major writing, *Khyentse Melong Özer Gyawa,* an explanatory treatise on the *Lama Gongdü* cycle.

Guru Rinpoche, appearing in a vision, gave him the name Pema Wangchen. In a vision Mañjushrīmitra gave him blessings, which caused him to realize the meaning of symbolic wisdom (mTshon Byed dPe'i Ye Shes). Thereafter, he changed his maroon monastic robes to the natural garb of an ascetic, uncolored white robes and uncut long hair.

At twenty-eight, he discovered the extraordinary revelation of the *Longchen Nyingthig* cycle, the teachings of the Dharmakāya and Guru Rinpoche, as mind ter. In the evening of the twenty-fifth day of the tenth month of the Fire Ox year of the thirteenth Rabjung cycle (1757), he went to bed with an unbearable devotion to Guru Rinpoche in his heart; a stream of tears of sadness continuously wet his face because he was not in Guru Rinpoche's presence, and unceasing words of prayers kept singing in his breath.

He remained in the depth of that meditative experience of clear luminosity ('Od gSal Gyi sNang Ba) for a long time. While being absorbed in that luminous clarity, he experienced flying a long distance through the sky while riding on a white lion. He finally reached a circular path, which he thought to be the circumambulation path of Charung Khashor, now known as Bodhnath Stūpa, an important Buddhist monument of giant structure in Nepal.

In the eastern courtyard of the stūpa, he saw the Dharmakāya appearing in the form of a wisdom ḍākinī. She entrusted him with a beautiful wooden casket, saying:

> For the disciples with pure mind,
> You are Trisong Detsen.
> For the disciples with impure mind,
> You are Senge Repa.
> This is Samantabhadra's mind treasure,
> The symbolic scripts of Rigdzin Padma[sambhava], and
> The great secret treasures of the ḍākinīs. Signs are over!

The ḍākinī vanished. With an experience of great joy, he opened the casket. In it he found five rolls of yellow scrolls with seven crystal beads. At first, the script was illegible, but then it turned into Tibetan script. One of the rolls was the *Dug-ngal Rangtröl,* the Sādhana of Avalokiteshvara, and another was *Nechang Thukkyi Drombu,* the prophetic guide of *Longchen Nyingthig*. Rāhula, one of the protectors of the teachings, appeared before him to pay respect. As he was encouraged by another ḍākinī, Jigme Lingpa swallowed all the yellow scrolls and the crystal beads. Instantly, he had the amazing experience that all the words of the *Longchen Nyingthig* cycle with their meanings had been awakened in his mind as if they were imprinted there. Even after coming out of that meditative experience, he remained in the realization of intrinsic awareness, the great union of bliss and emptiness.

Thus, the *Longchen Nyingthig* teachings and realization, which were entrusted and concealed in him by Guru Rinpoche many centuries earlier, were awakened, and he became a tertön, the discoverer of the *Longchen Nyingthig* cycle of teachings. He gradually transcribed the teachings of the *Longchen Nyingthig* cycle, starting with the *Nechang Thukkyi Drombu*.

He kept all his discovered teachings secret from everyone for seven years, as the time had not yet matured to teach them to others. It was also essential for the tertön to practice the teachings himself first.

Although he was maintaining the life of a hidden yogī, respect for and faith in him grew spontaneously in the people around him, and he became a source of benefit for many people, as he had perfected the power of the four actions without needing to work to acquire them.

At thirty-one, he started to observe a second three-year retreat at Chimphu near Samye. First he started his retreat in a cave known as Upper Nyang cave. Then he discovered another cave and recognized it as the Sangchen Metok cave or the Lower Nyang cave, where King Trisong Detsen had received the Nyingthig teachings from Nyang and meditated on them. For the rest of his retreat he lived in the Sangchen cave.

During his retreat at Chimphu, the highest realization of Dzogpa Chenpo was awakened in Jigme Lingpa, and that awakening was caused by three pure visions of the wisdom body of Longchen Rabjam (1308–1363), the Dharmakāya in pure manifestation. In the Upper Nyang cave he had the first vision, in which he received the blessing of the vajra body of Longchen Rabjam. Jigme Lingpa obtained the transmission of both the words and the meaning of Longchen Rabjam's teachings. After moving to Sangchen Phuk (the Great Sacred Cave), he had the second and third visions. In the second vision he received the blessing of the speech of Longchen Rabjam, which empowered him to uphold and propagate the profound teachings of Longchen Rabjam as his representative. In the third vision Jigme Lingpa received the blessing of the wisdom mind of Longchen Rabjam, which awakened or transferred the inexpressible power of enlightened intrinsic awareness of Longchen Rabjam to him.

Now for Jigme Lingpa, because there was no objective reference point, all the external appearances had become boundless. There was no separate meditation or meditative state to pursue. As there was no subjective designator in his inner mind, all became naturally free and totally open in oneness. He composed *Künkhyen Zhallung* and some other writings as the true meaning of *The Seven Treasures* of Longchen Rabjam, which had awakened in his wisdom mind. He expressed his wisdom power in vajra songs to his devoted hermit companions, concerning various situations:

> The nature of the mind is like openness space,
> But it is superior, as it possesses the wisdom.

Luminous clarity is like the sun and moon,
But it is superior, as there are no substances.
Intrinsic awareness is like a crystal ball,
But it is superior, as there are no obstructions or coverings.[148]

And:

Son, mind watching mind is
Not the awareness of the innate nature.
So, in the present mind, without modifications and
Waverings, just remain naturally.

Son, apprehending [anything] with your recollections
Lacks crucial skills of meditation.
So, in the natural and fresh state of the intrinsic awareness,
Remain without any grasping.

Son, people think that [one-pointed] dwelling [of mind] is meditation,
But it lacks the union of tranquillity and insight.
So, without accepting and rejecting either dwellings or projections of the mind,
Let the intrinsic awareness dwell freely without any reference point.[149]

And:

Son, the rigid, clear and stable visualization
Is not [perfect] Mahāyoga.
Dissolving the [mind of] grasping at the faces and arms [of the deities], dwell in the vastness,
The Great Perfection of the evenness of intrinsic awareness and emptiness.

Son, clinging to the experiences of four joys
Is not [the perfect] Anuyoga.
Having admitted the mind and energy into the central channel,
Remain in [the union of] bliss and emptiness, the great freedom from thoughts. . . .

Son, mere understanding of the spontaneous accomplishment of the three kāyas,

Is not the ultimate Atiyoga.
In the nature of vajra-chain insight,
Let the falsehood of mental analysis collapse.[150]

And:

Sicknesses are the brooms sweeping your evil deeds.
Seeing the sicknesses as the teachers, pray to them. . . .
Sicknesses are coming to you by the kindness of the masters and the Three Jewels.
Sicknesses are your accomplishments, so worship them as the deities.
Sicknesses are the signs that your bad karmas are being exhausted.
Do not look at the face of your sickness, but at the one [the mind] who is sick.
Do not place the sicknesses on your mind, but place your naked intrinsic awareness upon your sickness.
This is the instruction on sickness arising as the Dharmakāya.

The body is inanimate and mind is emptiness.
What can cause pain to an inanimate thing or harm to the emptiness?
Search for where the sicknesses are coming from, where they go, and where they dwell.
Sicknesses are mere sudden projections of your thoughts.
When those thoughts disappear, the sicknesses dissolve too. . . .
There is not better fuel [than sicknesses] to burn off the bad karmas.
Don't get into entertaining a sad mind or negative views [over the sicknesses],
But see them as the signs of the waning of your bad karmas, and rejoice over them.[151]

Then he received the transmissions of the *Seventeen Nyingthig Tantras, Vima Nyingthig, Lama Yangtig,* and some other Nyingma transmissions and teachings from Drubwang Ogyen Palgön (Shrīnatha) of Mindroling Monastery, who was also a distant relative of Jigme Lingpa's. Earlier he had also received the transmissions of Nyingthig teachings and Longchen Rabjam's writings from Thangdrokpa and Neten Künzang. However, the absolute and short line of transmission of the ultimate Nyingthig teachings came to him from Longchen Rabjam directly in the three pure visions.

When he came out of his retreat, he found that his body had totally exhausted its strength, because of scarcity of food and lack of proper clothing during years of cave living. He writes:

> Because of having little food and being exposed to a harsh environment, all the residues of bad karmas and karmic debts of my previous successive lives had started to ripen upon my body. Because of the humors of air *[rlung]*, my back hurt as if someone were hitting me with a rock. As a result of the stirring up of air and blood circulation, my chest was in pain, as if someone were driving nails into my body. Because of bam ailment [elephantiasis], my body was too heavy for my legs to hold up. Like a hundred-year-old man, I had worn out all my physical energies. I didn't have much appetite for food. . . . If I took three steps, my body would start shaking. [But I thought,] "If I die, I will be fulfilling the advice given by the early masters, which says: 'Entrust your mind to Dharma. Entrust your Dharma practice to the life of a beggar.' " As I had attained confidence in the realization of Dzogpa Chenpo, no thought of worry was even a possibility in my mind, but it aroused in me a great compassion for those who are [suffering from] old age and sicknesses.[152]

Then he had a pure vision of Thangtong Gyalpo, a sage of longevity, and for Jigme Lingpa all the happenings merged into the union of bliss and emptiness. Thereupon, he sang the power of his realization in the following words:

> I bow to the lord, the Great Sage [Thangtong Gyalpo]!
> I have realized the summit of the views, the Dzogpa Chenpo.
> There is nothing on which to meditate, as all is liberated as the
> view.
> I have unfurled the banner of meditation, the king of activities.
> Now I, the beggar, have no repentance, even if I die. . . .
> I, the beggar, who knows "how to turn sicknesses into the path,"
> Visualizing the lama, the source of the virtues,
> At the blissful chakra of my head,
> I meditate on the profound path of Guru Yoga.
> Since sicknesses and pain are the brooms for sweeping the evil
> karmas,
> By realizing sicknesses as the blessing of the master,

I meditate on the sicknesses as the lama and receive the fourfold empowerments from them.
Finally, by realizing the lama as my own mind,
I release [all] into the true nature of the mind, which is primordially pure and free from any reference points.[153]

He realized the face of the ultimate Samantabhadra, the Dharmakāya, and all the sicknesses dissolved into the ultimate sphere. Quickly, his physical body also gained strength without any more pain or obstructions.

Then the time for revealing the *Longchen Nyingthig* teachings to the disciples arrived, after seven years of secrecy. Although no one had a clue of the discovery of *Longchen Nyingthig,* his teacher-disciple Kongnyön Bepe Naljor,[154] because of his clairvoyance, beseeched Jigme Lingpa to transmit his mind ter teachings. As an auspicious sign, he also received requests to reveal the teachings with offerings from three important tülkus from Southern Tibet.

On the tenth day of the sixth month of the Wood Monkey year (1765), for the first time Jigme Lingpa conferred the empowerments and explanations of the *Longchen Nyingthig* cycle on fifteen disciples. Gradually but swiftly, the *Longchen Nyingthig* teachings reached every corner of the Nyingma world, and they became the heart core of meditation instructions for many realized meditators and for ceremonial liturgies to this day.

At thirty-four, Jigma Lingpa moved from Chimphu to Tsering Jong, the Long Life Land in Tönkhar Valley of Chongye in Southern Tibet. There, with the patronage of the house of Depa Pushü,[155] he built a hermitage with a meditation school and named it Tharpa Chenpö Trongkhyer Pema Ö Ling, the Garden of Lotus Light of the City of Great Liberation. He did not want to have a big institutional structure, and frequently quoted the verse from *Thirty Pieces of Essential Advice* by Longchen Rabjam, as his guide:[156]

To assemble numerous associates by various means,
To have a monastery with comfortable accommodations—
If you try, it will come about for a while, but it distracts the mind.
So my advice from the heart is to remain alone.

Tsering Jong became the residence of Jigme Lingpa for the rest of his life. A stream of great disciples came to this very simple hermitage to receive the profound, nectarlike teachings and transmissions from the greatest master of Dzogpa Chenpo, Rigdzin Jigme Lingpa, but the disciples returned to their own places to share the teachings with others. So Tsering Jong remained a simple hermitage and Jigme Lingpa a simple hermit.

He took no interest in wealth or power and spent all that was offered to him for religious purposes. Also, throughout his life, he was active in ransoming the lives of animals from the hands of hunters and butchers. He said:[157]

> I care not for any activity of business or harvest.
> I do not roam about performing ceremonies in towns [for donations].
> I keep no more than ten *khals*[158] of barley [as living subsistence] with me.
> As long as I am alive, I vow to continue this ascetic life.

Sometime after Jigme Lingpa's time, Tsering Jong hermitage became a nunnery, and it remained so till around 1959, when everything disappeared in the political turmoil. Since the beginning of the 1980s, once again Tsering Jong has been reestablished as a nunnery.

Jigme Lingpa's character was profound, forceful, and direct, but he was also loving, simple, and easy to be with. He writes:

> My perceptions have become like those of a baby. I even enjoy playing with children. When I encounter people with serious shortcomings, I throw their personal faults in their faces, even if they are respected spiritual leaders or generous Dharma patrons. . . . In every action of sitting, walking, sleeping, or eating, I secure my mind [in the state, that is] never dissociated from the brilliance of the ultimate nature. If it is the service of the Dharma, I dedicate myself to its completion, even if it is thought to be an impossible task.[159]

At fourty-three, he gathered together and commissioned the copying of the Nyingma tantras in twenty-five volumes, and he composed *The History of Nyingma Tantras.*[160] Later, on the advice of Jigme Lingpa and Dodrupchen, the king and queen-regent of Dege commissioned the wooden blocks of his Nyingma tantra collection, and those blocks are still in use for printing.

At fifty-seven, at the invitation of Ngawang Palden Chökyong, the Sakya Trichen, he went to Sakya and gave teachings and transmissions to the Trichen, his brother, and Ānanda Shrībhava, the sitting khenchen of Sakya, and many others.

On his return from Sakya, Lama Sönam Chöden, who later became known as Dodrupchen (1745–1821) came from Kham to receive teachings from Jigme Lingpa.[161] Dodrupchen saw him as Thangtong Gyalpo, and Jigme Lingpa in turn recognized Dodrupchen as the tülku of Lhase Murum Tsepo and gave him the name Jigme Thrinle Özer. Through Dodrupchen, the third Dzogchen Rinpoche, and the king of Dege sent messengers to invite him to Kham, but he refused to go because of his age and health, as well as his concern for the hardship for the horses during the arduous trip.

Barchung Gomchen Rigdzin and Mange Pema Künzang from Kham came to receive teachings and transmissions. Pema Künzang later became Jigme Lingpa's renowned diciple Jigme Gyalwe Nyuku (1765–1843). While Rigdzin and Pema Künzang were in Lhasa, before they reached Tsering Jong, someone stole a piece of silver, the only material they had for their living and traveling expenses. Jigme Lingpa wrote a poem to console them:

> If you know how to take [sufferings] into the path of equal taste,
> All unfortunate circumstances will arise as the support of virtues.
> So refrain from entertaining reversed views.
> If you practice as I teach you,
> Your minds and my mind will unite as one.
> There will arise the realization that transcends all the concepts, and
> You will remain in the vast nature of Dharmakāya, in which there
> is no duality.
> May all your wishes be fulfilled.[162]

In 1788, when he was sixty,[163] Jigme Lingpa gave teachings and transmissions to the king and queen of Dege at Samye. They became his devotees, and the queen became one of the main patrons.

At sixty-two, at the request of Göntse Tülku, he visited Göntse Gönpa of Tsona in Mön and gave teachings and transmissions.

At that time, Jigme Lingpa had an eye problem.[164] Textual transmissions (lung) had to be given by Dodrupchen on his behalf to his disciples, who included Götsang Tülku Jigme Tenpe Gyaltsen. They sent Jigme Gyalwe Nyuku to get a doctor, who performed a successful operation.

When he was sixty-three, in 1791, military forces of Nepal attacked Western Tibet, and many people suffered. Jigme Lingpa performed a number of ceremonies and sent offerings to various temples for peace and protection.

When he was sixty-five, he and his consort, Gyalyum Drölkar from the house of Depa Pushü,[165] had a son called Gyalse Nyinche Özer (1793–?).

Jigme Lingpa was unable to accept the numerous invitations offered to him. However, through Gyantse he went to Thekchok Chöling Monastery in Tsang and gave teachings and transmissions to many disciples headed by Khenpo Ogyen Palgön, and at many places on the way. This monastery became a follower of the Longchen Nyingthig lineage. At Dorje Trak Monastery, he gave a series of teachings and transmissions to Rigdzin Chenmo and others.

He received messages of prayers and offerings from the Mongolian king, Chögyal Ngawang Dargye (1759–1807),[166] a disciple of Dodrupchen and the teacher of Zhapkar Tsoktruk Rangtröl (1781–1851).[167]

Meanwhile, based on a communication between the last Dzogchen Rinpoche and Jigme Lingpa, the lamas of Dzogchen Monastery were strongly inquiring whether his son could be the tülku of the third Dzogchen Rinpoche, but Jigme Lingpa didn't indicate any possibility. Gyalse himself remembered his past life and had kept saying, "I am going to Drikung," since he was small.[168] Then Sakya Trichen recognized him as the tülku of Chökyi Nyima (1755–1792), the fourth Chungtsang,[169] one of the two heads of the Drikung Kagyü tradition.

At sixty-nine, with huge ceremonial pomp arranged by Drikung followers, Jigme Lingpa traveled with his son to Drikung for the son's enthronement. It was an amazing opportunity for people at different places along the way to see and hear him, the great master. But it was physically exhausting for the old and frail master to travel for days and perform endless religious activities. Soon, because of the change of water and environment, he fell seriously ill, and for a while people even lost hope for his recovery. Then unexpectedly, a disciple of his brought a Tibetan medical pill called karpo chikthup from the sacred place of Yama Lung, and after taking it he miraculously recovered and even appeared younger, like a new person.

At seventy, he returned to Tsering Jong from Drikung, stopping at a great number of holy places on the way and performing ceremonies, making offerings, and giving teachings. His health appeared good, but cared little about eating or sleeping. Day and night, he remained sitting up in either the Vairochana posture or the sage posture. His eyes didn't blink. He said that his body remained alive owing to his control over his life-force energy. Many times, he gave hints that he would die before long. But when his disciples became overwhelmed with grief, he would change the subject or sometimes would even say: "Oh, there will be no danger to my life." He told a close disciple in private that he was dying and that he would reincarnate, but there was no need to search for his new incarnation. They should hold a simpler funeral ceremony, but he hinted that they should preserve the body by explaining the ways that it is done. When his disciples expressed their wish to bring a doctor, he would say, "Yes! If you wish, you can bring one; but as there is no sickness in me, what is there for a doctor to do? Anyway, don't get one from a far distance; it will only cause hardship for people and animals."

Still, in a quiet way, he kept seeing people and giving blessings and teachings as requested. For days there was a rain of flowers around his residence and mild earthquakes again and again. One day he moved to Namtröl Tse, the new upper hermitage, and expressed his great joy at being there. He entertained some visitors and gave teachings.

On the very next day, the third day of the ninth month of the Earth Horse year (1798), he gave a teaching on White Tārā meditation. From early morning a strong, sweet fragrance filled the whole hermitage. The sky was totally clear and there was no touch of wind, but a gentle rain sprinkled continuously from the blue sky. All were amazed but worried. Then, in the early part of the night, he asked for new offerings to be arranged on the altar. As he sat in the sage posture, all expressions of his manifestation merged into the primordial nature.

His disciples discovered two different testaments, hidden at different places. They included meditative teachings to his disiciples and instructions about his funeral ceremony and reincarnation. One of them included the following lines:

> I am always in the state of ultimate nature;
> For me there is no staying or going.
> The display of birth and death is mere relativity.
> I am enlightened in the great primordial liberation![170]

After months of ceremonies at Tsering Jong and at many monasteries and temples in Central and Eastern Tibet and Bhutan, his body was placed in a small golden stūpa in Tsering Jong hermitage, and it was preserved there until Tsering Jong nunnery was destroyed a couple of decades ago.

After his death, his well-known incarnations included: Do Khyentse Yeshe Dorje (1800–1866), known as his body incarnation; Paltrül Rinpoche (1808–1887), the speech incarnation; and Jamyang Khyentse Wangpo (1820–1892), the mind incarnation.[171]

Jigme Lingpa produced nine volumes of written treatises and discovered ter texts. The prominent ones among them are *Longchen Nyingthig,* a collection of meditation instructions and ritual texts in two (or three) volumes, which were discovered as ter teachings; *Phurba Gyüluk,* one volume of liturgy on Vajrakīla, considered as both ter and canonical; *Yönten Rinpoche Dzö* with its two-volume autocommentary, his most famous scholarly work; and *Yeshe Lama,* which has become the most comprehensive manual of Dzogpa Chenpo meditation in the Nyingma tradition.

The *Longchen Nyingthig* remained as an important ter tradition, and with his scholarly writings, Jigme Lingpa's lineage became one of the most popular subschools of the Nyingma school till the present. In the Longchen Nyingthig lineage, all the disciples and grand disciples were equally great adepts, as Jigme Lingpa himself prophesied:

> In the lineage of my Nyingthig of Luminous Clarity, there will come children [disciples] who are greater than their fathers and grandchildren who are greater than their grandparents.[172]

Among his many great disciples, the main ones are prophesied by Guru Rinpoche in *Nechang Thukkyi Drombu,* the prophetic guide of Longchen Nyingthig:

> By the incarnations of Namkhe Nyingpo, Nyang, Chok-yang,
> And the Divine Prince, the door of the teachings will be opened.[173]

The disciples are[174] Nyangtön Trati Ngakchang Rikpe Dorje (aka Kong-nyön Bepe Naljor),[175] the incarnation of Namkhe Nyingpo: Loppön Jigme Küntröl of Bhutan, the incarnation of Nyang Tingdzin Zangpo; Thekchen Lingpa Drotön Tharchin (Dri Med Gling Pa, 1700–1776), the incarnation of Ngenlam Gyalwa Chok-yang; and Dodrupchen Jigme Thrinle Özer, the incarnation of Prince Murum Tsepo.

Thekchen Lingpa, Thangdrokpa, and Trati Ngakchang were both teachers and disciples of Jigme Lingpa.

Among his disciples, the masters who were most effective in propagating the *Longchen Nyingthig* teachings were the following. The first Dodrupchen, Jigme Thrinle Özer (1745–1821), was the principal Doctrine-holder (rTsa Ba'i Ch'os bDag) of *Longchen Nyingthig*. Dodrupchen built three monasteries:[176] Drodön Künkhyap Ling at Shukchen Tago in Do Valley, Ogmin Rigdzin Phelgye Ling at Getse Tö in Dzachukha Valley, and Yarlung Pemakö in Ser Valley. Jigme Gyalwe Nyuku of Kham Dzachukha remained in Tramalung hermitage for many years and later moved to Dzagya monastic hermitage. Jigme Küntröl of Bhutan built the Dungsam Yonglha Tengye Riwo Palbar Ling[177] Monastery in Eastern Bhutan. Today it is known as Yongla Gön under Pema Gatsal District in Eastern Bhutan. The names of other main disciples of Jigme Lingpa are listed in the lineage tree (see pages 334–335).

Among his main patrons, Depa Pushü sponsored the building of his hermitage at Tsering Jong, and the king and especially Queen Tsewang Lhamo of Dege, who was prophesied as the incarnation of Phokyongza Gyalmotsün, the queen of King Trisong Detsen,[178] commissioned wooden printing blocks of *Old Tantras (rNying Ma rGyud 'Bum)*, many volumes of Longchen Rabjam, and the nine volumes of Jigme Lingpa. Also, Tatsak Tenpe Gönpo (d. 1810), the regent of Tibet, and the thirteenth Karmapa Düdül Dorje (1733–1797) with great respect consulted him through correspondence.

Although disciples who were prominent members of Tibetan society flocked to Jigme Lingpa, he was only concerned to find true lineage holders, who come mostly from people of simple background. Quoting past masters, he expresses his view:

> It is better to have a single beggar who can hold the lineage
> than to have a thousand prominent people as your disciples.[179]

Jigme Lingpa's life was full of miracles, but he kept his mystical power hidden and his rich life simple. He was a born scholar who didn't train in traditional disciplines, but all his expressions turned into teachings and all his activities were in the service of others. He remained hidden as an ascetic in an isolated place in Tsering Jong, but the light of his wisdom reached all corners of the Nyingma Buddhist world, and it still shines in many open hearts around the world. He was born with physical marks of auspicious signs, an ĀḤ letter on his tooth, a HYA letter on his thumb, a vajra design at his heart, and a ritual bell image at his navel. He had visions of the Buddhas, deities, and lineage masters, and received teachings and blessings as from person to person. From his tooth[180] and his hair[181] came ringsels as the sign of his high Dzogpa Chenpo attainments. The most important imprint that he left for us is the words of the Dharmakāya, the ultimate truth in the form of his writings and discovered ter teachings.

12

First Dodrupchen Jigme Thrinle Özer
1745–1821

The First Dodrupchen Rinpoche Jigme Thrinle Özer[182] was the principal doctrine-holder (rTsa Ba'i Ch'os bDag) of the *Longchen Nyingthig* cycle of teachings.

He was known by many names, including Künzang Zhenphen, Sönam Chöden, Changchup Dorje, and Drubwang Dzogchenpa.

He was born in the upper Do Valley of Golok Province in Eastern Tibet in the Wood Ox year of the twelfth Rabjung (1745). Do Valley is situated in Golok Province on the border of the Amdo and Kham regions. Dodrupchen's father, Zönkho, was from a warrior clan called Puchung in the Mukpo Dong lineage. His mother, Sönamtso, was from the Nizok (Nubzur) tribe.

His birth was prophesied by Guru Rinpoche:

> In the east there will come a person named Özer,
> Endowed with strong devotion, extraordinary actions, powerful
> mind, and full of wisdom.
> He will uphold the discovered heart treasure teachings
> And propagate them with the support of many fortunate people.[183]

At about three, Dodrupchen started revealing his memories of his past lives. His parents wouldn't let him repeat them, as they were afraid that he was possessed by a demonic force. At about four or five, now and then, he witnessed amazing lights of Thögal visions, and he would remain absorbed in them with a feeling both of joy and sadness.

At six and seven, he saw and then remembered the sufferings of people from poverty, illness, old age, and death. Because of this, an unbearable sadness occupied his tiny heart, and his little face was always soaked in tears.

At seven, his parents sent him to his uncle, who was a lama, to study Tibetan and scriptures. He was able to read the prayers after he was taught them once, whereas others could learn them only by repeating them many times. Although Dodrupchen took birth as great masters in his past lives, he was not recognized as a tülku in his youth. Thus he was given the chance and challenges of passing through his studies and trainings as an ordinary trainee does in Tibet.

At ten, he revealed some ter teachings, but none survived, as no one thought them of any importance. He had numerous visions and dreams of masters who entrusted teachings and blessings to him and also warned him of any danger that was coming. Still, as his mind was always filled with compassion, when his parents were not noticing, he would cry profusely over the sufferings that people were experiencing and would try to help them, at least by saying prayers for them. He never had ill will toward anybody, even people who were trying to hurt him. He was always frank, bold, and powerful in expressing his thoughts. He was generous and energetic in offering his services to improve others' lives.

At fourteen, he entered Gochen Monastery of the Palyül lineage and received teachings from Sherap Rinchen until that teacher's death. Sherap Rinchen was a student of Pema Lhündrup Gyatso (1660–1727), who studied with Künzang Sherap (1636–1699), the founder of the Palyül lineage. Sherap Rinchen gave him the Dharma name Sönam Chöden. He studied and meditated on many teachings, mainly Dzogpa Chenpo and Tsalung, and fulfilled the requirements of various recitations and trainings. However, there was not much progress in his spiritual experience beyond what he already had.

At twenty-one, Dodrupchen left for Central Tibet through Dege with six other monks. On the way he received teachings from Situ Chökyi Jungne (1700–1774) at Palpung Monastery in Dege.

Finally they reached Taklha Gampo, the monastic seat of Gampopa (1079–1153), the main disciple of Milarepa (1040–1123). At Taklha Gampo, the Fifth Gampopa Jampal Thrinle Wangpo (Mipham Wangpo,

1757–?) named Dodrupchen as Sönam Chöden. With master Tamchö Wangchuk, a disciple of the Third Gampopa Zangpo Dorje, Dodrupchen studied Ngöndro, Chakchen Chödruk, and Phowa of both the Takpo and Zatsön traditions and many other teachings. Then he went on a pilgrimage to Tsāri, one of the most sacred places in Tibet, with much physical hardship. There, in a vision, he received the blessings of Vajravārāhī, a Buddha in female form. Soon all the voices, fears, and hardships he was experiencing on his pilgrimage turned into an experience of great joy, and he felt very happy and fulfilled.

On his return from Tsāri to Taklha Gampo, Tamchö Wangchuk sent him to a cemetery to spend the night practicing Chö and said: "Whatever happens, do not leave!" So Dodrupchen went to the cemetery and did his evening Chö practice. In the middle of the night, when he woke up, he saw that the rock behind him had turned into a huge and terrifying monster with long hair and sharp teeth. Dodrupchen was frightened, and his body was trembling. He couldn't go back to sleep, but remembering the lama's words, after performing another Chö practice, he remained lying there, his back against the monster. Before dawn he performed his third and last Chö practice. Soon day broke and there was nothing but the rock. He felt so happy, as if he had been granted another chance to live. From there, he went straight to the lama. By his clairvoyance the lama knew what had happened and was waiting for him. With a broad smile, the lama asked, "Was your good meditation still there?" Dodrupchen answered, "No, it has disappeared!" The lama said, "You did well! You were attached to your so-called good meditative experiences, which will cause rebirths in the higher realms of saṃsāra. I sent you to the cemetery to dissolve those attachments. So don't feel regret that you have lost your experiences. You did well by not leaving the cemetery." Then the lama, using this incident as the means of introduction to the ultimate nature, asked, "Is there any truly existing entity in those fears? Didn't they arise and dissolve in their own [openness] nature [free from limitations]?" Then in Ösal Phuk, the Cave of Luminosity, Dodrupchen did a long retreat with very little food.

With his companions Dodrupchen went on pilgrimage to Samye, Lhasa, and other holy places in Central Tibet. Then they journeyed toward home. On the way, in Dege, Dodrupchen received teachings from Künzang Namgyal (1713–1769), the Second Rabjam of Zhechen Monastery, who gave him the name Künzang Zhenphen. He also received teachings from Küntröl Namgyal (1706–1773), the First Jewön of Dzogchen Monastery, and Karma Tashi (1728–1790), the First Karma Kuchen of Palyül Monastery.

From the ages of twenty-five through thirty he stayed around his home valley because an old uncle had urged him in the name of Dharma not to leave until he died. As Dodrupchen belonged to a powerful tribal group, traditional obligations forced him to take care of tribal responsibilities. He was a forceful orator with a fearless heart and a powerful personality, which made him a most admired tribal figure. One day, he was traveling across a valley to collect some debts, riding one of the best-known horses in the tribal community. Suddenly strong remorse over saṃsāra overwhelmed his mind. This instantly caused all the appearances before him to transform into the Pure Land of Amitābha Buddha. It was a beautiful atmosphere, unimaginable by the mind. All the graspings and cravings of his mind had dissolved. Then, in a most enchanting voice, the blissful Buddha Amitābha said, "Son of good family, do not stay here. Go wherever you like. Your purposes will be fulfilled." Then he emerged from his realm of spiritual vision and experience into ordinary life, as if he had awakened from a deep sleep. Dodrupchen writes, "This experience might have lasted only for the time it takes to drink two cups of tea," perhaps about twenty minutes. "Since then my feelings toward even the best kinds of worldly prosperity, power, and gain became as if they were rich food before a sick person who has no appetite at all." Then he adds, "Although this experience might not seem of any great significance, yet it is the best part of my life story."

Dodrupchen went to Dzogchen Monastery, where he received *Khandro Nyingthig* transmissions and teachings from Pema Sang-ngak Tendzin (1731–1805), the Second Pönlop, and he meditated on them.

Then with four other monks he set off on his second trip to Central Tibet. On the way he got very sick, and doctors and friends had little hope of his recovering, but he refused even to take any medicine. Nevertheless, after some time he recovered, solely by the power of his pilgrimage and inner meditative strength.

Finally, he reached Taklha Gampo again and received teachings from the Fifth Gampopa Jumpal Thrinle Wangpo (Tsültrim Palbar). Then they went on pilgrimage to Yarlung, Samye, Tashi Lhünpo, Sakya, Tsurphu, Lhasa, and Drikung. He also received teachings from the Thirteenth Karmapa Düdül Dorje (1733–1797), who gave him the name Karma Wangtrak.

Then he returned to Dzogchen Monastery. Because he felt uneasy meditating in the monastery because of so many distractions, he went to Kangtrö Ogma, the Lower Snow Mountain, not very far from Dzogchen Monastery.

At thirty-five he started a three-year retreat in a cave in the solitary mountain of Kangtrö Ogma, practicing Könchok Chidü and many other teachings, and especially Thögal in summer and Tsalung in winter. He enjoyed the great peace of the atmosphere, but he vowed to dedicate himself to the training without letting himself be distracted even for a second by his enjoyment of the surroundings. However, after a month or so, a great shaking up *(Lhong Ch'a)* arose in him. It became hard for him to stop the turbulent waves of thoughts, emotions, and illusions. He now started having disturbances of the life-force energy *(Srog rLung),* symptoms that brought him to the brink of insanity. All appearances arose as enemies. He even saw fearful animals in his teapot. He felt he was involved in fighting with weapons. One night in a dream he heard a very frightening shout, and he felt that it almost split his heart. Even after he awoke, he kept hearing the same cry and then saw a pillarlike dark light linking the ground and the sky. His body was trembling violently. He felt an unbearable terror and feared that the sky and earth were being turned upside down. But then in an instant, all the disturbing appearances dissolved into himself, the "I," which was merely projecting and experiencing all those appearances. Then the concept of "I" was also gone beyond any elaboration. The fearful mind and the objects of fear all had merged into one taste, the taste of ultimate nature, the total openness. The fears of his dreams and experiences had vanished without even a trace. At that point, he writes, "I experienced a realization in which there is no designation of any view to realize or any meditation to follow. By just being in the realized state, my fear over negative experiences as well as joy over the experiences of bliss have gone."

Just before reaching a high realization, it is normal for many meditators to experience the final mental, emotional, and habitual struggles in various forms or degrees of temptations, fearful illusions, threatening sounds, or painful feelings. Many great masters have had the same kinds of experience just before they entered into high states of realization. If you do not succumb to these kind of last-minute disturbances created by hidden subtle habits and get beyond all those final encounters by remaining in the realized nature, like shaking the dust from a rug for good, you will attain total freedom from mental and emotional obscurations with their traces. A person who is having a so-called smooth meditative experience might think, "I am doing so well that I have no shaking-up experiences," but the truth could be that he has not yet destroyed his mental and emotional defilements and their habits from the root.

After some time, Dodrupchen's food was exhausted and for a long time, except for some tea, he didn't have much to eat. He became physically weak, like a man in a sickbed. He could hardly move, and his breathing became heavy and his chest congested. One day, as his water pot was empty, he went out to collect some water from a pond outside the cave. On the way back, while climbing up to the cave, because of the weight of the pot he fell down and lost consciousness. After a while he regained consciousness and tried to get up, but he could not. Thoughts came to his mind: "Now there is no way to escape from death. What to do?" Then another thought came into his mind: "It would be sad if I were dying while doing unvirtuous deeds, but I am dying while doing Dharma practice, so I should be rejoicing." This thought brought a feeling of joy in him, and his joy gave him the strength to get up. He went back to the cave, treated himself with the smoke from burning a little tsampa[184] that he had saved for medicinal use to calm down his violent air humors. Then he took a smaller pot and got some water. He made some tea and drank it, but as he had had no solid food for a long time, the tea made his body shake violently and he had a hard time calming it down.

Then he thought, "It would be better to go to Dzogchen Monastery and get some food. Otherwise I shall die, and that will be an obstacle to the practice." He left the cave and climbed a little way down the hill, but he was so weak that he fell down again. Getting up, he thought, "How foolish I am. My lamas instructed me to practice. To follow the instructions of the lamas is my main practice. To go and look for food will be wrong. Even if I die, I shall not leave the meditation cell, until I finish my retreat."[185] He returned to the cave and resumed his meditation as usual. After a while he heard a knock on the door, but ignored it as he was practicing. At the break in practice, at the door he found a pot of yogurt, which he brought inside and ate. The yogurt had special healing qualities, which helped not only to restore his health but to assist his meditation. The yogurt was said to have been offered to him by the Dharma protectresses Tseringma, the Long-Life Sisters. Since then the environs of the meditation cave are known as Tsering Phuk, the Cave of Tseringma. A few days later his Dharma friends brought him provisions of food. The pot of yogurt left by Tseringma, made of copper gilded with gold, was preserved till the late 1950s in a stūpa in Dodrupchen Monastery.

At thirty-eight Dodrupchen moved to Shinje Cave near Dzogchen Monastery, and there he did another four-year retreat, except for a short break when he had to go the monastery. He practiced the five-deity Chakrasaṃvara of the Takpo lineage, *Wrathful Guru Mekhyil* and *Vajrakīla Yangsang La-me,* both discovered by Ratna Lingpa. Then he meditated on Shinje (Yamarāja) and one day wrote the mantra on a rock with his finger as if in mud. Since then the cave became known as Shinje Cave, and I was told that the mantra is still visible on the rock.

Then he received the transmission of *Tsasum Sangwa Nyingthig* from the third Dzogchen Rinpoche (1759–1792), and he did a short retreat on it with many experiences and visions. During that retreat, the third Dzogchen Rinpoche sent him a copy of *Yönten Rinpoche Dzö.* His reading it gave him "uncontrived devotion" to its author, Jigme Lingpa.

Dodrupchen went to Dzogchen Rinpoche, who encouraged him to go see Jigme Lingpa, saying, "Seeing him will be more beneficial for you than staying in retreat." Dzogchen Rinpoche also urged Dodrupchen to invite Jigme Lingpa to Kham on his behalf or at least to bring the transmission of *Longchen Nyingthig* for him and others. From Dzogchen Rinpoche he received the transmissions and teaching of *Nyingthig Yabzhi* and many other teachings.

Somewhere in Dege, Dodrupchen came to a big river but couldn't find any way of crossing. He remained in the meditation of seeing the river as earth and walked across the river as if on dry land. When he was almost at the other shore, he thought, "Oh, my meditation is quite good," and at that moment he sank into the river and almost drowned. So later he kept saying, "Thoughts are dangerous."[186]

At forty-one[187] Dodrupchen left for Central Tibet for the third time. He met Jigme Lingpa, his karmic guru, for the first time at the house of Depa Pushü near Tsering Jong hermitage in Yarlung Valley in Southern Tibet. It was a time of great joy, like the reunion of a long-lost father and son.[188] Jigme Lingpa said, "Last night I dreamed of meeting with a bodhisattva, and it must be you." Dodrupchen saw Jigme Lingpa as Thangtong Gyalpo and experienced many visions and revelations.

Dodrupchen took the bodhisattva vow with Jigme Lingpa. That night, in his luminous dream[189] Dodrupchen saw bowls of ringsel and remains of Buddha Kāshyapa being withdrawn from a white stūpa. It was the sign that Dodrupchen was renewing the vow that he took before

Buddha Kāshyapa, when he was the son of King Kṛikrī at the time of Buddha Kāshyapa.

While receiving the empowerment of *Lama Gongdü,* Dodrupchen remembered clearly, without any doubt in his mind, that Jigme Lingpa had been Nyang Nyima Özer (1124–1192) and he himself had been Sangye Lingpa (1340–1396).

Jigme Lingpa gave Dodrupchen the complete transmission of both kama and terma teachings, including *Longchen Nyingthig, Yönten Dzö,* with its autocommentary, *Dzödün, Shingta Namsum, Trölthik,* and *Nying Gyü.* Jigme Lingpa gave him the name Jigme Thrinle Özer, Rays of Fearless Enlightened Action.

When Dodrupchen was at Samye, Barchung Gomchen Rigdzin and Mange Pema Künzang from Kham arrived on pilgrimage. With a letter Dodrupchen sent them to Jigme Lingpa for teachings. Later Pema Künzang became Jigme Lingpa's renowned disciple Jigme Gyalwe Nyuku. Having received teachings for two weeks, Rigdzin and Gyalwe Nyuku returned to Dodrupchen at Samye. Together they all went on pilgrimage in Central Tibet. Then they went to see a great meditator, Rigdzin Pema She-nyen, in Tsang and received many Changter (Northern Treasure) transmissions.

Then Dodrupchen returned to Lhasa from Tsang accompanied by Gyalwe Nyuku, who was on his way to Kham. While they were crossing a no-man's land in the Yadrok area of Central Tibet, Dodrupchen got seriously sick, but his mind remained very cheerful. Gyalwe Nyuku writes:

> When we, teacher and disciple, were going downward in Yadrok valley, the Lord Lama [Dodrupchen] got seriously sick with air and rheumatism. He was in constant excruciating pain and became so weak that he was almost dying. We didn't have much to eat except a piece of rotten animal fat and a pot of oil. We didn't have even a spoonful of tsampa. We drank some black tea. After he sat down to rest, in order for him to stand, I had to help him by pulling him up with the full strength of my two hands. Although physically he was in critical condition, instead of being depressed, he would say: "Oh, today I have a chance to pursue a little austerity in the practice of Dharma by putting some burden on my mortal body and by taming my greedy mind. I am achieving the goal for my precious human life. . . . There is no doubt that the experiences of

hardship I am going through are the fortunate fruitions produced by the accumulation of merits and purification of obscurations in my numerous lives in the past." There was great joy in his mind. I too was joyful, thinking, "It is wonderful that this Lord Lama is putting into practice [what the Buddha taught]":

> Preserve Dharma [realization] forever,
> Even at [the cost of] crossing [a mass of] flames or [a field of] razors.

Also, sometimes when the lama wasn't watching, I cried a lot, thinking:

> This holy person is going to die in this place where no other human being will even notice.[190]

From Lhasa, Gyalwe Nyuku went back to Tsang, Western Tibet, and Dodrupchen left for Kham, Eastern Tibet. But after a few days' journey, Dodrupchen could not bear leaving his teacher without seeing him once more. So he turned south and went to see Jigme Lingpa, to the great surprise and joy of his teacher. Dodrupchen received more transmissions and teachings. Jigme Lingpa recognized him as the incarnation of Prince Murum Tsenpo, son of King Trisong Detsen, and empowered him as the principal doctrine-holder of the *Longchen Nyingthig* teachings, as prophesied in *Nechang Thukkyi Drombu:*

> An incarnation of the Lhase [Divine Prince]
> shall open the door of the [*Longchen Nyingthig*] doctrine.[191]

On his return to Do Valley, at the request of Akyongza Paldzom, the lady chieftain of Upper Do Valley, Dodrupchen laid the foundation of a gompa at Shukchen Tago, which is about ten miles down from the present Dodrupchen Monastery. But soon he left for Dege and construction stopped.

At Dzogchen Monastery, he gave the textual transmissions of *Longchen Nyingthig* to the Third Dzogchen Rinpoche (1759–1792) and the Second Pönlop (1731–1805) of Dzogchen Monastery. Again with the approval of Dzogchen Rinpoche, Dodrupchen went to Central Tibet for the fourth and last time, with huge offerings. He was accompanied by Getse Lama Sönam Tendzin (Jigme Ngotsar)[192] and a few others. This time he saw Jigme Lingpa at the house of Depa Lha Gyatri (Gyari).

Then with Jigme Lingpa he traveled to Samye.[193] In the main temple of Samye, Dodrupchen sponsored and arranged a huge tsok offering ceremony presided over by Jigme Lingpa. He took bodhichitta vows again from Jigme Lingpa, and they recited many *Zangpo Chöpe Mönlam* together. He sponsored a mendrup, the preparation of "blessed medicine," for seven days under the mastership of Jigme Lingpa. Remember that the main temple of Samye is the place where Guru Rinpoche entrusted *Longchen Nyingthig* teachings to King Trisong Detsen, a previous incarnation of Jigme Lingpa's, and transmitted teachings to Prince Murum Tsepo, a previous incarnation of Dodrupchen's, a number of centuries previously.

Then they traveled together to Tsering Jong. Jigme Lingpa gave many empowerments, but as he had problems with his eyesight, Dodrupchen gave the textual transmission (Lung) of *Nyingma Gyübum* and others to the tülku of Tsele Götsang Tülku, Jigme Tenpe Gyaltsen of Thangdrok, and many others on behalf of his master.

In 1791, when Dodrupchen was at Samye, the Gurkha forces of Nepal ransacked many places in Western Tibet, including the town of Shigatse and Tashi Lhünpo Monastery. People in Central Tibet were frightened of being overrun by Gurkha forces any day, and many were fleeing their towns and monasteries.

As requested by fearful people, after having completed prayers at the main temple of Samye, Dodrupchen went to Hepori Hill and made a Sang offering. He invoked the Dharma protectors and reminded them of their vows to protect Tibet made before the very eyes of Guru Rinpoche. The smoke of the Sang formed the shape of a garuḍa (an eaglelike mystical bird) in the sky and was carried in the direction of the invaders. At sunset he threw a torma (offering cake) toward the West. At that moment, a dark cloud and a strong storm were coming from the West, but as soon as he threw the torma, miraculously the cloud turned back toward the West.

Then, in a poem, Dodrupchen gave his prophecy that there would be nothing more to fear from Nepalese forces, and he sent it to the government in Lhasa. Because of his assurances, people in Samye stopped fleeing. He wanted to go to see Jigme Lingpa but couldn't, as no boat was available to cross the Tsangpo River. Then he went to Kordzö Ling, the temple of the Dharma protectors at Samye. First he said prayers and performed ceremonies. But suddenly his manner totally changed. He shouted at the image of Pehar, the main Dharma protector of Tibet, hit it with his shawl, pulled down the coverings of the image, and challenged the Dharma protector's promises to protect Tibet before the eyes of Guru Rinpoche. Finally, he felt peaceful and remained in contemplation in that peace for a long time. (I have heard stories that the image was seen to tremble, and smoky mist came from its mouth and nose and rose into the air, causing hailstorms and epidemics among the invading forces.)

Kalön Dzasak Lama Kalzang Namgyal, one of the high authorities of the Tibetan government, sent a special emissary to Dodrupchen for his prophecy about the Nepalese danger. Dodrupchen wrote his prophecy in a poem that included the following lines and sent it to Kalön Lama:

> In [my mind, which is] crystal-clear primordial purity,
> Appear the following words and expressions:
> When you are at ease, O arrogant people
> Who are swollen with pride,
> Do not listen to any unsubstantiated voice.
> Do not flee to any unknown land. . . .

As the four provinces of Central Tibet were facing the threat of severe drought, Dodrupchen performed a fire-offering ceremony (homa), and that produced heavy rain, bringing great relief for many from the danger of famine.[194]

From Samye, Dodrupchen went to Tsering Jong. At that time, Jigme Lingpa couldn't read much because of eye problems, possibly cataracts. Jigme Gyalwe Nyuku sent for an eye doctor, who performed a successful operation. Before taking his final leave, Dodrupchen offered everything he had, including his cherished old hat, to Jigme Lingpa. He experienced great joy and peace as a result of this action.

Praising Dodrupchen, Jigme Lingpa gave his advice in writing, including the following lines:

> A person who can heal the disturbances of [physical and
>   environmental] elements,
> Who is able to tame the negative circumstances, and
> Who can accomplish whatever [the teacher] orders him to do—
> Isn't he called a fortunate disciple?
> Because of our past karmic relations,
> Which began many previous lives ago,

Jigme Thrinle Özer,
You came here from a long distance,
From a place that is difficult to see or hear about.
Carrying as precious gifts the treasures of profound and vast teachings,
Which are hard to find,
You are returning toward your homeland.
You are like a successful trader returning across the ocean.
If there were no karmic relations,
Even if you lived in the same part of the country,
How could you see me
As a bodhisattva, who takes care of others? . . .
As prophesied in *Nechang Thukkyi Drombu,*
While building the temple of Samye,
We were related as father [the king] and son [the prince].
Pure visions of that fact you saw by yourself.
From your childhood,
While remaining in solitary places,
As I did in my life,
You have received the prophecies about [discovering] ters.
Now the treasure of kama and terma teachings
I am entrusting to you, and
I prophesy that you will spread it in the barbarous lands.
As long as the [realization of the] true nature is not being lost to delusions,
There is no need to spend one's life in retreats. . . .
Between you and me there is no separation.
By the truth of the union of my mind and your mind,
By the compassionate blessings of the three Jewels,
By the power of the three roots, and
By the actions of the Dharma protectors,
May there be no negative circumstances in your Dharma activities, and
May there be not even a trace of any obstruction.[195]

Jigme Lingpa said, "Tonight you stay in my house. I have some advice to give to you." So Dodrupchen spent his last night in the presence of Jigme Lingpa. Jigme Lingpa said:

> All the instructions that I have received on both canonical and terma teachings are the inheritance of both you and me. When I

> was entrusted with the yellow scroll [of *Longchen Nyingthig*] by the Ḍākinī of the Ultimate Sphere, she told me that these are the Dharma inheritance of the king and his son. Also, in *Nechang (Thukkyi Drombu)* it is said, "The door of the teachings will be opened by the incarnation of the Divine Prince." So, without any doubt, you are the incarnation [of the Divine Prince]. So to propagate the teachings for the benefits of the tradition and beings is your main mission. We are inseparable. In future there will come a time that your enlightened activities will become very successful, but there will also be many obstructions from negative forces. Pray to me, and your obstructions will be pacified. When in you a new faith arises toward me, if a new opportunity arises, we, father and son, will meet again.[196]

The meaning of the last line was that Jigme Lingpa would take rebirth as Do Khyentse and would meet Dodrupchen again as his teacher.

Dodrupchen expressed his wish to remain as a hermit. Jigme Lingpa, rejecting that aspiration, advised:

> I have given you the vow of the bodhisattva, the pledge of taking the responsibility of [providing happiness for] all beings on your shoulders. If you just enjoy the peace and joy of a cave, you could be neglecting your vows. Never waver from propagation of the teachings. I have no doubt that even unvirtuous situations will turn into virtues for you.[197]

The next day, touching the warm bare feet of Jigme Lingpa with the crown of his head, Dodrupchen, a stream of tears glowing on his face, said, "In all successive future lives, may I never be separated from you, my protector lord. May every action and thought of my body, speech, and mind become a powerful source of benefit for the Dharma and beings." Jigme Lingpa, with great affection touching the forehead of Dodrupchen with his own forehead, said, "It is a promise; we have no separation. Please travel joyfully." Dodrupchen, with the feeling that his heart was leaping out of his chest, stepped backward and left the room and the hermitage.

Now that Dodrupchen had become known as an important lama, he had to perform ceremonies of blessings at Samye, Depa Lha Gyatri, and many other places.

At Döjo Palkhyim (Döpal) in Lhasa, as requested by the government, under the personal supervision of Changtrung Khenpo (aka Kudün Khenpo), Dodrupchen performed ceremonies[198] for many days for the welfare of the government and the country and then for Kudün Khenpo himself. While effectuating a dö (mDos) ceremony of Magön, with just his right hand Dodrupchen miraculously raised a two-story-high dö and then threw it. The Tibetan government paid him great respect and gratitude for his protection and prophecy for the country. Since that time, Dodrupchen became known by the name of Dodrupchen, the Great Adept (Mahāsiddha) of Do (Valley). People of Lhasa said, "There are many adepts (Grub Thob), but there is only one Great Adept (Grub Ch'en, Drupchen)."

Dodrupchen also brought back Gyalwe Nyuku with him to Kham. On the way they faced many dangers, but he conquered them all either by heroic courage or by spiritual powers. It all only strengthened his inner realization. For example, one day they lost their way in the snow, and Dodrupchen experienced a feeling of sadness. From that sadness arose an amazing vision of Milarepa. Milarepa, singing, gave him the *Ngetön Nyingpo* sādhana of Milarepa and merged himself into Dodrupchen.

In 1793, Dodrupchen was invited by the Dege Palace for the first time. He performed ceremonies and gave teachings accompanied by many mystical signs. From that time Dodrupchen became one of the main preceptors of Queen-Regent Tsewang Lhamo and her son, Prince Tsewang Dorje Rigdzin (1786–1847?) of Dege. The Dege court requested him to stay as their preceptor, but Dodrupchen immediately refused, for going to Wu Tai Shan in China in order to spend the rest of his life there was his primary goal (although it was never realized).

Now Dodrupchen was dedicating his life solely to the propagation of Dharma, so that the teachings would reach the hearts of many trainable beings. In his autobiography Jigme Lingpa expressed his joy on receiving a message about Dodrupchen's success in the propagation of Dharma.

> Dola [the Lama from Do, i.e., Dodrupchen] has given the explanatory teachings of Nyingthig [in Dege] three times. On the first occasion, two thousand disciples received teachings; on the second, three thousand; and on the third, five thousand. Many laypeople took vows of not hunting, whereby many animals were given the "gift of fearlessness." I feel happy that I have brought about this small result by staying in a remote place and developing bodhichitta. This is the fulfillment of the prophecy that said:

> The incarnations of Nam-nying, Nyang-ben, Chok-ying,
> and the Divine Prince will open the door of [*Longchen Nyingthig*] teachings.[199]

In the same year, as requested and sponsored by the queen-regent of Dege, Dodrupchen laid the foundation of Ogmin Rigdzin Phelgye Ling Monastery[200] at Getse Tö in Dzachukha Valley. But after laying the foundation, he left for Amdo because of his long-standing aspiration to go to Wu Tai Shan. He made a winter-long retreat at Trakkar Treldzong, a sacred place in Amdo.

In the monastery of Chöje Rinpoche in Go-me Province, Dodrupchen transmitted the *Longchen Nyingthig* and other teachings to Chöje Rinpoche, a celebrated Geluk scholar, who had studied Nyingma teachings and had become one of Dodrupchen's disciples. Dodrupchen received some transmissions from Go-me Chöje also.

Dodrupchen gave teachings and served many Tibetan and Mongolian communities of that region. He displayed many miracles, such as causing a stream to flow out of dry land for a community that was without water. For the Mongols of the Blue Lake region he became known as Harhan Dalai Lama.

Because of the fame of Dodrupchen's enlightened power, old Chönang Dzasak, a powerful Mongol chieftain, invited him to his domain, although Nyingma practice had been prohibited there for the last two years. The chieftain had many children, but none ever survived, although he took the spiritual protection of the lamas of Kubum Monastery. Dodrupchen blessed him and prophesied that the chieftain would have another child. When a child was born, the baby was so sick that no one expected him to live. But through Dodrupchen's spiritual protection the child survived. First he was named Yamathar, and later his name was changed to Garwap Gyalchok and Yizhin Wangyal. The spiritual power of Dodrupchen caused a new attitude of tolerance in the minds of people toward other lineages of Buddhism in that area.[201]

Dodrupchen was also invited by the Mongol king, Ching Wang Ngawang Dargye (1759–1807), also known as Chögyal Ngaki Wangpo. Ngawang Dargye was the most important chieftain in the Blue Lake region at that time. Dodrupchen gave the transmissions and instructions of *Longchen Nyingthig, Khandro Yangtig,* and commentaries of *Yönten Dzö* to between forty and a hundred important people in addition to the king and queen.

Dodrupchen gave the *Longchen Nyingthig* transmission to Drupchen Tülku Jigme Namkha Gyaltsen of Gön Lakha,[202] who became a Longchen Nyingthig lineage holder. Before 1959, it is known that Gön Lakha had more than nineteen hundred tantric residents. Dodrupchen also taught to Ngawang Tendar Lharampa (1759–?) of the Alaksha Mongols.[203]

Then a problem arose for Dodrupchen involving the Amban, the representative of the emperor of China at Sining, the capital of the state of Blue Lake (Qinghai). Dodrupchen was summoned to the Amban's camp and accused of belonging to a group of Khampas who were fleeing from their homeland. Dodrupchen was helping them, but he didn't belong to that particular group. Another accusation was that Dodrupchen had been in the Blue Lake region for a few years without informing the Amban, which was true. Further, it was said that he was wearing the hat of a Khenpo, an abbot, without official recognition, which was partially true since he hadn't received such recognition from the Geluk school, which was the official religious institution of that particular region. Through two interpreters, the Amban questioned Dodrupchen for a whole day amid a huge assembly of Tibetan and Mongolian dignitaries of the Blue Lake region, including King Ngawang Dargye and Jonang Dzasak. All of them, as Dodrupchen describes it, "sat as if they were receiving a religious discourse." At the end of the day, not only was Dodrupchen released, but the Amban was so impressed that he even requested him to say prayers for a sick friend of his. The problem was thus miraculously avoided, to everybody's surprise. Otherwise there could have been a real danger to Dodrupchen's life and to the positions of many Mongol princes, who were his patrons.

Many months later, the Amban sent another messenger to invite Dodrupchen to Sining. In Sining, with great respect the Amban said to Dodrupchen, "Usually, when people get a letter from the emperor, they stand and listen to it facing east. You, however, may remain sitting, but listen carefully and face east." Ceremoniously he opened the letter from the Emperor Chia Ch'ing (r. 1796–1820), which included the following lines:

> If the lama is beneficial to people, there should be no problem about his being a lama of the Red Hat [Nyingma] sect. He [Dodrupchen] must stay in the Blue Lake region. He mustn't leave for Wu Tai Shan, for Lhasa, or for his own home. If he should leave,

> he must consult the emperor first. The chieftains [of the Blue Lake region] must pay respect and service to the lama.[204]

The people of that area saw that the emperor's recognition of Dodrupchen as a lama of the twelve divisions (mDa' Tshan) of Mongols of the Blue Lake region was a great honor. They were joyful because their prayers that he would stay with them were granted. But Dodrupchen's dream of going to Wu Tai Shan was shattered. (There are stories that Dodrupchen's disciple-chieftains were instrumental in the emperor's edict that he must remain in that area.)

Realizing that now he could not travel toward Wu Tai Shan against the emperor's edict, Dodrupchen wanted instead to go to Central Tibet to see Jigme Lingpa once again. But his devotees persisted in opposing this plan, citing the emperor's order. So Dodrupchen sent Jigme Chötrak in his stead to Central Tibet with huge offerings, everything that he possessed. The travelers also took many gifts from King Ngawang Dargye for Jigme Lingpa.[205]

The Chonang chieftain requested Dodrupchen to build a gompa (monastary) and promised all the necessary financial and political support. But Dodrupchen refused to accept the offering, reminding himself of a wise old saying, "Don't stay too close to your patrons."

Arik Geshe Chenmo Champa Gelek Gyaltsen (1726–1803)[206] of Ragya Monastery, a preeminent Geluk scholar, profusely praised Dodrupchen and made generous offerings to him. He also received transmissions from Dodrupchen.

An epidemic in Arik Ragya Gompa, a large Geluk monastery in Amdo, killed about half of its four thousand monk residents. All the survivors fled to a nearby valley, except one monk, who chose not to leave, as it would disrupt his saying the prayer of *Mañjushrī-nāma-saṃgīti*. One day he heard the sound of bells and saw some people with an unusual tigerlike animal entering the abandoned monastery. When one of them came to his house, before he could warn him of the epidemic, the man said, "Dodrupchen is here. He wants to get the message to the monks that there will be no more danger and they can return. We are disposing of the abandoned bodies." Later, Dodrupchen performed a fire-offering ceremony (homa) and stopped the epidemic, enabling the monastery to revive. He also miraculously drew a stream of water from the rock of Amye Khyung-gön, the hill behind the monastery, which is still a healing stream today.

An uncle of Dodrupchen and others came from Do Valley in Golok and urged him to return home. Citing and emperor's order, the chieftains and people of the Blue Lake region, who were his devotees, objected to his departure. But Dodrupchen's uncle suddenly got sick and refused to take medicine or go to any monastery for prayers unless Dodrupchen would go back home with him. Thus the chieftains were forced to allow Dodrupchen to return home. He left Lama Pema Tamchö behind as his representative to show that he was not abandoning the area.

Dodrupchen returned from the Blue Lake region to Do Valley in 1799. There he resumed building his Drotön Lhüntrup Gompa at Shukchen Tago in Do Valley.

Jigme Gyalwe Nyuku also came to Do Valley to help Dodrupchen build the monastery. Dodrupchen, accompanied by Gyalwe Nyuku and others, visited the King Tsewang Lhündrup (d. 1825) of Dzigak at the Phüntsok Dzong, the king of Chötse, and many places in Dzika Valley to transmit teachings, perform ceremonies, and raise funds for the monastery.

Nüden Dorje, a young nephew of Dodrupchen's, who later became the famous Khangdong (or Khordong) Terchen, came to see his uncle.[207] Dodrupchen gave him a vajra and a phurbu and asked him to stand up. Holding them in his hand, Terchen turned around and said HŪṂ HŪṂ HŪṂ. At that moment, the memories of Terchen's having been Düdül Dorje (1615–1672) in the past awakened. Then Dodrupchen conferred on him the empowerment of *Yumka Dechen Gyalmo,* and Terchen heard the sound of the mantra OṂ PADMOYOGINĪ JÑĀNAVĀRĀHĪ HŪṂ coming from all the trees, flowers, and vegetation he could see around him.

In 1801, on a visit to Mar Valley, Dodrupchen met Do Khyentse (1800–1866), who was then about a year old. The child was insisting his parents take him to someone named Sönam Chöden, adding that otherwise he would be going home, meaning that he would die. Sönam Chöden was one of the early names of Dodrupchen, but hardly anybody but he knew it. When Dodrupchen met the child, he tearfully held him and assured him, "I will take care of you." Khyentse wrote years later that when he met Dodrupchen, he saw him not in the form of an ordinary person, but as Guru Rinpoche.

At the advice of Dodrupchen, Do Khyentse was brought to Shukchen Tago and started to receive blessings and teachings. Do Khyentse kept seeing Dodrupchen in various forms and surrounded by various men and women in mysterious forms. After growing up, he realized that those appearances were not normal forms of the lama or his surroundings.

After a few years' stay, the involvement of the chieftain of upper Do Valley in shielding a thief was discovered. That incident disappointed Dodrupchen greatly, as he was not only a great lama, but a wise, ethical, and highly respected tribal leader. Soon, he refused to stay at Shukchen Tago, although it remained as a hermitage for many years. Paltrül Rinpoche (1808–1887) read the Kanjur there for a long time and memorized many sūtras.[208] However, I saw only the ruins of Shukchen Tago when I used to pass by the place as a child.

Dodrupchen kept receiving urgent invitations from the king of Dege and Dzogchen Monastery. He went to Gyarong Monastery, Dzogchen Monastery, and places in Dzachukha Valley. He was received with great ceremonial processions at each place. At Dzogchen Monastery he gave empowerments to the young Fourth Dzogchen Rinpoche. When he heard that the queen-mother regent of Dege was seriously sick, he rushed to Dege Palace. The queen mother had just recovered from her sickness. Dodrupchen gave her teachings on *Yeshe Lama* and other teachings. To the king he gave empowerments of Hyagrīva, and *Vajrakīla of Gyüluk*. Later he also transmitted to him the ter teachings discovered by Dodrupchen himself.

Dodrupchen transmitted many teachings, including *Yabzhi, Longchen Nyingthig, Nyingma Gyübum,* and *Dzödün* to many disciples, including high lamas of Nyingma monasteries of Kham, such as Dzogchen, Kathok, and Zhechen. Among the recipients were the Fourth Dzogchen Rinpoche, Do Khyentse, the Third Zhechen Rabjam, Kathok Situ, Gotsa Tülkus, Gomchen Ngawang Chöjor, and Thartse Khenchen Namkha Chi-me of Ngor.[209]

Till then, Do Khyentse was staying under the care of Dodrupchen and had unofficially been recognized as the tülku of Jigme Lingpa by Dodrupchen himself. Then approval of the recognition by Sakya Kongma and Drikung tülkus, who were close disciples of Jigme Lingpa, was brought by the representatives from Drikung, who came to bring the tülku to Central Tibet. With elaborate arrangements by the Dege Palace, Do Khyentse was then sent to Drikung, where Jigme Lingpa's son was one of two heads of the Drikung lineage.

In 1806, as an uncle of Dodrupchen was dying, he rushed back to Golok from Dege. But until 1809, he went back and forth a few times between Dege, Dzogchen, and Golok, performing ceremonies and mostly giving transmissions and teachings at many monasteries and other places.

With Jigme Gyalwe Nyuku, Dodrupchen built Dzagya Monastery[210] in Dzachukha Valley, which later became the main seat of Jigme Gyalwe Nyuku himself and of his famous disciple, Paltrül Rinpoche.

I would like to note here that there was a sectarian resistance against the influence of Nyingma lamas headed by Dodrupchen in the Dege court. However, there is no basis for the assertion made by some Western writers that Dodrupchen was imprisoned and then exiled from Dege during the revolt in Dege in 1798.[211] In fact, Dodrupchen was not in Dege during this period. Between 1793 and 1799 he remained in the Blue Lake region giving teachings to Tibetans and Mongols. He returned from Amdo to Golok only in 1799 and built Shukchen Tago Gompa. It was only from around 1802 until 1809 that he made frequent visits to Dege, giving teachings to the queen-mother regent and the prince, who became king in 1806. Dodrupchen made many visits and spent a lot of time in Dege after his return from Amdo, compared with his single visit of many months in 1793. According to numerous documents, not only the queen-mother regent but also her son, King Tsewang Dorje Rigdzin (1786–1847?, r. 1806–1847?), remained ardent devotees of Dodrupchen.

Dodrupchen inspired the palace of Dege[212] to commission the wooden blocks of the nine volumes by Jigme Lingpa, and also the twenty-five volumes of the *Nyingma Gyübum* and more than ten volumes by Longchen Rabjam.

Finally in 1809 Dodrupchen returned to Golok. A prophecy of Rongtön Dechen Lingpa (17th century) says:

> An incarnation of the Divine Prince, the heroic bodhisattva,
> Will appear, with teachers and meditators of Dzogchen Ati.
> He will build about three monasteries in upper, middle, and lower
> Ser Valley.

In 1810, at the age of sixty-six, he established a meditation center at Yarlung in the Trakchen gorge of Ser Valley. He named it the Pemakö Tsasum Khandrö Ling. Later, it became known popularly as Yarlung Pemakö Monastery.[213]

After building Yarlung Pemakö, Dodrupchen vowed never to leave it, so he didn't go anywhere, but stayed there for more than the next ten years of his life. While Dodrupchen was living there, music with no visible source could be heard in Yarlung Pemakö on almost every tenth and twenty-fifth day of the lunar calendar. People believed that the music was played by the assembly of ḍākas and ḍākinīs. On those days when the music was heard, people were reminded that this was one of the ceremonial days of the month.

At Yarlung Pemakö, Dodrupchen taught and gave transmissions to a great number of disciples, many of whom went on to become famous masters. Frequently, when Dodrupchen would give the transmission of empowerments and the instructions, Jigme Kalzang would give the textual transmission (Lung) on his behalf.

In 1812, Do Khyentse returned from central Tibet to see the aging Dodrupchen. Again and again the king of Dege strongly urged both Dodrupchen and Do Khyentse to come to Dege, but Dodrupchen couldn't go, as he had vowed never to leave his monastery.[214]

At the age of twenty,[215] the Fourth Dzogchen Rinpoche (1793–?) visited Yarlung Pemakö to receive further teachings from Dodrupchen. Dodrupchen transmitted to him the empowerment, texts, and instructions belonging to Longchen Rabjam and Jigme Lingpa, as well as *Vima Nyingthig* and *Nyen-gyü Dorje Zampa.*

Dodrupchen blessed Dzogchen Rinpoche by giving him a skull cup full of chang (beer). With the drink, the teacher's realization was spontaneously transferred to Dzogchen Rinpoche, and he attained the state of the dissolution of relative phenomena into the absolute nature (Ch'os Nyid Zad Pa). Thereafter Dzogchen Rinpoche became a famous adept who made no distinctions and who had no hope or fear of good or bad. There are many amazing stories of his life and wisdom.

When Gyalse Zhenphen Thaye (1800–?) first saw Yarlung Pemakö from afar, he got off his horse. Making many prostrations, he cried like a child. He said, "This place of my teacher is nothing but the true Unexcelled Pure Land of the Dharmakāya." When he reached Dodrupchen, the lama was blessing people by touching them with a small banner made of silk ribbons of five colors, and Gyalse saw Vajrapāṇi in a light body adorning the banner.

In 1815, Dodrupchen sent Do Khyentse to Central Tibet with huge offerings. He returned in 1816.

In 1817/18, Jigme Gyalwe Nyuku came to Yarlung Pemakö to see the aged Dodrupchen[216] for the last time. It was a time of great joy and sadness for both the Dharma father and son or brothers. Dodrupchen summed up the reunion by saying, "It is [as rare and joyful as] the meeting of a dead and a living person." Dodrupchen gave teachings on Ngöndro and many other teachings to Gyalwe Nyuku and others. He also prophesied where Gyalwe Nyuku should establish his main seat, with detailed descriptions of a place that he had never seen.

In Yarlung Pemakö, many great masters came to receive transmissions from Dodrupchen. Among them were Gyalwe Nyuku, Fourth Dzogchen Rinpoche, Do Khyentse, Kathok Getse Mahāpaṇḍita, Dola Jigme Kalzang, Repa Tamtsik Dorje, Chöying Tobden Dorje, Zhichen Sönam Palden, Sönam Gyaltsen, Changlung Namkha Jigme Dorje, and Gyalse Zhenphen Thaye.

In 1819, Dodrupchen advised[217] the representatives of Dege Palace, Dzogchen Monastery, Kathok Monastery, and Drikung to allow Do Khyentse to be a hermit tāntrika, as he wished in order to fulfill his enlightened activities. So they did allow Do Khyentse to assume the life of a wandering yogi. Do Khyentse recalls the life of the aged Dodrupchen in those days:

> The Precious Lord Dharma King was in better health than before. Occasionally he would suddenly sing yogic songs, but we did not have the opportunity to write them down. Sometimes he would describe his visions of the Sambhogakāya pure lands, and at other times, various circumstances of beings in the six realms. He also gave prophecies of the future of the Dharma propagation and of individuals. Some of us kept seeing his body in various forms, and sometimes we saw no body but only his clothes on his seat. There were endless wonders. Whenever we remembered any question we had on important points of teachings, he would answer spontaneously without our needing to ask him.[218]

At the age of seventy-seven, in the early morning[219] of the thirteenth day of the first month of the Iron Snake year (1821), he changed into Sambhogakāya costume. He gave instructions to some disciples individually. Then, without being sick, he merged into ultimate peace, while describing his experience of the phases of withdrawal of energies of the elements in the body. Beams and circles of rainbow lights and a rain of flowers filled the sky. When his body was cremated, many ringsels emerged as the sign of high attainment. His followers built a golden stūpa in which they preserved his remains at Dodrupchen Monastery till

1959. Ngawang Tendar Lharampa, a famous Geluk writer and a disciple of Dodrupchen from Alaksha, Mongolia, writes:

> There are masters who are able to attain the realization . . . that dissolves [their bodies into rainbow-light bodies] but who choose instead to attain the state of knowledge-holder with residue. The reason is that some of them have not ended their karmic force, in order to dedicate themselves to turning the wheel of activities in the service of Dharma and beings. Others leave physical remains in the form of dungs and ringsels, so that these at least remain as sources of blessing for the disciples. An example is [the manner of death of] our precious refuge, the glorious Jigme Thrinle Özer, the illusory manifestation of Samantabhadra, the primordial Buddha arisen in the perceptions of trainable beings as the lord of the sages and the embodiment of the hundred Buddha families.[220]

On the very night of Dodrupchen's death, his spiritual testament was received by his principal disciple, Do Khyentse, who was at a distance of many weeks of travel. In the latter part of the night of the thirteenth day of the first month of the Iron Snake year, Dodrupchen appeared in the sky in a radiant light body and an attire of lights. He was floating on a carpet of light, which was held up by four ḍākinīs. In a very enchanting voice he sang the verses of his testament, which include the following lines, and then he merged into Do Khyentse.

> I am going into the expanse of the Wisdom of the Ultimate Sphere,
> Which is the state that transcends thoughts and expressions.
> I am going into the state of Mirrorlike Wisdom,
> Which is the ceaseless clear glow, fresh and open.
> I am going into the expanse of the Wisdom of Evenness,
> In which all the thoughts of grasping and grasper have vanished
> into the ultimate sphere.
> I am going into the Wisdom of Discriminative Awareness,
> Which is the clarity, the dawn of six kinds of foreknowledge.
> I am going into the state of the Wisdom of Accomplishment,
> Which emanates various manifestations in accordance with [the
> needs of] trainable beings.
> I am going to Zangdok Palri, the pure land of knowledge-holders.
> As my mind becomes the same as the mind of the Heruka,
> I will manifest three incarnations as your companion.

This testament, until it clearly appears
As the secret drawings of the ḍākinī symbols,
Keep sealed tightly like the mouth of a dead body.
May these symbols never vanish. TIṢHṬHA-LHEN!
Son, please stay healthy.
Now you have won over the obstructions of your life.
Until all the phenomenal existents are liberated as the signs and
teachings [of Dharma],
[You should be] aware of saṃsāra and nirvāṇa as dreams and
illusions.
Dedicate yourself to the meditation where there is no reference
point.
This is the empowerment of total entrustment and aspiration.
This is the supreme empowerment of empowerments.[221]

Dodrupchen discovered many teachings as mind treasure, under the title of *Tamchö Dechen Lamchok,* the Excellent Path of Supreme Joy, the Holy Teachings. It includes Outer, Inner, and Secret sādhanas of Amitābha, a most sacred sādhana of Hayagrīva, and the sādhanas of the twelve Dzogchen Masters, Milarepa, Machik Labdrön, and Mahādeva. He also discovered a famous Chö liturgy, entitled *Chuwo Chigdre.* Among his writings were *Gyatsö Chuthik* (A Drop from the Ocean), a short and a long version of commentaries on *Yönten Rinpoche Dzö,* a brief commentary on *Chö Khandrö Kegyang,* a sādhana of purification of samaya, and compilations of Mahākala liturgy and of the Vajrakīla sādhana discovered by Sangye Lingpa.

Dodrupchen wrote many prophecies. It is known that Labrang Monastery in Amdo had a one-volume collection of his prophecies. I myself have seen a collection of a couple of hundred pages, but now only one section of a few pages seems to have survived.

Dodrupchen was renowned for the clarity and accuracy of his prophecies. Usually lamas write their prophecies as they are told of the events by a ḍākinī, a lama, or a Buddha in a pure vision. But the uniqueness of Dodrupchen's prophetic writings is that he foretells the events as a natural or self-arisen vision that appears in his realized wisdom state itself. For example:

In the mirror of the Ultimate Sphere [of my wisdom mind], which
is free from thoughts,

Arise the situations of the world in general, and
Of Eastern Tibet (mDo sMad) in particular,
In the form of interdependent arisings without any
confusion. . . .[222]

He foretold many events related to Dharma propagation, various provinces, and individuals. For example, he prophesied the births of Khyentse Wangpo (1820–1892), Zhapkar Tsoktruk Rangtröl (1781–1851), Pema Siddhi (d. 1957), and hundreds of other great lamas. He foretold that China would become "red," although in his time "red" didn't signify what it does today. He also foretold what could happen to a regent of Tibet from Redring (died in 1947) and the consequences of that event.

Soon after Dodrupchen's death, Do Khyentse returned to Yarlung Pemakö to pay respect to the remains, ashes, and ringsels of Dodrupchen, which were kept in a vase. Dodrupchen's disciples urged Do Khyentse to stay as Dodrupchen's successor (gDan Tshabs), but he refused.

Later, Gyalse Zhenphen Thaye (1800–?) of Dzogchen Monastery, a celebrated scholar and one of the main disciples of Dodrupchen, came to stay as Dodrupchen's successor for a while. Gyalse instituted a forty-five-day annual teaching and practice of *Guhyagarbha-māyājāla-tantra* at Yarlung Pemakö. Paltrül Rinpoche acted as the teaching-assistant to Gyalse for the first year, and then he himself presided over it for two more years.[223] Paltrül Rinpoche and Nyoshül Lungtok (d. 1902?) stayed around Ser and Do Valley, the seats of Dodrupchen, for about nine or ten years.[224]

Among his disciples were the lineage-holder masters, who are prophesied in *The Confidential Prophecy of Lama Gongdü*.[225] They are the four lineage-holders named Dorje (rDo rJe'i gDung bZhi), the thirteen named Dorje (rDo rJe'i Ming Chan bChu gSum), and the six named Sangye (Buddha mCh'ed Drug).

There are different interpretations for specifying the four lineage-holders named Dorje. One way is: (1) Dola Jigme Kalzang Dorje (Chökyi Lodrö) in the east, like the sound of a white conch full of spiritual fame, (2) Repa Tamtsik Dorje of Khyunglung (who was renowned for having a thousand yogī and a thousand yoginī disciples) in the south, with many tantric disciples like a heap of white rice, (3) Gyalse Rikpe Dorje (Zhenphen Thaye) in the west, with many monk meditator-disciples like a garden of red lotuses, and (4) Chöying Tobden Dorje (a great writer and propogator of Nyingthig teachings in Amdo, especially in Rekong) in the north, like an iron phurbu with many powerful tantric disciples.

Another way is: (1) Do Khyentse, (2) Fourth Dzogchen Rinpoche, (3) Gyalse Rigpe Dorje, and (4) Kyebu Yeshe Dorje (Dola Jigme Kalzang).

A third way is: (1) Do Khyentse, (2) Dzogchen Rinpoche, (3) Repa Tamtsik Dorje, and (4) Chöying Tobden Dorje.

Kongtrül Yönten Gyatso (1813–1899) writes,

> To you who are known as the Radiance [Özer] of the East, the Nirmāṇakāya,
> With four [disciple] yogīs, as prophesied by the Guru [Rinpoche],
> Who acted for the benefit of beings, the wisdom incarnation of Murum (Tsepo),
> Changchup Dorje [Dodrupchen], Lord of Sages, I pray.[226]

The thirteen named Dorje are listed variously, but one way is: (1) Mingyur Namkhe Dorje, (2) Do Khyentse Yeshe Dorje, (3) Jigme Mikyö Dorje (Namkha Tsewang Choktrup, 1744–?) of Gyarong Gön, (4) Repa Tamtsik Dorje, (5) Chöying Tobden Dorje, (6) Jigme Palkyi Dorje, (7) Rigdzin Jampal Dorje of Zhechen, (8) Kyilung Thukchok Dorje of Golok, (9) Jigme Pawo Dorje, (10) Zhönu Yeshe Dorje (aka Dola Jigme Kalzang, (11) Wangda Dorje Palzang of Golok, (12) Rigdzin Palkyi Dorje of Troshül, and (13) Rolwe Dorje of Barchung.

Nyoshül Lungtok provides another way of categorizing the main disciples of Dodrupchen:

> The chief of all the Khampa disciples of the great knowledge-holder [Jigme Lingpa] was Jigme Thrinle Özer, the Dodrupchen. Among Dodrupchen's [principal] disciples were four lineage-holders named Dorje, six named Buddha, thirteen named Namkha, and one hundred maṇḍala-holders. The chief among the thirteen named Namkha is Mingyur Namkhe Dorje.[227]

Jigme Gyalwe Nyuku and Jigme Ngotsar were both colleagues and disciples of Dodrupchen. Also, when Paltrül Rinpoche was little, Dodrupchen confirmed him as the tülku of Palge Lama, and with his foreknowledge he said to Dola Jigme Kalzang: "I am bestowing the mind entrustment and aspirational transmission of the complete *Longchen Nyingthig* teachings upon him, with the name of Ogyen Jigme Chökyi Wangpo."

As explained before, the Nyingthig lineages of King Ngawang Dargye and his disciple Zhapkar Tsoktruk Rangtröl came through Dodrupchen. Kuyang Lo-de,[228] a disciple and teacher of Zhapkar, writes in a lineage prayer:

> Künkhyen Jigme Lingpa,
> To you I pray, please bestow your blessings.
> Künzang Zhenphen, the Supreme among the Adepts,
> Dharma King Ngaki Wangpo, and
> Omniscient Tsoktruk Rangtröl,
> To you I pray, please bestow your blessings.[229]

The Longchen Nyingthig lineage of Dharma Senge (d. 1890) also came through Dodrupchen, as Dharma Senge writes:

> May the sacred aspirations of Rigdzin Jigme Lingpa be fulfilled.
> May the sacred aspirations of Jigme Thrinle Özer be fulfilled.
> May the sacred aspirations of Ngadak Yeshe Gyatso be fulfilled.
> May the sacred aspirations of the root teacher be fulfilled.[230]

Among Dodrupchen's many incarnations were Jigme Phüntsok Jungne, the Second Dodrupchen (1824–1863), and Se Sherap Mebar (1829–1843),[231] a son of Do Khyentse.

13

Jigme Gyalwe Nyuku
1765–1843

Jigme Gyalwe Nyuku[232] was a great meditator, bodhisattva, and adept. He was one of the two masters who were responsible for the spread of *Longchen Nyingthig* teachings all over Tibet, especially in Eastern Tibet. In his youth he was known as Pema Kunzang and later as Jigme Gyalwe Nyuku, the Fearless Son of the Victorious One (Buddha).

Gyalwe Nyuku was born in the Wood Bird year of the thirteenth Rabjung (1765) in the Getse nomadic group of Dzachukha Valley. His father was Ogyen Tashi of the Mange tribe of the Dong lineage, and his mother was Tashi Kyi of the Awö tribe. Dzachukha is the valley around the source of the Dza (Nyak Ch'u/Yalung) River. Gyalwe Nyuku was the second of nine children. From childhood he never had any interest in worldly enjoyments. In the spring, whenever he saw rainclouds floating in the sky and heard the sound of gentle thunder, he experienced an unbearable urge to go to a solitary place atop a high mountain and devote himself to Dharma meditation. Everybody in his family just wanted him to be a good householder, with the exception of his mother, who was very religious and who tried to support him in his Dharma aspirations.

At twelve he got the chance to learn to read. At fourteen he made a pilgrimage to Lhasa, Samye, and many other places and returned safely.

At fifteen he received instructions on Dzogpa Chenpo and on *Tsasum*

Sangwa Nyingthig from Getse Lama Rigdzin Gyatso (?–1816).[233] The lama told him, "What you need in order to perfect your meditation on the nature of the mind is only to maintain what you have already realized." He had amazing visions and was able to foresee many events that took place later.

At sixteen he was obliged to join his elder brother on his business trips. During these travels he was overcome with a strong revulsion for the lying and cursing practiced by laypeople.

At seventeen he took his mother on a pilgrimage to Lhasa with some friends. While they were in Central Tibet, he and a friend tried to run away to practice Dharma, but friends caught them and brought them back to Kham.

At eighteen he did a hundred-day meditation retreat. At nineteen, his elder brother died. This, more than any other single event, turned his mind resolutely toward Dharma, but Lobzang Chökyong, the chieftain of the Getse tribal group, and his relatives started to put great pressure on him to get married and to take care of the family. Yet he yielded not an inch in his determination to leave the householder's life.

Since there was no way to devote himself to a life of Dharma if he stayed in Kham, he ran away to Central Tibet with a friend named Rigdzin, a Dharma meditator from the Barchung tribal group. He had managed to take a silver brick for their expenses. Traveling through Chabdo, Drikung, Gaden, Yamalung, and Samye, they reached Lhasa. Gyalwe Nyuku was not only endowed with spiritual wisdom, but was also very intelligent and practical. His friend Rigdzin was very trusting and spiritual but impractical and didn't have much ability even to collect wood for fuel in the mountains. In Lhasa a thief in monk's garb learned that they wanted to exchange the silver brick for money. One day when Gyalwe Nyuku was away, the thief came to Rigdzin and offered to change the silver brick into coins at the rate they wanted. Rigdzin handed over the silver, and the thief vanished. Thus, except for some donations that people gave them, they had nothing to live on. Instead of scolding his friend, Gyalwe Nyuku consoled him, saying, "We lost the silver because we didn't have the merits to own and use it."

After passing through Drak Yangdzong, they reached Samye. There they met the first Dodrupchen, whom Rigdzin had known in Kham. Dodrupchen advised them:

> You are young children of rich families. . . . You could meditate at Chimphu with me, as I am going there, but before doing medita-

> tion you must receive proper instructions. There is a lama who knows all without any obscuration, and also he gives teachings according to the needs of the disciples without depending on whether or not they have material offerings. He is my lama, Khyentse Rinpoche [Jigme Lingpa]. I will send you to him with a letter. By happy.

Following Dodrupchen's advice, they went to Tsering Jong and saw Jigme Lingpa. Gyalwe Nyuku writes that when he saw Jigme Lingpa, for a while all the feelings of this life dissolved and he experienced joy as if he had attained the path of insight. Then for fifteen days they received the empowerment of *Rigdzin Düpa,* the lung of *Yönten Dzö,* and detailed instructions on meditation on Dzogpa Chenpo according to the maturity of their minds (sMin Khrid).

Then they returned to Dodrupchen at Samye. After a brief pilgrimage, they went to Tsang to see the famed Gomchen Kuzhap, Rigdzin Pema She-nyen. On the way, although they didn't know how to swim, they put Rigdzin between Dodrupchen and Gyalwe Nyuku and crossed the Kyichu River. Gyalwe Nyuku thought later that they had succeeded only by the blessing of the Triple Jewel. In Tsang they received many Changter transmissions from Pema She-nyen and Chö transmissions from Drupchen Thupten Tendzin.

Then Dodrupchen was planning to leave for Lhasa alone to meet his friend and return to Kham. Gyalwe Nyuku insisted on accompanying him as far as Lhasa. On the way Dodrupchen got seriously ill, but he accepted his illness with great joy, and this greatly inspired Gyalwe Nyuku.

From Lhasa Gyalwe Nyuku went to Dorje Trak Monastery to join Pema She-nyen, who was giving transmissions of Rigdzin Chenmo. Then they returned to Tsang. After completing a retreat of two years and nine months, Gyalwe Nyuku and Rigdzin returned to Lhasa.

At Trak Yerpa, Gyalwe Nyuku met a lama with ragged, patched clothes. The mere sight of that lama aroused a strong faith in him, as if he were seeing Guru Rinpoche in person. The lama gave him clarifications on his meditation and prophesied that in the early part of his life Gyalwe Nyuku would not stay at one place but that in the latter part of his life he would have no wish to leave a valley that faces southeast, and there he would accomplish the goals for himself and others.

Gyalwe Nyuku went to Tsering Jong and received many transmissions and instructions from Jigme Lingpa. According to the advice of Jigme Lingpa, after receiving the *Yumka* empowerment he undertook the difficult journey to the sacred mountain of Tsāri. On the way he meditated at many sacred places for a week or more. As he had given his shoes to a beggar long before, when he got close to Tsāri he had to walk barefoot, even in snow. His feet became hard and deformed, so that when some children saw his footprints on the path they turned back, fearing that they were the footprints of a monster. In such circumstances of hardship, he went to circumambulate Tsāri Mountain, which takes many days. At one place, sacrificing his own safety, he saved the lives of some people who were being buried under snow in the course of their circumambulation. Instead of much pain or sorrow, he continuously experienced all appearances as the Sambhogakāya, the Buddha bodies of light and rays, which appear naturally without dualistic concepts.

For nine months he meditated in total seclusion in Tsāri. At the beginning he ate a little tsampa three times a day with a soup made from the bark of a tree. After some time, he ate tsampa once a day. Then all the tsampa was exhausted, and he boiled the old *tormas,* or dried offering cakes, that he had offered earlier and drank the soup of it once a day. When that also was exhausted, there was nothing to eat. After some time, he was able to see sunlight even through the joints of his bones. He boiled some nettles and drank the liquid, but it injured his throat. Then he found an old hip bone of a lamb. He boiled it and drank the soup, which brought some calm to his system.

After completing his nine-month retreat, he was ready to leave. Relying on the support of a walking stick by grasping it with both hands, he started to leave the cave. At every step he felt that he was about to lose consciousness and fall down. He couldn't straighten his body, as he felt that his intestines were stuck to his spine. His neck was very long, and the joints of his neck and spine were easy to count. Drinking a cup of water would help him to walk a few more steps, but then the water caused him great trouble when he urinated. After walking this way for four days, he finally met some people who gave him food, and slowly he started to regain his health without any complications.

After traveling for many days, he reached Jigme Lingpa and received a brief blessing. Then he went to the hermitage of Ogyen Ling for a six-month retreat, during which he had many experiences and visions. One day he went out into the sunlight. He looked at the sky in the direction of his teacher, and a strong remembrance of his root master, Jigme Lingpa, and other teachers arose in his mind. He prayed to them with strong devotion. He experienced a revulsion toward saṃsāra stronger than he had ever felt before. For many sessions of practice he kept crying. Then, thinking this experience might be an obstruction, he contemplated the ultimate nature. For a while it was as if he had become unconscious. When he awakened, he found that there was nothing to view or meditate upon, as all the apprehensions of doing meditation had dissolved. Before he had had a subtle point of reference for his view and meditation, but now everything was gone.[234]

Then Gyalwe Nyuku got a message from Dodrupchen to come to meet him at Tsering Jong, where he had just returned. Gyalwe Nyuku rushed to Tsering Jong and saw both Jigme Lingpa and Dodrupchen. He offered a detailed account of his meditative experience, in which he felt that there was no meditator who apprehended any meditation. Jigme Lingpa was pleased and he said:

> That is right! Realization [of the ultimate nature] has to come through one of the four different ways. Some devotional, diligent, compassionate, and wise meditators realize it when they receive the "bestowal of wisdom" in an empowerment. Some realize it when they receive the "attainment of accomplishments," when they have perfected the meditation and recitation of a sādhana of the yidam. Some realize it by transferring the realization of the lama to themselves by developing a strong faith in the lama, by seeing the lama as the actual Buddha. Some realize it when they successfully pacify the shaking-up disturbances that arise owing to the influence of negative forces in sacred or haunted places such as cemeteries. Now you have realized the ultimate nature through both the blessing of the lama and the accomplishment of the yidam. So from now on, as Lord Tampa [Sangye] Rinpoche says:
>
> > When I am sleeping alone hidden,
> > I remain in the naked intrinsic awareness.
> > When I am in the midst of many people,
> > I look at [the face of] whatever arises.[235]
>
> Let nirvāṇa be attained in the primordial state, without entrapping the realized intrinsic awareness, which is [the union of] openness and clarity arisen from its primordial state, in the nets of elaborations of characteristics.

At that time, Jigme Lingpa was experiencing an eye problem, and Gyalwe Nyuku was sent to get a doctor. The doctor performed a successful operation on Jigme Lingpa's eyes.

At Dodrupchen's insistence, Gyalwe Nyuku agreed to return to Kham with him. Gyalwe Nyuku's mother was sick but expressed happiness about Gyalwe Nyuku's dedication to Dharma. She said, "If you can succeed in your Dharma practice, there is no need to worry about me." After getting permission from Dodrupchen, Gyalwe Nyuku did a recitation retreat at Barchung Latrang. That was in 1793.

Gyalwe Nyuku next went to Dodrupchen's camp at Mamö Do in Dzachukha, but Dodrupchen had gone to the Dege Palace. He did a hundred days' retreat in a cave near the camp and had many spiritual experiences and visions. After the retreat, when he saw Dodrupchen, who had returned from the Dege Palace, Dodrupchen said, "In a dream I saw myself on a high mountain leading along a small herd, and then I saw you down below, bringing up numerous animals. So you will benefit a greater number of beings than I will."

For a while, Gyalwe Nyuku served Dodrupchen, who was teaching around Dzachukha. Then Dodrupchen left for Amdo and Mongolia in order to go to Wu Tai Shan, and sent Gyalwe Nyuku and Dodrupchen's nephew, Jigme Changchup, to Dzogchen Monastery.

Gyalwe Nyuku did retreat in Tsering Phuk, near Dzogchen Monastery, where Dodrupchen had once done his own retreat. Soon after the retreat, he traveled to Central Tibet to see Jigme Lingpa once more.

At Tsering Jong, he experienced the great joy of seeing once more the omniscient Jigme Lingpa, who now no longer had any eye problems. He also met Gyalse, the young son of Jigme Lingpa. He received profound teachings for two and a half months. Jigme Lingpa told him, "Before, I wasn't aware that you were so intelligent. . . . If you stay with me for three years, I will make you a special person." Gyalwe Nyuku explained frankly that he had to go back home because of obligations to his friends. Jigme Lingpa replied:

> That is fine. Trustworthiness is the quality of a supreme friend. In fact, for practicing true Dharma, there is no need to know many things. Information does not necessarily benefit the mind. A good attitude benefits the mind. Nevertheless, you have sufficient wisdom in learning, analyzing, and meditation to be independent. There is no need to depend on monastic structures. You must try

> to meditate in caves or huts, where no negative circumstances will arise. If people come to you for teachings, instruct them with confidence. As your attitude is as excellent as pure gold, you will be helpful to others.

Then Gyalwe Nyuku returned to Kham. He did many years' retreat around Dzogchen and a three-year retreat at Getse in Dzachukha.

In 1799, he went to Shukchen Tago to help Dodrupchen build his new gompa. With Dodrupchen he went to King Tsewang Lhündrup (?–1825) of Tsakho at Phüntsok Palace, to the king of Choktse, and to many places in Dzika Valley to help Dodrupchen with his teaching and raising funds for building the gompa.

Later Gyalwe Nyuku visited Phüntsok Palace by himself. The king asked him to stay as the head of either Chupho Gompa or Namgyal Teng Gompa, but he refused.

Gyalwe Nyuku wanted to go to Nakshö Sinmo Dzong to stay, but at the insistence of Dodrupchen he promised not to go anyplace farther than five or six days' journey.

At Lhalung Khuk he attended the enthronement of Do Khyentse and saw Dodrupchen. Inspired by Gyalwe Nyuku, the queen-regent of Dege wished him to remain at Dege Palace, but thanks to Dodrupchen's skillful intervention he was able to avoid this obligation.

In 1804, at the age of forty, Gyalwe Nyuku settled at Trama Lung, the Valley of Dry Twigs, in Dzachukha. After some time, he received a message from Dodrupchen that the queen-regent of Dege wanted him to come to the Dege palace. He wrote to Dodrupchen for help, Dodrupchen obtained release from her order for him. As a subject of the queen-regent, Gyalwe Nyuku had to be diplomatic.

At Trama Lung, with a few hermits Gyalwe Nyuku lived meditating and teaching for over twenty years,[236] and he became known as Dza Trama Lama, after the name of the place. During that time, he didn't go into total seclusion as many retreatants usually do, but taught and gave empowerments at Trama Lung and nearby places to meditators, monks, and the lay population.

In 1812 he had many experiences, such as turning the whole of phenomena into a ball of blue light and then merging it into himself, upon which his body melted into a phenomenon that appeared but was not apprehensible, and then came back together again as his body. He received empowerments from Kathok Getse Mahāpaṇḍita, who visited his hermitage.

In 1814 at Norbu Ri Gompa he gave teachings to Do Khyentse, the reincarnation of his teacher, and many others. Do Khyentse vowed to recite the Avalokiteshvara mantra one hundred million times.

In 1815 Do Khyentse was passing through Dzachukha on his second and last visit to Central Tibet, and Gyalwe Nyuku went to see him off. Afterward he went to Gyarong Monastery to receive a long-life empowerment from the master Namkha Tsewang Chokdrup (1744–?). He was also visited by Jigme Kalzang, the regent of Dodrupchen, and received empowerments from him. Around this time, one of his two main teachers in Kham, Getse Lama Rigdzin Gyatso, died.

In 1816 Gyalwe Nyuku went to welcome Do Khyentse, who was returning from his visit to Central Tibet. He saw both Do Khyentse and Dzogchen Rinpoche and received empowerments from them.

In 1817/18, after receiving a message from Dodrupchen to come to see him, he went with about ten monks to Yarlung Pemakö in Ser Valley. The Dharma father and son (or brothers) had a joyful reunion. Gyalwe Nyuku and his companions received all the teachings and empowerments they wished. Responding to Gyalwe Nyuku's request, Dodrupchen gave a prophecy with a detailed description of a place where Gyalwe Nyuku should have his main residence. It said:

> In the West of the five-peaked Dagyal [Dzagya] Lhünpo, a solitary site,
> There is a place like a flower blooming.
> The mountain behind is like a great meditator in contemplation.
> The mountain in front is like a vessel being held up.
> The mountain at the right is like [a roll of] cloth unfurled in the sky. . . .
> Falling water sings vowels and consonants.
> The land is colorful with vegetation and flowers.
> Arrange to live in that excellent place.

As soon as Gyalwe Nyuku returned to Dzachukha, he moved to Gyagö Photrang, the place endowed with the characteristics prophesied by Dodrupchen. There he stayed for over ten years.

One night, Gyalwe Nyuku had a dream of peaceful and wrathful deities in the sky, and a ḍākinī was telling him that this was the time for him to leave. Then four beautifully ornamented ḍākinīs of four different colors lifted him and the first ḍākinī into the sky on an unfurled roll of silk. But at that moment he saw Dodrupchen coming down from the sky, telling the ḍākinīs to take him back, as this was not his time to leave, so they brought him back. Then the Buddhas dissolved into him, and he woke up from his sleep. Even when awake during the daytime, he kept having various experiences. For example, he saw all appearances turning into peaceful and wrathful deities; they merged into him; his body burst into a phenomenon that appeared but was not apprehensible; or sometimes everything became total emptiness.

One night, in a dream he was led by a ḍākinī into an amazing palace. In it he sat between Jigme Lingpa and Dodrupchen. He was so happy that he requested them to let him stay, but they said, "No, you are only a visitor. This is not your time to come. Without being discouraged by the people of the dark age, maintain your two bodhichitta vows. Fill your life with the wheel of Dharma activities. There is no separation between us and you."

In 1820, at Dzogchen Monastery, he received many empowerments from the fourth Dzogchen Rinpoche. He also gave teachings to Dzogchen Rinpoche and others.

On the seventeenth of the eighth month of the Iron Snake year (1821), Do Khyentse, who was visiting another part of Dzachukha, told his followers that he had received a prophecy that he would be leaving his body on the twenty-fifth of the same month. Only one person, who belonged to the Lotus family and was named Pema, could avert it. Do Khyentse said that that person was Gyalwe Nyuku. As soon as Gyalwe Nyuku heard these words, he traveled all night to get to Do Khyentse, who was in good health. With about fifty monks, he started to arrange a ceremony. On the twenty-fourth, Do Khyenste suddenly got sick. All night Gyalwe Nyuku performed the Sündok ceremony of *Yumka Dechen Gyalmo*. Do Khyentse was dying and people were crying. With strongest devotion, deepest meditation, and boldest prayers Gyalwe Nyuku did the best that he could, and finally signs of the clearing of obstructions appeared in the ceremonial rites, and instantly Do Khyentse showed signs of reviving.

In 1821 Gyalwe Nyuku attended the funeral ceremony of the third Pönlop (1806–1821?) at Dzogchen and dispelled the life obstructions of the fourth Dzogchen Rinpoche and gave him teachings.

In 1830 he moved his residence from Gyagö Photrang to Dzagyal Dünlung. Gyagö Photrang was a very beneficial place for him, an auspicious place where he and his disciples achieved great meditative accomplishments, but now, because of a change in climate, the ground had become wet and it was unhealthy to live there any longer.

In 1833 Gyalse Zhenphen Thaye came to receive more teachings from him. In 1834 Gyalwe Nyuku gave the transmissions of *Longchen Nyingthig* to the second Dodrupchen (1824–1863/64) and empowered him as the supreme vajracharya.

He ends his autobiography at the age of seventy-four (1838).

At the age of seventy-nine, on the twenty-fifth day of the first of the month of the Water Hare year (1843), he passed away. The fourth Dzogchen Rinpoche, in a pure vision, received Gyalwe Nyuku's testament.[237] His physical remains were preserved at Dzagya Monastery in Dzachukha.

As advised by Jigme Lingpa, Gyalwe Nyuku devoted the entire latter part of his life to teaching whoever came to listen to him, giving empowerments or meditation instructions to all who were devout and sincere in meditation. For example, Paltrül Rinpoche received teachings on the Ngöndro of *Longchen Nyingthig* twenty-five times from him. Paltrül Rinpoche wrote down Gyalwe Nyuku's teachings on the Ngöndro as the *Künzang La-me Zhalung*.[238]

His tülku was Künzang Dechen Dorje, who was recognized by the fourth Dzogchen Rinpoche.

14

Dola Jigme Kalzang

NINETEENTH CENTURY

Dola Jigme Kalzang[239] was a great meditator, scholar, and bodhisattva. He propagated the Longchen Nyingthig tradition in Kham and Amdo. He was also known as Chökyi Lodrö and Zhönu Yeshe Dorje.

Once, in a cave by the Ma (Yellow) River, he started a three-year retreat in strict seclusion to practice Vajrakīla sādhana. The very first night of his retreat a pilgrim took shelter at the door of Jigme Kalzang's cave. Playing a hand drum and a bell, the pilgrim chanted *Khandrö Kegyang,* a Chö liturgy. Jigme Kalzang heard the chant in the cave and was so moved by its deep meaning and beautiful composition that he could not resist coming out of seclusion in the morning to meet the pilgrim. He inquired who wrote the Chö liturgy and learned that it had been discovered by Jigme Lingpa as a ter but that he was no longer alive. Jigme Kalzang inquired whether any of Jigme Lingpa's major disciples were still living. The pilgrim replied that his greatest disciple, Dodrupchen Rinpoche, was living and teaching in Golok. Just by hearing Dodrupchen's name, Jigme Thrinle Özer, because it was the name of his karmic guru, Jigme Kalzang acquired unmodified devotion and left at once to meet him.

From Dodrupchen he received teachings in general and particularly the *Longchen Nyingthig* transmission. He became one of the main lineage holders of Longchen Nyingthig.

Jigme Kalzang recognized Paltrül Rinpoche as the tülku of Palge Lama of Dzogchen Monastery, and later the first Dodrupchen confirmed it. During the last years of Dodrupchen's life, he gave transmissions of empowerments and instructions, and Jigme Kalzang gave the recitation of scriptures (Lung) on behalf of Dodrupchen. Also, as Dodrupchen did not leave his hermitage, Jigme Kalzang was the lama who went on his behalf to propagate the *Longchen Nyingthig* and many other Nyingma transmissions of the Dodrupchen lineage in Dege and Amdo.

Jigme Kalzang transmitted Nyingma tantras and Nyingthig teachings to many important lamas of Kathok, Dzogchen, and Zhechen monasteries, and in the latter part of his life he propagated the teachings in Amdo and among the Mongolians in the Blue Lake region.

Jigme Gyalwe Nyuku writes that in 1815/16, "the Lord Lama Jigme Kalzang, the ultimate regent of the lord father Dodrupchen and the master of learning and attainment, arrived at Dzachukha to serve the Dharma. I invited him to my hermitage and received empowerments."[240] Again, he writes that in 1820, "with many offerings I went to welcome Jigme Kalzang, the master of learning and attainments, as he had arrived [in Dzachukha] from his visit to China."[241]

At the end of his life, when he was walking alone on a street in a town in China, he saw a thief about to be executed by being burned upon a copper horse that was heated by fire from within. The thief was screaming for help. Feeling great compassion, Dola Jigme Kalzang told the authorities that the prisoner was not guilty and that he himself was the actual thief. When his disciples found him, it was too late. He underwent the execution in the thief's place. Thus he ended his life displaying the real practice of a bodhisattva by giving his life to ransom the life of an unknown suffering person in an unknown street.

Among his incarnations were Yukhok Chatralwa Chöying Rangtröl in Ser Valley and Kalzang Dorje of Sanglung Monastery of Dzika Valley.

15

Fourth Dzogchen Mingyur Namkhe Dorje
1793–?

The Fourth Dzogchen Rinpoche, Mingyur Namkhe Dorje[242] (Jigme Khyentse Wangchuk), was one of the most amazing and eccentric adepts, one who possessed clairvoyance and had no discrimination between good and bad.

He was born in 1793 in the Dan Valley. His father was Sönam Rapten, a chieftain of Rakho, and his mother was Namkhadzin Wangmo. In prophetic verses Jigme Lingpa pinpointed where the fourth Dzogchen Rinpoche would be found, and also the third Dzogchen Rinpoche himself indicated where he would be born. From infancy, while beating a drum he kept saying the Guru Rinpoche mantra and repeating the word *Dzogchen.*

At the age of seven, he demonstrated his recollections of his past life before many great lamas, and amid great joy he was ceremoniously brought to and enthroned at Dzogchen Monastery by the monks of Dzogchen Monastery and the Dege Palace. Namkha Tsewang Choktrup of Gyarong Monastery performed the ceremonial cutting of his hair and gave him the name Jigme Khyentse Wangchuk. He received many transmissions from the third Nyima Trakpa Mingyur Phende. In particular he received *Khandro Nyingthig, Sangwa Nyingthig,* and *Dorsem Nyingthig* transmissions from Namkha Tsewang Choktrup, and he accomplished various trainings.

From the age of twelve, every year for seven years, he remained in strict retreat for at least six months. He received teachings and transmissions from Namkha Tsewang Choktrup, the first Dodrupchen, Cheyö Rigdzin Chenmo, the third Zhechen Rabjam, the first Zhechen Gyaltsap, Khenchen Rigdzin Zangpo, Gyalwe Nyuku, Jigme Ngotsar, and Gyalse Zhenphen Thaye.

At the age of twenty, Dzogchen Rinpoche went to see Dodrupchen again at Yarlung Pemakö. With Do Khyentse, Dzogchen Pönlop, and about sixty others, he received many transmissions, including *Nyingthig Yabzhi, Gyü Chudun, Damchö Dechen Lamchok,* and *Nyen-gyü Dorje Zampa.*

One day Dodrupchen gave a skull cup full of chang (beer) to Dzogchen Rinpoche. Being a monk, he had never tasted alcohol before, but he took it because it was a blessing from the lama. By drinking it, the realization of Dodrupchen was spontaneously transferred into Dzogchen Rinpoche, and he attained the state of Chönyi Zepa, the dissolution of the perceptions of relative phenomena into the absolute nature. Thereafter Dzogchen Rinpoche became the most renowned adept, who knew everything and made no discrimination. He had no hope for good or fear of evil. There was a popular saying: "The impact of other peoples' alcohol wears off, but the impact of Dodrupchen's alcohol never does."

At the beginning, the authorities of Dzogchen Monastery were upset with Dodrupchen for transforming Dzogchen Rinpoche into a person who had lost all diplomatic and administrative skills, which were thought to be important qualities for presiding over a great monastery with many branches. But later, realizing the greatness of Dzogchen Rinpoche's spiritual wisdom and power, they all became most grateful.

At the age of twenty-two, he went to Central Tibet on a pilgrimage. He met the ninth Dalai Lama, who was a distant cousin of his. He went to all the important sacred places and made offerings and did meditation. He received teachings and transmissions from Longchen Rölpatsal, Terchen Dawe Özer, Khardo Chökyi Dorje, Chakla Thukse of Dorje Trak, Trichen Pema Wangyal of Mindroling, and Chakzam Choktul. He was given full monastic ordination by Temo Regent Lobzang Thupten Gyaltsen.

He gave teachings and transmissions all the time to anyone who came to request them. Sometimes he would explain the most difficult texts very clearly in detail. But at other times he would teach even easy texts in a way that had nothing to do with the real meaning. Sometimes during ceremonies, after he began playing the hand drum, someone would have to hold his hands and take the hand drum away, or else he wouldn't stop, as he was beyond ordinary discrimination.

One day he was invited to a grand ceremony in another valley. He was sitting on a high throne, and the best kinds of food were being served. He suddenly said, "I am not going to eat." His attendant pleaded with him, saying, "Please eat something, otherwise our hosts will feel bad." After eating the meal, he said, "Now I am going to die." People were shocked and asked, "Why?" He said, "The food was poisoned. I didn't want to eat, but you asked me to. Now I have to die." People requested him to do something to avoid this, for he had the power. Then he said, "Shall I expel it?" People begged, "Yes, please!" Then on the throne itself he expelled it, and he survived without even getting sick.

For many years he went to the Dege Palace every third year to teach and preside over an important ceremony. Then at the age of fifty (in 1842), when he was leaving the monastery for Dege, his foot slipped on the threshold and he uttered a typical local expression of irritation: "May I never set my foot on you again." And then he added, "Oh, yes, I won't have to anyway!" Then in Dege, the night before the beginning of the seven-day ceremony, he kept talking in his sleep, but people only caught one phrase, "Gönla [the performer of the dharmapāla ceremony] flew away." Then next day he said, "I have to go back. Dege was benefitted by my presence and Dzogchen Monastery needs me." He wouldn't say anything more, and his attendants requested him to stay, as this was an important ceremony for the Dege Palace and the kingdom. Then after a few days they got the news that Dzogchen Monastery had been almost totally destroyed by an earthquake in which many died. Gönla, about whom he had been talking, was thrown some distance and survived with a broken leg.

Then with the generous support of Dege and other patrons, and especially under the guidance of Gyalse Zhenphen Thaye and other lamas, he rebuilt the monastery, making it even grander than before.

Then under the guidance of Dzogchen Rinpoche and the personal supervision of Zhenphen Thaye, Shrīsiṃha, a monastic scripture college, was established. It later became the model institution for studies and training in the Nyingma world.

When the wicked chieftain of Nyak-rong, Gönpo Namgyal (?–1865), captured Dzogchen Monastery, Pönlop instructed Dzogchen Rinpoche to say how great the chieftain was, how poor Dzogchen Monastery was, and so on. When the chieftain came to Dzogchen Rinpoche, he repeated everything as he had been taught. Then he added, "That is what Pönlop taught me to tell you," and then he gave all the true details of Dzogchen Monastery. The chieftain asked, "Where will I take rebirth?" He said, "In hell." Instead of being offended or confiscating the property of the monastery, the chieftain left with an offering of a silver brick to Dzogchen Rinpoche with the request, "Please take care of me when I die."

However, when it was not proper to reveal things, he was able to hide them. One morning he said, "Last night someone stole the golden top of the banner in the assembly hall." People rushed to check and found that it was true. They requested him to tell who had done it. He said, "I know him. While the thief was climbing down with the golden top, he almost fell down, and he prayed to me saying, 'O Mingyur Namkhye Dorje.' I saved him. However, I am not going to tell you, for if I tell, you will punish him."

I have not found in any sources information about when or how he died.

16

Do Khyentse Yeshe Dorje
1800–1866

Do Khyentse Yeshe Dorje[243] was the mind incarnation of Jigme Lingpa. He demonstrated the power of his enlightened mind in the form of amazing miracles, and in this respect he was the greatest master of the Tibetan tantric Buddhist tradition during the last many centuries.

He was conceived by a nonhuman father, born with miraculous signs, started speaking and showing power in his infancy, receiving blessings and teachings from Buddhas and masters in pure visions, discovering many hidden objects and teachings as ter, awakening realization in many disciples, propagating esoteric Dharma tirelessly, and guiding many human and nonhuman beings into Dharma. He was protected and supervised by nonhuman presences, vanished with his body for days to visit pure lands, traveled with his mind for days to pure lands, brought many dead or killed beings back to life, and left imprints of his body on numerous rocks as if on mud.

Do (mDo) Khyentse was also known as Yeshe Dorje, Rigdzin Jalü Dorje, and Trakthung Lekyi Pawo. He was born in and belonged to a Golok clan, but he lived most of the latter part of his life around Tartsedo (Dar rTse mDo, now known as Kanding), so he became known as Khyentse of Do (mDo). *Khyentse,* meaning "the One with Omniscience and Compassion," was one of the names of Jigme Lingpa, Do Khyentse's previous incarnation.

While his parents were in Lhasa on pilgrimage, at the Machik Pal-lha shrine two women led his mother through a wall, which she perceived as a door, and she entered a rich and beautiful palace. After experiencing an intimacy with the youthful noble person of the palace, she was brought back by the same women and found herself at the same shrine. Her husband and others had been searching for her for three days. That young man was Nyenchen Thanglha (the divine presence at Thanglha mountain range of Tibet), one of the most important land protectors of Tibet.

Soon, Do Khyentse's mother became a medium, and ceaseless phenomena of lights, visions, voices, and messages were witnessed by all members of the family. Do Khyentse's parents and friends were happy but frightened and confused. They hoped for the blessing of a Buddha manifestation and feared being haunted by a harmful demonic force.

Do Khyentse was born on the fifteenth day of the tenth month of the Iron Monkey year of the thirteenth Rabjung (1800) at Kongser Khado in the Ma Valley, a vast and beautiful field where the Machu (Hwang, or Yellow) River flows by. His adoptive father was Sönam Phen of the Chökor tribal group of the Golok Akyong clan, and his mother was Tsewang Men of the Dawa clan.

Immediately after his birth, which took place in the early morning of a full-moon day, Do Khyentse sat in the meditative posture and, touching the sunbeams entering the tent, he chanted the Sanskrit alphabet.

Three days after his birth, he vanished from the lap of his mother, but on the third day he reappeared sitting on her pillow. During that period, as he wrote later, a red woman took him to a pure land. In a crystal-like palace, many lamas and ḍākinīs purified him by washing him with pure water from a crystal vase. They gave him blessings and prophecies. Thereafter, he always kept seeing around himself beams of light and circles of light with images of Buddhas in them. He always felt that there were a couple of children with him to play with.

One day, standing up with the support of the hands of the invisible children, he looked through the sky and saw Zangdok Palri, the pure land of Guru Rinpoche. In the pure land Guru Rinpoche and the assembly of knowledge-holders and ḍākinīs were enjoying a feast offering (Tshogs) ceremony. Seeing this, his mind was filled with devotion and his eyes were filled with tears. At that moment his mother saw him and exclaimed loudly, "Baby is standing!" That sound woke him up from his experience, and he fell to the ground. After that he became a little bit more like a normal baby.

Whenever his nomadic parents moved around to different campsites, he would see amazing forms of beings who saw him off with sadness and others who welcomed him to their new places with great joy and gaiety. He was always guarded by dharmapālas, who cleaned, fed, and blessed him.

One day he saw a tantric yogī who said he was Nyang Nyima Özer (1124–1192) and who told him to search for Lama Sönam Chōden, who was Sangye Lingpa (1340–1396) returned to the human world. After that, he started to demand that his parents take him to Lama Sönam Chöden, saying that otherwise he would die. But no one knew who the lama was.

The first Dodrupchen was visiting a place nearby, and Do Khyentse's father told him stories about his son and asked him, "Do you know who Lama Sönam Chöden is?" Dodrupchen stared into the sky for a while and then, folding his hands at his heart in the gesture of devotion, said, "Yes, I know him well. He is a Dharma friend of mine. Anyhow, I will be coming to see your son."

On his arrival, Dodrupchen asked the baby, "Do you know me?" Do Khyentse, a little over a year old, said, "Yes, you are Sönam Chöden. I know you. Have you deserted me?" Dodrupchen picked up the baby in his arms and with tears said, "Yes, you are right. I can understand why you feel that way. But until now I couldn't find you. Now I will take care of you." Do Khyentse later wrote that he saw Dodrupchen in the form of Guru Rinpoche. Dodrupchen said the necessary prayers and gave blessings to the child, and told the parents, "Sönam Chöden was my name, but with the exception of one lama no one knew it. Now you all should come to my place; otherwise your son might not survive."

According to Jigme Lingpa's autobiography,[244] at the time of Dodrupchen's departure from Jigme Lingpa, Dodrupchen asked him to take rebirth in his region so they could be together. So there was an obligation to be fulfilled by Dodrupchen; besides, Do Khyentse was his teacher's rebirth.

So Do Khyentse's parents, against the arguments of their irreligious relatives, took him to the Shukchen Tago Gompa of Dodrupchen. Do Khyentse kept seeing Dodrupchen in various forms in the midst of different kinds of beings and mysteries, and he only realized later that these were not normal perceptions. Later, Do Khyentse, his sister, and their parents followed Dodrupchen when he traveled to Dzogchen Monastery and Dege Palace.

His sister, Ḍākinī Losal Dölma (1802–1861), was a Tārā in human form, a great master and adept. From childhood till her death, she dedicated her life to Do Khyentse as his close disciple, friend, and guide.

While he was staying near Dzogchen Monastery, a friend told him, "That is the way to go to Lhasa." That phrase awakened in him a feeling of great sadness, and then the memories of Tsering Jong and Chimphu flashed into his mind. During the night, he dreamed of the protector of Samye Chimphu, a white man riding a white horse, who requested him to return to Central Tibet to be at his hermitage with his wife, son, and disciples.

From Dodrupchen, along with the third Zhechen Rabjam, the first Kathok Situ, and about a hundred people, he received the textual transmissions and empowerments of the *Nyingthig Yabzhi, Dzödün, Longchen Nyingthig,* and Jigme Lingpa's writings.

Although Dodrupchen had recognized him as the reincarnation of Jigme Lingpa, this was kept secret, for it was proper to have the official approval from Central Tibet, from the seat and family of Jigme Lingpa.

Then the confirmation of Do Khyentse's recognition as the tülku of Jigme Lingpa by Sakya Kongma Wangdüd Nyingpo and the Drikung tülkus arrived with people who came to take him to Drikung. Sakya Kongma was a disciple of Jigme Lingpa, and the two heads of Drikung were the sons of Jigme Lingpa and his chief disciple, Kong-nyön. Then, in the presence of Dodrupchen, the queen regent, and the crown prince of Dege, with the representatives of Kathok, Dzogchen, Zhechen, and Drikung, Do Khyentse passed his formal tests by recognizing religious objects that had belonged to Jigme Lingpa. Everyone was filled with joy and devotion. Then in Lhalung Khuk in Dege, an elaborate enthronement ceremony was performed under the patronage of the Dege Palace and the monasteries.

The Dege Palace made all the necessary arrangements for his long trip to Central Tibet. At the time of departure, Do Khyentse was so sad to leave Dodrupchen that it seemed as if his heart were splitting, and he kept clutching Dodrupchen with both his tiny hands. Jigme Changchup, a nephew of Dodrupchen, had to take him away by force.

Do Khyentse and his parents and sister arrived with a big party at Yang-ri Gar in Drikung after a journey of many months. He was received by the two heads of the Drikung lineage, Zhaptrung Tendzin Pema Gyaltsen (1770–1826), a son of Kong-nyön, and Gyalse Nyinche Özer (or Chökyi Gyaltsen, 1793–?), the son of Jigme Lingpa. There he was enthroned in an elaborate ceremony. Then he made Photrang Dzongsar of Drikung his main residence. Gyalyum Drolkar and Özer Thaye, the consort and nephew of Jigme Lingpa, came to see him from Tsering Jong. After some time, his parents and sister left for Golok.

While he was learning to read books, he was able to memorize a page a day, which is good. But he was able to repeat all the oral teachings given by a scholar, which is exceptional. The scholar said, "Do Khyentse will become a person who is learned in the meaning rather than in the words." First Changchup, a nephew of Dodrupchen, stayed as his tutor, and then Dodrupchen sent one Nyima Gyaltsen to relieve Changchup.

He received many transmissions from Zhaptrung, Gyalse, and Gyaltsap of Tsurphu and experienced many visions.

In 1810, passing through Samye, Chimphu, Densathil, Zang-ri Kharmar, and Yarlung, he visited Tsering Jong, and he returned to Drikung Dzongsar through Palri, Sheltrak, and Yama Lung. "In the cave of Sheltrak," he wrote, "from the heart of Guru Rinpoche's 'Like Me' image, a beam of light came and touched my heart. I felt the experience of remaining for a while in the primordially pure intrinsic awareness, free from expressions. But at that time I wasn't aware of what it actually was." At Yamalung he saw Longchen Rölpatsal, one of the chief disciples of Jigme Lingpa and received long-life empowerment.

In 1811, his father and others returned from Golok with a message from Dodrupchen asking Do Khyentse to visit him. Do Khyentse went to Lhasa and received permission from the government to return to Kham. He was given the hat and dress of a khenpo and was recognized as such by Temo Thupten Jigme (d. 1819), the new regent of Tibet.

In 1812, he had a reunion with his mother and sister on the way to Yarlung Pemakö, to which he then returned.

In 1813, with the fourth Dzogchen Rinpoche, the third Pönlop, and about sixty disciples, he received *Nyingthig Yabzhi, Gyü Chudün, Damchö Dechen Lamchok,* and many other transmissions from Dodrupchen. With Shichen Lama Ogyen Norbu, Repa Tamtsik Dorje, and others he received *Gewa Sumkyi Donkhri, Machik Nyen-gyü,* and other teachings. With Changlung Palchen Namkha Jigme (aka Trupwang) of Rekong he received *Münpe Naljor Yangti Nagpo Serkyi Druchik, Dzogchen Ati Zabdön,* and other transmissions from Dodrupchen.

In 1814, he visited the Dege Palace and conferred the empowerment of *Longchen Nyingthig*. In Dzachukha he met Gyalwe Nyuku and Gilung Lama Jigme Ngotsar, both of whom were chief disciples of Jigme Lingpa. On his return to Yarlung, he received teachings on *Yönten Dzö, Takpö Thargyen,* and *Yeshe Lama* from Dodrupchen.

In 1815, at the age of sixteen, he was sent by Dodrupchen with about a hundred people to Central Tibet to take offerings to the lamas and monasteries. Instructing him to return in a year, Dodrupchen gave him five major goals to fulfill on this trip: (1) to receive empowerments of Hayagrīva and Long Life from Ra-nyak Gyalse, (2) to make one hundred thousand maṇḍala offerings at Samye, (3) to do a seven-day retreat at Chimphu on the prayer of Guru Rinpoche, (4) to eliminate the stirring up of obstructions at Kordzö Ling at Samye at all costs, and (5) to establish a spiritual relationship with the sacred place of Chakpori.

On the way, Do Khyentse went to see Ra-nyak Gyalse, who was displaying wild behavior. Do Khyentse was then a novice and at first could not appreciate what he was seeing, but as it had been his teacher's instruction to go to Ra-nyak Gyalse, Do Khyentse asked him for an empowerment of Hayagrīva. Instead, Gyalse pointed a gun at his heart and shot at him. The bullet didn't hurt him but turned into a Hayagrīva image. When Do Khyentse asked for a Long-Life empowerment, he was given some ashes from Gyalse's pipe mixed with spit in a cup, which instantly turned into pure nectar.

On their way to Lhasa, one day Do Khyentse took Riktsal and Özer to a notorious nomad camp in the Gegye area to buy meat. A white and a black dog got loose and attacked them, and Do Khyentse cut them in two with his sword. When nomads arrived to fight them for killing their dogs, Do Khyentse placed the upper body of the white dog with the lower body of the black dog, and the upper body of the black dog with lower body of the white dog, and the two animals got up and ran away. The astonished nomads immediately apologized and promised to adhere to proper conduct. After the dogs died, in memory of this miracle their skins were kept at a monastery called Gegye Dzogchen.

At Drikung, Do Khyentse was joyfully reunited with Zhaptrung and Gyalse and received empowerments from them. At Lhasa, Regent Temo was very helpful, and Do Khyentse received transmissions from Longchen Rölpatsal again. He went on pilgrimage to many sacred places and made offerings.

At Samye, in front of the Jowo, he accumulated one hundred thousand maṇḍala offerings. In Parkhang Yuzhal Barwa in the main temple of Samye he prayed one-pointedly for one week on retreat. One night, a frightening yogī suddenly came dancing in and gave him prophecies. Another night, a woman took him upstairs and he saw four Vairochana images sitting back to back. They said in harmony:

> By the mysterious play of knowing and unknowing [the reality],
> Saṃsāra and nirvāṇa are divided back to back.
> From the delusions created by discursive thoughts
> Is established the so-called world of six realms.
> In the pure manifestation of the four Buddha bodies,
> There is nothing but the pure lands of the three Buddha bodies. . . .

The four images gave him teachings, empowerments, and prophecies. He returned to his bed with great bliss in his body and extraordinary realization in his mind.

At Tragmar Keutsang cave he made one hundred tsok offerings before the "Like Me" image of the Guru. After having dream visions, he woke up and saw the image of the Guru in the form of light emanating luminous rays that filled the whole shrine. Beams of white, red, and blue light touched him. He heard the sound of many voices chanting of *The Seven-Line Prayer* in high registers, and people who had been sleeping nearby thought that Do Khyentse was singing in the middle of the night.

Then he moved to the lower Sangphuk cave of Chimphu. He intensely experienced the impermanence of life, and, finding no other solution, he concentrated on praying with one-pointed devotion to Guru Rinpoche. One night three fearful ḍākinīs appeared and said, "In the human world, you are defiled by the human womb. By grasping at the 'self' of the delusory appearances, ignorance of grasping and grasped have manifested. There is no other way but to separate you from your evil body." They cut his body into pieces and ate it all, including his consciousness; thus he fell into unconsciousness. When he regained consciousness, he saw the Vajrasattva consorts before him. By the touch of the lights from the Vajrasattva consorts, he felt that he had a body of light. Lamas and ḍākinīs gave him blessings and prophecies of his mind ter discoveries.

Then he spent seven nights at Kordzö Ling, the Dharmapala temple at Samye, to practice chö in order to eliminate the shaking up of negative emotions and concepts from the root. The next day, the oracle of

Samye, while possessed by the Dharmapāla, came and locked him in the cellar. It was totally dark. He performed a chö practice and meditated as best as he could. He saw various forms and heard sounds threatening him and calling him by name, and it was frightening. He thought, "This is what Dodrupchen, the lord of Dharma, instructed me to do. So for doing this practice, even if I lose my life, there is no fear or regret. If I have no fear of dying, then even if the whole world arises as my enemy, it won't bother me at all." Then all the stirrings-up *(Slong Tshad)* were eased. Soon, the oracle possessed by the Dharmapāla opened the door, brought him out, and paid him respect.

At Tsering Jong, he made offerings before the remains of Jigme Lingpa. He wanted to stay for a while, but it didn't work out. Then at Palri Monastery, from Tsogyal Tülku he received transmissions of *Trölthik* and other teachings.

After visiting Mindroling and Dorje Trak monasteries, he went to Chagzam Chuwo Ri and in the sacred cave made tsok offerings. In a dream he saw Thangtong Gyalpo and received blessings, which filled him with the experiences of bliss, clarity, and emptiness. There, Do Khyentse discovered a Guru Rinpoche Kutsap image as a ter, and the protector of the ter asked him not to show it to anybody until he met Dodrupchen.

He made offerings for the Mönlam prayer ceremony at Lhasa and was shown great respect and acknowledgment by the Temo regent.

As Dodrupchen was old and it was very important to receive complete teachings from him, the Drikung tülkus sadly had to agree to let Do Khyentse return to Kham for the time being. When he and his party reached the western part of Kham, they were met by a messenger from Dodrupchen telling them to come faster. Leaving the representatives of Drikung and Dege behind with the main party, Do Khyentse and ten companions rode fast without stopping, except for a day's rest at Gyalwe Nyuku's hermitage in Dzachukha.

After a few days, on the tenth day of the seventh month of the Fire Bird year (1816), Do Khyentse found himself in the presence of Dodrupchen in Yarlung Pemakö. Dodrupchen said, "I had many prophetic dreams, and also my health wasn't good. But all the obstructions to my life have been reversed for a while by the power of Döpa Khamkyi Wangchugma, except that my visions are obscured." He added, "During the winter you should go to Kathok Monastery to receive some necessary teachings from Getse Mahāpaṇḍita and also Zhingkyong Tülku. I would like to see you complete your necessary studies before I die." Do Khyentse received more clarifications and instructions on tsalung and *Guhyagarbha-tantra* teachings.

At Kathok, Do Khyentse received many empowerments, teachings, and trainings from Getse Mahāpaṇḍita. These included the elaborate empowerment of *Düpa Do* for fifteen days and other kama and terma transmissions. Getse said, "As prophesied by the previous Khyentse [Jigme Lingpa], Kathok Monastery is a lineage holder of the *Longchen Nyingthig* teachings. So in future you should serve the Dharma by combining both [the Kathok and *Longchen Nyingthig*] traditions together." Do Khyentse also received teachings from Zhingkyong and Moktsa tülkus of Kathok, and Namkha Tsewang Choktrup of Gyarong Monastery.

He received the lung of the *Nyingma Gyübum* from Jigme Ngotsar of Kilung Monastery, a disciple of Jigme Lingpa. During that transmission, in a dream he received teachings and the entrustment of the *Guhyagarbha-tantra* from Vimalamitra, and for a month he felt that he remembered all the words and meanings of the tantra.

In 1818, while he was in Dzachukha, he had an experience that a woman with a large retinue led him into a crystal palace where he saw Guru Rinpoche in union with his consort. Do Khyentse received four empowerments from the Guru's consorts, and then they merged into Do Khyentse. For a while Do Khyentse was absorbed into the ultimate nature free from expressions. When he left the crystal palace, he was met by the protectors of Ling, who also gave him blessings. Then, riding a white horse, he came back to his place and woke up. Gyalwe Nyuku and Lobzang Norbu, who were anxiously waiting, said, "You went to sleep and didn't wake up for three days. Dzogchen Rinpoche came to say prayers, and he said, 'There is no problem.' " Intervening, Gyalwe Nyuku said, "Whatever visions you had, please do not tell anybody, including Dzogchen Rinpoche, until the time comes. If you don't keep the visions secret, there could be many obstructions. If you keep them secret, attainments will come swiftly." Although Do Khyentse didn't tell anything, Gyalwe Nyuku knew through his clairvoyance what the visions had been. Do Khyentse discovered the *Cycles on Pema Gyalpo* as ter.

Do Khyentse spent more time at the palace of Tsewang Dorje Rigdzin, the king of Dege, than was necessary, because his attendants preferred being there than at Dodrupchen's monastic hermitage, owing to the prosperity, nobility, and power. One day Do Khyentse instructed his sister and an attendant, "There is an old beggar woman in that valley;

give her this tsampa, meat, and chang for me." When they got there, the old woman angrily threw away the tsampa but enjoyed the meat and chang. The sister saw the woman in a light body and smelled a sweet scent from her urine. Wildly scolding her, the woman gave the sister something to drink and sent some dütsi (a blessed medicinal substance) for Do Khyentse with the message: "My dear son, do not stay in this region too long. Here the auspicious causations have become murky." The next day, they went back to the woman's place with some more food, but there was not even a trace that anybody had ever stayed at the spot where they had found her the day before.

The king of Dege and Do Khyentse's attendants became disturbed, fearing that Do Khyentse might become a hermit or a wild yogī. People didn't have great respect for his enlightened realization and power. They were of the opinion that the way for him to be a great lama was to remain a strictly disciplined monk and a learned scholar.

Do Khyentse bluntly told the court of Dege that he was not going to remain an important lama, so either they must let him become a hermit or they would have to keep him in prison. The king said, "The Sakya Kongma of Central Tibet and Dodrupchen Rinpoche of Kham and many other important divine powers of Tibet agreed that you are the tülku of the Omniscient Khyentse Özer [Jigme Lingpa]. From my late mother's time, you have been recognized as the preceptor of Dege and the crown ornament of the Nyingma tradition. So how can you leave to be a hermit—and how can I prosecute you for going for Dharma? Now I myself and Dzogchen and Kathok monasteries will send our representative to Dodrupchen to have his opinion. We cannot violate whatever order the lama gives us, nor will you." Do Khyentse agreed. He and the representatives of Dege, Dzogchen, Kathok, and Drikung traveled to Yarlung to present their case before Dodrupchen.

Dodrupchen didn't say a word for three days. Then he told Do Khyentse, "People want to see you a monk who upholds the monastic tradition. But from your past activities and the prophecies, I can say that it is not going to happen. For a while you should become a hermit and later a Vajradhara, a master of esoteric discipline. . . . Some people also want me to tell you to stay as my regent. That would become an obstruction to you, and would be against your wish. . . . At the end of the Dragon year [1821] I am also going to go to my own place [die]. So stay here for the winter and spring to get more clarifications on instructions. At the end of next summer, do whatever you like. [In other words, leave before I die.] Otherwise, [if you don't leave before I die,] people could blame you for not obeying my wishes." Do Khyentse could only say yes, as he was so shocked at hearing that Dodrupchen would die soon. Then Dodrupchen conveyed the same decision to the representatives.

The very next day, on the tenth day of the seventh month of the Earth Hare year (1820), after the tsok offering ceremony, Do Khyentse offered Dodrupchen all the possessions he had brought with him. Dodrupchen blessed Do Khyentse's hair, so that from then on he could keep it long, and also he blessed a new set of white robes and gave it to him, saying, "For two and a half years, wear this costume; then you will discover a new one." Instantly, Do Khyentse transformed himself into a white-robed tantric.

Then, with the representatives, Do Khyentse went to Dege to convey the decision to the king, who said, "When the Protector Lord Dodrupchen gives such an order, I dare not tell you anything but 'Please do whatever you wish.' " Do Khyentse sent half the property he possessed to Drikung, and the other half he entrusted to Dege.

Now Do Khyentse returned to Dodrupchen as a humble ascetic with two companions. Dodrupchen was very happy to see him in this form, and he said, "Now you are a hermit. Maintain a low position without any desire for power or fame. Wear patched old robes. Practice as it is said: 'Give all profit and victory to others. Take all loss and defeat upon yourself.' " During the day he received from Dodrupchen empowerments of *Khandro Yangtig* and detailed teachings of *Yeshe Lama.* At night, in the dream of luminosity, from Longchen Rabjam he received detailed instructions on the meaning of *Khandro Yangtig.*

Dodrupchen appeared joyful and in good health. Sometimes he would suddenly sing yogic songs. He would describe his various visions. Do Khyentse and others kept seeing his body in various forms, and sometimes there was no body but just his clothes on his seat. Amid these endless wonders, if anyone remembered any question about teachings, he would answer spontaneously without needing to be asked.

On the tenth day of the sixth month of the Iron Dragon year (1821), with great sadness the master and disciple bade goodbye for this lifetime. On the pass of Garlung, Do Khyentse and Palge made a hundred prostrations toward Dodrupchen with prayers. Do Khyentse changed his name to Repa Yongtrak and with a few people went to Thugje Chenpo of Trokyap Province and then to various places in Amdo, including

Amchok, Latrang, and Tso Ngönpo and Rekong. Then he sent all his companions home except Lhaksam Rapkar.

In Rekong, he went to a cemetery to practice for three nights and showed signs of success in shaking up emotions and concepts and pacifying them, but then he came down with smallpox. He seemed to enter an unconscious state for over two weeks. During that time, he saw different realms of the world. He experienced his body being eaten by wrathful deities to purify the impurities of his physical form. In Zangdok Palri pure land he participated for seven days in the performance of tsok offerings with Guru Rinpoche and many great masters of the past. At the end of the tsok, Guru Rinpoche entrusted to him seven caskets of ter with mind-mandate transmissions and prophecies. Guru Rinpoche said:

> Son, after realizing the nontruth of perceptions,
> There is little benefit in dwelling in solitude.
> When the falsehoods of phenomenal appearances have collapsed into their own place,
> And the uncontrolled innate nature of phenomena has been recognized,
> Without [falling into] discrimination of the subtle forms of grasping and grasped
> And attachment to contaminated virtuous deeds,
> Please maintain the strong hold of the vast expanse of primordial purity.

Then he experienced going to see Dodrupchen, who, in the great joy of seeing him again, said, "I will be leaving in the first month of the coming year. I will leave my advice for you with your sister. . . . Now the obstructions of your life are averted." Do Khyentse saw a white ĀḤ letter at Dodrupchen's heart. By concentrating his awareness on it, his mind merged into an inexpressible state. Then, when he felt that he was touching his own body, he returned to physical consciousness. His sickness had gone, but it took about a month for him to regain his full strength.

On the thirteenth day of the first month of the Iron Snake year (1821), Do Khyentse saw Dodrupchen in the sky in the midst of lights and rays in an amazing radiating light body clad in lights. Dodrupchen was sitting on a brocadelike blanket held up by four ḍākinīs, and with a most enchanting voice he gave his testament. (For the lines of the testament, see chapter 12, page 158.) Beams of light of five colors emanated from the white ĀḤ letter at Dodrupchen's heart and merged into Do Khyentse. Then from the ĀḤ a second ĀḤ letter came out and merged into the heart of Do Khyentse. For a while, Do Khyentse became unconscious and merged into the experience of vajra waves. When he regained consciousness, the lama had disappeared. For three days he remained in a state in which all the gross and subtle thoughts had dissolved and the intrinsic awareness had spontaneously awakened. After that he felt great sorrow, realizing that Dodrupchen had passed away.

He met Pema Rangtröl, Kyanglung Gönpo Gyal, and Chöying Tobden Dorje, disciples of Dodrupchen, and gave them teachings. After many months his sister and others arrived from Yarlung Pemakö with the news of Dodrupchen's death, and his sister relayed the advice that the lama had left with her for him. He went to Yarlung to pay his respects to the remains of Dodrupchen, but refused to stay as Dodrupchen's regent.

Around this time he had changed from the white robes of a tantric into layman's dress. He briefly visited Dege, where everyone was shocked and puzzled by his new outlook. There he met Gyalwe Nyuku, who requested him to wear a tertön's (or tantric) robe. Do Khyentse answered, "I am neither a tertön nor an observer of monk's vows, so the proper thing for me is layman's dress." Despite this, Dzogchen Rinpoche praised him, and Pönlop dedicated the remainder of his life to extending Do Khyentse's life. Do Khyentse wandered in the no-man's-lands of Golok as a hunter and restored to life many killed or dead animals and people.

In 1823, his consort, the daughter of Akyong Lhachen, gave birth amid miraculous signs to a daughter named Khaying Dölma. Khaying Dölma married the king of Trokyap in 1841 but died, childless, in 1855.

Do Khyentse started giving transmissions and teachings of *Longchen Nyingthig* to his sister and others. He stayed sometimes at Dordzong (rDo rDzong) in Golok. Later he established a gompa of the Longchen Nyingthig tradition, which belonged to the Muk-yang tribal group. Then he taught at many places in Gyalmorong, Dzika, and Ser Valley.

Now his fame as a master reached Dege, and at the insistance of the king he briefly visited Dege again. But Do Khyentse refused to stay as a preceptor because he had been doubted the last time, when he turned up as a layman, and that had damaged the auspicious circumstances.

Instead, he offered to stay as a dünhor (councillor), which other lamas discouraged, as it was not a proper designation for a great lama.

Do Khyentse went to Dzachukha and suddenly got seriously sick, as had been prophesied earlier. Through the intense prayers of Gyalwe Nyuku, he recovered.

In 1825, accompanied by his sister and others, he went to Ma Valley and discovered the treasures of Ling. Then he went to Phuntsok Dzong, the palace of King Tsewang Lhündrup (d. 1827) of Gyarong, and gave teachings. After that he went to the pilgrimage place Kaukong Senge Yongdzong and gave teachings to King Namkha Lhündrup of Trokyap in Gyarong. They had an excellent master-disciple relationship and built a temple, which later became known as Gomsar (New Gompa).

One day, in the Murdo Mountains of Gyarong, Do Khyentse took his son Raltri to a cave in a steep mountain and asked him to wait for him. Do Khyentse returned to their camp while Raltri waited in the cave. When it became dark and his father had still not returned, Raltri could hardly move for fear of falling to his death. Suddenly he heard his father calling him to come and saw a carpet of light before him. Without hesitation or doubt, he sat on it and instantly found himself at the camp.

Once Do Khyentse was traveling on a very narrow mountain path in Trakwar in Dzigak of Gyarong. He told Riktsal Thogme, "If you are brave, push me and my horse down!" Riktsal pushed them and they fell into the Gyalmo Ngülchu (Chinese, Dadu) River, hundreds of feet below. Riktsal thought, "Now my lama is dead," and he jumped after them. The marks of Do Khyentse, his horse, his sword, and Riktsal were imprinted on the rock as if on mud, and they are still visible in winter, when the river is low. Then Do Khyentse asked Riktsal to get on the horse behind him, and they climbed up the steep rock mountain, making marks at every step. Since then, it is said, death by falling ceased to occur on that dangerous path.[245]

In 1829, Do Khyentse's son Sherap Mebar, a tülku of Dodrupchen, was born, as prophesied by Dodrupchen himself with amazing signs. From childhood he would not eat meat. Unfortunately, he died at the age of fourteen, in 1842. Do Khyentse's second son, Rikpe Raltri (1830–1874), was a tülku of Gyalse Nyinche (1793–?), the son of Jigme Lingpa, and was the father of Zilnön Gyepa Dorje, the second Do Rinpoche (1890–1953).

In 1831 Do Khyentse was invited by the king of Chakla to Tartsedo and other places of that region. From that time, Do Khyentse mainly stayed in the Tartsedo region, and the king of Chakla became one of his main patrons.

In 1832, in a dream vision he received teachings and prophecies from Machik Labdrön accompanied by five ḍākinīs. Afterward, all obstructions from negative aspiration were pacified, and he began to function as the Lord of Yogīs.

Once, when he was camping in the Zhak-ra Mountains, the king of Chakla came to see him. One day, riding horses and holding butter lamps in their hands, Do Khyentse, the king, and Tongza Özer rode into a lake. When the water reached the horse's mane, the king grew frightened and turned back. Do Khyentse and Özer disappeared. After a while they both emerged safely. According to Özer, they had gone under water without wetting their clothes or extinguishing the lamps. Then they reached a many-storied house surrounded by three walls with all kinds of animals around it. He stayed outside the house while Do Khyentse was led inside by people in white clothing, and then they led him out again. No one knew what Do Khyentse brought out with him.

One day in the Datha area, two young shepherds saw Do Khyentse and his group traveling by. They wanted to test whether Do Khyentse really had clairvoyance or not. One of the shepherds pretended to be dead, and the other ran to the lama's party for prayers for the dead. Do Khyentse came to the body and smoked three pipes, putting the ashes on the shepherd's head. Then he left without saying any prayer. After the party had left, the boy found that his friend actually was dead. He ran after the party and confessed the truth and prayed the lama to revive him. Do Khyentse returned, and saying "Dza," he made a summoning gesture and left again. Soon the boy regained consciousness and expressed his sorrow over being brought back, as he had been sent to a joyful pure land. Immediately he followed Do Khyentse and later became an accomplished meditator.

Once in the early summer, Do Khyentse was camping overnight at Dora Karmo in Minyak on his way to Tartsedo. He shot a marmot and told Özer to bury the body, which he would need on his way back. In the fall, when they returned to that place, he asked Özer to bring the body without leaving even a hair behind. It had almost disappeared, but Özer collected all the pieces and put them together in front of him. Do Khyentse touched the marmot's body with his hand, and it ran away squeaking. Özer remarked that he had seen many cases of the dead being brought back to life, but this was such an instance in which an animal had been dead for so long.

One day the Chakla king requested an empowerment. When Özer had finished his preparations, they found that they hadn't brought the text that was to be recited from their hermitage, which was quite far away. Do Khyentse said, "No problem." The next day, just before sunrise, people halfway to the hermitage saw him walking by, and at sunrise people saw him at the hermitage. At breakfast time, the palace attendants reported to the king that Do Khyentse had just entered the palace barefoot, at which the king said, "No, he is having breakfast." But having doubts, the king and attendants rushed into Do Khyentse's room, and they saw him perspiring, and the text was on the table. Do Khyentse said, "I am tired. I went to get the text!"

Thereafter Do Khyentse established Kyilung Gompa in the Geshe region of Gyarong, gave empowerment of *Longchen Nyingthig,* and taught ngöndro, tsalung, and *Yeshe Lama* to about a hundred disciples. Later Kyilung Gompa became the seat of the first Zenkar Rinpoche and one of the main seats of the present Zenkar Rinpoche, Thupten Nyima (b. 1943), the incarnations of Do Khyentse.

Do Khyentse went to meet Gönpo Namgyal (d. 1865), the wicked chieftain of Nyarong, who caused many sufferings to many parts of Kham. One day the chieftain said to Do Khyentse, "You carry a gun—now shoot that crow." Do Khyentse did so. Then the chieftain said, "You claim to be a compassionate Buddhist, but you are killing animals. How can that be?" Do Khyentse snapped his fingers, and the crow flew away. The chieftain remarked, "What a gun—couldn't even kill a crow." Another day, they were riding together in the snow. Do Khyentse's horse didn't make any tracks. The chieftain said, "Oh, you have a good horse. Let's exchange horses." When they did, again the horse that Do Khyentse was riding didn't make any tracks, and the chieftain remarked, "You are a good horseman."[246] Having inspired both admiration and peace in the chieftain's mind, Do Khyentse was instrumental in getting many prisoners released.

Once when they were staying in the Zhak-ra Lhatse Mountains of Minyak, a wild man (Mi rGod, yeti?) carried Do Khyentse away. He was left in a cave in the middle of a steep rock hill. There he merged into absorption, in which he had a vision of a ḍākinī who gave him teachings, prophecies, and nectar. When he came out of absorption, his sister and others led by a stranger had arrived at the foot of the hill and were shouting his name. It was impossible for them to climb up or for him to climb down. With one-pointed mind his followers prayed to the Buddhas and lamas, and instantly he appeared at the bottom of the rock hill. Then he gave transmissions of *Longchen Nyingthig* and *Khandro Yangtig* with amazing signs and visions.

In 1836, he went to Lauthang and gave transmissions of *Longchen Nyingthig*. Lauthang became one of the seats of Do Khyentse. In the recent past, Lauthang Gompa was the seat of Lauthang Tülku Drachen (d. 1959), a tülku of Dodrupchen.

While they were at Lauthang, Do Khyentse led his son Raltri into an amazing house. Many ḍākinīs served them various kinds of food and showed them an astonishing display of treasures. Do Khyentse gave a phurbu to Raltri, and then they came out of the house. When Raltri looked back, the house was gone, but the phurbu was still with him.

In 1844 Khyentse visited Yarlung Pemakö and gave the *Longchen Nyingthig* transmissions to Jigme Phüntsok Jungne, the second Dodrupchen. Then he revealed his own ter teachings to the public. They include *Yangsang Khadrö Thukthik* and *Chö Dzinpa Rangtröl.*

In 1847 at Lauthang he enthroned Tri-me Trakpa of Yuthang as the tülku of his late son Sherap Mebar, a tülku of Dodrupchen. Tri-me Trakpa, who also refused to eat meat from childhood, later became known popularly as Do (mDo) Rinpoche.

In 1856/57, while he was visiting the Yutse Mountains in Golok, Paltrül Rinpoche came to receive the empowerment of *Yumka Dechen Gyalmo.* Then, with the second Dodrupchen, the three of them made sang (incense-burning) offerings.

Despite all the evidence, some were skeptical of Do Khyentse's enlightened power. An uncle of his wouldn't believe in Do Khyentse's way of discipline. One day when Do Khyentse shot a marmot, his uncle scolded him, saying, "How can a tülku be killing animals like a sinner?" Then Do Khyentse struck the body with his whip,[247] and the marmot ran away. At that his uncle rebuked him, "Now you have learned magic tricks too!"

In the Yutse Mountains, Do Khyentse enjoyed playing games by day and meditating by night. It is believed that he brought many human and numerous nonhuman beings to the peaceful path of Dharma. At the invitation of the king of Samang of Gyarong, he gave teachings to the king and his subjects. Now he had become the preceptor of all eighteen principalities of Gyarong.

In 1858 he started to write his autobiography at Kaukong Senge Yongdzong in Trokyap, and in 1860 he concluded it while giving Dzogpa Chenpo instructions to the king of Trokyap and others. All experienced high realization and witnessed amazing signs.

While he was at Kaukong, in the early morning of the eighth day of the first month of the Earth Sheep year (1860), he saw Dodrupchen in the form of Milarepa and heard the following:

> The views of Madhyamaka, Mahāmudrā, and Dzogpa Chenpo
> Are of the nature of the basis, the path, and the result.
> Freedom from the elaborations of four extremes
> Is called the outer gross Madhyamaka.
> That [view] with a sharp knowledge, free from faults,
> Wisdom with the spirit of essence,
> Which is the Buddha nature, the continuum basis,
> Is the subtle inner Madhyamaka.
> Having that [view], by relying on skillful means that bring forth the realization, and
> Through the trainings of fourfold yogas,
> Perfecting the meditationless result
> Is the way of proceeding along the path of Mahāmudrā,
> The meaning [or the union] of emptiness and clarity, free from grasping, of the mind. . . .
> In natural Dzogpa Chenpo,
> Recognizing the intrinsic awareness directly
> Undoes all the knots of grasping and grasper.
> Then, by recognizing images and circles [of lights],
> The manifestative power of intrinsic awareness will be perfected as the Sambhogakāya.
> When the luminosity of the four visions is perfected,
> Phenomena dissolve into the great expanse of the ultimate nature,
> And the liberation into the ultimate sphere of the "youthful body in a vase" will be attained. . . .[248]

Then lights with heat came from the master and entered through Do Khyentse's head, filling all his body and purifying even his most subtle defilements, and filling him with the wisdom of great bliss.

In 1866 he came back to Tartsedo and gave teachings to people everywhere, even in the streets of the town. Then, on the twentieth day of the second month, sitting in the posture of the Dharmakāya, he dissolved his physical tülku into the ultimate nature. Instantly, various sounds were heard, earthquakes were experienced, and rainbow lights in the shape of stripes, circles, and pillars filled the sky for days. At his cremation, in the ashes his disciples found many ringsels, including one egg-sized ringsel in five colors.

Among his tülkus were Pema Ngödrup Rolwe Dorje (1881–1943), the first Alak Zenkar of Kyilung Monastery of Gyarong, and Khyentrül Dzamling Wangyal (?–1907), a son of Düdjom Lingpa.

17

GYALSE ZHENPHEN THAYE
1800–?

GYALSE Zhenphen Thaye[249] was one of the most important masters of the Nyingma school. He was born in the Iron Monkey year of the thirteenth Rabjung (1800) in the Gemang tribal group of Dzachukha. He was also known as Gyalse Rikpe Dorje. He was recognized by many as a tülku of Minling Terchen. He received teachings from, among others, the first Dodrupchen, Jigme Gyalwe Nyuku, Dola Jigme Kalzang, the fourth Dzogchen Rinpoche, and Shengtruk Pema Tashi and many masters of Mindroling Monastery.

He studied at Dzogchen and Mindroling monasteries and became a celebrated scholar. He also meditated at many sacred places, from Mount Kailasha in Western Tibet to Mount Ome (gLang Ch'en) in China, and became an accomplished adept.

Gyalse Zhenphen Thaye went to Yarlung Pemakö to receive teachings from Dodrupchen again. He saw the place as an Unexcelled Pure Land of the Dharmakāya. After the death of Dodrupchen, Gyalse returned to serve as the Dodrupchen's regent for a while. Gyalse started a forty-five-day annual teaching and practice of the *Guhyagarbha-māyājālatantra* at Yarlung Pemakö, Dodrupchen's main seat. Paltrül Rinpoche acted as the teaching assistant to Gyalse for the first year, and then he himself presided over it for two more years.[250]

Gyalse assumed the responsibility of rebuilding Dzogchen Monastery after it was almost totally destroyed by an earthquake in 1842. However, the main significance of his life is the three major contributions he made to the Nyingma school.

He built the famous Shrīsiṃha Shetra (scripture college) of Dzogchen Monastery, and there he and his disciples taught sūtras and tantras. This shetra became an institution for learning and a model for scripture colleges at many other Nyingma monasteries.

He made Vinaya, or monastic discipline, into the practice of daily life and established annual rainy-season retreats for the monks at Dzogchen Monastery, a custom that was also followed by many other Nyingma monasteries.

At the request of Sangye Künga, the seventh Throne-holder of Mindroling, and Paltrül Pema Wangyal, he assembled the kama teachings of the Nyingma tradition in one collection. Then he initiated the practices of the thirteen kama sādhanas in monastic assemblies in Dzogchen Monastery, from which they spread to many other Nyingma monasteries in Eastern Tibet.

Unfortunately, I don't think there has been adequate acknowledgment for the great services he rendered to the heart and core of the Nyingma tradition. Among his many great disciples were Khenchen Pema Dorje, Paltrül Rinpoche, and Do Khyentse.

He died relatively young, but I have no information about when or how he died. His tülku was Gyakong Khenpo Chökyi Nangwa (Zhenga, 1871–1927) of Dzogchen Monastery.

18

Dzogchen Khenpo Pema Dorje
NINETEENTH CENTURY

KHENCHEN Pema Dorje[251] was a great master of both sūtra and tantra. He was also known as Pema Vajra, Pema Badzar, and Pema Tamchö Özer. He was one of the most famous khenpos, or masters of learning, of Dzogchen Monastery. He studied at the feet of Gyalse Zhenphen Thaye, the fourth Dzogchen Rinpoche, Khenchen Sengtruk Pema Tashi, Paltrül Rinpoche, and many other masters. He was a scholar of both sūtra and tantra. He received the *Longchen Nyingthig* transmissions from Jigme Gyalwe Nyuku, the fourth Dzogchen Rinpoche, Khyentse Yeshe Dorje, and Gyalse Zhenphen Thaye.

Among his writings are *Nyingme Gal-len Rikpe Kyareng,* a refutation of attacks on the Nyingma views, and *An Instruction on the Recitation of Avalokiteshvara of Longchen Nyingthig.*

His tülku was Choktrül Dega Rinpoche of Dzogchen Monastery. Choktrül Dega's tülku is Tülku Kalzang, who has been spearheading the reconstruction of Dzogchen Monastery in recent years.

19

Paltrül Jigme Chökyi Wangpo
(1808–1887)

PALTRÜL RINPOCHE Ogyen Jigme Chökyi Wangpo[252] is the speech incarnation of Jigme Lingpa. He was one of the great Nyingma teachers and writers, whose life and writings are cited even by scholars of other schools. Although he was one of the greatest scholars and adepts of the Nyingma school, he lived as a most humble and simple hermit. He spoke directly and loudly, but every word of his was the word of truth, wisdom, and caring.

He was born in the Getse Kongma tribe of the Mukpo Dong lineage at Karchung Ko-ö in Dzachukha Valley in the Earth Dragon year of the fourteenth Rabjung (1808). His father was Lhawang of the Gyalthok group, and his mother was Dolma of the Tromza group. Soon after his birth, he tried to say OM . . . , but it wasn't clear. But on the fifth day he said OṂ MAṆI PADME HŪṂ, very clearly. Also, the letters of the mantra OṂ MAṆI PADME HŪṂ were visible on his neck, as was a HRĪḤ letter on his tongue.

Although he was a tülku of Jigme Lingpa, officially he was recognized as the tülku of Palge Samten Phüntsok by Dola Jigme Kalzang. Confirming the recognition, the first Dodrupchen said to Jigme Kalzang: "I am bestowing the mind entrustment and aspirational transmission of the complete *Longchen Nyingthig* teachings upon him with the name Ogyen Jigme Chökyi Wangpo." Soon, Palge Könchok, a nephew of the last

Palge, brought Paltrül Rinpoche to Palge Latrang, the residence of the last Palge.

Paltrül studied sūtric and tantric teachings with many teachers, including Dola Jigme Kalzang, Jigme Ngotsar, Gyalse Zhenphen Thaye, Sönam Palge, and Zhechen Thutop Namgyal. Sengtruk Pema Tashi of Dzogchen Monastery ordained him as a monk.

However, his root teachers were Jigme Gyalwe Nyuku and Do Khyentse. With Jigme Gyalwe Nyuku he studied from the ngöndro, the preliminary training, up to the teachings on tsalung and Dzogpa Chenpo. From Gyalwe Nyuku, he received *Longchen Nyingthig* ngöndro teachings twenty-five times, and undertook as many trainings on them. Later he wrote down the words of his teacher on the ngöndro as the famous text, *Künzang Lame Zhalung* (Words from the Mouth of the Samantabhadra Lama).

One day Do Khyentse, who was wandering while performing esoteric exercises, suddenly showed up outside Paltrül's tent. Do Khyentse shouted, "O Palge! If you are brave, come out!" When Paltrül respectfully came out, Do Khyentse grabbed him by his hair, threw him on the ground, and dragged him around. At that moment, Paltrül smelled alcohol on Do Khyentse's breath and thought, "The Buddha expounded on the dangers of alcohol, yet even a great adept like him could get drunk like this." At that instant, Do Khyentse freed Paltrül from his grip and shouted, "Alas, that you intellectual people could have such evil thoughts! You Old Dog!" Do Khyentse spat in his face, showed him his little finger (an insulting gesture), and departed. Paltrül realized, "Oh, I am deluded. He was performing an esoteric exercise to introduce me to my enlightened nature." Paltrül was torn by two conflicting feelings: shock over his own negative thoughts and amazement at Do Khyentse's clairvoyance. Sitting up, he immediately meditated on the enlightened nature of his mind, and a clear, skylike, open, intrinsic awareness awakened in him. Thereupon, clear and total realization like a rising sun awakened in him, over the dawnlike realization that he already had as the result of the introduction he had received from Gyalwe Nyuku. Since then, he jokingly kept "Old Dog" as his esoteric or sacred name.

When Paltrül was about twenty, Palge Könchok, the chief administrator of Palge Latrang, died and Paltrül closed the residence of Palge and started to live as a wandering hermit.

At Dzogchen Monastery he received the *Nyingthig Yabzhi* and *Longchen Nyingthig* transmissions from the fourth Dzogchen Rinpoche and

Gyalse Zhenphen Thaye. Then he meditated in long retreats at Shinje cave and Tsering cave near Dzogchen Monastery, where once Dodrupchen had done his years-long retreat.

Around 1851, from the great scholar Gyawa Do-ngak Gyatso, a disciple of both Paltrül and Zhapkar Tsoktruk Rangtröl (1781–1851), Paltrül heard the details of Zhapkar's highly inspiring life. When he reached Golok on his way to see Zhapkar, he heard the sad news that Zhapkar had just died. He turned back and came to Yarlung Pemakö, the seat of Dodrupchen. At Yarlung, he joined Gyalse Zhenphen Thaye (1800–?), who was living there as the regent of the late Dodrupchen and was starting a forty-five-day annual teaching and practice of the *Guhyagarbha-māyājāla-tantra*. Paltrül received teachings on the *Guhyagarbha-tantra* from Gyalse and acted as his teaching assistant for the first year. Then he himself presided over the annual teachings for two more years.

He went around Ser, Do, Mar, and Dzika valleys and numerous times gave teachings on the *Bodhicharyāvatāra* and inspired the whole population to recite OṂ MAṆI PADME HŪṂ. In those areas, he succeeded to a great extent in abolishing the system of serving meat to the lamas when they came to perform ritual services. He proclaimed rules against stealing and hunting. He brought Buddhism into everybody's life and into every home, so that it was not limited to monks or the monasteries and gompas.

He visited Shukchung Monastery, and then for a long time he stayed at Shukchen Tago, the formal residence of the first Dodrupchen. Although Dodrupchen had abandoned it about half a century before, it still was functioning as a hermitage. Here he recited the Kanjur three times and memorized many sūtras.

Then he lived at the foot of a tree at Ari Nak (aka Dhichung Phuk) for a long time. It was an elevated open field in the middle of a thick forest. No one ever went there, and the only people one might see occasionally were the travelers on the other side of the Do Valley, about a half mile's distance across the Do River. Ari Forest is situated on the bank of the Do River halfway between Shukchen Tago and the present Dodrupchen Monastery.

First, Paltrül and Nyoshül Lungtok, who lived around Paltrül and studied with him for twenty-eight years, stayed alone at Ari Forest for six months. A small bag of tsampa for food, the clothes on their backs, and a couple of books were their only possessions. At midday they would get together and eat a little tsampa. Then they would tie the tsampa bag to a tree and leave it till the next day. After that, Paltrül would give teachings on a couple of verses of the *Bodhicharyāvatāra* to Lungtok. Then, wearing the white rag that was his only garment, with a cane in his hand Paltrül would disappear into the woods, loudly uttering, *Ha! Ha! Ha!* as a meditation exercise. The next day at midday, they would get together again and do the same thing.

Soon, many disciples arrived at Ari Forest, and Paltrül started to teach *Semnyi Ngalso* and *Yönten Dzö* and other teachings.[253] Paltrül Rinpoche would give teachings, and then the disciples would meditate on them in the forest. As they weren't paying much attention to their living arrangements, they had very little to eat. Although it was a thick forest, there was no edible vegetation. The tea that they drank was strong and tasty when they first made it with fresh tea leaves; but later they would add more and more water to the old tea, so that it had less and less taste and color. They joked about the different strengths of tea, calling it the "three-kāya tea." Strong tea was the tea of the elaborate Nirmāṇakāya, weak tea was the tea of the simple Sambhogakāya, and tasteless tea was the tea of the emptiness Dharmakāya. Paltrül saw that property and desirable conditions, such as having plenty of food, good clothing, comfortable dwellings, and compliments and fame are more hindrance than support in spiritual progress. He wrote:

> Suffering is good and happiness is not good.
> Happiness enflames the five poisons of passion.
> Suffering exhausts the bad karmas accumulated in the past.
> Suffering is the grace of the lama.
> Criticism is good and compliments are not good.
> If I am complimented, I will be inflated with arrogance.
> If I am criticized, my faults will be exposed. . . .
> Poverty is good and prosperity is not good.
> Prosperity causes the great pains of earning more and preserving it.
> Poverty causes dedication and accomplishment of divine Dharma.

Next Paltrül went to Dzamthang Monastery, a great center of Jonang studies. There he gave lectures on *Uttaratantra* based on Künkhyen Dolpo's interpretations. In Minyak he met Dra Geshe Tsültrim Namgyal, a great Geluk scholar, who was amazed at Paltrül's scholarship. At Gyaphak Monastery, he gave empowerments and teachings of the complete *Longchen Nyingthig,* which he gave very rarely. In Golok, he tamed wild robbers and cruel hunters with the power of his presence and words of reason. In Marung he taught people to repeat the words of compassion, OṂ MAṆI PADME HŪṂ, for they didn't even know how to say it. Then he returned to the Ari Forest of Do Valley and stayed there for some time.

In 1856/57 Paltrül heard that Do Khyentse had arrived in the Yutse Mountains of Golok from Tartsedo. Paltrül went there, a distance of many days' travel, to see Do Khyentse. Paltrül requested Do Khyentse to give him an empowerment of *Yumka Dechen Gyalmo* of *Longchen Nyingthig*. Do Khyentse said, "I have been keeping it secret for many years, but now I will confer it upon you," and with great joy he transmitted it to Paltrül. Among the many prophecies given by Do Khyentse was one that Paltrül would live till the age of eighty. Then Do Khyentse, the second Dodrupchen, and Paltrül performed a sang ceremony together, which became a sign that they would be reborn as siblings. Paltrül returned to the Do Valley and gave teachings on the *Bodhicharyāvatāra* at many places.

After living for about ten years around the Do and Ser valleys, around the seats of Dodrupchen, Paltrül returned to Dzogchen Monastery. At Padme Thang, Nakchung hermitages, and Shrīsiṃha college of Dzogchen Monastery, he taught the *Bodhicharyāvatara, Abhisamayālaṃkāra, Madhyamakāvatāra, Mahāyānasūtrālaṃkāra, Abhidharmakosha, Guhyagarbha-māyājāla, Yönten Dzö, Domsum Namnge,* and many other texts for a number of years. He went to Kathok on pilgrimage and gave teachings on the *Bodhicharyāvatāra.* He received Tertön Chogyur Lingpa at Dzogchen Monastery and received transmissions.

Finally, he returned to Dzachukha, his home region. He visited almost every monastery and hermitage in Dzachukha Valley, especially Gekong and Changma hermitages, and taught the *Bodhicharyāvatāra* and other texts of Mahāyāna philosophy. But for most of the latter part of his life he lived around Dzagya Gön, the seat of his root teacher Gyalwe Nyuku, where Gyalwe Nyuku's remains are enshrined in a reliquary. At Dzagya, he established a three-month annual *Bodhicharyāvatāra* teaching and practice, and a one-week teaching and practice on the Pure Land of Amitābha, the Buddha of Infinite Light. Whenever he entered the shrine where the remains of his teacher are preserved in a reliquary, he would always say the following aspirations loudly:

> In all our successive lives, may we never be influenced by any evil friends. In all our successive lives, may we never violate even a

single hair of others. In all our successive lives, may we never be separated from the light of holy Dharma. [Followed by a verse from the scriptures:]

> Whoever receives teachings from me, and
> Even sees me, hears me, thinks of me, or relates to me in
> conversations,
> May the door of his rebirth in inferior realms be sealed,
> And may he take rebirth in the Potala Supreme Pure Land.

At Mamö Do in Dhachukha he dedicated many years of effort to expanding a famous *Dobum,* an amazingly huge complex of walls of stones, and on each stone OṂ MAṆI PADME HŪṂ is carved many times. This wall was started by Paltrül's predecessor. For the first time he started to accept all the offerings he was given and used every piece of butter as the pay for the people who were hired to carve the prayers. When the stone wall was completed, he sent a messenger to request Khyentse Wangpo to consecrate it. On that particular day, blessing grains of consecration, thrown by Khyentse Wangpo from a distance of eight days' journey by horseback, landed on the stone wall before everyone's eyes.

At Tramalung, he taught and led the practice of unique preliminary trainings, Trekchö and Thögal. Later, his chief disciple, Tendzin Norbu (Tenli), remarked, "I had some understanding of Dzogpa Chenpo before, but at Tramalung I attained a complete understanding and realization of it."

Around 1872, the third Dodrupchen, who was eight years old, came to Dzagya Gön to receive teachings and transmissions from Paltrül. After his teachings, at the request of Paltrül himself, Dodrupchen gave teachings on the *Bodhicharyāvatāra* to a huge public gathering, which included Paltrül himself. Then Paltrül sent the good news to Khyentse Wangpo saying, "Concerning the Dharma of learning, Dodrupchen has given teachings on the *Bodhicharyāvatāra* at the age of eight. As for the Dharma of realization, Nyakla Pema Düdül [1816–1872] has just attained the rainbow body. So the doctrine of the Buddha has not yet been diminished."

At that time, Dodrupchen heard the voice of Paltrül through the walls from time to time, saying: "Great Lord Padmasambhava, please watch over me. I have no others to depend upon . . ."—the words of invocation to Guru Rinpoche from the *Longchen Nyingthig* ngöndro text. This indicates that ngöndro must have been one of his main practices.

From the age of seventy-one, he began to save food, enough for about a week, which he had never done before. Beyond that, he wouldn't accept any offerings, or if he did accept any, he would send them immediately to the stone wall fund. Sometimes he would just leave food where it was offered to him, so that poor people used to follow him to collect offerings that he had left behind.

At the age of seventy-six, at the Dza Mamö field he gave teachings on *The Aspiration Prayer of the Pure Land* and *Maṇi Kabum* to about a thousand people. After that he didn't give any public teachings. Whoever came to him, he would send to Tendzin Norbu for teachings. If people insisted, he would scold them instead, but the more he scolded people, the more devoted to him they became. That was because of his compassionate heart and unpretentious words.

At seventy-seven, he went to Dzagya Gön and invited the fifth Dzogchen Rinpoche, who was visiting Dzachukha, and they celebrated the tenth day of the Monkey month of the Wood Monkey year, the birthday of Guru Rinpoche.

At the age of seventy-eight, Paltrül returned to Ko-ö, his birth place. At the age of eighty, on the thirteenth of the fourth month of the Fire Pig year (1887), he started to have some health problems. On the eighteenth of the month he took his morning tea as usual. Then, before noon, he sat up naked in the Buddha posture and placed his hands on his knees. Khenpo Künpal was present, and Khenpo tried to put the clothes back on Paltrül, but Paltrül didn't react. After a while, with his eyes open in the meditative glance, he snapped his fingers once and rested his hands in the gesture of contemplation, and his mind merged into the primordial purity. On the twentieth of the month, Tsamtrül Rinpoche performed the ceremony of awakening Paltrül's mind from the absorption.

At his death, no materials of any value were left behind. There was one set of monk's robes, an alms bowl, a yellow shawl, a lower garment, enough food for about ten days, a set of the five texts by Asaṅga, and a copy of the *Madhyamakāvatāra*. There were five silver coins and a few scarves, which he hadn't yet sent to the stone wall fund. That is all he had.

The third Dodrupchen describes the teachings of Paltrül as follows:

> Whatever teachings he gave, he never presented them with any trace of showing off his scholarship but with the intention that they

should suit the listeners' understanding. If his teachings are analyzed, they are seen to be logical and meaningful. If they are heard even by a dull mind, still they are easy to understand. As they are condensed, they are easy to grasp. They are of adequate length, related to the subject, enchanting, and tasteful.

Describing Paltrül's personality, the third Dodrupchen writes:

> Paltrül uses fearful and overwhelmingly tough words, but there is no trace of hatred or attachment in them. If you know how to listen to them, they are directly or indirectly only teachings. Whatever he says is solid like gold—it is true. He treats all people equally, neither flattering them in their presence nor backbiting in their absence. He never pretends to be something or someone else. So everybody, high or low, respects him as an authentic teacher. He is not partial to high people, nor does he have any disregard for ordinary people. Whoever is involved in unvirtuous activities, unless the person is unchangeable, he digs out that person's faults at once and exposes them. He praises and inspires people who are pursuing a spiritual life. He seems hard to serve, yet however close you are to him, it is impossible to find a single instance of dishonesty, dubiousness, instability, or hypocrisy in him. He is unchanging in friendship, easy and relaxing to be with. He has patience concerning both good and bad happenings. It is hard to separate from him. Although he remained a hidden practitioner all his life, he was wholesome from every point of view, as he never deviated from the *bodhisattva* activities. As a proverb says: "Even if the gold remains underground, its light radiates into the sky." To the extent that you examine him, you will find him clean and pure. To the extent that you think about him, your faith in him increases.

Describing Paltrül's physical appearance, the third Dodrupchen writes:

> His head is broad like a parasol. His face is like a blossoming lotus, and his sense faculties are immaculately clear. Usually he has very little sickness. From childhood he has been endowed with great wisdom and compassion, and he is a brilliant orator.

Khenpo Künpal, who was with Paltrül for many years in his later life, writes that one of his main prayers was the *Mañjushrīnāmasaṅgīti*. Not only did Paltrül have no worldly possessions, but he did not have many religious books, which for a scholar-teacher are thought to be most important. Sometimes he had a copy of the *Bodhicharyāvatāra* and a *Mañjushrīnāmasaṅgīti,* which were his daily prayers. But even those he would sometimes give away, as he knew the texts by heart. He didn't have paper or a bamboo pen. So, wherever he was, when he stood up, he was ready to leave a place instantly.

Paltrül gave teachings on philosophical texts of sūtra, tantra, and Dzogpa Chenpo and awakened or transmitted ultimate realization to the minds of many fortunate disciples. However, it seems that only on very few occasions did he give empowerments or performed elaborate ceremonies.

He was nonsectarian in his teaching, writing, and practicing. He studied, practiced, and taught the complete Buddhist traditions of Tibet. He saw the masters of different schools equally as the Buddha of Wisdom:

> Lord Sakya Paṇḍita, who brought the dawn of the five
> knowledges,
> Lord Tsongkhapa, the source of the teachings of sūtra and tantra,
> and
> Longchen Rabjam, the master of the complete teachings of the
> Buddha,
> Are the true Mañjushrīs of the Land of Snow [Tibet].

A person of great humility and simplicity, he was nonetheless able to accommodate many noble, rich, powerful and famous scholars as his disciples. Many disciples in brocade attire surrounded by hosts of retinues came to the feet of this solitary dweller in old, ragged, patched cloth, who hardly had enough tsampa to eat or fuel to make tea. There were even occasions when his humility shamed the brocade-wrapped, horse-riding people and exposed their weaknesses.

Once, Paltrül traveled through a nomadic camp, on foot as usual. He stopped at a family with a huge tent and asked them to let him rest for a couple of days as he was exhausted. The family said, "Can you read prayers?" He answered, "A little bit." Then they gladly allowed him to come in and let him settle in the lower corner of the tent. Many people were busy making ritual objects, putting up tents, building high seats, and cooking good food for a great lama and his party who were coming to perform an important ceremony. After a couple of days, they got word that the great lama was arriving, and everybody rushed out to receive the lama. Paltrül didn't go out. People shouted at him and almost dragged him out to present himself before the lama. The lama, attired in brocade, came with all the pomp of about forty horsemen in attendance, holding banners in their hands, as if in a play. Paltrül had no choice but to go before the great lama, so he did. When the grand lama saw Paltrül, he jumped off his horse and fell at the master's feet, ashamed at his meaningless pompous display before the meaningful, humble presence of the great Paltrül. The lama was Minyak Kunzang Sönam, a disciple of Paltrül who wrote a famous commentary on the *Bodhicharyāvatāra.* From that day, the lama renounced his pompous way of life, became a hermit, and never rode a horse again, but walked whenever he traveled around. People believed that Paltrül had foreseen the outcome of this encounter through his clairvoyance, an ability he had shown many times.

His writings are collected in six volumes, on Dzogpa Chenpo, tantra, sūtra, advice, poetry, and drama. His best-known works are the elaborate instruction on the preliminary practice of *Longchen Nyingthig,* entitled *Words from the Mouth of Samantabhadra Lama;* a short but amazing instruction on Dzogpa Chenpo meditation, entitled *The Three Words That Hit the Crucial Points,* and a commentary on the *Abhisamayālaṃkāra.*

In Eastern Tibet, Paltrül was perhaps the most instrumental of anyone in making the *Bodhicharyāvatāra* (The Way of Bodhisattva Training) a handbook for many monks; *The Aspirational Prayer for Taking Rebirth in the Blissful Pure Land of Amitābha* a daily prayer for many laypeople; the *Guhyagarbha-māyājāla-tantra* the foundation of Nyingma tantric tradition; Dzogpa Chenpo teachings not only a textual tradition but a meditative realization; and above all, OṂ MAṆI PADME HŪṂ as the perpetual breath of many people.

Among his incarnations were Jigme Wangpo of Dzagya Gön and Namkha Jigme of Dzachukha, a son of Düdjom Lingpa.

20

Second Dodrupchen Jigme Phüntsok Jungne 1824–1863

The second Dodrupchen Rinpoche, Jigme Phüntsok Jungne,[254] was born in the Puchung clan of the Mukpo Dong lineage at Dilsham Kathok in Thangyak gorge in Do Valley. His father was Puchung Chöphen, and his mother was Apangza Tsomo.

One day, while he was in the womb, his mother slipped into the Thangyak River and was in danger of drowning. At that moment she heard her baby saying, "Don't be afraid, Mom." At his birth there was a rain of flowers, rainbows arched over the tent, and the sound of music was heard in the air. As a child, while playing he often inserted twigs into rocks as if into mud.

The first Dodrupchen prophesied his birth as his own reincarnation in the following lines:

> After this [life] through the power of three absorptions
> [I will be born as] Phüntsok Jungne,
> A messenger who will demonstrate the enlightened activities of the three Buddha bodies, and
> A creator of various miracles as the source of benefits.

His recognition as Dodrupchen was confirmed by Sakya Kongma, and he was enthroned at Yarlung Pemakö. Exceptionally bright, he mastered the common and uncommon studies without difficulty. He was highly skilled in composition and poetry and had very beautiful handwriting. He was so handsome, it is said, that one could find nothing imperfect in his physical appearance.

In 1834 he went to Dzachukha and received the teachings of Ngöndro, *Rigdzin Düpa,* and Dzogpa Chenpo teachings from Jigme Gyalwe Nyuku.[255] Jigme Gyalwe Nyuku, with many offerings, empowered him as the Supreme Vajrāchārya. In 1844, Do Khyentse came to Yarlung Pemakö[256] and gave him the transmission of all the empowerments, scriptures, and instructions of *Longchen Nyingthig.* He also received teachings and transmissions from the fourth Dzogchen Rinpoche and Paltrül Rinpoche.

From childhood he displayed numerous powers, so that wonders became regular phenomena for the people around him. Many times, he restored life to the dead bodies of animals. Whenever he performed phowa (the transference of consciousness) for the dead, the signs that are believed to be indications of the transferring of consciousness to the pure lands always occurred. He had the power of knowing the past and future and of reading others' minds. In the latter part of his life he dressed as a layman. Although he performed symbolic ceremonies and displayed miraculous powers, he refused to give any formal teaching or transmissions.

Once, when he was traveling with a large group of people in a no-man's-land, they were suddenly surrounded by a large band of robbers. Dodrupchen invoked the Dharmapālas, saying, "If you are enraged, rain down Zas [gZa][257] and planets on the ground." Suddenly, from the sky hundreds of Zas landed all around them. The robbers apologized to him and made offerings of many horses.

One day, Do Khyentse killed a ewe and invited the second Dodrupchen and Paltrül Rinpoche for lunch. Paltrül's attendants were afraid that he would get very upset, because he was violently opposed to eating meat and especially to killing any creature, even the smallest. But the three of them sat together on one seat and cheerfully enjoyed the meat, to the astonishment of Paltrül's disciples. Later, Paltrül said to his disciples, "How could a ewe get such benefit from her own body? As these knowledge-holders enjoyed her body, there will be no more inferior rebirths for her."

In the Yutse mountains Do Khyentse made a sang offering on a stage. Then Dodrupchen performed the same ceremony on the same stage.

Finally Paltrül Rinpoche also did the same. Then Paltrül Rinpoche said, "I wish that I could die before the knowledge-holders, but this omen tells us that Do Khyentse will die first, then Dodrupchen, and I will be the last. Also, as we performed the offerings on the same stage, we will be reborn as the children of the same parents." As it turned out, Dodrupchen died earlier owing to unexpected circumstances, but they all took rebirth as the sons of Düdjom Lingpa.

When Gönpo Namgyal (?–1865), the wicked chieftain of Nyak-rong Province, was preparing to attack Ser Valley, he wrote to Dodrupchen saying that he was going to destroy Ser Valley but that he would do no harm to Yarlung Pemakö, through which the troops would pass. The second Dodrupchen answered that the people of Ser Valley were his dependents (Lha sDe) and that if they were harmed, it would be the same as harming his own monastery. The chieftain wrote back saying that when his troops came to Ser Valley, he would first destroy Yarlung. Upon hearing this news, all the residents of Yarlung Pemakö fled, leaving it empty.

Because of his followers' insistence, Dodrupchen had no choice but to abandon Yarlung. Then in accordance with prophecies of ḍākinīs, he moved to Tsangchen plain in the upper Do Valley. (It is believed that the first Dodrupchen also had built a retreat place on Tsangchen plain in the past.) On Tsangchen plain there is a sacred rock hill called Jikche Barma, the Frightening Blaze, which is believed to be the residence of a powerful protectress. Dodrupchen, holding a phurbu in his hand, suddenly flew into the hill without hindrance. Inside the hill, he reported, there was a fearful town. In a palace within it, he was asked to share the throne of the chief, a woman of wrathful appearance. At his request, she gave him permission to build a gompa.

In 1862, he laid the foundation of the gompa, which many decades later became the famous Dodrupchen Monastery. Soon, he took Gyaza (or Tsaza) Tamtsik as his consort, and this angered the Chökor Kalzang Gelek, a powerful local leader, who was hoping that his niece would become the consort of Dodrupchen. Because of this, Dodrupchen soon after departed for Tartsedo (now known as Kanding), leaving the construction of the gompa to his followers.

He stayed in and around Tartsedo as one of the preceptors of the king of Chakla. In 1863, many people in Tartsedo died in a smallpox epidemic. Dodrupchen was extremely saddened by the suffering that people were going through in the town. In order to stop the suffering, he took the epidemic on himself. As soon as he got sick, the epidemic stopped in the town. He said, "In this life, I had so many problems because of women. Next life, I will take rebirth as a person who will not even look at the face of a woman." (His tülku was Jigme Tenpe Nyima, a very strict monk.) Then he said, "A yogī should die like a stray dog," and lying on a street of Tartsedo, pointing his head downhill, he died.

Soon Do Khyentse arrived with his son, Rikpe Raltri. Do Khyentse shouted at Dodrupchen's body, "Why are you dying like a stray dog?" and he kicked the body. Dodrupchen's body sat up in the meditation posture as if he were alive and remained in absorption for a week. When three-year-old Rikpe Raltri saw Dodrupchen's body sitting up, he experienced a great shock, and that shock awakened the realization of the ultimate nature in him. Since then, Rikpe Raltri always said, "My supreme lama is Dodrupchen Jigme Phüntsok Jungne." Dodrupchen's body was cremated, and the remains were brought back to Dodrupchen Gompa and preserved in a golden stūpa until the political turmoil in 1959.

Among the incarnations of the second Dodrupchen were Jigme Tenpe Nyima, the third Dodrupchen Rinpoche, the second Pema Norbu Künzang Tendzin (1887–1932) of Palyül, Tülku Drachen (d. 1959?) of Lauthang, and Tsangpe Se Tülku of Dzika. There is also a story that the fifth Jamyang Zhepa (1916–1946) of Labrang Monastery was an incarnation of Dodrupchen.

21

Jamyang Khyentse Wangpo
1820–1892

According to Nyingma tradition, Jamyang Khyentse Wangpo[258] is the body incarnation of Jigme Lingpa.[259] He became one of the greatest masters, in whom the lineages of all of Tibetan Buddhism find their confluence. He became a prominent propagator of Nyingma, Sakya, Kagyü, and other teaching lineages. He was recognized as the rebirth of Jigme Lingpa (1730–1798) by the Nyingmapas and the Nesar Khyentse (1524–?) and Thartse Champa Namkha Chi-me by the Sakyapas. As Jigme Lingpa, he was also the manifestation of King Trisong Detsen, Vimalamitra, and many other masters. He was the master of thirteen lineal orders and was regarded as one of the five kings among the hundred major tertöns of the Nyingma tradition.

He was also known as Dorje Ziji, Pema Do-ngak Lingpa, Jigpa Mepe De, Tsokye Lama Gyepe Bang, Kunkhyen Lama Gyepe Bang, Jigme Khyentse Dökar, Mañjughoṣha, and Kün-ga Tenpe Gyaltsen.

He was born near Khyungchen Trak in a family of the Nyö clan from the village of Dilgo in the Terlung Valley of Dege amid wondrous signs on the fifth day of the sixth month of the Iron Dragon year of the fourteenth Rabjung (1820). His father was Rinchen Wangyal, an administrator of the Dege Palace, and his mother was Sönamtso, from a Mongol background.

Once his father asked the first Dodrupchen whether he should become a monk. Dodrupchen replied, "Do not become a monk. If you don't become a monk and get married, a great tülku will be born among your offspring. He will become a great source of benefits for the Dharma and beings."

From childhood he could recall his previous lives, and Ekajaṭī and Mahākāla were visible in forms and in energies around him to offer their protection.

At the age of eight he started to study Tibetan, astrology, medicine, and other disciplines with his father and Lamen Chötrak Gyatso. He was very intelligent, and he perfected his recitation and writing studies without the slightest difficulty. He also understood the meanings of the profound texts merely by reading them.

One day when he was seriously sick, in a vision he was given Vajrakīla empowerment by Guru Rinpoche and Yeshe Tsogyal, and the obstructions of his life were pacified.

At about age eleven, he went to Kathok Monastery, and his uncle Moktön named him Jigme Khyentse Dökar, which indicated that he was the tülku of Jigme Lingpa.

At twelve, Thartse Khenpo Kün-ga Tenzin (1776–?) recognized him as the tülku of his teacher and uncle, Ngor Thartse Khenchen Champa Namkha Chi-me, who was a great Khenpo of Ngor Monastery in Central Tibet and who then taught and died at Lhundrup Teng in Dege. Kün-ga Tenzin named him Jamyang Khyentse Wangpo Kün-ga Tenpe Gyaltsen.

At fifteen, in a pure vision he went to Bodhgayā and was entrusted with the treasures of the *Prajñāpāramitā* and *Anuttaratantra* teachings by Mañjushrīmitra. In front of the Bodhgayā temple, he purified the defilements of gross body by burning it and transforming it into a pure body like that of Vimalamitra.

At sixteen, in a pure vision, he went to Zangdok Palri, and from Guru Rinpoche, with hosts of ḍākinīs, he received the introduction to the three Buddha bodies and the prophecy that he would become the "receiver of seven orders" (bKa' Babs bDun). Then Guru Rinpoche and the ḍākinīs merged into Khyentse, saying:

> Maintaining the emptiness intrinsic awareness nakedly,
> Unstained by the grasped objects or
> Unpolluted by the grasper thoughts
> Is the vision of the Buddhas.

At eighteen he went to the hermitage of Zhechen Monastery and studied Sanskrit, poetry, and other subjects with Gyurme Thutop of Zhechen.

At nineteen, from Jigme Gyalwe Nyuku he received the transmissions of the *Longchen Nyingthig* cycle with miraculous signs. Then Lama Norbu, a disciple of the first Dodrupchen, gave him the introduction to the nature of the mind while transmitting the teachings of Amitābha discovered by Dodrupchen. Even in the latter part of his life, Khyentse Wangpo would say, "There is no more to progress [in the realization of the nature of the mind] than he realized then."

At twenty, at the request of Thartse Khenpo, he went to Ngor Monastery in Central Tibet. There he discovered many teachings and objects as earth ter. They included *Thugje Chenpo Semnyi Ngalso,* discovered at Tragmar Drinzang; *Lama Kuzhi Drupthap* at Damshö Nyingtrung; *Tsasum Gyutrül Trawa* at Singu Yutso; and *Tsasum Chidü* at Yarlung Sheltrak.

At twenty-one, he took full monastic ordination from Khenpo Rigdzin Wangpo at Mindroling Monastery in Central Tibet. He received bodhichitta vows from Sangye Kün-ga, the seventh Throne-holder of Mindroling.

Before the Jowo image at the Jokhang Temple in Lhasa, the rice he threw as offering instantly turned into white flowers, and a hundred butter lamps burned without needing to be lit. While he was saying prayers for the benefit of others, someone requested him to make an aspiration for himself. He said:

> Without having any leader here [in me] or any servant over there,
> Without having enemies to subdue or friends to protect,
> In a solitary place, by taming my own mind,
> May I accomplish the vast deeds of the bodhisattvas.

At twenty-four, at Oyuk, his memory of having been Chetsün Senge Wangchuk and his subsequent attainment of the light body of great transformation was awakened, and he discovered the profound *Chetsün Nyingthig* teachings. He made an extensive pilgrimage as an ascetic in Tsang, Ngari, and Central Tibet. At many places he perceived the images as the real Buddhas or the masters, and he beheld pure visions and had realizations. By the end of his twenty-fourth year, he returned to Kham and studied the teachings of the Ngor tradition at Dzongsar Tashi Lhatse.

At twenty-nine, he went to Central Tibet again for three years. At Gegye in Changdrok, as he was receiving the blessings from Guru Rinpoche in a pure vision, he discovered *Sangdrup Tsokye Nyingthig* as mind ter. At Samye, he saw the Tsokye Dorje image transform itself as the actual Guru Rinpoche and merge into him. As a result, he discovered *Tsokye Nyingthig*. At thirty-five, while he was meditating on white Tārā, he had the vision of the Tārā. As the result, he discovered *Phagme Nyingthig*.

At forty, as a result of pure vision, he received blessings from Guru Rinpoche, which enabled him to see all the tertöns and all the ter teachings that had appeared in the past, were appearing then, or would appear in the future in Tibet. Since that time he became the master of all of the ters.

From Khenpo Pema Dorje he received many transmissions including *Longchen Nyingthig, Gyutrül Zhitro, Düpa Do,* and the seventeen tantras. Also, from the fourth Dzogchen Rinpoche he received the common and uncommon ngöndro teachings of *Longchen Nyingthig*. He also received *Longchen Nyingthig* transmissions from Jigme Gyalwe Nyuku and Jetsün Sönam Chokden.

Then he received the teachings of all the lineages that exist in Tibet from about one hundred and fifty lamas over a period of some thirteen years. He studied or received the transmissions of more than seven hundred volumes. They included the traditions of Nyingma, Kadam, Sakya, Drikung, Taklung, Kamtsang, Drukpa, and others.

His main teachers were Trichen Tashi Rinchen of Sakya, Thartse Kün-ga Tendzin (1776–?), Champa Naljor, and Ngawang Lektrup of Ngor in Tsang Province in the west, Trichen Gyurme Sangye and Jetsün Thrinle Chödron of Mindroling, and Lhatsun Rinpoche of Drepung Monastery in Ü Province, and Zhechen Gyurme Thutop, Jigme Gyalwe Nyuku, Migyur Namkhe Dorje, Khenpo Pema Dorje, and Kongtrül Lodrö Thaye of Kham Province in the east.

He accomplished everything that he studied. However, according to Kyabje Dilgo Khyentse, Khyentse Wangpo's "main practice was the guru yoga of Longchen Nyingthig."[260]

He made Dzongsar Tashi Lhatse Monastery of the Sakya tradition in Dege his main seat and rebuilt it after the destruction caused by Nyakrong forces.

According to the Nyingma tradition, he received the transmissions or became the receiver of the seven orders (bKa' Babs bDun) of teachings:

1. He received the transmissions of both the Old Tantras and New Tantras.
2. He discovered many earth treasures (Sa gTer).
3. He rediscovered many earth treasures that had been discovered by earlier tertöns.
4. He discovered many mind treasures (dGongs gTer).
5. He rediscovered or reawakened many mind treasures that had been discovered by earlier tertöns.
6. He discovered many Pure Vision teachings (Dag sNang).
7. He received oral-transmission teachings (sNyan brGyud) in pure vision from many divinities.

The third Dodrupchen, who studied with him, describes his personal experiences of Khyentse Wangpo:

> Wherever he lived, a very strong sweet scent always filled the surroundings, which was believed to be the sign of his strict monastic discipline. Even a movement of his fingers was inspiring and meaningful, and people became powerless not to appreciate every gesture he made. Wherever he lived, you would always feel a pleasant heat, as if from a fire in the cold. Numerous people saw him in different forms of Buddhas or early masters. Whatever the season, people in his presence always had the feeling of being in the joy and prosperity of summer. He was exceptionally caring of poor people and spoke to them very gently. Arrogant and cruel people who were known as brave men would run from him without looking back, like escapees, or would submit as if their heads were falling off. Before him, every great master or powerful person became insignificant and humble. He was humble, honest, and kind. He was skilled in both Dharmic and secular ethical values. Before him, no one dared to express flattering or deceptive words. He taught all kinds of assemblies with great confidence, like a lion among other animals. In the midst of hosts of disciples, he was simple, and harmonious with all, and he spoke at the right moment and for the right length of time. His reasoning mind was swift like a river coursing down a steep mountain. His voice would fill the atmosphere as if it were the waves of the ocean. Sometimes he taught without caring to eat his meal. Because of the rush of disciples and the load of teachings, visitors sometimes had to wait weeks

> or even months to see him, but everyone felt joy in waiting for him.

Khyentse Wangpo constructed many temples and libraries, and inspired thousands of people to undertake activities on behalf of Dharma. He commissioned the building of about two thousand statues, the copying of about two thousand volumes of scripture, the carving of wooden blocks for about forty volumes, the making of more than a hundred copper statues gilded with gold, and the repair of many historical temples and monasteries.

For many decades he gave teachings and transmissions to disciples of different traditions. For example, he gave the empowerments of Vajrasattva discovered by Minling Terchen about fifty times and the empowerment and instruction of *Longchen Nyingthig* about twenty times.

At seventy-three, at the beginning of the first month of the Water Dragon year (1892), he said that he kept seeing Amitābha Buddha in the midst of an ocean of disciples. After the completion of an elaborate ceremony on the twenty-fifth day of the first month, he said to his offering master (mCh'od dPon), "From now on you don't have to do anything." The next day he started to show ill health. His disciples asked, "What prayers should we do for your longevity?" He replied, "None. Around the twentieth of next month, I will have recovered." When they insisted, he said, "It will be good if you say as many hundred-syllable mantras of Vajrasattva as you can."

Then in the morning of the twenty-first of the second month, he washed his hands and said, "Now take everything away [from my table]. All my work is completed." Then, uttering lots of prayers of auspiciousness, he threw grain flowers, which is a sign of completion. Later that day, he was withdrawn into the expanse of the enlightened mind of Vimalamitra. In the surrounding land there were gentle earthquakes. Even after death, his face looked radiant like the face of the moon. His body became as light as if it were made of cotton.

His main Nyingma disciples are listed in the lineage tree (page 340). Among Sakyapas, they are Sakya Dakchen, three Jetsünmas of Sakya, Kün-ga Tenzin of Ngor, Thartse Zhaptrung, Zhalu Losal Tenkyong, and Ngor Thartse Pönlop Loter Wangpo (1847–1914). Among Kagyüpas, they are the fourteenth and fifteenth Karmapas, Taklung Ma Rinpoche, Situ Pema Nyinche (1774-1853), Dazang Tülku, Dokhampa, Paṇḍita Karma Ngedön, Kongtrül Yönten Gyatso (1813–1899), and Samding

Dorje Phagmo. Among Gelukpas, they are Könchok Tenpa Rabgye of Tashi Khyil, Lhatsün Töndrup Gyaltsen, Hor Khangsar Kyabgön, and Lithang Champa Phüntsok.

Khyentse Wangpo manifested many incarnations simultaneously. They include Chökyi Wangpo (1894–1909) of Dzongsar, Chökyi Lodrö (1893–1959) of Kathok, Karma Khyentse Özer (1896–1945) of Palpung (Beri), Guru Tsewang (1897–?) of Dzogchen, Künzang Drodül Dechen Dorje (1897–1946) of Dza Palme, and Dilgo Khyentse Tashi Paljor (1910–1991) of Zhechen. Among them, Kathok Khyentse Chökyi Lodrö was the most outstanding teacher. After the death of Dzongsar Khyentse, Kathok Khyentse moved to Dzongsar Monastery, the seat of the previous Khyentse Wangpo, and since then Kathok Khyentse became known as the Dzongsar Khyentse. Since the early 1960s, Dilgo Khyentse Rinpoche, single-handedly upholding the unique tradition of Khyentse incarnations, propagated Dharma tirelessly in India, Bhutan, Nepal, Tibet, and the West.

22

Nyoshül Lungtok Tenpe Nyima
1829–1901/2 [261]

Nyoshül Lungtok Tenpe Nyima[262] was one of the greatest meditation masters of Dzogpa Chenpo in the *Longchen Nyingthig* lineage. He was the greatest realized disciple of Paltrül Rinpoche. There is a saying, "If there is no Lungtok, Paltrül is childless."

He was known as the tülku of Shāntarakṣhita, Kong-nyon Bepe Naljor, and Jewön Küntröl Namgyal. He was born in the Nyoshül tribe of the Mukpo Dong lineage as the son of Chösung Tadrin.

He studied with Gyalse Zhenphen Thaye, Khenchen Pema Dorje, the fourth Dzogchen Rinpoche, and later with Khyentse Wangpo. He was ordained as a monk by Gyalse Zhenphen Thaye, who named him Lungtok Tenpe Nyima.

Lungtok's root teacher was Paltrül Rinpoche. Living with Paltrül for twenty-eight years without separation, he received the transmissions of various teachings and especially Nyingthig teachings of Longchen Rabjam and Jigme Lingpa. He received the instructions of Trekchö teachings, which introduced him to the primordial purity that is present as the ultimate nature of all phenomenal existence. He received the instructions of Thögal teachings, which introduced him to the luminous appearances as the three Buddha bodies. He stayed about ten years around the seats of Dodrupchen in Ser and Do valleys with Paltrül Rinpoche.

At the Ari forest in the Do Valley, a few miles from the present Dodrupchen Monastery, Lungtok and his teacher Paltrül stayed alone together for six months. A small bag full of tsampa as food, the clothes they were wearing, and a couple of books were the only things they possessed. At midday they would get together and eat a little tsampa. Then they would tie the tsampa bag to a tree and leave it till the next day. After that Paltrül would give teachings on a couple of verses of the *Bodhicharyāvatāra* to Lungtok. Soon, many disciples arrived at Ari Forest, and Paltrül started to teach *Ngalso Korsum* and *Yönten Dzö* and other teachings. Paltrül Rinpoche would give a teaching, and then the disciple would meditate on it in the forest for days. First they had a little tsampa to eat every day, but soon their tsampa ran out. Then they collected food given to dogs by nomads or left behind, and they lived on that for a while. They didn't want to go around nomad camps to beg for food, but were happy to live with what was left unwanted.

At Ari forest, one day Paltrül asked Lungtok, "Do you remember your mother?" Lungtok said, "Not much, sir." Paltrül said, "It is because you haven't meditated on compassion. Now go into those willow trees and meditate on 'recognizing motherhood' and 'remembrance of mother's kindness' for seven days." Lungtok meditated as Paltrül had instructed, and the bodhichitta of loving-kindness and compassion naturally developed in him without any need of further efforts.

At Ari forest, after Paltrül's teachings, Longtok meditated on the meanings of *Relaxing in the Illusory Nature (Gyuma Ngalso)* by Longchen Rabjam. His concepts of grasping at truly existing entities collapsed, and all phenomenal existents arose as unreal like illusions. Later Khenpo Ngachung asked him, "Is it a realization?" He answered, "No, but a good experience" (Nyams).

With Paltrül, Lungtok left Golok for Dzogchen Monastery. Lungtok did a three-year retreat at Kangtrö near Dzogchen Monastery for the longevity of the fourth Dzogchen Rinpoche. He didn't have much food to eat. He had no clothing except his robes. He used a flat stone as his cushion to sit on for his three-year retreat.

Then Lungtok stayed with Paltrül at Nakchung hermitage near Dzogchen Monastery. Every day at dusk, Paltrül would do a meditation session on the training of Namkha Sumtruk, stretched out on his back on a new woolen carpet on a piece of grassy field the size of himself. One evening, while Paltrül was lying there as usual, he asked Lungtok, "Lungche [Dear Lung]! Did you say that you do not know the true nature of the mind?" Lungtok answered, "Yes, sir, I don't." Paltrül said, "Oh, there is nothing not to know. Come here." So Lungtok went to him. Paltrül said, "Lie down, as I am lying, and look at the sky." As Lungtok did so, the conversation went on as follows:

"Do you see the stars in the sky?"

"Yes."

"Do you hear the dogs barking in Dzogchen Monastery [at a far distance]?"

"Yes."

"Well, that is the meditation."

At that moment, Lungtok attained confidence in the realization in itself. He had been liberated from the conceptual fetters of "it is" or "it is not." He had realized the primordial wisdom, the naked union of emptiness and intrinsic awareness, the Buddha Mind.

Lungtok and his esteemed Dharma brothers, Tendzin Norbu, Khenpo Könchok Özer, Minyak Künzang Sönam, and Naktha Tülku, requested Paltrül to allow them to remain as wandering hermits for the rest of their lives. But Paltrül made Könchok Özer a khenpo of Dzogchen Monastery; he told Tendzin Norbu to teach at Gemang Monastery and the other three to return to their own home regions and maintain hermitages. So Lungtok came back to his home region and stayed at many hermitages, but mainly at a hermitage named Jönpa Lung.

At Shuku Shar hermitage, Lungtok meditated on *Bodhicharyāvatāra* for ten years and on *Ngalso Korsum* for three years. Later, he jokingly would say, "For thirteen years by projecting and withdrawing thoughts, I tried to discipline my thoughts so they wouldn't be increased. If I had meditated on Dzogpa Chenpo from the beginning, I could have realized a good view and meditation by now."

In 1883, when he was at Gyaduk hermitage, a five-year-old boy was brought to see him by his father. That boy was the future Khenpo Ngawang Palzang (1879–1941), his main lineage-holder.

Around 1895, Lungtok moved to Pema Ritho and established an encampment of hermits, and Ngawang Palzang formally became his disciple by studying ngöndro and other teachings with many others.

Lungtok said, "I haven't done anything against Paltrül Rinpoche's advice, except one thing, which is that he told me not to teach Dzogpa Chenpo before the age of fifty. Then, if I could, I should teach it. But before the age of fifty I had to teach a little to Önpo Tendzin Norbu, as he insisted. So my samaya with my teacher is an unbroken golden chain."

Later, he would tell his disciples, "If you meditate properly, the best meditators will make daily progress, the mediocre meditators will make monthly progress, and the lesser meditators will make yearly progress. For meditation the important thing is to know the crucial skills [*gNad*] of meditation. Even if you meditate, if there is no progress, it is a sign that you lack the understanding of the crucial skills of meditation."

Throughout his life he shared the teachings of Paltrül with all who came to him, and especially after the age of fifty he gave Dzogpa Chenpo teachings. However, like Paltrül Rinpoche, he hardly gave any transmissions of empowerment except to Sershül Khenpo Ngawang and Anye Khenpo Tamchö of Dodrupchen Monastery, Lama Ngawang Tendzin, Lama Dorli, Khenpo Ngawang Palzang, and a kama empowerment at Khangtsik Gar.

He wrote a detailed instruction on Trekchö meditation for Nyakla Rangrik, who was then in Central Tibet, and he asked him to burn it after reading it. Nyakla Rangrik did burn it as his teacher told him to do, but the messenger saw it on the way and copied it before it reached Nyakla Rangrik. Many of the amazing writings of Khenpo Ngawang Palzang are also the very words of Nyoshül Lungtok, which originally came from Paltrül Rinpoche.

At the age of seventy-two, Nyoshül Lungtok died on the twenty-fifth of the fifth month of the Wood Ox year of the fifteenth Rabjung (1925). Rainbow lights arched overhead, there was a gentle rain of flowers, and the sound of sweet music was heard. After the cremation, ringsels appeared from the ashes as signs of his attainment and as objects of reverence for his disciples.

His reincarnation was Shedrup Tenpe Nyima (1920–?).

23

Önpo Tendzin Norbu

NINETEENTH CENTURY

Önpo Tendzin Norbu[263] was one of the greatest scholars among the closest disciples of Paltrül Rinpoche. He was also known as Önpo Tenli or Tenga. He was an önpo (nephew) of Gyalse Zhenphen Thaye (1800–?).

He studied *Madhyamakakarika, Domsum, Bodhicharyāvatāra, Semnyi Ngalso, Yönten Dzö, Guhyagarbha-tantra, Ösal Nyingpö Gyü,* and many other texts with Paltrül. Especially at Tramalung in Dzachukha, Paltrül taught him and a few selected disciples the Dzogpa Chenpo teachings, starting from the unique preliminary trainings and main trainings of Trekchö and Thögal, stage by stage, according to the training experiences of the disciples. Paltrül not only taught them, but he himself participated in the trainings. Later, Tendzin Norbu told the third Dodrupchen, "Before, I tried to meditate on Dzogpa Chenpo and teach it to others, but these were just general ideas. But since we were trained at Tramalung, I think that I have a perfect understanding and realization of Dzogpa Chenpo."

He wanted to become a wandering hermit, but Paltrül Rinpoche advised him to teach at Gemang Monastery in Dzachukha, and he did so for the rest of his life.

He would say to his disciples, "Why are we not able to practice

Dharma? Because we don't believe in karma. If we gain trust in karma, we will become like my gracious Abu [elder brother, Paltrül]."

From 1883, Paltrül Rinpoche didn't give public teachings. Whoever came to him, he would send them to Tendzin Norbu for the teachings.

After the death of Paltrül, Önpo Tendzin Norbu took care of the arrangements of the funeral ceremonies. He also collected the writings of Paltrül and organized them in six volumes.

24

Adzom Drukpa Drodül Pawo Dorje
1842–1924

Adzom Drukpa Drodul Pawo Dorje[264] was one of the greatest lineage holders and propagators of the *Longchem Nyingthig* teachings. He was also known as Natsok Rangtröl.

He was born on the fifteenth day of the sixth month of the Water Tiger year of the fourteenth Rabjung (1842). His father was Atra from a Mongol family background. He was recognized as the tülku of Adzom Sangye Tashi by Tri-me Zhingkyong Chökyi Dorje, and he was also recognized as a tülku of Pema Karpo (1526–1592), the celebrated master of the Drukpa Kagyü school, by Gyalwa Changchup of Trom. Thus he became known as Adzom Drukpa.

He was given the refuge vow by Öntrül Thutop Namgyal of Zhechen. When he was thirteen, at Kathok Monastery, the first Kathok Situ Chökyi Lodrö taught him the ngöndro of *Dorje Nyingpo*. By practicing it, he developed a strong experience of the impermanence of life, and he emphasized his meditation on purification for a number of years. Then from Kathok Situ he received tsalung and Dzogpa Chenpo teachings. At the age of twenty-one, he realized the true nature of the mind, the intrinsic awareness. From then till the age of thirty-four, he concentrated on the meditation on dwelling in the realized nature of the intrinsic awareness and reached the ultimate stage of attainment.

Situ Chökyi Lodrö also gave him the empowerment of *Do Gongpa*

Düpa, the *Cycle of Khakhyap Rangtröl* and many others. He served Pema Düdül (1816–1872) of Nyak-rong, who eventually attained the rainbow body, and he received teachings of the *Khakhyap Rangtröl* cycle and many others. Since that time, in keeping with the strong advice of Pema Düdül, Adzom Drukpa kept his hair long and wore tantric dress.

From Gyatrül Do-ngag Tendzin he received transmissions of the *Namchö* cycle and *Zhitro Gongpa Rangtröl.* From Alak Chushö Tsang, he received the teachings of *Changchup Lamrim* of the Geluk tradition and studied many writings of Je Tsongkhapa, which clarified his many questions.

From Khyentse Wangpo he received *Nyingthig Yabzhi, Longchen Nyingthig, Khandro Sangwa Kündü, Gongpa Zangthal,* and many other transmissions. From Kongtrül Yönten Gyatso he received *Rinchen Terdzö* and *Kagyü Ngakdzö.* From Khenpo Pema Badzar he received the teachings on *Lama Yangtig.* From Paltrül Rinpoche he received the teachings on *Kunzang Lame Zhalung, Yeshe Lama,* and many others. From Nyoshül Lungtok he received teachings on *Ngalso Korsum.* From Ju Mipham, he received explanations on *Deshek Nyingpö Tongthün, Ngeshe Drönme,* and others.

Throughout his later life he taught the great lamas of Kathok, Dzogchen, Zhechen, and Palyül monasteries. He edited and published many important Nyingma texts, including the complete writings and ter teachings of Longchen Rabjam and Jigme Lingpa. He discovered many teachings as ter under the name of *Ösal Dorje Sangdzö* (Treasure of Vajra Luminosity). He established his main seat at Tashi Dungkar Khyil, the Auspicious Spiraling Conch Shell, popularly known as the Adzom Chögar, the Dharma Encampment of Adzom.

At the age of eighty-three (1924), with wondrous signs of circles of light, beams of light, and various sounds, he dissolved into the ultimate basis.

He had two sons, Gyurme Dorje (also known as Agyur Rinpoche, 1895?–1959?), a great Dzogpa Chenpo master, and Pema Wangyal, and a daughter, Semo Chi-med. His tülku, Druktrül Rinpoche (b. 1926), still lives at Adzom Chögar in Kham.

25

Lushül Khenpo Könchok Drönme
1859–1936

KHENPO Könchok Drönme[265] (Könme) was one of the famed four great khenpos of Dodrupchen Monastery. He was a great learned master and accomplished adept. Khenpo was also known as Lushül Khenpo, Dowa Khenpo, Könme Khenpo, and Lobzang Künkhyap. He was known as tülku of Tri Kongthang Tenpe Drönme (1762–1823) of Labrang Monatery.

Khenpo was born in the Earth Sheep year of the fourteenth Rabjung (1859) in the Lushül tribal group of Dzachukha in a family that had migrated from the Do Valley of Golok. From childhood he had a gifted mind for learning texts just by a glance or a single hearing.

From Paltrül Rinpoche he received many teachings, including *Bodhicharyāvatāra.* One day he went to see Paltrül Rinpoche, who was staying in a small tent near a family with a big tent. At that time Paltrül wasn't seeing people, and the family had many ferocious dogs that wouldn't let anyone get near. But Khenpo wasn't going to stop anyway. He sneaked along a little narrow ditch and ran into Paltrül's tent without being detected by people or dogs. Paltrül was bold and direct, but Khenpo was fearless. Paltrül said, "Are you a robber or something?" Khenpo said, "Yes, Abu Tsang [the Elder One]! I want to steal some pure gold of instructions from you." Paltrül liked people who talked directly and boldly rather than being diplomatic, polite, or flattering, so Khenpo got the answers to his questions. Also, while Khenpo was with him, Paltrül completed his famous giant stone wall of prayers and Khyentse Wangpo's blessing grains of consecration landed on the stone wall. With Önpo Tendzin Norbu, Khenpo studied the two-volume autocommentary of *Yönten Rinpoche Dzö.*

Soon with his family, following the third Dodrupchen, Khenpo returned to Do Valley, the homeland of his ancestors. With Gyawa Dongak Gyatso, a principal student of Zhapkar Tsoktruk Rangtröl and Paltrül Rinpoche, he studied most of the Mahāyāna texts by Asaṅga, Nāgārjuna, Chandrakīrti, Dharmakīrti, and Dignāga and many tantric texts. Later he also received many inner transmissions and instructions from the third Dodrupchen.

Khenpo became a great scholar of sūtric and tantric texts of both the Nyingma and Geluk traditions. He also knew medicine and was busy diagnosing and giving free medicine to the local people. He was learned in astrology and astronomy as well.

His main tutelary deity was Chakrasaṃvara of the Mahāsiddha Luyipa tradition. He had recited over three hundred million mantras of Chakrasaṃvara. He was well known for having attained the illusory body (sGyu Lus) through Chakrasaṃvara practice. One who attains the illusory body can transfer his mind into the divine body of the deity and travel to various pure lands and then return to his ordinary body. Khenpo, however, would not acknowledge such attainment publicly and would only say, "Because of my strong devotion, whenever I remember my tutelary deity, instantly I feel a hair-raising joy. I am highly satisfied with such an attainment." He had many pure visions of Buddhas and deities and received blessings and attainments.

He was able to see beings in various forms that are invisible to us. For example, in his youth he had a consistent vision of an old, ugly, and angry-looking woman, but as a meditator Khenpo viewed her as a divine image. In later years, she transformed into the pure image of Ekajaṭī, the source and preserver of the tantras.

He also had many encounters with Nyiwa, a harmful spirit force who always kept harassing him. This force is said to have caused the illnesses of both Düdjom Lingpa and the third Dodrupchen. One day, the spirit force again came to him. With great compassion in his mind, Khenpo repeated three times, "I will never abandon you with my compassion until you become enlightened!" After that, not only Khenpo but even his disciples were left alone by the spirit.

One day, a disciple was trying to light a butter lamp for a long time without success. Then Khenpo laughed, and the wick immediately caught fire. The disciple asked Khenpo, "What happened?" Khenpo said, "With the thought that the lamp is a body of water, I merged into meditative absorption."

During the latter half of his life, Khenpo mainly lived at Dodrupchen Monastery as one of the four major Khenpos and concentrated exclusively on teaching and meditating. He was not only a great scholar but a quick reader of his students' minds. His lectures were lively to hear, easy to comprehend, detailed in explanations, and profound in meaning.

He was tall and big-boned, with a wide skull and high cheekbones like a lion's. For many decades of his later life, he became very heavy and couldn't go out of his house on the hill without two powerful men assisting him with their full strength.

Khenpo lived in a two-story house filled with books and religious objects. His house was situated between rocks and juniper trees, in the middle of the hill behind Dodrupchen Monastery, overlooking the whole monastery and Tsangchen field. He stayed alone in his house. In the early dawn he would start his practice of meditations and recitations. Then he would have yogurt and cake (zhun) for his breakfast. Soon he resumed his meditation session, which would continue until the arrival of some of his students at about eleven o'clock. The students would clean and fill over six hundred offering bowls with water, some would make his daily offering of one hundred butter lamps, and one would make lunch (or just tea) for him. By the time the students had finished their offering arrangements, he would have finished his lunch, and together they would say an offering prayer. Then he would start teaching.

When my teacher, Kyala Khenpo, was studying with him, Khenpo Könchok Drönme would teach two or three classes, or occasionally even as many as seven classes a day. Most of the time, he had about seventy students studying with him. There was no particular course to take, but he taught according to the wishes and needs of the students. He could be teaching tantras to the most advanced students; Madhyamaka, Prajñāpāramitā, or Abhidharma to advanced students, logic to beginners, and simple texts to ordinary students on the same day. Both the words and meaning of the root texts by Nāgārjuna, Asaṅga, Dharmakīrti, Chandrakīrti, and others were in his memory. He also remembered the meaning of many of their commentaries. Usually he didn't finish his teachings till dark. Then some students would light the butter lamps and would say an offering prayer together. Then Khenpo would have his tea. When the butter lamps had burned out, some students would clean the lamps and leave Khenpo alone till the following noon. About the structure of his courses, Lauthang Tülku Drachen, a principal disciple of Khenpo, writes:

> First he taught the texts of *The Collected Elementary Topics* (*bsDus Gra*), *Science of Intellect* (*Blo Rigs*), *Science of Reasoning* (*rTags Rigs*), and *The Five Texts* (*bKa' Bod lNga*),[266]
> Then the commentary on the discipline chapter of bodhisattvabhumi,
> And after that *The Fifty Verses on Having a Teacher* and texts on tantric precepts,
> The commentary on *The Five Stages of Guhyasamaja* on empowerments and the development stage, and
> Then the tantras of *Vajrabhairava, Chakrasaṃvara,* and *Kālachakra.*
> These were followed by *Guhyagarbha-māyājāla-tantra.*
> He concluded them with the sacred introduction of *Dzogpa Chenpo.*
> This was the teaching tradition of the Omniscient Noble Lama.[267]

Because of the Khenpo's nonsectarian approach to scholarship and the fact that his teachings were on both Nyingma and Geluk texts, some Nyingma scholars felt uncomfortable. A rumor spread that when Kathok Situ Chökyi Gyatso (1880–1925) visited Khenpo, Situ's attendants witnessed that the writings of Tsongkhapa were wrapped up in silk and brocade and the writings of Longchen Rabjam were covered with dust. That was totally untrue. Longchen Rabjam's writings were wrapped in double covers, both silk or brocades and cotton, as were the writings of Tsongkhapa.

Visiting many monasteries and places in Golok, Khenpo taught scholarly texts and conferred the tantric transmissions. He ordained hundreds of monks and nuns and established annual rainy season retreat traditions in many monasteries.

At Tarthang Monastery of Golok for six months he gave complete teachings on *Abhisamayālaṃkāra* and other major texts to Choktrul Rinpoche, Thupten Chökyi Dawa (1894–1959), and other selected students, and Akong Khenpo acted as his teaching assistant (sKyor dPon).

For the young tülkus and monks of Tarthang he gave teachings on *Bodhicharyāvatāra*. At Göde Dzogchen Namgyal Ling Monastery, the seat of Chöying Tobden Dorje in Rekong, he taught and established the annual rainy season retreat.

After the deaths of the other three great khenpos and then the passing away of the Dodrupchen in 1926, the whole responsibility for upholding the unique level of scholarship of Dodrupchen Monastery landed on Khenpo's shoulders. For over a decade he taught ceaselessly and did not allow the monastery to be affected by the great losses. Indeed people hardly felt any effect in terms of the scholastic importance of the monastery. There were hardly any scholars in the Golok and Ser areas in those days who weren't students of Dodrupchen Monastery and of Khenpo himself. After Khenpo's death, although there were great khenpos at Dodrupchen Monastery, the good students who came from other monasteries and places went back to their own areas, and Dodrupchen Monastery went through a great decline for almost two decades. Thinking back, I can see how far it had fallen by the time I arrived at the monastery.

Khenpo didn't live as a hermit, as Amye Khenpo and Garwa Khenpo of Dodrupchen Monastery had done. He was known for the comforts of a nice house, rich food, and beautiful clothing, besides his huge private library and good collection of old and new religious objects. However, he used all the other materials that were offered to him by people to finance his free medicine, to fund his daily butter lamp offerings, and to pay for the printing and hoisting of Long-Life mantra flags that filled the hill around him. Dodrupchen Monastery was situated in a poor area, but later the living standard of that area improved. Many believed that it was due to the merits stimulated by Khenpo's year-round generous offerings. Also, for years, Dodrupchen Monastery suffered from epidemics. The third Dodrupchen, in accordance with his dream signs, advised Khenpo to surround the monastery with Long-Life mantra flags. Khenpo did this and maintained them year after year, and from then on the population was free from epidemics.

Khenpo himself acknowledged his successful service to Dharma. Kyala Khenpo quoted him as saying, "I have no feeling that we left anything undone in order to spread the Dharma, both the sūtras and the tantras, in Do-me [Eastern Tibet], with Rinpoche as the trunk and we, the khenpos, as the branches of a tree."

Among his major writings were an *Outline of Abhisamayālaṃkāra* and a *Commentary on Logic,* but both disappeared during the political changes. Today what we have among his major writings are *La-me Gonggyen* (Ornament of the Visions of the Lama), a text that elucidates the important points of the basis, path, and result of Mahāyāna and especially of the inner tantras; *A Notation on the Outline of Guhyagarbha-tantra;* and *A Notation on the Yumka Dechen Gyalmo.*

In 1934, Khenpo started to give lessons to the two Dodrupchen Rinpoches. After finishing the classes on elementary texts, he was teaching them *Yönten Rinpoche Dzö* with its commentaries. He finished the section of the text on sūtra and was starting the section on tantra. Suddenly, at the age of seventy-seven, Khenpo came down with some sort of cold or flu. It didn't seem serious, but he stopped teaching for a while. He moved to the Guhyagarbha-tantra temple to be close to the assembly of monks, who were performing many days' ceremony for his longevity. Then early in the night of the twenty-eighth day of the twelfth month of the Wood Pig year (1936) he told his students, Khenpo Jamtön, Kutruk of Gunang, and Kulo of Rekong, who were present with him at that moment:

> "I had a dream [although his disciples who were watching him were sure that he hadn't slept]. A woman told me: 'Sokhe Chomo says: "The present luminous absorption is the realization of emptiness. Because, if this is not the emptiness which is the nature of primordial knowledge, then the primordial wisdom of the ultimate sphere of the final Buddhahood and the present luminous absorption will not be able to be established as indistinguishable. This [present luminous absorption] is the precious majestic virtue [Yon Tan Rin Ch'en rGyal Po]. Because, if all the virtues of the result are not spontaneously present [in it] without [need of] seeking, then the primordial wisdom of the Buddhas and the present luminous absorption will not be able to be established as undifferentiable." '
>
> "I told the woman: 'Yes, that is a perfect understanding. In any case, if one extends it further by meditating on it through the path of unmodified natural contemplation [Ma bChos Chog bZhag], and if one realizes the total perfection of the intrinsic awareness, then this [luminous absorption] becomes as the five primordial wisdoms. The clarity and no-concept which has not arisen as either of the two obscurations is the mirrorlike primordial wisdom. The

freedom from falling into partialities and dimensions is the primordial wisdom of evenness. Knowing all the phenomenal existents without confusion is the discriminative primordial wisdom.' "

Then Khenpo took a sip of saffron water, and sitting in the posture of "relaxing in the natural state of mind" said, "What are you thinking?"[268]

With those words, he merged into the luminous absorption of the ultimate nature, about which he was speaking. He remained in the luminous absorption for a couple of days, as is common for many great meditators. During that period, although his heartbeat had stopped and there was no movement of the pulse, he held up his head, kept his body straight, and maintained a touch of heat at his heart, which are signs that he was still in the luminous absorption, or that he had a good experience of the luminous absorption. A meditator who realizes and maintains the luminous absorption of his or her own mind can unite it with the universal or outer luminous absorption so that all the appearances spontaneously arise as the manifestative power of his or her mind itself. That is the attainment of Buddhahood or Dharmakāya, the ultimate truth.

According to tradition, after a few days, Khenpo's body was cremated with ceremonies and prayers in a stūpa that was a temporary construction, which was then sealed off. After a few days, when the disciples opened the stūpa to collect his ashes, they found hundreds of ringsels in white, red, yellow, and blue colors, which had emerged and were emerging from the burned bones. Ringsels of multiple colors are rare and are a sign of great accomplishment through Dzogpa Chenpo meditation. Later, the disciples built a golden stūpa and placed most of the ringsels in it. I had a set of four of these ringsels in four colors in my locket, but at about the same time that the golden stūpa in the Dodrupchen Monastery in Tibet was destroyed, I lost my locket in India. It seems that when the time comes, everything that is supposed to go goes, in one way or another.

At Dodrupchen Monastery, Kyala Khenpo was appointed as a khenpo, to fill the position of his late master. Ta-re Lhamo (Namkhe Pumo, b. 1937), the daughter of Apang Tertön Ogyen Thrinle Lingpa (?–1945); and the author of this book, Tulku Thondup (b. 1939), were recognized as the tülkus of Lushül Khenpo.

26

Third Dodrupchen Jigme Tenpe Nyima (1865–1926)

The third Dodrupchen Rinpoche, Jigme Tenpe Nyima[269] was born on the evening of Monday, the eighteenth day of the second month of the Wood Ox year of the fourteenth Rabjung (1865) in the Chakong tribe of the Nup clan of the Achak Dru lineage. He was born at Chakri Öbar, a sacred hill in the upper Mar Valley of Golok, where his mother, Sönamtso, lived. His father was Dudjom Lingpa (1835–1903), a famous adept and a great tertön, who was then living at Dröphuk, a hermitage in a small gorge about a mile away from Chakri. His father named him Sönam Tendzin.

Dodrupchen had seven younger brothers, all of whom were famous tülkus. Khyentse Tülku Dzamling Wangyal (1868–1907), a tülku of Do Khyentse, was enthroned at Dodrupchen and Nizok monasteries but remained with his father. Tülku Tri-me Özer (aka Pema Drodül Sang-ngak Lingpa, 1881–1924) became a great scholar and tertön whose consort was the famous teacher Dewe Dorje of Lhasa, popularly known as Sera Khandro. The tülku of Cheyö Rigdzin Chenmo died young. Tülku Pema Dorje, a tülku of Satsa Lama, lived at Dodrupchen Monastery and took care of Dodrupchen and the monastery. Tülku Lhatop (1885–?) was a tülku of Shichen (gShi Ch'en) Monastery. Tülku Namkha Jigme (1888–?) was recognized as a tülku of Paltrül Rinpoche and lived in Dzachukha. Tülku Dorje Dradül (1892–1959?) remained at Dartsang

Ritrö in the Li gorge of Do Valley, Düdjom Lingpa's seat in the latter part of his life.

Dodrupchen was recognized by the fourth Dzogchen Rinpoche, Mingyur Namkhe Dorje (1793–?). In his prophecy there is a line that identifies the third Dodrupchen as the "adornment of the excellent iron casket," an allusion to the Chakong, or "iron casket," tribe.

In 1810 he was enthroned at Yarlung Pemakö Monastery in the Ser Valley. For many years he spent the summers at Yarlung Pemakö and winters at Dodrupchen Monastery, which is also known as Tsangchen Gön, or the monastery at Tsangchen field. Later, Dodrupchen Monastery became his main seat. At the beginning, Tülku Tri-me, a six-year-old younger brother of his, came to stay with him. After a few years Tülku Tri-me no longer wished to live in a monastic structure and returned home. Then another brother, Tülku Pema Dorje, came to stay with Dodrupchen. Later on, Tülku Pema Dorje became the administrator of the monastery and the devout caretaker of Dodrupchen's projects until his death. Tülku Pema Dorje said, "[Dodrupchen] Rinpoche would hardly say anything directly about what to do, but listening to his hints, I would try to fulfill his aspirations."

Dodrupchen went to Dzogchen Monastery and studied with Khenpo Pema Dorje. At the beginning it was difficult for him to understand the meaning of philosophical texts. He often cried himself to sleep, and in the morning he found that his head was stuck to the pillow because of his tears. One morning he said to his tutor, "Last night in a dream I saw three lamas in ascetic costumes in a temple. The middle one was holding a volume in his hand. I asked him, 'Who are you? What is this volume?' He replied, 'I am Do Khyentse Yeshe Dorje. This volume is for helping people who cannot learn their lessons.' I asked him to give me the book. He did so, and I felt extremely happy. So I have confidence that if I study today, I shall learn." Thereafter, the breadth of his understanding suddenly burst forth, and he had no difficulty in understanding the meaning of the texts.

The next year, he went to the great master Paltrül Rinpoche (1808–1887) in the Dzachukha Valley. He received many teachings from Paltrül. He was able to grasp the meaning of the texts the first time he heard something, and he did not require a teaching assistant (sKyor dPon) to review the lesson with him. Dodrupchen was only eight years old when Paltrül Rinpoche sent messengers all over Dzachukha Valley inviting people to hear him, for he would be giving the annual teaching on the

Bodhicharyāvatāra. Before a big assembly of monks and laypeople at Dzagya Monastery, Paltrül Rinpoche himself offered the ceremonial maṇḍala and requested the teaching. Dodrupchen presented the discourses, and everyone was astonished by his understanding and confidence. At first, Dodrupchen's little voice didn't reach people who were sitting far away, but slowly his voice became stronger and all were able to hear it. Paltrül expressed his joy in a message to Khyentse Wangpo, saying:

> Concerning the Dharma of scholarship, the tülku of Dodrupchen has given the explanatory teachings on the *Bodhicharyāvatāra* at the age of eight. As for the Dharma of realization, Nyakla Pema Düdül [1816–1872] has just attained the rainbow body. So the Doctrine of Buddha has not yet declined.

Paltrül was very kind and respectful to Dodrupchen, and he would let him sit on his pillow during his teachings. One early morning Paltrül heard that Dodrupchen was crying. Later he was told that Dodrupchen had dozed during his dawn prayers and his tutor had given him a spanking. Paltrül was so upset at what the tutor had done that he told Dodrupchen, "When you die, don't go to Zangdok Palri, for if you do, Guru Rinpoche will send you back again, as he is always worrying about Tibetans. You just go to Dewachen [Amitābha's pure land], and don't come back to these people." Paltrül didn't like the tutor, as he was too harsh for little Dodrupchen. On Dodrupchen's next visit to Paltrül, he had Akhu Lodrö, a gentle, respectful, gray-haired monk, as his tutor. Paltrül was happy with him and he said, "Oh, he looks like a tutor of an important lama." Whenever Akhu Lodrö had to discipline Dodrupchen, first he would make three prostrations to him. So, even many years later, when Akhu Lodrö made prostrations in order to receive teachings from him, Dodrupchen said, "It still makes me nervous to see Akhu Lodrö doing prostrations to me."

From many teachers, mainly Khenpo Pema Dorje, Paltrül Rinpoche, Khyentse Wangpo (1820–1892), the fourth Dzogchen Rinpoche (1793–?), Mura Tülku Pema Dechen Zangpo, Zhechen Thutop Namgyal (1787–?), Gyarong Namtrül Künzang Thekchok Dorje, Ju Mipham Namgyal (1846–1912), Gyawa Do-ngak Gyatso, Kongtrül Yönten Gyatso (1813–1899), and Tertön Sögyal (1856–1926), Dodrupchen received teachings on Vinaya, Madhyamaka, Nyāya, Prajñāpāramitā, Abhidharma, and the Old Tantras and New Tantras. He received the transmission of the complete Nyingma teachings, with particular emphasis on *Yabzhi* and *Longchen Nyingthig* from Khyentse Wangpo, Khenpo Pema Dorje, and the fourth Dzogchen Rinpoche. He became a great master and holder of many lineal transmissions.

He received visions of many masters and divinities and achieved many attainments. But little is known of his inner realizations because he hardly disclosed any. When he mentioned any visions, he always portrayed them as dreams. That might have been true because, for a realized person, dreams are illusory and luminous clarity of one's own wisdom mind, and so too, all pure visions are manifestations of that illusory and luminous clarity.

When he was fifteen, as political dangers kept people in a turmoil of great fear, Rokza Lama Palge asked Dodrupchen to check his dream signs. He did so for three nights. On the first night he saw a fearful bird in a cage. Other birds were trying to oppose the caged bird, but they all collapsed when they arrived before it. Then someone told Dodrupchen, "If many yellow swans surround him and fly over him, he will faint and fall." On the second night he was in a dense forest. Someone said, "At the edge of the forest, a dangerous tiger is ready to jump and eat everyone. But at present, only his head is raised to look around, while his body is still lying on the ground. If powerful tāntrikas throw tormas, he will lower his head to the ground." On the third night, he was given a message from Khyentse Wangpo that explained the ultimate danger to Buddhism and the peace of Tibet. This message will be given later, in the life of the fourth Dodrupchen, Thupten Thrinle Palzang. "The dreams indicate," he said, "that if all the religious people collectively perform rites of averting negative forces now, the dangers will be avoided. Otherwise, the peace and wisdom of Buddhism will be diminished before long." Then he emphasized that it was very important for each and every person—monks, nuns, or laypeople—to say OṂ MAṆI PADME HŪṂ, the mantra of the Buddha of Compassion and Guru Rinpoche, in groups or individually, as many times as they could, with compassion and devotion. That would be the best way of averting such dangers. Some great lamas of that area tried their best to follow his advice, but many said, "Rinpoche told us to say OṂ MAṆI PADME HŪṂ. That means there is nothing we can do but say the mantra and prepare for death," and they didn't do much. Among illiterate or less educated people, there is a popular notion that meditation on compassion and saying peaceful mantras are preparations for death or for the attainment of enlightenment, while for averting great dangers you have to perform exorcism. But the truth is that any form of Buddhist practice must be based on compassion and serve all.

At the age of twenty-one (1875), Dodrupchen composed his first scholarly writing, *Lekshe Gaton,* a commentary on *Guhyagarbha-māyā-jāla-tantra,* a most important Nyingma tantric scripture. Scholars were amazed by his scholarship at such a young age. However, many years later, he discovered that his commentary had been influenced by the views of the Sarma[270] tradition of Tibet, and he wrote a second commentary on the same subject.

When he was thirty, his tutor Akhu Lodrö asked how long he himself would live. That night in a dream Dodrupchen opened a book and there were two lines: "Your tutor yogī will live for five years. He will not stay longer than that. There will be no change." His gentle old tutor passed away after five years.

At the age of twenty-two, Dodrupchen stayed with Ju Mipham Namgyal for a long time at Dzongsar Monastery, where Khyentse Wangpo was living. Before Dodrupchen's departure for Dodrupchen Monastery and Mipham's departure for Karmo Taktsang, Dodrupchen went to Mipham to bid him goodbye. Mipham came to the door of the room to see Dodrupchen off and gave him a scroll. Later Dodrupchen found in the scroll a thirty-seven (Me Ri) verse instruction on crucial philosophical points. At the end of the verses, Mipham said, "Please do not show it to others." So he could not do so. In that scroll were two lines of prophecy for Dodrupchen:

> If the flame is not blown out by the wind,
> At thirty-five, the obstructions will be cleared and you will uphold
> your own lineal tradition.

At this, Dodrupchen thought: I am trying to uphold the tradition of my own Nyingma and especially the Nyingthig lineage, and what new thing could happen then? But at the age of thirty-five, for no particular reason, Dodrupchen wanted to read *Kagye Deshe Düchen.* When he read it, somehow he realized that his earlier understanding of Nyingma views (as he had presented it in his first commentary on the *Guhyagarbha-māyājāla-tantra*) were influenced by Sarma views, and a new understanding of Nyingma views and a strong confidence in them awakened in him. Then for five years he studied a great number of Nyingma writings, and from the age of forty his confidence in the ultimate view was fully affirmed in terms of the unique views of Nyingma as interpreted by Longchen Rabjam and Jigme Lingpa. That was what Ju Mipham had meant by his two lines of prophecy.

Tuktsa Tülku of Dephu, a Sakya monastery in Amdo, told Ju Mipham that he wanted to study Nyingma teachings, but he wasn't sure whether to study with Dodrupchen, as his views might have been influenced by Sarma views. Mipham assured him, "At the beginning Dodrupchen's Nyingma views had some influence from Sarma views, but now his Nyingma views definitely are pure Nyingma views. You should go and study with him." And Tuktsa did.

At Dodrupchen Monastery, Dodrupchen rebuilt the main temple and a huge stūpa. With the support of other great khenpos, he gave teachings for a number of years without rest or intermission, including delivering discourses on the *Bodhicharyāvatāra* one hundred times by himself alone, as Paltrül had made him promise to do. Later, he would point to a small but beautifully made wooden throne (which I have seen) and say to people, "From that wooden seat I have given teachings on the *Guhyagarbha-tantra* over forty times." As a result, Dodrupchen Monastery became a famous center for study and practice of the whole of exoteric and esoteric Buddhism.

One day while he was giving teachings, a strong storm suddenly swept across the area. As the storm touched Dodrupchen, he felt sick, and thereafter he remained sick and unable to walk. As the result, he moved to his hermitage and remained in seclusion for the rest of his life. The hermitage is called Gephel Ritrö, the Hermitage of Fostering Virtues, which in his writings he sometimes referred to as the Forest of Many Birds. This hermitage is situated below the summit of a sky-touching mountain about two miles from Dodrupchen Monastery, in the middle of a lawn fenced by tall pine and juniper trees. The big three-storied house in which he lived was filled with wonderful religious objects and many rare books, so that the entire house resembled a library, temple, museum, and residence in one. He describes the hermitage:

> It is raised as the crown of a high mountain,
> Crowded with youthful men, the trees,
> In whose laps women, the gentle birds,
> Are singing their melodies.

In it there is a temple where virtuous fruitions are being fulfilled.
Its walls are smooth with the color of the moon.
Young plants of the forest are visiting to decorate it,
As if they are making curtsies of respect.

There were a few resident monk-scholars who looked after him and the hermitage. Although he was ill, he never rested apart from the hours during which he slept, and he was constantly engaged in writing, study, or meditation.

In 1904, he was asked for his dreams about whether his brother Tülku Pema Dorje should take administrative charge of Dodrupchen Monastery. That night he dreamt a line in a book that said, "Until death he will exhort in Dharma." His brother looked after the administration until his death.

When he was forty-one (1905), half of the Lagya tribal group, who were the lay subjects or parishioners of Dodrupchen Monastery, were expelled from Ser Valley by chieftain Washül Kadö. Dodrupchen Monastery was forced to consider moving to another region. But then Pema Bum, one of the three major tribal divisions of Golok, offered Tri Valley to Dodrupchen for his lay subjects. Subsequently Lagya settled in Tri, and Dodrupchen Monastery remained where it was.

As Dodrupchen lived in seclusion in his hermitage, with the exception of his attendants, the four great khenpos, and a few of the tülkus of Dodrupchen Monastery, very few people ever had an audience with him. Among the few visitors who were received for teachings were Tertön Sögyal, Rigdzin Chenpo of Dorje Trak, Kathok Situ, Khyentse Chökyi Lodrö, Garwa Tertön Long-yang (d. 1910), Tarthang Choktrül, Tülku Tsultrim Zangpo, and Sera Rintreng.

Tertön Sögyal (Lerab Lingpa, 1856–1926) was a frequent visitor, and he and Dodrupchen exchanged teachings. In 1916, when Dodrupchen wrote his second commentary of the *Guhyagarbha-māyājāla-tantra,* called *Dzökyi Demik,* Tertön Sögyal transcribed what Dodrupchen dictated to him. Dodrupchen's *Terkyi Namshe,* the treatise on ter discovery, which is another original writing of his, was heavily based on clarifications he received from Tertön Sögyal.

Tertön Sögyal brought four symbolic scripts (brDa Yig), which he had discovered but couldn't decode yet. Together he and Dodrupchen decoded them. According to ter principles, if a teaching was entrusted to and concealed in many disciples by Guru Rinpoche, then not only the designated tertön but others also were authorized to decode the symbolic scripts.

At the age of fifty-nine (1914),[271] Tertön Sögyal moved to Golok and stayed close to Dodrupchen for the rest of his life. First he started to build a gompa at Khemar field in upper Do Valley among the Wang-röl tribal group, but before completion he left it for others to finish. Then he and his family were given special permission to live in Dodrupchen Monastery. But after some time, he chose to move to Dzongdün in Ser Valley, about a day's journey by horse from Dodrupchen Monastery, and he stayed there for the rest of his life.

Once when Tertön Sögyal was seriously sick at Dzongdün, he told his attendants to carry him to Dodrupchen. On the way, when his party reached Dilsham Kathok in Thang-yag Valley, he told his attendants to make prostrations to a tree in the field, where the second Dodrupchen had been born. When they got to the Do River, miraculously he was able to ride his horse, and after seeing Dodrupchen all his sickness had disappeared.

In the year of the Wood Ox (1925), Tertön Sögyal came to see Dodrupchen. At the conclusion of their meeting, they exchanged scarves, which they never had done when they parted on previous occasions. Then they told each other, "I shall see you in the Pure Land." The next year, in the year of the Fire Tiger (1926), they both died.

Rigdzin Chenmo, the head of the Dorje Trak Monastery, asked to be allowed to see Dodrupchen. Traditionally, since Rigdzin Chenmo was one of the two most important lamas of the Nyingma school, Dodrupchen was pleased to see him. On his arrival, Rigdzin Chenmo didn't even sit on the cushion but sat on the floor on a small carpet before Dodrupchen. Then they had lunch together with a long question-and-answer session in private. Rigdzin Chenmo later valued it as his most beneficial meeting with a lama.

Kathok Situ Chökyi Gyatso (1880–1925) came to see Dodrupchen with many questions on philosophy and meditation. Kathok Situ also made a famous statement to Dodrupchen: "Now at Dzogchen Monastery Gyakong Khenpo [Zhenphen Chökyi Nangwa] teaches the texts [gZhung] according to Indian commentaries, saying, 'Only Indian commentaries are reliable.' At your Dodrupchen Monastery, khenpos are teaching sūtras according to Geluk commentaries and tantras according to Nyingma tradition. So Kathok Monastery is the only institution where the pure Nyingma traditions are being taught." Dodrupchen inquried, "For *Abhisamayālaṃkāra,* what commentary are you using at Kathok?" Kathok Situ answered, "The commentary by Gorampa" (who was a famous Sakyapa master).

In 1920, Khyentse Chökyi Lodrö of Dzongsar (1893–1959) came to Dodrupchen's hermitage for a visit of several months to receive teachings and transmissions. One day Khyentse, alone as usual, went to Dodrupchen's shrine room to receive the *Rigdzin Düpa* empowerment. Dodrupchen was sitting on a higher seat. Khyentse was asked to sit on a cushion by the window. A monk who was the ritual assistant (chöpön) put all the empowerment materials on the altar and left the room. Dodrupchen kept saying the mantras. Soon the vase on the altar emitted white beams of light, filling the whole room. Then red lights covered the whole room, and it became hard for Khyentse even to see Dodrupchen. When the lights faded, he saw that a beautiful woman with ornaments was there, acting as the "action master" with dancing gestures. Khyentse, who was then a monk, thought, "It would have been better to have a monk doing the action-master performances at such an important time." At the end of the empowerment, the woman vanished. Dodrupchen told Khyentse, "Tülku Tsang! I had a supreme accomplishment to confer on you, but because of your concepts it couldn't happen today. But you will get it later. The lady was Dorje Yudrönma [one of the main Dharma protectresses of Longchen Nyingthig]." In the *Rigdzin Düpa* empowerment, Dodrupchen gave him the name Pema Yeshe Dorje, which scholars thought was an indication that Chökyi Lodrö was also the tülku of Do Khyentse Yeshe Dorje. At the time of *Ladrup Thigle Gyachen* transmissions, Khyentse saw Rinpoche as Longchen Rabjam.[272] Khyentse Chökyi Lodrö writes of his visit to Dodrupchen in verses.

> I went to the encampment of Do[drupchen] in the North and
> Met the omniscient Tenpe Nyima.
> I received the empowerments of *Rigdzin Düpa* and *Ladrup Thigle Gyachen,*
> The teachings on *Longchen Nyingthig,* and
> *The Outline of Guhyagarbha.*
> He constantly gave me instructions and advice.
> He gave me the permission to propagate
> His writings, with no need of having the verbal transmission [Lung].
> With great kindness, he gave me all the care.[273]

Tarthang Choktrül Chökyi Dawa (1894–1959) was a student of Khenpo Könchok Drönme, and at Khenpo's repeated request he arranged to have an audience with Dodrupchen. Tarthang Choktrül came to Rinpoche and sat on the cushion; they had lunch together, and he left without asking any questions on any important Dharma points. Later, others asked Tarthang Choktrül, "Why didn't you ask Rinpoche any important meditation or intellectual questions?" He answered, "I just went to see Rinpoche and receive a blessing—not to ask questions!"

Tülku Tsültrim Zangpo of Shukchung Monastery, a great scholar and adept, was a doctrine-holder of Tertön Sögyal's ter teachings, as Dodrupchen himself was. Also, he copied many texts for Dodrupchen. Because of the texts he was able to see Dodrupchen many times.

Sera Rintreng, a brilliant scholar, was one of those who got to see Dodrupchen by becoming one of his attendants. He spent three years as Dodrupchen's cook. One day, giving him a yellow-seed rosary, Dodrupchen told him, "Because of my health I can't give you any textual teachings. You must go to the east. You will become a great scholar of the Dharma." Accordingly, Rintreng went to Ditsa hermitage in Amdo and studied with Alak Zhamar and became a great scholar.

Many people found another way to see Dodrupchen. Every year Dodrupchen gave empowerments and a brief explanation of the Three Root Sādhanas of *Longchen Nyingthig* for the monks who were to enter into the one-year meditation school of the monastery. But the school took only eight monks, and most of them would repeat the same program for years in order to see Dodrupchen. But sometimes, if a monk promised to do a strict year's retreat by himself, he could be admitted into the empowerment given by Dodrupchen. Among those monks were my teacher Chöchok of the Kyala family, who later became known as Kyala Khenpo of Dodrupchen Monastery, and Lobzang Dorje (aka Lo-de) of the Akong family, who later became known as Akong Khenpo of Tarthang Monastery.

Kyala Khenpo (we will talk about him in chapter 34) received the empowerments for three successive years, which turned out to be the empowerments of Dodrupchen's last three years.

From his childhood Akong Khenpo had a great urge to see Dodrupchen. Once he was grown up, he came to Dodrupchen Monastery to find a way to see him. Khenpo was a good scribe, so first he copied eight volumes for Dodrupchen by sending manuscripts back and forth through the attendants. He refused to accept any fees for copying, but requested in return to be allowed to do a one-year retreat program, so that he could see Dodrupchen. This he was allowed to do. Finally, when Khenpo saw Dodrupchen, he never felt even for a second that Dodrupchen was a human being, but only a Buddha. With total concentration and devotion, he received the long empowerments with many others. But after a while, for a fraction of a second, his mind was distracted by something else and suddenly Dodrupchen shouted PHAṬ!, an esoteric syllable. Khenpo felt that he had almost fainted. Shocked, he looked up at Dodrupchen, staring at him with wide-open eyes. At the end of the ceremony, Dodrupchen said, "In the ceremony of an empowerment, if a realized master and a devotional disciple meet together, the disciple could be introduced to the realization. Young monk of Akong, you have got such an introduction. Now you must meditate on it with diligence." Later Khenpo said that was how he realized the true nature, not by studying.

Many people constantly visited the hermitage in search of answers to their questions on philosophical points or meditation training, often seeking to pose their questions through intermediaries. One of them was Dodrupchen's scholar and adept brother, Tülku Tri-me, who came to him with questions. Dodrupchen declined to receive him, saying, "It is not fair to see my brother and not to see others." However, Tülku Tri-me was satisfied by the necessary clarifications he got through Rayop Rang-rik, Dodrupchen's brilliant attendant.

In Dodrupchen Monastery there were many great scholars, among them the four great khenpos whose appearance was foretold in *The Confidential Prophecy of Lama Gongdü*. Their names are Sershul Khenpo Ngawang Kün-ga, Garwa Khenpo Jigme Ösal (?–1926), Amye Khenpo Tamchö Özer (?–1927?), and Lushül Khenpo Könchok Drönme (1859–1936). Almost all the scholars of that time in Golok and Serta provinces of Tibet and also many from Nyingma monasteries of Kham, Gyarong, and Amdo were students of Dodrupchen Monastery.

Although Dodrupchen became a celebrated scholar and a perpetual refuge for a great number of people, his monastery remained simple and small, as he did not push for material prosperity, which could distract people from true Dharma. He was a hidden ascetic, so it was very difficult to know the depth of his inner realizations or views. Like a child, he was free from pride and easy to be with, yet his mind was profound and he spoke the truth. Because of the simplicity of his way of life, the richness of his qualities, the profundity of his scholarship, and the discipline that he had over his own mind, whenever intellectuals and powerful people came before him, they simply became humble, silent, and subdued in his presence.

Upon completion of the construction of a great stūpa at Gogen Thang in Ser Valley, he performed the consecration ceremony in his hermitage. The grains that he tossed in the ritual instantaneously landed on the stūpa, which was at a distance of one and a half days' journey by horse.

Although Dodrupchen never took the ordination of full monkhood and remained holding the vow of a novice monk (shrāmaṇera), he observed his novice monk vows very strictly, such as not eating after midday. He instructed the four great khenpos, the abbots of Dodrupchen Monastery, to direct the monastery in the strictest monastic laws, and it became a model monastic institution in the region of Golok and beyond.

Dodrupchen preserved his hermitage also as a monastic residence. Once Tertön Sögyal asked him, "My consort strongly wishes to have an audience. Is it possible for her to come to see you?" Dodrupchen thought for a while and said, "Is it OK if people take me to my doorstep to meet her? For no woman has ever crossed my doorstep yet." So, one day, people helped Dodrupchen downstairs to the door, and he gave teachings to the consort of Tertön Sögyal. It is believed that one of the reasons why he was so strict about his monastic discipline is the aspiration that the second Dodrupchen made at the time of his death, as mentioned earlier.

Although Dodrupchen was not healthy, he consistently kept reading and studying. Once his brother, Tülku Pema Dorje, anxiously asked him, "Rinpoche, when will you finish your studies?" He paused and said, "When I attain Buddhahood." Pema Dorje complained, "Oh, that will be too long!"

Dodrupchen produced five volumes of scholarly treatises on both exoteric (sūtra) and esoteric (tantra) teachings. Among these, his text on *Changchup Sempe Zung* (Memories of the Bodhisattvas)[274] was profusely praised by scholars as a work of unprecedented originality. This text was written much earlier, but he put it into final form in the Water Dog year (1922). His *Dzökyi Demik* (An Outline of the Guhyagarbha-māyājāla-tantra)[275] became one of the important texts of the Nyingma on the studies of *Guhyagarbha-tantra,* which is the root text of Mahāyoga and also of the Nyingma tantras in general. Also among his other important writings are *Terkyi Namshe,* a detailed description of the discovery of the hidden mystical teachings,[276] and *Kyiduk Lamkhyer,*[277] a short but profound piece on turning happiness and suffering into the training of Buddhism.

When Jampal Rölpe Lodrö, popularly known as Amdo Geshe, a great Geluk scholar and also a teacher of Khyentse Chökyi Lodrö, saw Dodrupchen's text *The Memories of the Bodhisattvas,* he said, "This is not written by a human mind. This could only be written by a person who has the blessings of the Wisdom Deity, Mañjushrī." Amdo Geshe offered a copy of this text to the thirteenth Dalai Lama, who said, "Today, a writer of this quality is very rare in this land." Amdo Geshe stayed with Khenpo Tamchö at Dodrupchen Monastery for a winter, but he was unable to see Dodrupchen. However, when Amdo Geshe saw Dodrupchen's commentary on the *Guhyagarbha-māyājāla-tantra,* he objected to the uniquely Nyingma views given in it, and he wished to debate with Dodrupchen. On hearing this story, Sera Rintreng, a scholar of both Nyingma and Geluk texts, said, "I know Amdo Geshe. He is a great scholar and a wonderful lama. But he is a human being after all. I know Rinpoche. We don't know what a Buddha could be, except to say, 'A Buddha is a very special one.' Rinpoche is not a human being. He is a very special one. That I witnessed myself." Then he added, "If Amdo Geshe wishes, I will debate with him. He is contradicting himself. He praised Rinpoche's first writing as a work of a person with the blessings of Mañjushrī. If that is so, there must be the blessing of Mañjushrī for Rinpoche's next writing!"[278] However, they never got the chance to debate.

The present, fourteenth Dalai Lama has also praised the works of the third Dodrupchen Rinpoche in his private interviews and public speeches as the greatest scholarly works on the Nyingma view, and he has recommended reading them in order to learn the unique views of the Nyingma. He has said that the lineage of his own understanding (or realization) of Dzogpa Chenpo and Nyingma first came to him from the third Dodrupchen by reading his writings.

Among the four great khenpos of Dodrupchen Monastery, Garwa Khenpo was the closest to Dodrupchen. One day Khenpo returned to the monastery from a visit to the hermitage unusually late. A disciple of his asked the reason for his being late, and he answered, "We talked about some happy things and some sad things." The disciple asked, "What are they?" Khenpo said, "Rinpoche wanted to die first, and I urged him to let me die first." When asked, "What did you decide?" he answered, "I will die a little earlier." After about a year Khenpo died, and after a few months Dodrupchen died too.

Just a few months before Dodrupchen's death, he gave his last annual empowerments for the retreatants. According to Kyala Khenpo, who was one of the recipients, Rinpoche's health appeared unchanged. However, for the preceding two years, at the end of the empowerment, without saying any aspiration or auspicious prayers, he had always made a gesture that the ceremony was over, and then everyone would leave. But this time, at the end of the empowerment, Garwa Khenpo walked in from next door as he was waiting there to conclude the ceremony, although the disciples didn't know it. Then Dodrupchen said, "It is said, 'Don't be humble in making aspirations,' so we should say an elaborate aspiration prayer." Led by Khenpo, Dodrupchen and the disciples said many long aspiration prayers together, followed by a long auspicious prayer by Dodrupchen himself. Kyala Khenpo told me that he thought, "Oh! This is a sign that Rinpoche will not be giving any more empowerments," and certainly that was his last transmission of empowerments. Garwa Khenpo and Dodrupchen had planned all this in advance.

Then one day, while Dodrupchen was composing a commentary on *Me-ngak Tatreng* (Garland of Instructions on View) by Guru Rinpoche, he told his attendant to wrap up the manuscript and return it to the shelf, saying, "For the time being this is the end of my writing. In the future a person who says he is my tülku will come and complete this text." (However, no one has written a new commentary yet.) Thereafter he started to appear ill, and one evening he suddenly passed away at the age of sixty-two, in the Fire Tiger year (1926). There were the usual signs at the deaths of great masters, including earth tremors, rainbow rays, and warm weather. After forty-nine days his body was cremated, and the remains were preserved in a two-story-high golden stūpa at Dodrupchen Monastery.

27

SHUKSEP LOCHEN CHÖNYI ZANGMO
1865–1953

JETSUN Lochen Chönyi Zangmo[279] of Shuksep nunnery was one of the foremost lady teachers of the last many centuries of Tibetan Buddhism.

She was born on the fifteenth of the first month of the Wood Ox year of the fourteenth Rapchung (1865)[280] near Rewalsar, Himachal Pradesh, India. When she was born the earth shook mildly, the sound of OṂ MAṆI PADME HŪṂ was heard from the air, and a rain of flowers was seen. Also, in the same hour, the family servant bore a girl and the family's lamb gave birth. Her father was Töndrup Namgyal, alias Thonglek Tashi, from Tibet, and her mother was Penpa Dölma from Bhutan. Her parents met while they were each on pilgrimage and were staying in India. Although her parents came from prosperous families, they went to India leading the simple life of pilgrims who sustained themselves with alms. Her parents separated soon after her birth, and she grew up with her mother amid material poverty but spiritual wealth. From childhood Jetsün was very respectful to her mother and the elders, harmonious with friends, devout in Dharma, kind to all beings, accompanied by miracles, and richly gifted with wisdom.

In Tibet there were a number of people who died, went through the bardo experiences, saw different worlds of beings and/or pure lands of the Buddhas, and then, after many days, returned to their bodies. Thereafter they lived healthy lives and told the stories of their experiences for years. They are called Deloks, returners from death. Jetsün read the Delok stories of Karma Wangdzin and Nangza Öbum. By reading them a couple of times, she memorized every word and its meaning.

One night in a dream, Jetsün saw a Delok woman singing OṂ MAṆI PADME HŪṂ in various enchanting melodies; Jetsün sang along with her and proved to sing as well as the other woman. After waking she still remembered the melodies and sang them, to the amazement of her companions.

With her mother, she traveled to gathering places such as markets and fairs, where the gifted young lady would display her paintings of the stories of Deloks, tell their stories, and sing OṂ MAṆI PADME HŪṂ in her enchanting voice in various melodies from morning till evening. Everywhere she went, she attracted crowds, and those who listened to her were inspired to belief in karma and devotion to Dharma. Many would cry remembering their own misdeeds, many forswore doing any more evil deeds, many committed their lives to Dharma training, and many also made generous offerings.

At the age of thirteen, as advised by a nun from Amdo named Lobzang Dölma, Jetsün and her mother went to Ökar Trak near Kyirong to see the nun's uncle, Pema Gyatso (aka Chi-me Dorje, 1829–1890?),[281] a master from Amdo. Pema Gyatso turned out to be one of Jetsün's karmic lamas. He was a disciple of both Zhapkar Tsoktruk Rangtröl and Thatral Dorje.[282] Thatral Dorje was a direct disciple of the first Dodrupchen. From Pema Gyatso she received the teachings on *Künzang Lame Zhalung* and empowerments of *Longchen Nyingthig*. The lama gave her all the teachings but treated her strictly, as Marpa had treated Milarepa. She also received teachings from Jinpa Norbu and Nangdze Dorje, disciples of Zhapkar.

At Heri hermitage in the Nupri area, she did a three-year retreat in the caves and completed her ngöndro training and recitations of the complete *Longchen Nyingthig* cycle. In this retreat she realized the true nature and sang her realization to her teacher:

> The meaning is beyond comprehension of the mind.
> The clarity of the natural glow [power] is unceasing.
> It is resonating, but beyond the utterances of speech.
> It is clear, but beyond description in words.
> Because of the ease in my mind, I gained natural confidence in it.

The experiences of bliss, clarity, and freedom from concepts are joyful.
All the fabrication of inviting [future experiences] or running after [past experiences] has dissolved.
Not just once, but again and again I am experiencing it.
I felt laughter as it naturally arose in me.
I gained confidence that there is nothing to seek from somewhere else.[283]

With Pema Gyatso she went to Lhasa, and they received teachings together from Dharma Senge. In 1890,[284] Pema Gyatso died, and after a month Dharma Senge also passed away. Dharma Senge told his disciples to give his hand drum, bell, and trumpet for chö rites to Jetsün, but she was given only the trumpet.

She also received teachings from Trülzhik Künzang Thongtrol of Dongak Ling, Tertön Rang-rik Dorje (a disciple of Nyoshül Lungtok) of Nyakrong, the fifth Dzogchen Rinpoche and Lama Sangye Tendzin, a disciple of Paltrül Rinpoche. She received *Longchen Nyingthig* and other transmissions from Matrül Thekchok Jigme Pawo, a disciple of Khyentse Wangpo, and *Rinchen Terdzö* from Zhechen Rabjam. Every day without exception, she was constantly in Dharma meditation and Dharma activities.

At Zangri Kharmar she received the transmission of the *Taphak Yizhin Norbu* from Thekchok Tenpe Gyaltsen, the tülku of Zhapkar, and was given the name Rigdzin Chönyi Zangmo. *Taphak Yizhin Norbu* was the main teaching and practice of Chögyal Ngaki Wangpo and Zhapkar Tsoktruk Rangtröl. She meditated on this teaching in retreat and experienced many events. They included solid things becoming ethereal, ethereal things becoming solid, and all kinds of forms and images appearing before her. In addition, wherever her concentration went she could reach there; she was able to speak in the languages of various realms; she saw the happenings of the world as if she were looking at the lines on her palm; her body was filled with heat; her mind was filled with bliss; she could hardly stop singing or dancing; her mind never was separated from contemplative absorption; and her intrinsic awareness remained in the oneness, where there is no distinction of center or extremes.

One day she wished to see the Karmapa Khakhyap Dorje (1871–1922) in Tsurphu, and she instantly found herself before him and received blessings. Neither the attendants of Karmapa nor her own companions were aware of her visit to Karmapa's place or her absence from her retreat hut.

Then at Zang-ri Kharmar, she herself experienced Delok, returning from death. One day she fell down on the ground, her body became cold, and her breathing ceased. First her mother and friends thought that she had died, but then her mother saw that her face was the face of a living person, not a dead one (as indeed there had been miracles throughout her life). They checked her heart, and there was warmth in it, the amount of warmth in a bird's body. That confirmed her mother's belief. During her death experience, which lasted three weeks, she went to Zangdok Palri, the pure land of Guru Rinpoche, and received blessings and prophecies from Guru Rinpoche. She also experienced the hard travel through the bardo process, faced the Lord of Death, and saw the sufferings of beings in various realms.

From Semnyi Deyang Rinpoche she received the complete empowerment and textual transmissions of *Longchen Nyingthig* twice and also teachings on *Yönten Rinpoche Dzö*. She practiced the teachings in retreats, including a three-year recitation retreat on *Longchen Nyingthig*.

In accordance with Taklung Ma Rinpoche's divinations, Jetsün and her mother made their permanent residence at Shuksep, where their teacher Semnyi Rinpoche was also living.

Then her mother, who was ninety-nine years old and had said OṂ AMIDEVA [TABHA] HRĪḤ, the mantra of Amitābha Buddha, billions of times, facing the west, the direction of the pure land of Amitābha Buddha, said:

> In this life, in the next life, and in the intermediate life,
> In my mind, may there arise revulsion [from saṃsāra],
> extraordinary attitude [of love for all], and pure perception;
> May I perfect the attainment of the three sacreds;
> And may I become one with the Guru Amitābha.

And she died.

Later in her life Jetsün lived at Shuksep nunnery near Kangri Thökar, the main hermitage seat of Longchen Rabjam. She taught numerous people and especially nuns and laywomen of the nobility of Central Tibet as well as ordinary people for many years.

She also received transmissions from Kathok Situ Chökyi Gyatso,

Gyarong Namtrül Drodul Karkyi Dorje, Khyungtrül Rinpoche, Dzogchen Khenpo Chösö, and Lingtsang Gyalpo.

Advising her disciple Nordzin Wangmo, Jetsün writes:

> Realization of [the nature of] one's own mind by oneself is called intrinsic awareness.
> By purifying the confused ignorance into its primordial purity,
> Spontaneously accomplishing the self-arisen three Buddha bodies,
> And perfecting all the virtues, you will reach the dissolution [of phenomena in the ultimate nature].
> The meaning that transcends mental concepts is the view.
> Remaining [in that view] without distraction by circumstances is meditation.
> To release all, whatever you do is the Dharma action.
> To ripen the fruition of the practice is result. . . .
> By [starting your meditation] with pure attitude at the beginning,
> Maintaining the intrinsic awareness as the main practice in the middle, and
> Dedicating them with the wisdom of freedom from concepts at the end,
> May you perfect the three sacred aspects [of meditation] and attain liberation.

Her autobiography ends in the Earth Ox year (1949/50). At the age of eighty-nine, at the end of the Water Dragon year of the sixteenth Rabjung (1953), she passed away at Kangri Thökar.

Jetsün Pemala (b. 1955?), the daughter of Mr. and Mrs. Sönam Kazi of Sikkim, India, and Dorje Rapten (b. 1954), a son of Traring house of Lhasa have been recognized as the tülkus of Jetsün Lochen.

28

Fifth Dzogchen Thupten Chökyi Dorje
1872–1935

THE fifth Dzogchen Rinpoche Thupten Chökyi Dorje[285] was born in the Water Monkey year (1872) near Chabdo in Kham. He was recognized by Khyentse Wangpo and other lamas as the tülku of the fourth Dzogchen Rinpoche and enthroned at Dzogchen Monastery in 1875.

Rinpoche received teachings and esoteric transmissions from Paltrül Rinpoche, Khyentse Wangpo, Kongtrül Lodrö Thaye, Khenpo Pema Dorje, and many other masters.

With the support of Gyakong Khenpo, Zhenpen Chökyi Nangwa, and other great scholars, he transformed Shrīsiṃha, the scripture college of Dzogchen Monastery, into one of the most famous institutions of learning. Gyakong Khenpo was the incarnation of Gyalse Zhenphen Thaye and the author of notations on the "thirteen major scholarly textbooks."

He dedicated his life to developing his monastery and numerous branch monasteries, traveling and teaching without rest. His active life was filled with miracles and clarivoyance. Through his prophetic power, he recognized most of the important Nyingmapa tülkus of Eastern Tibet who were born in the last three decades of his life. No one who knew him doubted that he was a Buddha in human flesh.

In the latter part of his life, Rinpoche lived with about twenty or thirty young tülkus. Like a parent, he educated them and fed and dressed them with his own hands—all very unusual for a high lama. These young tülkus later became of great service to the monasteries and many people.

One day, Rinpoche sent for Nera Geshe of Dege and asked him to go to the forest and see if there was enough wood to build a monastery. Nera Geshe went to the forest because Rinpoche had asked him to, but barely looked around, thinking there was no point in looking for wood since he could see no possible reason to build a monastery. But he reported to Rinpoche that there was enough wood in the forest to build a monastery. Shortly thereafter, at the age of sixty-four (1935), Rinpoche suddenly died. The following year, the entire Dzogchen Monastery was consumed in a huge fire. Nera Geshe then realized why Rinpoche had sent him into the forest, and he dedicated the rest of his life to rebuilding the monastery.

His tülku, the sixth Dzogchen Rinpoche, Jigtral Changchup Dorje (1935–1958/9), died at an early age during Tibet's political turmoil. The seventh Dzogchen Rinpoche Jigme Losal Wangpo (b. 1964) lives in his new Dzogchen Monastery in exile in South India.

29

Gekong Khenpo Künzang Palden
1872–1943 [286]

Khenpo Kunzang Palden[287] was born in Dzachukha Valley in Kham in the Water Monkey year of the fifteenth Rabjung (1872). He was also known as Thupten Künzang Chökyi Trakpa and Gekong Khenpo Künpal.

From his youth he received teachings of both sūtra and tantra and of Nyingthig, in particular from Paltrül Rinpoche, who cared for him as his own son. Until Paltrül Rinpoche's death, Khenpo lived around Paltrül. Khenpo used to read the scriptures aloud while Paltrül Rinpoche listened. Khenpo was ordained as a monk by Khenpo Yönten Gyatso (Yön-ga) of Dzogchen Monastery and became one of the greatest propagators of monastic discipline. He studied most of the scholarly texts with Önpo Tendzin Norbu, the nephew of Gyalse Zhenphen Thaye, and also with Ju Mipham Namgyal. He became one of the great scholars.

He received many transmissions, especially of *Longchen Nyingthig,* from Khyentse Wangpo, the fifth Dzogchen Rinpoche, the third Dodrupchen, and Dechen Dorje. Thereby he became one of the great Longchen Nyingthig lineage holders. He also received teachings and transmissions from Adzom Drukpa, Kongtrül Yönten Gyatso, and Kathok Situ Chökyi Gyatso. In Ser Valley, from Düdjom Lingpa (1835–1903) he received the transmissions of new ter teachings discovered by Düdjom Lingpa.

He made Gekong Monastery of Dzachukha his main seat. He was the first teacher who taught at the new scripture college of Khathok Monastery, with Khenpo Ngawang Palzang as his teaching assistant.

In 1937, both fourth Dodrupchen Rinpoches came to Dzachukha to receive the transmissions of Nyingthig teachings from Khenpo. As his eyesight had become bad, with much hardship he gave the transmissions of both *Nyingthig Yabzhi* and *Longchen Nyingthig* to the Dodrupchens. Expressing his joy, he said, "My transmissions of Nyingthig teachings are unique in their authenticity and closeness. Now I have been able to hand over the inheritance of the father to his sons!"

He composed many important writings, including the commentaries on *Ngeshe Dronme, Bodhicharyāvatāra,* and *The Stories of Vinaya.* At the age of seventy-two, in the Water Sheep year (1943), with many wondrous signs, he passed away and left many ringsels as objects of devotion for his disciples.

30

Yukhok Chatralwa Chöying Rangtröl
1872–1952

Chatralwa Chöying Rangtröl[288] was a true Vimalamitra in human form. He was born in the Water Monkey year of the fifteenth Rabjung (1872) in Yukhok Valley. His father was Khyishül Tratse, and his mother was Adzi Zawalo.

He was known as Yukhok Chatralwa, the Hermit from Yukhok Valley. Chöying Rangtröl, the Natural Liberation in the Ultimate Sphere, was his given name. He was known as a tülku of Dola Jigme Kalzang.

At the age of eleven, he was admitted to Lhatse Monastery of the Palyül lineage in Lower Ser Valley. Because of his gifted intellect, his studies advanced quickly. He received many transmissions from Lhatse Kyabgön.

Once, as he was traveling on a dangerous path in Lower Do Valley to collect alms for the sustenance of his future studies and meditation, he was attacked by a mother leopard with her two cubs and survived being devoured only by the power of his prayers. For a long time afterward he had nightmares about the leopards. One night in a dream a woman bringing the leopards to him said, "These leopards are my apparitions, but you didn't realize it." Then the leopards dissolved into the woman, and she also dissolved into a letter and then vanished. Later Kyabgön told him, "Your experience of leopards was a shaking up [sLong Tshad] of your hidden concepts and emotions, but it took until now for you to realize it. Now you have been able to overcome them." Chatralwa read the biography of Milarepa and for five days he experienced having no reference points in his mind, and since then his mind rested at ease.

Once his teacher Lhatse Kyabgön was seriously sick, and he invited a powerful ter master, Rolwe Dorje, popularly known as Chagmo Tülku. By Chagmo Tülku's blessing, his teacher recovered from his sickness.

Chatralwa became aware that Chagmo Tülku possessed unique Dzogpa Chenpo instructions. He requested Chagmo Tülku to give him the instructions. Instead, Chagmo Tülku advised him to go to his own teacher, the third Dodrupchen, for the instructions. But Lhatse Kyabgön would not allow Chatralwa to leave. Finally Chagmo Tülku gave him the instructions on Dzogpa Chenpo, including teachings on *Yeshe Lama,* saying, "These are the essence of Dodrupchen's instructions." Chatralwa meditated with great diligence upon what he had been taught. After a week, he felt many experiences. The karmic air (or energy) created by subjective-objective grasping dissolved into the ultimate sphere, and he remained in the absence of thoughts. It wasn't an unconsciousness or neutral state of mind. Like the light of a lamp in a vase, ceaseless Buddhas and pure lands as well as the ultimate sounds were spontaneously present as the luminosity of the intrinsic awareness (the true nature of the mind), the primordial wisdom.

Many years later, after the death of Lhatse Kyabgön, Chatralwa went to see Düdjom Lingpa (1835–1903) and received *Nangjang* and other teachings for many months. Following Düdjom Lingpa's prophecy, he went to see his karmic teacher, Adzom Drukpa (1842–1924), and received teachings starting from ngöndro up to the Trekchö meditation of primordial purity and Thögal meditation of luminous clarity, which had been entrusted to Adzom Drukpa by Khyentse Wangpo. He was also given the transmissions of *Nyingthig Yabzhi, Longchen Nyingthig, Chetsün Nyingthig, Gongpa Zangthal,* and many others.

According to the prophecy of Adzom Drukpa, he came to Lower Ser Valley to propagate the teachings. On the top of a high, steep, conchlike mountain, he built his hermitage, which became known as Yage Gar, the Encampment of Excellence. It is a few miles from Tsi village, where the fourth Dodrupchen Rinpoche was born. Chatralwa stayed there for the rest of his life, teaching mainly Dzogpa Chenpo meditation.

After some time, Tertön Sögyal (1856–1926) moved from Dodrupchen Monastery to Upper Ser Valley, and Chatralwa spent a long time with him. Tertön Sögyal taught him *Dzökyi Demik,* a commentary on

Guhyagarbha-tantra by the third Dodrupchen, by day and *Ösal Nyingpo,* a commentary on *Guhyagarbha-tantra* by Mipham Namgyal, by night. He also taught Chatralwa many other commentaries on *Guhyagarbha,* and instructions on Dzogpa Chenpo.

Whenever Tertön Sögyal returned from his visits to the third Dodrupchen, the tertön would pass on the important teachings he received or discussions he had with Dodrupchen to Chatralwa. When Chatralwa told us this, I remember his saying, "*A-we!* I haven't forgotten them. How I could forget such golden teachings? I am not mad." His devotion to the third Dodrupchen was enormous, but he never got the chance to see him.

At the age of twelve (1951), I went to see Chatralwa with my teacher Kyala Khenpo and some others. At his hermitage there were about two hundred monks. Most of them lived in tiny huts and caves outfitted with a small bed-cum-seat on which they could sleep, sit, meditate, and study. Next to their beds they had small stoves on which they made tea while sitting in bed. Next to their pillows they had little altars with some books. Many could hardly stand up in their cells. Many of the disciples were practicing Dzogpa Chenpo meditation, and Chatralwa himself guided them. But the majority of students were studying texts of sūtra and tantra under the mastery of his senior students.

The first time I saw Chatralwa, the strongest impression I had was of his being so ancient, his timelessness and agelessness. A thought came into my mind, "Oh! Rigdzin Jigme Lingpa must have been like this." He was sitting on his seat wrapped in cloth. He had thin gray hair that was long and a little matted. I remember his saying, "My teacher Adzom Drukpa told me that I should lead a tantric life, and he prophesied that I would become a tertön. But I want neither to be married, as it could lead to a life of struggle, nor to discover any new ter teachings, as there are so many authentic golden ter teachings available. So, as a symbolic observance of my teacher's words, I kept this long hair as a tantric costume." Although he never met the third Dodrupchen, half of his teachings were quotes of Dodrupchen's words, which he had received through Chagmo Tülku and Tertön Sögyal.

Chatralwa had a rather big, comfortable house, with lots of sunlight, filled with religious objects and books. One day a well-known lama called Rinchen Dargye visited him. After entering Chatralwa's room, the lama kept looking around instead of sitting down. Chatralwa sharply asked him, "*A-we!* What did you lose?" The lama answered, "I heard you are a Chatralwa, a hermit. But in fact you have collected enough to be called a rich man." Chatralwa replied, "*Chatralwa* means someone who has got rid of his or her emotional attachments to worldly materials or to life itself. It does not mean being poor and hankering for them, as many do."

If you offered him a present, most probably he would express his rage, and he might even throw you out. But if you made a nice dish and took it to him, he would always appreciate it with his famous line, "*A-we!* It is worth hundreds of horses and thousands of oxen [mDzo]."

In his earlier years he taught scholarly texts of sūtra and tantra to his students. But in later years he wouldn't teach any text. He gave only the clarifications on various questions that disciples would bring to him and especially the instructions on Dzogpa Chenpo meditation.

His style of teaching Dzogpa Chenpo meditation was called Nyamtri, instructions according to one's experiences. He would instruct his disciples individually on how to start the meditation. After that, he would give the instructions or clarifications only according to the experiences, problems, or progress that the disciples were having. So he gave the blessings, keys, and supports, but he would let the disciples themselves awaken, open, or realize the true nature of their own minds by themselves.

Most of his disciples were living from hand to mouth, but they were cheerful, content, calm, and compassionate. If you witnessed the joy on their faces, the peace in their voices, the calmness in their movements, and their kindness and helpfulness to others, you would get a feeling that the so-called prosperity of material wealth has no relevance to the true joy of life.

Around 1940, Chatralwa was seriously sick with phlegm. Unannounced, Dodrupchen Thupten Thrinle Palzang arrived, and after an hour or so, Chatralwa started to eat and then recovered, having no more symptoms or need of medicine. Chatralwa insisted on pouring the tea for Rinpoche, saying, "I am said to be an old disciple of Dodrupchen, so I should serve him." Chatralwa was never recognized or enthroned officially as tülku, but he became known as the tülku of Jigme Kalzang. His words about being an old disciple of Dodrupchen were thought to be an admission of his being the incarnation of Jigme Kalzang.

In their later meetings, Chatralwa gave the essence of all his teachings and transmissions to Dodrupchen Rinpoche, as if pouring water from one vessel into another.

At the age of eighty-one, Chatralwa's health deteriorated, and he told his disciples to invite Dodrupchen Rinpoche, who was then at Dzogchen Monastery. He said that until Dodrupchen's arrival there was no need to do any ceremonies, and that when he came, they should let him do whatever he liked. Then, on the twenty-second of the first month of the Water Dragon year (1952), he passed away into the ultimate peace. A couple of days after his death, Rinpoche arrived from Dzogchen Monastery and performed all the traditional ceremonies. Many of Chatralwa's disciples returned to their own hermitages and monasteries, and some came to Dodrupchen Monastery. Yage Gar hermitage was almost dissolved. All the great days were gone in a few months' time. Celebrating his realization, Chatralwa wrote:

> Inseparable from the nature of the Lord of Oḍḍiyāṇa [Guru Rinpoche],
> O father, the accomplished lama, please dwell on the crown of my head.
> The phenomenal objects appear as the power [of the wisdom], pure from sudden stains, and
> The all-pervading nature [of the mind] is the union of the original purity and the spontaneous perfection.
> With such recollections, although there is no beauty of poetry,
> I like to sing the song of realization of the basis, which is the liberation from the beginning.
> By realizing the inner intrinsic awareness, which is openness and no-self,
> External appearances have been liberated as freedom with no reference point.
> Having purified the intrinsic awareness and the appearing objects as the union in evenness,
> The attainment of the stronghold in the primordially liberated basis is assured.
> Having transcended all the discriminating hopes and fears of "it is" and "it is not,"
> To sleep naked, careless of any moral activities, is joyful!
> The accounts of the paths and stages, and the distinctions of the views and meditations—
> All those eggshell-like coverings of doubting mind are broken.
> The extraordinary quality of the path is the effortless and spontaneous accomplishment.

The uncontrived intrinsic awareness of the nature is the
spontaneously accomplished primordial wisdom.
The equalness of saṃsāra and nirvāṇa in their purity of the result is
the freedom from distinctions.
Thus I have realized the nature of the primordial Buddha-at-the-basis, and
Now there is no need of striving for the attainment of
Buddhahood.
Please meditate on Dzogpa Chenpo. There are extraordinary
virtues to attain.
At the mountain of Sangdzong, the beggar called Chö[ying
Rangtröl]
Has spontaneously proclaimed this song of joy.

31

Kathok Khenpo Ngawang Palzang
1879–1941

Khenpo Ngawang Palzang[289] of Kathok Monastery was one of the greatest writers, teachers, and transmitters of *Longchen Nyingthig* in this century. He was known as a tülku of Vimalamitra, and there is no exaggeration in calling him the second Longchen Rabjam.

He was popularly known as Khenpo Ngachung (the Junior Ngak), and in many writings he signed himself as Ösal Rinchen Nyingpo Pema Ledreltsal or Pema Ledreltsal.

I offer here a short summary of Khenpo's autobiography, *Ngotsar Gyume Rölgar* (An Amazing Magical Play). If you are interested in reading a biography of a lama of scholarly and spiritual attainments, this should be your choice. It presents a magnificent life in a most beautiful classical style of writing that is rarely seen.

Khenpo was born on the tenth day of the tenth month of the Earth Hare year of the fifteenth Rabjung (1879) amid wondrous signs of rainbow rays and sounds of music from the sky. His father was Namgyal of the Nyoshül tribal group, and his mother was Pematso of the Juwa tribal group.

His days and nights were filled with amazing lights, experiences, visions, sounds, and communications with divinities. On the third day of his life, sitting in the meditative posture, he recited the Vajrakīla mantra. During the first winter, in freezing weather, the baby was sleeping with his mother. But his mother couldn't sleep with him, as he was generating so much heat through his spiritual energy. The mother said, "What are you, a child of demons?" The child sang:

> I came from the direction of Latrang in the east,
> I have self-control over energy and heat.
> I have accomplished the attainment of Guhyasamaja.
> If you recognize me, I am Alak Rigdra.

At this his mother said, "Who knows? Keep quiet." His parents and relatives worried about their unusual child and tried to keep his display of miracles secret from others.

When he was two, his father took him to Nyoshül Lungtok at Gyaduk Hermitage. Lungtok expressed great joy in seeing him and gave blessings and also gifts.

When he was five, his family was facing great hardship from a flood, and one day he fashioned a twig into the form of a phurbu, a sacred dagger, and said,

> I, as Vimalamitra in India,
> Reversed the Ganges River.
> There is no problem for a creek in a gorge.
> Mother, look at the great wonder!

Then, pointing the phurbu at the river, he recited the Vajrakīla mantra, and the river changed its course as if it had been propelled by a storm.

At seven, his uncle taught him to read prayer texts. When his uncle taught him one syllable, he would say the next one instead of repeating after him. His uncle became upset and said, "Why are you jumping ahead? You are not recognizing the syllables." Then he studied slowly and took about twenty days to learn the first page of the prayer, and that satisfied his uncle. Then one evening, half asleep, he read the whole *Zangpo Chöpa,* and his uncle realized that he was dealing with an unusual person. His uncle brought him a number of new texts, and Khenpo read them all with no difficulty. His uncle stopped giving him any reading lessons.

From the age of eight, he started to receive teachings and empowerments from many lamas. At the age of fifteen, he was ordained as a novice by Khenchen Gyaltsen Özer, and Nyoshül Lungtok advised him on the importance of observing the vows.

With Nyoshül Lungtok he moved to the hermitage called Pema Ritho. There he received detailed instructions on ngöndro practice from Lungtok and completed the ngöndro accumulations. During the maṇḍala practice of ngöndro, he saw Longchen Rabjam in a dream. Longchenpa, putting a crystal on Khenpo's head, said:

> Ah! The nature of the mind is the enlightened mind. Ah!
> Ah! The great emptiness is the sphere of Samantabhadra. Ah!
> Ah! The openness intrinsic awareness is the Dharmakāya. Ah!
> Ah! From the five glows arises everything. Ah!
> Ah! The nature of intrinsic awareness transcends view and
> meditation. Ah!
> Ah! Today may they be established in your heart. Ah!

Because of the force of devotion, Khenpo fainted for a while. From the statue of Longchen Rabjam on his altar came ringsels. Nyoshül Lungtok told others that Khenpo could be the tülku of Vimalamitra of this century, as Vimalamitra had promised to send a major incarnation to Tibet in every century to spread the Nyingthig teachings.

Before the guru yoga of ngöndro practice, he received the empowerment of the two-volume *Longchen Nyingthig* cycle from Lama Atop, one of the principal disciples of Nyoshül Lungtok. Like his teacher Paltrül Rinpoche, Nyoshül Lungtok gave only a few empowerments in his whole life. Lungtok gave Khenpo the instructions on *Longchen Nyingthig* in general and guru yoga in particular.

Khenpo recited the siddhi mantra thirty million times and made one hundred thousand prostrations together with acts of homage. Since Khenpo started to receive teachings from Nyoshül Lungtok, he never for a second had a thought of his teacher being an ordinary being, but always saw him as a fully enlightened Buddha. He also could not remember ever speaking improperly to any of his Dharma brothers and sisters.

During the ngöndro trainings, he kept experiencing that his mind had merged into a thoughtless state and that then all the objective appearances had dissolved. His teacher minimized its importance, saying, "It is the universal ground," a neutral state, but not the enlightened nature.[290]

After guru yoga practice, Lungtok gave detailed teachings on tantra including the three roots and many other texts. Khenpo did a forty-nine-day strict recitation retreat on *Rigdzin Düpa*. He achieved great clarity in the development stage, reciting the siddhi mantra ten million times and the *Rigdzin Chitril* mantra one hundred million times. Then he did a month retreat on *Yumka Dechen Gyalmo* and practiced day and night. He was able to hear the sound power of the mantra without any efforts. He had an extraordinary realization that the visions of divinities or ordinary appearances are mere apparitions and designations created by the mind.

At the age of twenty, as strongly advised by Lungtok, Khenpo took the vow of full ordination as a monk from Atop. Thereafter he observed every one of the 253 vows of a monk and kept no extra materials for himself. When he had to keep any extra materials for the service of the Dharma or for others, he kept them only after reciting tütren (Dus Dran), a formula for reminding oneself of the "mindfulness of the purpose," written by Panchen Lobzang Chögyen.

His teacher gave him detailed teachings on life and longevity. Then Khenpo did a hundred-day retreat on the long-life practice of *Longchen Nyingthig*. After many days of doing the recitation, he saw lights being emitted from the long-life pills on the altar, and then they melted into lights. By emphasizing his training on energy (air), he experienced the accomplishments of entering, dwelling, and perfection of his energies in the center channel. Through heat yoga, he experienced great bliss and heat in his body and the union of bliss and emptiness in his mind. The touch of either cold or heat in the external temperature caused him to generate heat and bliss. Through the training on subtle essence, before long his mind and mental events had ceased. He remained in a thick, sleeplike thoughtless state, but first it was with openness and then that mind, too, merged into the state of union of emptiness and clarity. He was able to remain in such a state for the whole period of a meditative session.

When Khenpo was twenty-one, Nyoshül Lungtok gave him a few lines of the innermost teachings of Nyingthig every day. After every teaching, Khenpo meditated on the meanings of the instructions for many days, and this was followed by discussions and clarifications.

Lungtok explained that he had received the Nyingthig transmission from the fourth Dzogchen Rinpoche that came from Jigme Lingpa through the lineage of Dodrupchen. He also received the transmission from both Paltrül Rinpoche and Khyentse Wangpo that came from Jigme Lingpa through the lineage of Gyalwe Nyuku.

During these trainings, he developed an unquestionable confidence that what he had experienced during his ngöndro trainings, namely that his experience of a thoughtless state, after which all the objective appearances had dissolved, was not a mere absence of thoughts but the naked union of intrinsic awareness and emptiness.

He presented his conviction to his teacher. The teacher laughed and said, "During the preliminary mind trainings [Blo sByong] of ngöndro practice, you were talking of a contemplation [of a thoughtless state] and the dissolving of the objective appearances. That is what it is. There are two kinds of thoughts, subjective thoughts and objective thoughts. In contemplations of the realized ones, first their subjective grasper dissolves. At that time, as the objective thought is not yet dissolved, there will be thoughts of appearances. Then what they objectively grasped will dissolve, and then even the mere appearances will not be there before the contemplative mind."

Khenpo, being a most gifted person, had the experience of the true nature in his early meditation trainings. However, his teacher would not tell him that this was the important realization. If he did so too early, there could arise a subtle conceptual grasping in the mind of Khenpo, an attachment to the so-called "important realization," and instead of Khenpo's being encouraged by having his realization confirmed, he could be distracted from the journey. That is the very reason why Paltrül Rinpoche says: "Do not rush to call it Dharmakāya!"

Then Nyoshül Lungtok gave one of his most rare empowerments, a Yeshe La-me Tsalwang, the empowerment of the power of the intrinsic awareness (or the introduction to the nature of the mind) as given in *Yeshe Lama*. It was followed by teachings on innermost instruction of Dzogpa Chenpo, including *Chöying Rinpoche Dzö*.

Then his teacher told Khenpo that now he should go to Dzogchen Monastery to study scholarly texts. He had heard that Mipham Namgyal was also coming to the monastery to teach. Khenpo didn't want to leave but had to follow his teacher's words. With a gift of thirteen brown sugar cakes and a long scarf, the teacher bade farewell to his disciple by saying prayers and then adding, "I am inspiring you, empowering you, and recognizing you as the holder of the thirteenth stage, the state of Vajradhara." With a heavy heart, Khenpo prayed and left his teacher for the last time.

In the fall of his twenty-second year, Khenpo arrived at Dzogchen Monastery. With Minyak Lama Rigdzin Dorje and others, he studied

Madhyamakālaṃkāra by Shantarakshita, *Tsema Rikter* by Sakya Pandita, *Don Namnge, Kagye Namshe,* and Ösal Nyingpo on *Guhyagarbha* by Mipham.

With Khenpo Losal he studied *Domtik Paksam Nye* by Dharmashrī, *Mahāyāna-sūtrālaṃkāra, Madhayānta-vibhaṅga,* and *Dharmadharmatā-vibhaṅga* with Rongtön's commentaries, *Uttaratantra* with Dölpo's commentary, *Guhyagarbha* with the commentaries by Longchen Rabjam, Rongzom, and Yungtön, *Thekchen Tsüljuk* and *Nangwa Lhadrup* by Rongzom, *Yönten Dzö* with the commentaries by Dodrupchen and Tentar Lharampa, and *Semnyi Ngalso* and *Gyuma Ngalso.*

With Khenpo Sönam Chöphel he studied *Abhisamayālaṃkāra* with the commentaries by Je Tsongkhapa and Paltrül, *Bodhicharyāvatāra* with the commentaries by Ngülchu Thogme and Künzang Sönam, and *Norbu Ketaka* by Mipham, *Prajñānāma-mūla-madhyamaka, Chatuḥshataka-shāstra, Dültik Rinchen Trengwa, Dülwa Tsotik, Longchen Nyingthig Tsalung, Sangdak Gonggyen,* and others.

From Mura Tülku Pema Dechen he received many empowerments and teachings on *Yeshe Lama* and other scriptures. From Khenpo Konchok Norbu he received unique instructions of Paltrül on *Bodhicharyāvatāra.*

With Apal he studied *Abhidharmakosha* with auto-commentary and commentaries by Gyalpö Se, Chimchen, and Chimchung. Khenpo had a hard time comprehending Apal's elaborate style of teaching. He went to the rock in Shrīsiṃha, where Paltrül once taught *Abhidharmakosha* and made aspirations that he might understand what Vasubandhu envisioned in his text. He fell asleep and in a dream was blessed by Vasubandhu, and Khenpo remembered his having been Sthiramati, the principal student of Vasubandhu. After that he was able to understand the teachings.

Then Mipham Namgyal arrived and stayed at Nakchung hermitage of Dzogchen Monastery to compose his *Khepala Jukpa.* One day Khenpo went to see him, and that very day Mipham had completed *Khepala Jukpa.* Mipham entrusted the text to Khenpo and inspired him to teach it. Also, Khenpo received the empowerment of *Jampal Gyüluk.*

He also received the empowerments of *Könchok Chidü* from the fifth Dzogchen Rinpoche and *Gongpa Düpa* and *Khandro Nyingthig* from Drukpa Kuchen of Dzogchen Monastery.

In the fall of his twenty-fourth year (1902), he returned to his teacher's hermitage and was shocked to learn that he had died on the twenty-fifth day of the fifth month of the previous year. He made a three-month recitation retreat on *Vajrakīla Düpung Zilnön* of *Longchen Nyingthig*. He also performed feast offerings and gave teachings to people. Then he went to Kading hermitage and did retreats on *The Peaceful and Wrathful Māyājāla Sādhana* and *Jampal Gyüluk* and gave teachings. He meditated on Thögal and saw the lights and images of the Buddhas filling the atmosphere, and then the power of intrinsic awareness in the form of the vajra chain, the subtlemost wisdom, dissolving into the inner ultimate sphere. By doing so he reached the ultimate nature of the primordial wisdom, the naked union of intrinsic awareness and emptiness. All the shells of experiences had vanished. All the subjective and objective grasping had been shattered. For an entire half day he remained in luminous clarity free from thoughts. As a sign of his realizing that the appearances are not real as they are supposed to be, his bell fell onto a stone, and instead of the bell breaking as it normally would, there was a mark of the bell on the stone and also a mark of the stone on the bell.

While meditating on *Khandro Yangtig,* in a vision he went to the unexcelled pure land in the form of Lhacham Pemasal and received the empowerments from the chief of ḍākinīs and was given the name Ösal Rinchen Nyingpo Pema Ledreltsal. Also, as Longchen Rabjam, he received transmissions from Rigdzin Kumārādza.

When he was twenty-nine, his mother died amid signs of light and earthquakes. From Terchen Ngawang Tendzin he received the textual transmissions of *Nyingma Gyübum.*

Then once again he went to Dzogchen Monastery. With Khenpo Lhagyal of Dzogchen he studied *Pramāṇavārttika,* and with Khenpo Zhen-ga he studied the commentaries of *Madhyamakāvatāra* and many other scriptures.

Then Dzogchen Rinpoche wanted to make him a khenpo, an abbot of Dzogchen Monastery, but he refused, as he had been instructed by Lungtok to teach not at Dzogchen Monastery but at Kathok Monastery.

He returned to Jönpa Lung, the seat of his teacher, and started to give more teachings. During the empowerment of *Yumka Dechen Gyalmo,* the nectar boiled on the cool altar, and seed letters written on the mirror with colors appeared in relief ('Bur Dod). During the *Dzödun* text transmission, an unknown woman with rich ornaments attended for a while and then vanished. While Khenpo was giving teachings on *Semnyi Ngalso,* the whole valley was filled with rainbow lights.

From Adzom Drukpa, he received the empowerment of *Gongpa*

Zangthal, Khandro Yangtig, and *Lama Yangtig* and the teachings of ngöndro and actual practices of *Dorje Nyingpo.*

At the age of thirty, invited by the second Kathok Situ Chökyi Gyatso (1880–1925), he went to Kathok Monastery. There he was appointed as a teaching assistant (sKyor dPon) in the newly opened shedra, or scripture college. Khenpo Künpal taught *Domsum Rabye, Pramāṇavārttika, Tsema Rikter, Yizhin Dzö, Men-ngak Dzö,* and *Chöying Dzö,* and Khenpo Ngachung reviewed the teachings for the students.

When Khenpo Ngachung was thirty-one, Khenpo Künpal had to return to Dzachukha. Khenpo Ngachung took over as the khenpo of the shedra and taught various texts for thirteen years. Every day he gave at least three lectures and sometimes seven. He also gave empowerments, including *Nyingthig Yabzhi* and *Longchen Nyingthig* twenty-seven times, *Dorje Nyingpo* three times, and the text transmission of *Dzödun* thirteen times. He fully ordained over four thousand monks.

While teaching he received *Rinchen Terdzö, Düdül,* and many other transmissions from Kathok Situ, Jewön Rinpoche, and Khenpo Gyaltsen Özer. From Detso Khenpo Sönam Palden of Golok, he received the teachings of *Lamrim Chenmo* and many other Geluk teachings. From the second Pema Norbu (1887–1932), he received *Namchö, Ratna Lingpa, Changter, Minling Terchö, Jatsön,* and *Trölthik.*

Again, he returned to Jonpa Lung and, as advised by Kathok Situ, established a monastery.

Then he went to Palyül Monastery to start a shedra. He gave many short teachings, including *Bodhicharyāvatāra.* Then he went to Tralak Shedrup Ling Monastery in Da Valley at the invitation of Chaktsa Tülku and gave the empowerment of *Rinchen Terdzö,* combined with many other teachings and transmissions.

At Namoche in Upper Nyi Valley he gave the empowerments of *Nyingthig Yabzhi* and *Longchen Nyingthig* in a camp and gave teachings of ngöndro and *Yeshe Lama.*

When he was forty-seven (1925), at the behest of Kathok Situ a gathering of a thousand monks who were followers of the Kathok tradition was called at Kathok Monastery. Khenpo and many others gathered, but Kathok Situ was seriously sick and soon passed away. Khenpo gave *Rinchen Terdzö* empowerments.

At the age of forty-nine, he meditated on many of the major sādhanas of Nyingma in retreat and experienced many attainments and visions. Especially during the meditation on *Ladrup Thigle Gyachen,* he had a vision of Longchen Rabjam and was inspired to write texts on Nyingthig. As a result he wrote his most famous works, *Künzang Thukkyi Tikka* on *Yeshe Lama, Nyen-gyü Chuwö Chüdü* on Trekchö, *Khandro Thukkyi Tilaka* on Thögal, and *Nyime Nangwa* on both Trekchö and Thögal.

At the age of fifty-one, he visited Markham and gave the empowerments of *Nyingthig Yabzhi, Longchen Nyingthig, Rinchen Terdzö,* and teachings of *Ngalso Korsum* and *Yeshe Lama.* Then at Gyalse Monastery he gave many empowerments and teachings and recognized and enthroned the tülku of Gyalse. He also visited the camp of Nyakla Changchup Dorje and ordained sixty-four candidates as novices or monks.

At the age of fifty-four (1932), he went to Tralak Monastery in Da Valley to establish a shedra. Soon thereafter, he felt that the second Pema Norbu was dying, and Khenpo visited him in his meditative body and talked about the future. Pema Norbu told him that as his body was worn away due to sickness, he would be dying. Khenpo suggested that he go to Amitābha's pure land, but Pema Norbu wanted to go to Pema Ö, the pure land of Guru Rinpoche, and come back to spread the Nyingthig teachings. Soon Khenpo received a message that Pema Norbu was in serious condition, and he quickly set out to reach him. As it was many days distant, by the time he got there Pema Norbu had already died five days earlier.

At the request of Khyentse Chökyi Lodrö, Khenpo went to Kathok to preside over the enthronement ceremony of the tülku of Kathok Situ.

At the age of fifty-five (1933) he made a recitation retreat on the Vajrakīla *Yangsang La-me* discovered by Ratna Lingpa, had a vision of Yeshe Tsogyal, and received Vajrakīla accomplishments. His autobiography ends at his fifty-fifth year.

At the age of sixty-two (1941), he passed away with amazing signs. Tents of light arched over the place, sounds of music were heard, and tremblings of the earth were felt. Shedrup Tenpe Nyima, the tülku of Nyoshül Lungtok, and Gyurme Dorje, the son of Adzom Drukpa, led the cremation ceremony.

32

Alak Zenkar Pema Ngödrup Rölwe Dorje
1881–1943

The first Alak Zenkar Pema Ngödrup Rölwe Dorje,[291] the incarnation of Do Khyentse, was born in Rekong, Amdo. More than six decades before his birth, the first Dodrupchen had predicted his birth, saying:

> From the region of Ah there will come a person named Pema Ngödrup,
> The incarnation of Khyentse, in the form of an ascetic.
> Whoever is connected with him will attain liberation from the six realms.

Alak Zenkar received transmissions from Gurung Tülku Rinpoche, who was a student of Mipham (1846–1912). Later, his teacher sent him to Dege, saying, "Your main karmic teacher is Mipham Rinpoche. You might not be able to see him, but you must try!" He added, "Then, in a monastery situated below a reddish rock, you will receive the transmissions of the ter teachings of Do Khyentse. That will also be the place where you should settle."

When he had nearly reached Zhechen Monastery, he had a dreamlike vision in which he saw a crystal chöten. A lama in scholar's attire was sitting in the window of the chöten's vase. He heard pith instructions on meditation from the lama. Then the lama and the chöten melted into light in the form of symbolic scripts. Finally the symbolic scripts of light merged into him. At that very moment, he experienced his whole being merging into his own innate intrinsic awareness nature, and the whole of phenomena arose as the body, speech, and mind of the Buddha, all inseparable from his own realized wisdom. That was the ultimate transmission he was to receive from Mipham. Then he went into Zhechen Monastery and paid his respects to the remains of Mipham, who had already died.

After that he went to Dzogchen Monastery and received transmissions from the fifth Dzogchen Rinpoche and studied *Guhyagarbha-tantra* with Gyakong Khenpo. He also received teachings from Kathok Situ Chökyi Gyatso and Dzom Drukpa.

Remembering the prophecy of Gurung about the place where he should be settled, he went to the Geshe area of Gyarong. When he reached Mirha (Maha) and saw the Kyilung (sKyid Lung) Monastery, one of the main seats of Do Khyentse located below a reddish rock, he became certain that this was his destination.

Do Khyentse had advised his disciples at the time of his death, "Do not try to find my tülku in a pompous way. I myself will come as an ascetic from somewhere to take care of the monastery." Nevertheless, for a long time, no one knew that Alak Zenkar was the one. Alak Zenkar, who was then in his thirties or older, sat at the end of the rows of monks in the temple. He received the transmissions of the ter teachings of Do Khyentse from Khenpo Rikten. People named him Alak Zenkar, the Master with the White Shawl, as he was wearing a white shawl. Soon, people became aware of his profound scholarship and realization. He would remember Do Khyentse's many past activities at the monastery, which were recalled by only a few old disciples still living. Also, he had the name that Dodrupchen had prophesied. All these signs convinced people that he was the tülku of Do Khyentse for whom they had been waiting for decades.

He taught and took care of the Kyilung Monastery and its thirteen branch monasteries. Then he built a hermitage called Ogyen Khachödo, at which he mostly lived. Later in his life he kept his door open to all, monks, and nuns, laymen and laywomen alike. He taught them and performed tsok ceremonies with them, dancing with yogic songs, sharing food and drink from the same cups and plates, which was unusual for Tibetan culture. One of his many popular yogic songs begins:

In the ultimate sphere of original purity
The [self-appearing] colors do not exist as real.
Having perfected the naturally arisen power of intrinsic awareness,
The attainment of freedom from grasping at "self" is the
    Dharmakāya.

He never rode a horse but always walked. Yet on many occasions he appeared by his miraculous power in a short time, from a distance of many days' travel, and there was no way to tell how he had got there.

At the age of sixty-three (1943), in an unusual gathering, drinking from a cup, he said, "This cup is only for me. I must drink it by myself." After drinking it, he said, "That drink was contaminated with poison. I was offered poison by the same person for the third time. This time I took it, for the time of my death has also arrived." Then he compelled everyone who was present to promise not to harm the person by any means and wrote a will stating the same demand. And he passed away with wondrous signs.

His tülku, the second Alak Zenkar Thupten Nyima Rinpoche (b. 1943), has become one of the preeminent lights in the resurgence of Buddhism and Tibetan literature in Kham in recent decades.

33

DZONGSAR KHYENTSE CHÖKYI LODRÖ
1893–1959

KYABJE Khyentse Chökyi Lodrö[292] of Dzongsar was the greatest master of many lineages of this century.

He was born in the Water Snake year of the fifteenth Rabjung (1893) at Rekhe Ajam near Kathok Monastery. His father was a tantric master called Gyurme Tsewang Gyatso, the grandson of Tertön Düdül Rölpatsal of Ser Valley of Amdo, and his mother was Tsültrim Tso of Ser Valley of Amdo. His father named him Jamyang Chökyi Lodrö. At the age of six, Khyentse learned to read texts with his uncle with little effort.

When he was seven, Kathok Situ Chökyi Gyatso, the nephew of Khyentse Wangpo, brought him to Kathok Monastery and recognized him as the action-manifestation of Khyentse Wangpo, as prophesied by Kongtrül Yönten Gyatso. Situ performed the hair-cutting ceremony and named him Jamyang Lodrö Gyatso.

Situ assigned his own tutor, Khenpo Thupten Rigdzin, to Khyentse, and under his tutorship Khyentse studied prayers, grammar, astrology, Sanskrit, and many scriptures. From Kathok Situ he received the transmission of *Nyingthig Yabzhi, Longsal* cycles, and many other scriptures, and Situ became the most important person for his spiritual path and secular life.

From Adzom Drukpa in Trom Valley he received *Longchen Nyingthig,*

Gongpa Zangthal, Lama Yangtig transmissions, and the introduction to Trekchö meditation.

When Khyentse was thirteen, his tutor, who took care of him like a parent, died after being seriously ill for three years. During those final years, Khyentse took care of him personally with his own hands, cooking, washing, fetching water for him, and so on. Khyentse believed that his service not only pleased his tutor but also purified qualities within himself. After his tutor's death, Khyentse studied *Domsum, Yönten Dzö, Yizhin Dzö, Khenjuk,* and the texts by Asaṅga with Kathok Situ, Khenpo Kunpal, and many others.

When he was fifteen, because of the death of the young Khyentse Tülku at Dzongsar Monastery, Chökyi Lodrö moved his residence to Dzongsar, the seat of Khyentse Wangpo. At such a young age it was a difficult challenge to find himself in a new environment, facing a great deal of opposition to his taking over the main seat. But slowly he calmed everything down with the power of his skill, fearlessness, tolerance, and compassion. With Khenpo Champa Wangchuk he studied *Abhidharma, Abhisamayālaṃkāra,* and *Madhyamakāvatāra.* Soon he himself started to teach many texts to selected students at Dzongsar.

At seventeen, from Thartse Pönlop Loter Wangpo he received the Sakya transmissions of *Lamdre Lopshe,* the tantra of *Hevajra,* and other scriptures. At eighteen, from his father he received the transmissions of *Rinchen Terdzö* and the ter teachings of Chogling. At nineteen, from Khenpo Samten Lodrö he received *Drupthap Küntü* and other transmissions. In that year his father, the master of tantras, passed away. At twenty, he received many transmissions from Thartse Zhaptrung Champa Künzang Tenpe Nyima, but then the lama died.

At twenty-six, he went to Dzogchen Monastery and received ordination as a monk from Khenpo Jigme Pema Losal. Also, from Zhechen Gyaltsap he received transmissions of *Changter, Minling* ter, and many other teachings. That same year, he established a shedra called Khamche at Dzongsar Monastery. He invited Zhenphen Chökyi Nangwa (aka Zhen-ga, 1871–1927) of Dzogchen Monastery as the first khenpo to teach at the new shedra. Later it became a famous institution from which many great scholars emerged.

At twenty-eight,[293] he went to Golok for many months' visit to see the third Dodrupchen, Jigme Tenpe Nyima. He received the empowerments of *Rigdzin Düpa* and *Ladrup Thigle Gyachen.* He also received teachings on *Yeshe Lama, Longchen Nyingthig,* and *The Outline of Guhya-*

garbha-māyājāla-tantra. From Könme Khenpo of Dodrupchen Monastery he received the transmissions of the *Damchö Dechen Lamchok* cycle discovered by the first Dodrupchen as a ter. From Tertön Sögyal he received Vajrakīla and Trölthik transmissions.

At thirty-two, at Zhechen Monastery, he again received many transmissions, including *Dam-ngak Dzö* and *Changter* from Zhechen Gyaltsap Pema Namgyal, who became one of his important teachers.

At thirty-three,[294] he went on a pilgrimate to Central Tibet. At Mindroling Monastery he took the ordination of a monk from Khenpo Ngawang Thupten Norbu for the second time, as his predecessor had been ordained at this monastery in the lower Vinaya lineage.

Just before his return from Central Tibet, Kathok Situ died. After that, for about fifteen years Khyentse also looked after the administration of Kathok Monastery. He built many religious monuments, restrengthened the scriptural college, and enthroned the new tülku of Kathok Situ, as recognized by the fifth Dzogchen Rinpoche.

He received many tantric transmissions of the Geluk school from Jampal Rolwe Lodrö, popularly known as Amdo Geshe, who lived in Golok. He received the Lamdre Lopshe, Vajrabhairava, and Mahākala cycles from Gaton Ngawang Lekpa. From Kathok Khenpo Ngawang Palzang he received transmissions of the *Khandro Yangtig, Longsal,* and *Düdül* cycles. In total, he studied with about eighty masters from all the different traditions of Tibetan Buddhism.

He accomplished many meditations and recitation of numerous sādhanas of both Old and New traditions of tantra, including the fivefold hundred-thousand accumulation of ngöndro (for prostrations he did only forty thousand accumulations) and the recitation of the sādhanas of *Takhyung Barwa, Sengdongma, Ladrup Thigle Gyachen, Vajrakīla, Tārā* and *Palchen Düpa* of *Longchen Nyingthig,* and the *Ladrup* of *Khandro Yangtig.*

He had many visions, accomplished many attainments, and manifested many spiritual powers, but because of his humility he only indicates a few of them in his autobiography:

> If I had been trained myself in logic,
> I could have acquired good knowledge of reasoning,
> But it would have brought little benefit.
> As I was able to memorize
> The Three-Root Sādhanas, the Magön, and other prayers of
> *Longchen Nyingthig,* and

Some assembly prayers of the Ngor tradition,
I had good habits [or memories] of the past lives. . . .
I remembered the glorious Sakya Monastery,
Clearly in my mind again and again, and
Taking birth in the Khön family,
In my past lives.
I remembered being Ngari Panchen, great Lhatsun,
Ngawang Lobzang Gyatso,
Tsang-yang Gyatso, Palkhyen, and others. . . .
Thangtong Gyalpo introduced me
To the nature of intrinsic awareness with the support of a crystal.
In dreams I saw Āryasthavira Aṅgaja,
Vimalamitra, and Longchenpa.
I received long-life empowerment from Khyentse Wangpo.
From the great bodhisattva Paltrül
I received instruction on the ngöndro of *Longchen Nyingthig*.
From Nupchen Sangye Yeshe I received entrustments of many
tantras.
I experienced or dreamed of the receiving of blessings
From some lamas of Lamdre, Milarepa, and Tsongkhapa.
I was shown the tantric disciplines
By Lhatsün Namkha Jigme.

There were many incidents of his displaying powers. Once he blessed a new image, and it became hot to the touch. When he blessed the Mahākāla image of the Dzang Mahākāla temple, the image moved as if it were alive. When he prepared ambrosia, beams of light arched around the temple. At the time of an empowerment of Vaishravana, gold dust rained through the air. Many times the distribution of a small amount of blessing pills or nectar became an inexhaustible supply for a huge assembly of devotees.

At fifty-six, he married Khandro Tsering Chödrön (b. 1925) of the Aduk Lakar family as his spiritual consort. According to his own prophecies and those of Khyentse Wangpo and Kongtrül Yönten Gyatso, this union was for dispelling the obstructions of his life and for promoting his enlightened activities.

He gave numerous transmissions of Nyingma, Sakya, and Kagyü teachings to disciples of various Buddhist traditions of Tibet, including the empowerments of *Yabzhi* three times and of *Longchen Nyingthig* many times and the teaching on *Yönten Dzö* three times.

At the age of sixty-three, traveling through Lhasa he reached India and survived the political turmoils of Tibet. He went on a pilgrimage to all the sacred places of Buddhism in India and Nepal. Then he made the Palace Chapel of the king of Sikkim his main temporary residence and continued to give endless teachings and transmissions to devotees from all walks of life.

At the age of sixty-seven, on the sixth day of the fifth month of the Earth Pig year of the sixteenth Rabjung (1959), he passed away amid signs of lights, earthquakes and sounds. Today most of his remains are preserved in a small golden stūpa at the Royal Chapel of Sikkim, which Khandro Tsering Chödron takes care of while dedicating her life to meditation and prayers.

His tülku is Thupten Chökyi Gyatso (Khyentse Norbu, b. 1961?), the son of Dungse Thinley Norbu Rinpoche and the late Jamyang La, and the grandson of Kyabje Dudjom Rinpoche and Lopön Sönam Zangpo of Bhutan.

34

Kyala Khenpo Chechok Thöndrup
1893–1957

Kyabje Kyala Khenpo Chechok Thöndrup (Chöchok), my teacher and tutor, was a living bodhisattva and a master of Dharma.

He was also known as Lobzang Champa and Mati. As an ordinary student he studied and trained through years of hard dedication and became a highly accomplished khenpo.

Khenpo was born in the Water Snake year of the fifteenth Rabjung (1893) in the Mar Valley of Golok. His mother was Sötso. His father was Yumko of the Kyala clan, who had migrated generations before from the Kyala village of Dzika Valley.

He grew up in Trang Nyi Ha ("between two mountain paths") in Upper Mar Valley of Golok. From childhood he was an unusual boy who had love and faith in his heart. In his youth, he spent most of his days as a shepherd, looking after his herds of yak and sheep among the mountains, which was the norm for boys in the nomadic camps. He spent most of his life with animals, singing sweet words or saying prayers into their ears, without hitting them with stones, as other herdsmen do. While caring for animals, sometimes he spent hours carrying little fish from small ponds formed by rain to bigger ponds, because the ponds were drying up and the fish were about to die.

He had an uncle (1865–?) who was an accomplished master. His uncle had gone with the third Dodrupchen as his child companion to receive teachings from Paltrül Rinpoche at the age of seven. From him, while taking care of the animals, Khenpo kept receiving lessons in reading texts and learning the meaning of Dharma and the lives of masters.

From the age of about fifteen, he was able to spend several months each year at the hermitage of Garwa Long-yang, a famous tertön, receiving Dharma teachings and trainings.

At the age of nineteen, after the death of Garwa Long-yang, Khenpo told his father of his determination to go to Dodrupchen Monastery in the next valley, about two days' journey by horse. His father would not say a word on the subject for days, a gesture of disapproval. This nonverbal communication went on for some time, but finally his father gave up his resistance.

At Dodrupchen Monastery, Khenpo started to study with Garwa Khenpo and then with Khenpo Könme, who became his main teacher.

At the age of twenty he was ordained as a monk. Soon he refused to accept any material assistance from his parents. If a serious beginner in Dharma training maintains close contact with his family or friends, he may not be able to dedicate his mind to the spiritual trainings, as he will be ensnared by his emotional bonds and obligations. As a result of his decision, Khenpo was up against the problem of livelihood. Nevertheless, he never revealed his problems to anyone, because he was afraid that someone might come to his assistance and a new tie would be created. Every autumn, when the nomads have collected their butter and cheese and the farmers have their crops in, as was the custom of many monks, Khenpo went for alms to some nearby nomadic camps or villages of farmers, and sometimes to both areas. The food collected during the few weeks of the alms round lasted him for the whole year.

With Khenpo Könme he studied the writings of Dharmakīrti and Dignāga on logic, the six texts by Nāgārjuna, five texts by Asaṅga, *Madhyamakāvatāra* by Chandrakīrti, and *Madhyamākalaṃkāra* by Shāntarakṣhita on Mahāyāna philosophy, and Guṇaprabha and Pema Wangyal on the vows of discipline. He studied the texts of *Lamrim Chenmo* and ngöndro on general trainings, *Guhyasamaja, Guhyagarbha,* and *The Three Roots of Longchen Nyingthig* on tantra, and *Yönten Dzö, Yeshe Lama, Dzödün,* and *Ngalso Korsum* on Dzogpa Chenpo.

In his student days, during the day he would attend classes, participate in discussions on the courses, and devote hours to memorizing texts. At night he pursued his own private studies and memorized texts in his own room. On moonlit nights he would go outside and read. Sometimes, as the moonlight advanced up the mountainside, he would follow along after it, reading his way up the slope. In the morning he had to climb back down from the very top of the mountain. He read by moonlight because he could not afford the materials for light. Khenpo was always busy with studies of deep religious and philosophical works, reciting prayers, and doing his meditation and sādhanas. He never rested, except for sleeping four hours or so at night.

He received teachings and transmissions from other khenpos and Tülku Pema Dorje of Dodrupchen Monastery. He also received transmissions from Kathok Situ Chökyi Gyatso, the fifth Dzogchen Rinpoche, Tertön Sögyal, and Rigdzin Chenmo of Dorje Trak, when they visited Dodrupchen Monastery.

At the age of about thirty-five, he started to concentrate on the trainings of tantra and Dzogpa Chenpo meditation. All together he spent nine years in long retreats in total seclusion. In some retreats he had breaks of a few days each year to receive empowerments from the third Dodrupchen Rinpoche and some instructions from Khenpo Könme, but in some retreats he didn't have any breaks. Throughout his life, he did many short retreats or less strict retreats, which lasted one hundred days or a month. He also did a few retreats of a month or two on enjoying the essence (bChud Len, rasāyana), sustaining himself solely with the elixir drawn from the essence of flowers and a white stone called Chongzhi.

His daily routine during most of his long, strict retreats consisted of about twenty minutes for a little breakfast, about half an hour for lunch at noon, and about fifteen minutes for tea in the evening. At night he slept about four hours. For all the rest of the day and night he concentrated one-pointedly in meditation.

The cottage in which he did most of his retreats was situated right above Khenpo Könme's residence on a rock, hidden behind trees. It was a small cottage, consisting of one little room, a tiny kitchen, a tiny verandah, and a latrine. At the start of a long retreat he closed the door of his cottage until the months or years of retreat were completed. He could not see anyone outside, nor could anyone see him. He could speak to no one. Of course, until the conclusion of the retreat, no one could enter. There was a wide-open space in the roof that provided light and through which he could see the sky and the tops of mountains and trees. Little birds would visit him through the open roof to enjoy his offerings. Occasionally, some words of people and sounds of ritual music being played in the monastery reached him. There was a small hole in the side of the house through which at regular times a monk would pass him food and water.

People were surprised to see him in good health when he emerged from his long retreats. Later he would say, "During those periods I never experienced any kind of discomfort. And after the first few months in retreat, I felt that I would never come out, because in the solitude I was attaining such peace and bliss. Even if I were not doing any meditation there, I would at least be removed from negative thoughts."

In 1926, Khenpo was in retreat. He didn't know that the third Dodrupchen had died. One morning during his breakfast he heard someone calling to another, "Come and join in cleaning around the temple. Rinpoche's body will be brought in from the hermitage." Unusually, the conversation was very clear and loud. He felt that he had been hit by lightning. For him the whole world had become empty and dark. He just wanted to go far away, as there was no reason to live around that place anymore. He had to rely solely on his meditation for his survival, and he meditated more, which brought greater progress and strength in his meditation. Since the very day on which he heard that Dodrupchen had passed away, for the remaining thirty years of his life, unless he was walking or riding, he always remained in the sitting meditative posture without ever lying down. At night, he slept sitting in his meditative posture. He would say, "By sitting up I sleep for four hours, but if I lay down I would sleep longer, and then the time would be wasted instead of being used for meditation."

In 1935, Khenpo went into a loose retreat instead of a strict one, as Khenpo Könme was sick. Before he went into the retreat he told Khenpo Könme, "When Dodrupchen died, I felt that I couldn't stay around anymore. If it weren't for the meditation, I would have left. So, when you die, I will not be able to live here. You are actually the person on whom I solely rely." On the morning of the twenty-ninth day of the twelfth month (1936), someone knocked on his door and said, "Khenpo [Könme] changed his pure land [died] last night." After performing the rites of conclusion of the retreat, he came out the next day and participated in the funeral ceremonies. This time he didn't experience much shock, as he had after the death of Dodrupchen, and he believed that Khenpo Könme must have prayed for him.

At the age of forty-two, after the death of his teacher, he reluctantly accepted appointment as one of the four major khenpos at the Dodrupchen Monastery. He started to give teachings at Dodrupchen and at other monasteries to students who included the two young fourth Dodrupchen Rinpoches.

In 1943, when I was recognized and enthroned at the age of four as the tülku of Khenpo Könme, it was my great good fortune to have Khenpo assigned to me as my tutor. Since 1944, I had the opportunity to study at his feet for almost fourteen years. He was not only my Dharma teacher but the parent whom I really knew. When I was little, I used to sleep in his room. Whenever I woke up, I would always see his joyful face, and he would be sitting in his meditation box, doing meditation or saying prayers, in the dim light of flickering butter lamps. An infinite energy of peace, warmth, and wonder always overwhelmed my simple mind and provided the feeling of total security, as many people might remember the wonderful feelings of being surrounded as a child by the warmth of a loving parent.

While I was around him, Khenpo's daily schedule, which resembled Khenpo Könme's routine, was more or less as follows. He got up probably around three A.M. and began his meditations. At around six he had breakfast, resuming his meditation after half an hour. At around eleven o'clock we all assembled, and after making the offerings and prayers together, we had lunch. After lunch Khenpo started his teaching, giving between one and three classes a day. He taught the deepest and most difficult texts in the simplest words, with detailed explanations. He, like any khenpo of Dodrupchen Monastery, never accepted any fees from the students. On the contrary, he used to give food and lend books to the poor students. He was so happy to teach that he did not mind giving them his time, which he always felt was so precious to him for his meditation. In the evening we again assembled at about six o'clock to light the altar lamps and offer prayers together, after which we had tea and conversed on various subjects. Afterward he resumed his meditation until about ten at night. Then he would sleep for about four hours.

Khenpo enjoyed telling stories of the past, but then he used to feel very bad for wasting his precious time in storytelling, which he thought worthless.

Tibetan tutors could be strict in disciplining their pupils, but Khenpo was exceptionally gentle, maybe too gentle. There was only one scary incident that I remember. When I was about six, I pulled a page out of a book, and the paper was so flimsy that it tore into two pieces. I knew I had done something wrong and wanted to hide it, so I made the page into a little ball and threw it into a hole. Later that day, Khenpo came to me, very upset, and asked, "Did you throw it into the toilet?" I didn't say a word. He picked me up, holding me very tight, and then put me down on the floor, saying, "Now I am going to get a stick to beat you." I was so scared that without thinking, the words just came out of my mouth, "I am your lama's tülku. If you beat me, it will create a terrible karma for you!" Anyway, he didn't beat me, I don't know why. Years later, I realized that piece of paper had been a page from *Gomchok Trilen* by Jigme Lingpa, one of the most important texts on meditation, and that where I had thrown it was an outdoor privy. So I had thrown the most revered text into the worst place.

In appearance he was very simple, humble, and easygoing. But in knowledge he was rich, his intellect was sharp and deep, and his mind was gentle and kind. He had very little knowledge of medicine but kept giving medicine to people without requiring any fees for himself or for the medicine, as this medicine distribution had been started by Khenpo Könme, who was a doctor. When sick people brought diagnoses from physicians, he would let his students give them the medicine.

He taught at many places besides Dodrupchen Monastery. He taught at Yarlung Pemakö in Ser Valley; Wang-röl Gompa of Do Valley; Kyala Gompa of Dzika Valley; Joro Gön, Dogar Gön, and Alo Gompa of Gyarong; Tertön Gar, Göde Gön, and Gon Lakha of Rekong; and Kongser Khado Gompa of the Trokho region. He established drupdras (meditation schools) at both Tertön Gar in Rekong and Joro Gön in Gyarong.

Explaining the meaning of *The Three Crucial Words* by Prahevajra (Garab Dorje), Khenpo wrote to Rinpoche, Thupten Thrinle Palzang:

> The spontaneously born luminous wisdom, which is primordially pure and free from elaborations,
> Dwells as the innate nature of various delusory cycles, the grasper and grasped [dualistic] thoughts,
> In the form of clarity, emptiness, freedom from grasping and openness, the aspects of the Dharmakāya.
> Please recognize the natural state itself, the naked [union of] emptiness and intrinsic awareness [of your mind].
>
> Having directly cut off all the apprehensions of the conceptual mind,
> In the state of freshness and openness intrinsic awareness, which has no reference point,

By remaining without modifications and elaborations,
You will see the face of self-awareness Dharmakāya, even if you do not seek it.

The happiness and sufferings of saṃsāra and nirvāṇa, the drawings of the mind,
In whatever mode they arise, their nature is free from the beginning.
Having [all the thoughts] spontaneously dissolved as the all-pervading sphere, free from grasping,
To rest in ease and peaceful mind is joyful.

If the innate intrinsic awareness, which is unmodified and openness wisdom,
Arises nakedly as the [union of] great bliss and emptiness, free from elaborations,
Then lethargy and exuberance [high and low], the foes of meditation, will be cleansed naturally, and
There will be no need to rely on any other means of dispelling the obstructions or developing experiences.

Whatever [form] appears is the glow of the unborn Dharmakāya, the [union of] emptiness and awareness.
Whatever sound resounds is the music of the indestructible roar [nāda].
Whatever thoughts arise are the universal [all-pervading] nature, free from grasping.
Please dwell in the sovereignty of Dharmakāya, the unchanging [state of] awareness and emptiness.

One day in 1957, Khenpo told me, "I don't care for my own safety, since I will have a very short life, like the length of a goat's tail. But I want to save your life. I requested Rinpoche [Thupten Thrinle Palzang] to let us accompany him, and he agreed. So we should leave, but we can't tell anybody except Loli," his brother. If people knew that Rinpoche was leaving, they might not let him leave, or else many people would want to leave and the authorities would stop us easily.

Rinpoche told us that thirteen people would be accompanying him and that they should be broken up into three groups. Khenpo and I should leave among the first group. He would come in the second.

To the people of our inner circle, with the exception of Loli, Khenpo and I had to say, "According to a divination, Khenpo and I should go to Mount Drongri, a sacred place, to do a month's retreat without letting other people know. So Loli will cover up for us, pretending that we are on retreat, and we will go with some friends as we have already arranged." They didn't question us, as such arrangements were usual in some circumstances, and they arranged for some horses and helped us to keep our supposed trip to Mount Drongri secret.

One evening, just two days before we left, Khenpo went to see Rinpoche Rigdzin Tenpe Gyaltsen, who was living in a temple. When Khenpo started to leave Rinpoche, Rinpoche asked everyone else present to stay behind, and he came out of his house in the dark to say goodbye to Khenpo. Then Khenpo walked away, but Rinpoche followed him again and said goodbye one more time. Then Khenpo left again and Rinpoche followed him to bid him goodbye for the third time. And then he turned back to the temple. Later Khenpo told me, "I didn't give even a hint of our departure. But Rinpoche was certainly feeling that we were seeing each other for the last time. He seemed to be very emotional and having a hard time separating. It could mean that I may not return in this lifetime."

At midnight on the thirtieth of the eleventh month of the Fire Monkey year (1957), when everybody was asleep and the whole community was blanketed in darkness, we quietly left the monastery. At Chungnyak pass, from where you could see the monastery for the last time, in darkness Khenpo and we made prostrations to the monastery, the seat of great lamas, and to Rigdzin Tenpe Gyaltsen, who could have been in his luminous clarity of sleep or just watching us with his all-knowing wisdom eyes. Loli stayed behind and covered up our escape by playing drums as if Khenpo and I were doing a retreat at our house.

Some time before, Lama Zhingkyong, a disciple of Kyala Khenpo, wrote me a prophecy without knowing that we would be leaving. In it a line says, "When the fire-egg breaks, you will reach Central Tibet." Accordingly, on the sixth of the first month of the Fire Bird year (1957), we reached Lhasa. Khenpo had become sick because of the traveling and the foot injuries he received on the way. We spent a few days in Lhasa and got some treatment for Khenpo from a Tibetan physician called Lhokha Amchi. We saw the Jowo, the most holy object in Tibet, and made some offerings. For Khenpo this was his second visit to Lhasa, the first having been a pilgrimage he had made with his parents at the age of seven.

After a few days' stay in Lhasa, following the plans we had made with Rinpoche, we went to Drak Yangdzong, a famous pilgrimage place, to wait for Rinpoche. Khenpo's health began to deteriorate, and he said, "Since I was young, I have always wished to live and meditate at a place blessed by Guru Rinpoche. Now I haven't got the time to meditate, yet I am happy to be able to spend my last days at this place."

At dusk on the second day of the second month of the Fire Bird year (1957), after reading the first three chapters of *Chöying Rinpoche Dzö,* he suddenly merged into the ultimate peace at death. The next day he was still in meditation, and a simple local lama came and performed the ceremony of awakening him from his meditative absorption.

Among his writings are *The Commentary on Rigdzin Düpa, A Brief Notation on Palchen Düpa, A Brief Notation on Vajrakīla, A Brief Instruction on the Three Words That Hit the Heart,* and *The Commentary on the Dagni Changchup Miche* (lost).

35

Dilgo Khyentse Tashi Paljor
1910–1991

Kyabje Dilgo Khyentse Rinpoche Tashi Paljor,[295] was one of the few great lineage holders, writers, teachers, and transmitters of the teachings and powers of Nyingma tantras in general and *Longchen Nyingthig* in particular who reached numerous disciples in Tibet, India, Nepal, Bhutan, and the West.

He is also known as Gyurme Thekchok Tenpe Gyaltsen, Jigme Khyentse Özer, and Rapsal Dawa.

He was born on the thirtieth of the fourth month of the Iron Dog year of the fifteenth Rabjung (1910) in the family of Dilgo, a minister (nyerchen) of the king of Dege in the Nyö clan in Dan Valley. His father was Tashi Tsering. It was the very day that the great master Mipham Namgyal and his disciples were performing the feast ceremony at the completion of his one-and-a-half-month teaching on his *Commentary on Kālachakra* at Dilgo. Mipham immediately gave pills of Sarasvatī, the female Buddha of wisdom, with the sacred letters DHIḤ and HRĪḤ to the baby to eat even before tasting his mother's milk. About a month after the birth, Mipham gave empowerments for purification and longevity and named him Tashi Paljor. Since then until Mipham died at the beginning of 1912, Khyentse was given blessed substances continuously.

When he was only four months old, Ngor Pönlop Loter Wangpo recognized him as the tülku of Khyentse Wangpo. At the time of the death of Mipham, Zhechen Gyaltsap Pema Namgyal (1871–1926) saw him and asked the family to give him to Zhechen.

At the age of six,[296] he was accidentally burned badly in fire and was seriously ill for about six months, which caused him to take ordination as a novice.

When he was fifteen, Gyaltsap recognized him as a tülku of Khyentse Wangpo, enthroned him at Zhechen Monastery, and named him Gyurme Thekchok Tenpe Gyaltsen. He also gave him numerous transmissions, including those of the *Dam-ngak Dzö* and *Nyingthig Yabzhi*. From Khenpo Pema Losal of Dzogchen he received the transmission of *Longchen Nyingthig*. From Adzom Drukpa, he received teachings on *Longchen Nyingthig Ngöndro*.

With Khenpo Zhenphen Chökyi Nangwa (Zhen-ga) of Dzogchen, Khenpo Thupten Chöphel (Thupga) of Changma hermitage, Dza Mura Dechen Zangpo, and other masters, he studied the texts of Nāgārjuna, Asaṅga, *Abhidharma, Yönten Dzö,* the commentaries of *Guhyagarbha-māyā-jāla-tantra,* and many others. Khenpo Thupga recognized him as the tülku of Önpo Tendzin Norbu (Tenli).

Then from Khyentse Chökyi Lodrö he received the transmissions of Sakya, Kagyü, Geluk, and Nyingma teachings, including *Rinchen Terdzö, Nyingthig Yabzhi, Longchen Nyingthig,* and *Lama Gongdü*. From Khenpo Tendzin Dargye of Zhechen, he received the transmission of the nine volumes of Jigme Lingpa. From Zhechen Kongtrül (1901–1959?), he received transmissions of the thirteen volumes of the Minling cycle. He received teachings of all the Buddhist traditions of Tibet from over seventy teachers. Among them, Zhechen Gyaltsap and Khyentse Chökyi Lodrö were his principal teachers.

Starting from the age of eighteen, for twelve years he stayed in solitary places and practiced various teachings, including the Three-Root Sādhanas of Minling Terchen and *Longchen Nyingthig*.

Throughout his life he dedicated himself to giving teachings and transmissions to all, whoever came to receive them. He wrote that by the age of sixty-four, he had given empowerments of *Nyingthig Yabzhi* and *Longchen Nyingthig* over ten times. From the age of forty till eighty-two he gave discourses on *Chokchu Münsel,* the commentary on *Guhyagarbha* by Longchen Rabjam, at least once a year, and gave extensive commentaries on Jigme Lingpa's *Yönten Dzö*. Among countless other teachings, he gave five times the transmission of the *Rinchen Terdzö,* four times those of the *Nyingma Kama,* thrice that of the *Dam-ngak Dzö,* and twice that of the *Kanjur.*

Rinpoche and his consort, Khandro Lhamo, had two daughters. His daughter Chi-me La's son is the seventh Zhechen Rabjam.

At the invitation of the royal family of Bhutan, he spent many years in Bhutan teaching and transmitting the teachings.

Since the early 1960s, he single-handedly maintained and propagated the unique nonsectarian tradition of Khyentses, and tirelessly with the continuity of a stream he spread the teachings by traveling, teaching, practicing, and building monuments without any pause, for the sake of Dharma and people.

In 1980, he built Zhechen Tennyi Dargye Ling Monastery (a name he took from his old monastery in Tibet) at Baudhanath in Nepal, an elaborate complex with over two hundred monk students. In 1988, he established a shedra at the new monastery, and there monks are studying scholarly texts.

Starting in 1975, he visited many countries in the West many times and taught various levels of teachings and transmissions. Also he established Thekchok Ösal Chöling, a Dharma center in France. He visited Tibet twice from exile to teach and to help in rebuilding the monasteries and the faith in his homeland.

He conferred on the fourteenth Dalai Lama many empowerments and teachings on the commentaries of *Guhyagarbha* and *Yönten Dzö* and oral teachings of Dzogpa Chenpo combined with the teachings on *Yeshe Lama.*

He discovered many teachings and sādhanas as ter and wrote many scholarly texts and commentaries on various subjects, totaling twenty-three volumes. Among his writings on *Longchen Nyingthig* are a commentary on *Palchen Düpa* and *Wangki Chokdrik.*

At the age of eighty-one, at three A.M. on the twentieth of the eighth month of the Iron Sheep year (September 28, 1991), his enlightened mind merged into the ultimate openness at a hospital in Thimbu, the capital of Bhutan. Since then, his new monastery in Nepal has been presided over by his Dharma heir and grandson, Rabjam Rinpoche, Gyurme Chökyi Senge.

He was one of the greatest learned and accomplished masters of Tibet of our age. He was tall and giant. When he was among other masters, he stood like a mountain in the midst of hills or shone as the moon among stars, not because of his physical prominence, but because of the breadth of his scholarship and the depth of his saintliness. When he gave teachings, it was like the flow of a river, with hardly any pause. If strangers heard his lectures, their first impression might be that he was reading a beautiful text from memory, as the words of his talks were poetry, his grammar was perfect, and the meaning was profound.

Another most astonishing feature was his memory. He remembered not only scholarly and liturgical texts and details about his teachers and friends, but also those people whom he had seen only once years earlier.

His kindness was boundless, and there was room for everybody. Whenever I had an audience, he gave me the feeling that there was a place for me reserved in his vast mind. If you watched carefully, you got the feeling that he was always in his meditative or realized wisdom of openness and reaching out to people with the power of compassion, love, and directness, without any alteration.

He practically held the transmissions of all the Buddhist teachings of Tibet, but was constantly searching for additional transmissions, no matter how minor they might be. He had a huge library collection but never stopped looking for even a page of a rare writing. He was also immensely loyal.

In his last trip from Bhutan to Kalimpong, instead of flying he insisted on making the arduous journey by car in order to see an old disciple of his on the way. While that effort might have exhausted the last drops of his physical strength, it would have been his joy and fulfillment, an act of compassion.

Urgyen Tendzin Jigme Lhundrup (b. 1993), the grandson of Tulku Ugyen Rinpoche (1919–1996) and the son of Kela Chokling Rinpoche and Dechen Paldron of Terdhe, has been enthroned as the reincarnation of Dilgo Khyentse Rinpoche.

36

Chatral Sangye Dorje
b. 1913

Kyabje Chatral Sangye Dorje Rinpoche[297] is one of the very few great masters of the Longchen Nyingthig lineage still living.

Rinpoche was born in the Abse tribal group of Nyak-rong Province of Kham and soon migrated to Amdo with his tribal group.

He received the transmissions of the ter cycles of Düdjom Lingpa (1835–1903), Sera Khandro, and others from the great master Sera Khandro Dewe Dorje (1899–1952?) herself and Tülku Dorje Dradül (1891–1959?), the youngest son of Düdjom Lingpa.

At the age of fifteen, he abandoned his ties with his family and went to many teachers to study and practice. He gave up riding and traveled on foot. He refused to enter houses or tents of household people, staying only in hermitages, caves, or his own little tent.

From Kathok Khenpo Ngawang Palzang (1879–1941) he received the transmissions and teachings of *Longchen Nyingthig* and many other teachings. Khenpo became his most important root master. He also received many transmissions from Khyentse Chökyi Lodrö and other masters of Dege. In Central Tibet, he became one of the principal disciples of Kyabje Düdjom Rinpoche, the tülku of Düdjom Lingpa.

Rinpoche transmitted rare teachings to Shuksep Lochen, Khyentse Chökyi Lodrö, Düdjom Jigtral Yeshe Dorje, and many other important masters. Gyaltsap Redring (d. May 8, 1947), who was then the regent of

Tibet, invited Rinpoche to Lhasa and received many transmissions and instructions on Dzogpa Chenpo meditation from him. As a result, a large number of people from the nobility and ordinary walks of life flocked to Rinpoche for teachings with offerings. He saw this as a distraction from his path and, suddenly leaving everything behind, ran away to the caves in the mountains blessed by Guru Rinpoche and other masters of the past. He then lived as a hermit for decades and became known as Chatral, a hermit, or one who has abandoned mundane activities.

At the end of the 1950s, he moved to Bhutan and then to India. He restored a simple temple above Jor Bungalow village near Darjeeling and started a three-year drupdra, where meditators trained in *Longchen Nyingthig* practice. A drupdra is a meditation retreat school where a group of people go into seclusion for one year, three years, or more. Today there are many drupdras all over the world established by Tibetan lamas, but when Rinpoche built this drupdra, it was the only one established by a Tibetan refugee lama.

Rinpoche also built many temples, stūpas, and a number of other drupdras in Nepal and India. Today, he lives primarily at Pharping, an important pilgrimage place in Nepal blessed by Guru Rinpoche.

Rinpoche resists any involvement in monastic or bureaucratic structures and maintains a hermit tradition. He has numerous disciples from Tibet, Bhutan, and Nepal as well as some from the West. Rinpoche and his consort, Kamala, a daughter of Tertön Tulzhuk Lingpa, have two daughters, Tārādevī and Saraswatī, a tülku of Sera Khandro.

On November 16, 1968, Father Thomas Merton met Rinpoche and described the meeting as follows: "The unspoken or half-spoken message of the talk was our complete understanding of each other as people who were somehow *on the edge* of great realization and knew it and were trying (somehow or other) to go out and get lost in it—and that it was a grace for us to meet one another."[298]

Harold Talbott, who was present at their meeting, recalls Merton remarking to him after the meeting: "That is the greatest man I ever met. He is my teacher."

37

Fourth Dodrupchen Rigdzin Tenpe Gyaltsen 1927–1961

Kyabje Rigdzin Tenpe Gyaltsen, the fourth Dodrupchen Rinpoche,[299] was an embodiment of great wisdom and miraculous power. Among his many names are Rigdzin Jalü Dorje, Natsok Rangtröl, Düdül Pawo Dorje, and Jigtral Düdül Namkhe Dorje.

Rinpoche was born in the Fire Hare year of the sixteenth Rabjung (1927) in the Upper Mar Valley of Golok in Eastern Tibet. His father was Gyurme Dorje of Wangda, one of the eight tribal groups of Pema Bum, which is one of the three divisions of the Golok clan. His mother was Melo of the Ling tribal group. He had the marks of the letters HA RI NI and SA at his heart, which was a sign from a ter prophecy, which says:

> The manifestation of the Lord Padma[sambhava] named Pawo
> Will tame the beings with his esoteric disciplines.
> At his heart, HA RI NI and SA letters appear clearly.
> Whoever is connected with him will be freed from inferior births.

At the age of four he was recognized as the tülku of the third Dodrupchen by many lamas, including Amdo Geshe Jampal Rölpe Lodrö, a great Geluk master, and Tülku Dorje Dradül (1891–1959?). Tülku Dorje Dradül was a great tertön, the youngest son of Düdjom Lingpa and youngest brother of the third Dodrupchen. However, Rinpoche himself later acknowledged that he was the tülku of Do Khyentse, and he also displayed mystical power similar to that of Do Khyentse.

When Rinpoche was four years old, with great ceremony he was enthroned at Dodrupchen Monastery simultaneously with Rinpoche, Thupten Thrinle Palzang, the other tülku of the third Dodrupchen. After that, the two Rinpoches had their reading lessons together, and they lived together until their late teens.

At the age of seven both Rinpoches studied the scriptural texts with Lushül Khenpo Könchok Drönme (Könme) until Khenpo died in 1936. Then they studied with Chökor Khenpo Kang-nam, Kyala Khenpo Chöchok, and other scholars of Dodrupchen Monastery for a number of years.

At the age of eleven, for many months the Rinpoches went to Dzachukha Valley to receive the *Nyingthig Yabzhi* and *Longchen Nyingthig* transmissions from the great Gekong Khenpo Künzang Palden (Künpal).

In his childhood, Rinpoche did not exhibit any miracles, but as he grew up and Rinpoche Thupthen Thrinle Palzang stopped displaying miracles, he started to display his own power.

At the age of nineteen, both Rinpoches went to Central Tibet for a year-long pilgrimage. Rinpoche did a short retreat at Kang-ri Thökar, the place where Longchen Rabjam lived. At many places he had visions and saw the ters to be discovered, but he chose to ignore them, as he was surrounded by serious-minded monks.

Sera Yangtrül (1926–1989/90), a famous tertön of Ser Valley, who was among the caravan of the pilgrim party of Dodrupchens, said:

> On our way back from Central Tibet, one day Rinpoche and I walked to the bank of a river. Rinpoche told me, "Dig up the sand. We will find something." After digging a little, I uncovered a prayer wheel. Rinpoche said, "Dig more; there should be something else." I dug more and discovered an image gilded with gold. Rinpoche said, "I need this image. You take the wheel." Thinking, "I'd like to have the image, but he is not giving it to me. What to do with this prayer wheel?" I said, "I don't need this prayer wheel." Rinpoche said, "Then throw it away." I did, and before it fell on the ground, it just vanished. Referring to the prayer wheel and the gilded image, I asked, "Rinpoche, what are these?" He just said, "Oh, some travelers must have left them here." It was the

fault of my being too young. It was a ter discovery, but I didn't realize it then.

Yangtrül tells another story.

Again on the way back, Rinpoche and I went for a walk into a canyon. First he wanted us to make many pegs with the twigs of a thorny bush. After making them, looking at a high, steep, and flat-faced rocky hill, he said, "In that rock there are ter. Shall we go to see them?" I said yes. When we got there, he put the pegs into the rock as if in mud and, using them, he kept climbing up, and I followed him. Then we reached a huge cave. In it we chanted *The Seven-Line Prayer* and *The Prayer for Spontaneous Accomplishment of the Wishes* of Guru Rinpoche. At that moment, a piece of the wall of the cave opened like a window. In the windowlike hole we saw many statues and "caskets." Also there was a stone in the shape of an arm. Rinpoche said, "Pull that stone. Your share of ter is there." When I tried to pull it, it just came open, like a lid. In it, there were many images and caskets surrounded by snakes. Rinpoche said, "Pick them up without any doubts." I put my hands in and took out one image and three caskets. After looking at them, he said, "Now put them back." I said, "I am going to take the image." Rinpoche warned, "No! The time of taking out has not yet arrived, and the protectors will not let us take them." As I put back the ter substances, the door in the rock spontaneously closed and sealed it off as before. It was all like magic. Then I climbed down first, and he came down afterward, taking out the pegs from the rock. I told him, "Rinpoche, let the pegs stay, we will need them when we return." He said, "No! If people see them, they will laugh at us, saying, 'Two crazy people have been here.' " When he had finished picking out the pegs, there was not even a trace of his having nailed the pegs into the rocks. Now I know that it was an amazing display.

Sometime after their return from Central Tibet, Rinpoche made his main residence at Gephel Ritrö, the Hermitage of Fostering Virtues, where the third Dodrupchen stayed for most of the last half of his life. This hermitage is situated below the summit of a sky-touching mountain in a mirrorlike field of green grass painted with wildflowers. The field was surrounded by walls of tall evergreen pine and juniper trees. Beyond the wall of trees, at a far distance, you can see the waves of ranges of high-rising mountains on the other side of the Do Valley. Some mountains are dressed in trees, some are covered with gray, reddish, or bluish rocks, and others are occasionally capped with snow. They give an illusion that they are forming a wall behind the walls of tall trees, or rather that day and night they are guarding you.

Rinpoche studied many texts, but the scope of his studies wasn't broad. Still, he was a scholar by nature, as Jigme Lingpa was. He was tall and slim compared with other lamas of Golok, with wide, bright, powerful eyes. He was an amazing speaker both for Dharma teachings and in social conversation. He was a good painter, a master of chanting, and skilled in making tormas and maṇḍalas. Even though he lived simply, he was highly dignified, and even when he talked silliness, it was teachings; even when he acted unpredictably, he was always a most trustworthy person, and even while he lived and died in prison, by his presence he brought the light of Dharma into the lives of many fellow inmates.

From about the age of twenty, except when he was giving empowerments or teachings, or was traveling outside the monastery, he would not sit on thrones or preside over ceremonies as the vajra master. He enjoyed sitting on a cushion and acting as the master of chanting or the master of performance, or sometimes playing the ceremonial flute, which are designations of lower rank.

In the woods at the hermitage there was a high seat of stones from which the third Dodrupchen once taught. For a long time, from this seat Rinpoche also taught Dzogpa Chenpo to Tülku Jigme Phüntsok (Jiglo) and about twenty selected disciples. Around this time he discovered teachings on Dzogpa Chenpo and on chö practice as ter.

Soon Rinpoche became seriously sick. He was thought to be affected by having been poisoned on his trip to Central Tibet a couple of years before. His face and tongue and urine became dark or bluish. Many of his teeth, including two front teeth, cracked. Many Lamas, including Khenpo Kang-nam and Kyala Khenpo, gathered at the hermitage and for many days prepared rinchen rilbu, a special healing or purifying medicine. On the day he was supposed to take the medicine, it just disappeared and the cup was empty. People interpreted this as a bad omen and started losing hope. But, as Rinpoche was always unpredictable, all the signs of his sickness slowly disappeared with no logical explanation. Later, on one of his trips to Amdo, he had gold caps put on his two front teeth. For many young people, gold caps were the fashion, but for him it was to preserve his cracked teeth.

One day he told his students to arrange clay for making images of Longchen Rabjam and Jigme Lingpa. When the clay was ready, he told them, "You make the image of Longchen Rabjam. I will do the image of Jigme Lingpa." The next day he built the seat and lower part of the image of Jigme Lingpa, which was about two feet high. When he reached the waist, he stopped working on the statue for days. His students kept asking him to finish it, because otherwise the clay would become dry and he wouldn't be able to work on it. He kept saying, "Whenever you finish the image of Longchen Rabjam, I will finish mine." When his students informed him that they had finished their statue, he told them, "Make preparations for consecration tomorrow. I will finish my statue then." The next day they saw that the upper body of Jigme Lingpa had completed itself and was very beautiful. It was hard to know whether it was made of clay or stone. At the heart of the image, they could all clearly see a small image of the Samantabhadra consorts in a ring of five colors. Khenpo Kang-nam saw images that looked like the eighty-four mahāsiddhas on different parts of its body. Different people saw different images: some saw Guru Rinpoche with consorts, while others saw eight vidyādharas, and so on. Later, this image was given to Tülku Jigme Phüntsok, and he witnessed many miracles and heard music where this image was kept on the ceremonial days. I myself saw the statue with a clear image of the Samantabhadra consorts and some unrecognizable figures on it.

Rinpoche wasn't happy with the location of the kitchen of the hermitage, as smoke from the kitchen was affecting the shrine room and library. One day he came to the kitchen and, making a circle with his foot on the huge stove made of stones, said, "The kitchen wasn't here during the third Dodrupchen's time!" and he went away. Then, next morning, when the cook came to the kitchen, every stone of the stove had disappeared. Suspecting that someone could have moved them, people looked in the woods around the hermitage for hours, but there was no trace of anyone, and they concluded that Rinpoche had done one of his demonstrations. I myself saw the place from which the stove had disappeared just a couple of days after it was actually gone.

During his stay in the hermitage, Rinpoche sponsored an annual ten-day ceremony of a hundred thousand tsok offerings (Tshogs 'Bum) with about thirty or forty selected monks. During those ceremonies, from the tsok offering cakes a stream of nectar in the form of a tasty white liquid kept dripping, and it filled many small pots. I attended one of those ceremonies when I was about seven or eight years old.

If Rinpoche wished, whatever object he concentrated on, such as a pot, a painting, or a table, would be possessed by the presence of a dharmapāla, and it would move. Frequently he would use a square table with four legs. On top of it there was a square box filled with mystic diagrams, precious or semiprecious stones and metals, and dry grain. Silk scarves of different colors were wrapped around the table and hung down loosely. On top there was a half dorje as the top ornament. When the time came, saying a particular prayer, two people facing each other held the legs of the table and picked it up. The table, shaking right and left, dragged the people so forcefully that after a couple of minutes even young people were out of breath. They did this to demonstrate the presence of dharmapālas, to predict what should be done by letting the table hit questions written on pieces of paper, to recognize a thief, and so on. When another prayer was recited, it would return to the altar. I was told that while the table was in the air, you couldn't let go of it, because you couldn't open your hands. I never tried to hold it because I was too scared of its force.

In Rekong, there was a tradition of making a dharmapāla enter a table and receiving prophetic indications. To prepare the table took many days of meditation and prayers. But Rinpoche made it happen by a mere gesture or by concentration. Also, for others there was the possibility of causing the presence of a negative spirit, but we believed that for Rinpoche they were dharmapālas, the followers and guides of the Dharma.

With very few attendants, Rinpoche went to Amdo. He gave teachings and transmissions at many monasteries, demonstrated a number of miracles, and gave many prophecies. At Köde Monastery in Rekong, during a long-life ceremony, Rinpoche asked Alak Zhiwatso, a tülku of Chöying Topben Dorje's son, to hold the end of an arrow made of dried bamboo, and he pulled it. The arrow was lengthened by about two feet.

One day he visited an old hermit in a cave, who was a disciple of the previous Dodrupchen. The hermit said, "Rinpoche, today you must display a miracle. Until you display a miracle, I won't let you go." He sat at the door of the cave, blocking the way out. Rinpoche told him, "If you let me go, I promise that I will display a miracle." Upon that assurance, the hermit allowed him to leave. When Rinpoche got out of the cave, he said, "I fooled you," and rode away. The hermit was disappointed not only because Rinpoche didn't display any miracle, but because he broke his promise. Then he saw a very clear imprint of Rinpoche's foot on the rock at the door of the cave. With great joy, the hermit followed Rinpoche's party and requested Rinpoche to give him the shoe with which the imprint was made. Both the rock and the shoe were enshrined in a temple in Rekong. In Me (rMe) Valley Rinpoche made a knot in an iron rod. He crushed a crystal ball as if it were dough and left his hand imprints on it. He healed many who were sick or were believed to be possessed by spirits.

At Tarthang Monastery in Golok, when he met Choktrül Rinpoche, he didn't have a scarf with him to exchange in the customary form of greeting. But, before the eyes of many people, he made a gesture of grasping something in the air and brought out a white silk scarf to offer.

Whenever Rinpoche went on trips to distant places, he demonstrated amazing miracles. But then he would make his attendants promise not to repeat the story when they got back to the monastery, for the khenpos and senior lamas would get upset. There are two main reasons why the khenpos held this strange position, rightly or wrongly. First, there was a belief that if a lama manifested his esoteric power publicly, many of the audience might not be receptive to such a display, and then they could have a negative reaction. If so, it would bring negative effects, stronger than other causes, as it was connected with esoteric power. The negative reaction includes shortening the life of the lama. Secondly, as the khenpos were the guides of monastic discipline, they thought that if an important lama of the monastery displayed supernatural power, young students could be swayed by wild characters and distracted from their serious studies and humble monastic vows, which are the appropriate way for common people. Although an enlightened person will know more than an intellectual mind, that was one of the traditional attitudes.

Rinpoche visited the branch monasteries of Dodrupchen in Dzika Valley. At Sanglung Monastery, while giving long-life empowerment to Lama Lhünpo, he pulled on a long-life arrow made of a dried branch and lengthened it by about one and a half feet. For years it kept growing, until it was destroyed.

Then he visited the branch monasteries of Dodrupchen in Gyarong. At Do Khyentse's temple at the Kaukong pilgrimage place in the Trokyap principality, Rinpoche tossed a drink to the image of Do Khyentse, and the image absorbed the drink. Rinpoche visited the temple of the self-arisen Avalokiteshvara image in Trokyap. Soon after Rinpoche left,

Tri Kongthang, an important Geluk lama, who still lives at Labtrang Monastery in Amdo, visited the temple. Tri Kongthang said to the image as a prayer, "You are Avalokiteshvara. Dodrupchen is Vajrapāṇi. I am said to be Mañjushrī. The Three Classes of Buddhas/bodhisattvas are gathered here. Please show a mystical sign." At that moment, before the eyes of all who were there, from the mouth of the image a stream of greenish nectar descended. I saw the greenish water kept in a bottle at the temple, just a couple of months after the event.

Rinpoche moved back to the monastery. The annual ceremony of a hundred thousand tsok offerings at the hermitage changed into an annual tsechu, or tenth-day public ceremony, at the main monastery. Hundreds of monks performed this great ceremony for one week. At the end of the week the young monks performed various stages of rites and meditations in the form of a mystical dance for four days. Now for Westerners such a performance is simply known as a lama dance. Rinpoche had prepared the most exquisite brocade and silk costumes and well-made masks for the performers. At first people thought that by making the simpler and private ceremony at the hermitage into a bigger and public ceremony at the monastery they would lose the miracles, such as the streams of nectar. But soon people witnessed other kinds of miracles. Once, rice pudding cooked for a few hundred monks did not run out, even after feeding hundreds of laypeople who came to see the performances. A small field was big enough for about a hundred performers to perform in and for about ten thousand to practice and watch. During the dharmapāla procession, about twenty tables and many lances with dharmapāla flags were possessed and moved here and there wildly.

Then, with an elaborate party, Rinpoche traveled to Mewa, Kubum, Sining, Rekong, Lanchow, and finally to Labtrang Monastery in Amdo. At Labtrang, he was given permission by the monastery to let his attendants train in performing the drama of King Songtsen Gampo. The monastery never taught others, but at the time of the death of the fifth Jamyang Zhepa (1916–1946),[300] he told his attendants, "One day from the south someone will come saying, 'I am the propagator of drama performances.' When he comes, you must teach him." So, his attendants remembering the words of the late Jamyang Zhepa, gave all the trainings to Rinpoche's students. Rinpoche returned to the monastery with magnificent costumes, makeup, and musical instruments for the drama. Rinpoche himself composed two additional performances, the lives of Trime Künden and of Drowa Zangmo. Because of the rich costumes and perfect training, the performances were a wonder in the Golok area, where people had never witnessed such performances before. All the performers were monks, playing the roles of both men and women wearing makeup. (Today, the tradition of Rinpoche's drama performances has been revived at many places in the Do, Mar, and Ser valleys.)

The khenpos had objections, thinking that the drama performances might be a distraction from serious studies, meditation, and discipline, but they themselves enjoyed them so much that the seniormost khenpo, Khenpo Kang-nam, even requested a special performance for himself.

At the age of twenty-five (1951), Rinpoche traveled with many monks to Tartsedo (Kanding). On the way, one night they camped in the valley next to the valley where the hermitage of Yukhok Chatralwa was situated. When Chatralwa heard this, he instructed ten young students, "A big caravan is camping in the next valley. Tomorrow you must stop them from coming here."

The next day, Chatralwa's disciples were caught in a dilemma. How could they prevent Dodrupchen from coming? But also, how could they not prevent Rinpoche, as it was the lama's request? So they went and waited by the mountain path, worrying about what to do.

Early the next morning, Rinpoche told his attendants, "Today I will lead the way." Instead of going directly along the mountain path, they traveled up the valley and turned down the valley of the hermitage and suddenly penetrated into the hermitage. The monks of the hermitage had no choice but to welcome him. But Chatralwa told his disciples, "Here we have no material goods to offer him, which are what he might have come for, as we are a group of beggars. I have no teachings to give him, and he might not even want them anyway, as I myself don't know anything. It is better for him to leave this ragged place right now for the sake of his horses, mules, and attendants." With tears in his eyes, Rinpoche asked the lama's disciples to tell the lama for him, "Because of my lack of karma, now I won't be able to see you in this lifetime. But I am praying that in the next life I will be able to see you and receive your nectarlike teachings."

When the lama heard the message, he smiled and said, "I was worried that I wouldn't be able to see the tülku of Dodrupchen in this lifetime, as I am too old. I was making a joke because I was so excited." Rinpoche came in, and the first thing he did was to give a long-life empowerment to the lama, as the lama was sick. Then for a few days they exchanged important points of tantra and Dzogpa Chenpo teachings. Later Rinpoche wrote a five-page poem in praise of Chatralwa's realization.

Then Rinpoche visited Minyak Garthar, Rashel Gön, Trakhar Gön, and many other places and gave empowerments and teachings. At one place he offered a cup full of liquid to an image, and the image absorbed it. At the ceremonies, the ceremonial substances flew into the air.

One evening when it was time to camp, there was a heavy rain. Until his attendants could put up the tents, Rinpoche took shelter under a rock, where he could not even sit up straight. When Tsamzang and others went to get Rinpoche, he was sitting up. Without knowing the truth, Tsamzang asked, "Rinpoche, you found a bigger cave?" He said, "No, but after some time I was too tired to sit bending my head." Then they noticed that Rinpoche's whole upper body had penetrated into the rock, as if into mud. They could see the imprint of his robe, head, and even every hair in the rock. According to Sönam Nyima, this imprint is still there.

In Tartsedo, Rinpoche stayed at Dorje Trak and the seats of Do Khyentse and gave transmissions and teachings to the king of Chakla and thousands of others. It is said that he discovered a number of earth ter, but I have no more information. When he visited Rikhuk Kushok, one of the important lamas of Tartsedo, Rinpoche crushed a glass and left the imprint of his hand. Tondrup, Rikhuk Kushok's nephew, told me that he saw it at his uncle's place. From Tartsedo, Rinpoche visited Chengdu and Chongqing, and he returned to Dodrupchen Monastery in 1952.

Soon, he established the Rigne Lobdra, the Science College. Rinpoche sponsored fifty students to study grammar, writing, poetry, rites, drama, chanting, maṇḍalas, tormas, painting, medicine, and astrology. He brought many famous Tibetan doctors and astrologers from other places to teach the students. He opened a free clinic with free distribution of medicine.

Rinpoche started to live anywhere, without maintaining any fixed residence for himself. Sometimes he would be found living in the corner of one of the shrines with a mattress and some religious objects, with curtains around him. He never locked himself up in the private sanctuary of a room. He was always there without even a door to lock, for all to come in, to see him, to listen to him, and to give all the help that he could provide. He was devoting his life to taking care of all, especially the poor and eager young monks. For years until I left the monastery in

1957, day after day, before dawn till late at night, he himself led people, mostly the poor ones, in prayers, ceremonies, meditations, and study. He shared with them his own room, food, and clothes. He entertained them by telling amazing stories, trained them in various skills, and enlightened them by giving Dharma teachings. Whatever treasures or possessions people offered him, he would accept them, but sometimes it seemed that he was so eager to be rid of them. A couple of times a year, he would distribute not simple things, but jewels, silk, silver, and clothes to needy people with his own hand. Many times it happened that he had disbursed all his funds for Dharma projects or given them to people, and he hadn't kept anything even for a proper meal.

The elder monks kept suggesting to Rinpoche that he should be more traditional. He should live in a dignified place appropriate to a Dodrupchen. He should choose senior monks as his attendants. He should save funds and treasures for the infinite future of the monastery. But Rinpoche calmed them down by saying, "It will be my greatest joy in life if I can help the lives of people, especially those who are really in need, in every possible way. We should be happy if we can spend all the things we are given for the purpose of benefiting the people. Soon we are going to have the days when we will not have the 'right' to enjoy even a cup of tea." I myself heard these very words from Rinpoche many times.

Rinpoche went to see Tülku Künzang Nyima (d. 1958/9), a grandson and speech tülku of Düdjom Lingpa (1835–1903). At the urging of Rinpoche, Tülku Künzang Nyima discovered a series of ter teachings of *Khandro Gongpa Düpa,* and they performed ceremonies together.

In 1957, a few months after we left for Lhasa, Rinpoche traveled to Amdo. He gave teachings and transmissions at many places. He visited Labtrang Monastery and made elaborate offerings. Then he visited Sining. At the golden stūpa of Je Tsongkhapa at Kubum Monastery, where Je Tsongkhapa was born, he performed a seven-day offering ceremony, inviting twenty-five geshes to participate. Every day he made prayers of aspiration for the development of Dharma, peace, and happiness for all mother beings.

According to the late Khenpo Ngawang Sherap and others, Rinpoche told his attendants, "If anybody wants to escape, this is the last chance to leave for Lhasa." At this his attendants urged him to leave, and at one point he gave in to their pressure. His attendants even made arrangements for his party to leave for Lhasa. Then, on one of those prayer days at Kubum, with great distress Rinpoche told Tsültrim Gyatso, one of his main attendants, "I saw a golden temple with three stories, and all of it disappeared behind a mountain. Now the life of Dharma and the happiness and peace of people are ended. I am not going to leave. I can't abandon my monks and people. I will return to the monastery and try to give the pure transmissions and teachings of *Nyingthig Yabzhi* and *Longchen Nyingthig* one more time, for the last time." Then, visiting many Nyingma monasteries and giving teachings on the way, he returned to the monastery.

In 1958, many important lamas of various places assembled spontaneously at Dodrupchen Monastery, without anything having been arranged. Rinpoche first gave teachings on ngöndro. Then, with elaborate arrangements, he and hundreds of monks performed a seven-day ceremony of *Ngensong Jongwa* on the peaceful and wrathful deities. It was followed by the empowerments of the *Longchen Nyingthig,* each empowerment accompanied by detailed explanations. Then he gave teachings on *Yeshe Lama* as well as on *Khandrö Kegyang.* Then he started to give the empowerments of *Nyingthig Yabzhi.* For each empowerment (with the exception of the vase empowerments), he divided the recipients into groups of not more than five people, according to the tradition. Each empowerment was accompanied by instructions and then meditation on them for days, to qualify for the next empowerment. While the empowerment was going on, he told his attendants, "At the end of these transmissions, we are going to perform an elaborate tsok offering ceremony. Every material thing that I own should be spent for that." At the completion of the empowerments, everybody performed an elaborate tsog ceremony together. Soon thereafter the army suddenly attacked the monastery. As people begged him, Rinpoche with many lamas escaped into the forest to hide. The monastery was totally ransacked. Some monks were killed and others were arrested.

After spending weeks in forests, Rinpoche surrendered to the authorities at Namda in Dzika Valley. Although he was assured by the authorities through emissaries that he wouldn't be arrested, he was immediately arrested. Then, as a prisoner, he was taken to Padma (Baima) County headquarters and kept there for some time.

In 1959, he was taken to one of the most infamous, massive prison camps in the barren landscape of Qinghai, about five hundred miles from home, to serve his life sentence. His kin and disciples didn't know where he was for years. He was one of those prisoners who had to work at hard labor. Because of the prison system and also the severe famine, prisoners mostly had to live on thin gruel for 1960 and 1961. However, it was a state prison, and if you didn't say or do anything against the rules and did your hard labor, then it was a place for slow death by hunger and labor, but not so much by the torture of beatings as it was in the local prisons. In this prison he was the only prisoner from Dodrupchen Monastery, but there were a number of his disciples from other regions, so later we heard about his life through some of those who survived and were released.

I heard that in both county and national prisons, even if he was mistreated, sick, and hungry, he seemed somehow cleaner and more cheerful than the others, always absorbed in peace. He seemed never to care about himself, but was sad because of what people were going through. In the national prison, sometimes he secretly shared his small amount of food with others who were weaker than himself. After he got sick, he didn't have to go to work, and his share of gruel was brought to his bed. With great joy, he would use it as a tsok offering and then would enjoy it.

In 1961, an operation was performed on him, and in the operation they used the blood of a Muslim butcher. Later, when he learned about the transfusion, he didn't want to live anymore. He wouldn't listen to the whispered pleading and hidden tears of his disciples. To Dzakhen Lama, one of the grieving disciples, he said, "I am not forced to be in this prison because of my past karma. [I am here for a purpose.] I have no difficulty going to any kind of pure lands, if I choose. Don't worry for me!" As soon as he died, his body was buried. Drubwang Rinpoche, a disciple of his, saw where they were burying his body. In 1979, Dodrupchen Monastery was able to recover the body with the help of Drubwang Rinpoche and a Chinese who had been in charge of burial.

From time to time, Rinpoche had a chance to whisper his teachings, his visions, and the events of his past lives to his disciples, Gyalse Padlo Rinpoche, Drubwang Rinpoche, Dzakhen Lama Rigdzin, and others. Also he wrote teachings in the form of small poems as his farewell gift when a disciple was released.

At the time of the release of Tülku Thrinle Künkhyab (aka Nangchen Gyalse Achen, ?–1990?), Rinpoche wrote the following advice and gave it to him to secretly take out of prison:

> At the bliss chakra at the crown of my head,
> O lama, the embodiment of the Buddha of the three times,

I pray to your compassion that is faster than lightning.
You are not far away, but in my own heart.

The vivid-awareness of the devotional mind
Free from reference points is the presence of the lama.
The presence of this in oneself is wonderful!
[Object:] Now, in the sphere of vast open space,
With the quality of no-grasping, please stay well.

[Subject:] Whatever conditions of struggling thoughts arise,
Like snowflakes on a heated stone,
Let them dissolve into the sphere of great openness of the basis.
Then such [thoughts] will have no [power] to harm or heal. It is joyful!

[Action:] In discriminating [things as] good and bad, virtues and unvirtues,
Like drawing lines in space,
Realize their self-purity, by seeing them moving but translucent,
Since they are primordially free from characteristics of hopes and fears.

[Result:] The "recollecting awareness" is the self-liberation at touch [or realization].
The three worlds are the supreme awareness, the liberation-at-the basis.
All the arisings are the play of the Dharmakāya power.
Both saṃsāra and nirvāṇa are solely intrinsic awareness.

In order to fulfill the request of Tülku Rinpoche Thrinle Kunkhyab, this is written by Jigtral Düdül Namkhe Dorje at the time of his release from prison.

Just after the death of Rinpoche, at the dawn of the tenth day of the seventh month of the Iron Ox year (1961), his disciple Dzakhen Rigdzin lamented with devotion and grief. At that time, Rinpoche appeared before him (in the sky) in heruka costume. Glancing at the sky, Rinpoche gave him his spiritual testament:

O Son, direct your ear to me.
I am the fearless lord of the hundred adepts,
I am the forefather, the universal basis of saṃsāra and nirvāṇa.

Today, our parting is the fault of compounded phenomena.
What is the use of your mourning for it?
Death is just a conventional term, like the sound of wind.
Please do not feel sad, but stay happy.

When the elements of my body were dissolved,
My outwardly projecting cognition returned inwardly,
Into the expanse of the basis, "the [youthful] vase body with six supreme qualities."
My unhindered [or clear] cognition, the appearances of the basis,
Merged into the unconfused innate subtle wisdom,
The ultimate sphere of the mind of the lord Guhyapati,
Which was like the moon in the new-moon sky,
Where the indescribable virtues,
Such as the spontaneously completed array of Buddha lands,
The food-of-absorption and self-appearing ornaments, are present.

Although the outward lama, my physical form,
The body manifestation, is dissolved into the sphere of luminous clarity,
The inward lama, my absolute meaning,
O son, will remain in the universal basis of your mind.
I, your father, the knowledge-holder Jalü Dorje,
Have never been separated from you even for a moment.

Your mind free from reference points, [the union of] clarity and emptiness, is me.
If you maintain the face of this itself, the accomplishments will arise:
Your outer and inner physical elements will become pure.
The maṇḍalas of the three seats will be completed in your own body.
Your appearances, speech [and thoughts] will become the body, speech, and mind of the lama.

This is the lord of action of all the glorious wrathful deities,
The great glorious deity Vajrakīla:
The phurba of enlightenment [is perfected] in the womb of the consort.
The phurba of the three existents liberates saṃsāra.
The phurba of ultimate nature is accomplished spontaneously.
With the groove of the phurba of subtle wisdom

The movements of air/energy and mind [are liberated] into the avadhūti,
And the heart channels of apprehended and apprehender are eliminated.
The phurba of freedom from elaborations is perfected at the basis.
This [attainment of phurba] is the heart essence of a thousand glorious ones [buddhas].
The array of saṃsāra and nirvāṇa is completed in his body.
These are arisen from themselves and unite into themselves.

From every pore of my body
I manifest hundreds of millions of manifestations.
Especially, my mind manifestation will appear in Ga-ge.
The body manifestation will appear in Puwo.
Soon [a word is missing here] appear in my native valley.
My [manifestations] and tantric traditions
Will appear as the light of the moon [compared with the sunlight].
You will have the fortune of serving them.

This glorious yellow scroll, from the precious casket,
Your share [of teachings], is concealed in your mind.
In future, decode it and provide benefits for others.
Do not forget the testaments I have given you in the past.
Now, for a while, I will go to the Unexcelled Pure Land.

Performing a Hayagrīva sādhana, from his three sacred maṇḍalas [forehead, mouth, and heart], he bestowed the four empowerments [in the form of beams of light] to Dzakhen Rigdzin, and then, dancing, he floated away through the sky.

Rinpoche was an exceptional person who dedicated everything to taking care of others, and especially the poor. He himself tried to live as one of the ordinary people. He hardly cared for his own needs.

Rinpoche wrote many teachings on Dzogpa Chenpo and many poems and pieces of advice, but almost all are lost. He discovered a complete cycle of trainings on Chö practice as mind ter teachings. Some parts of it have survived.

In Golok and Amdo there are about six young lamas who have displayed miraculous powers and unofficially have been acknowledged as his incarnations. However, Tülku Jigme Long-yang,[301] born in the Puchung Risarma tribal group in Do Valley, has been recognized by Dodrupchen Monastery as Rinpoche's tülku and has been living at the monastery.

38

Fourth Dodrupchen Thupten Thrinle Palzang
b. 1927

KYABJE Thupten Thrinle Palzang, the fourth Dodrupchen Rinpoche,[302] is a great master of Dzogpa Chenpo and a principal lineage holder and propagator of the *Longchen Nyingthig* teachings.

Rinpoche was born in the Fire Hare year of the sixteenth Rabjung (1927) in Tsi village in the Ser (Serta) Valley of Golok in Eastern Tibet. Tsi is a small village surrounded by rich green fields of wheat, barley, and peas. The green grassy mountain behind is dotted with trees and rocks. The gentle Ser River flows by slowly from right to left. Rinpoche's father was Drala of the Jekar clan, and his mother was Kali Kyi of the Kazhi clan.

Between his conception and the age of six, Rinpoche displayed many miraculous signs. Lushül Khenpo and Lauthang Tülku made a record of these signs up to the age of four. In my childhood, with great curiosity, I read them many times, and the following are some of those that I still remember.

Around the time that he was conceived, his father had a dream in which he was brandishing a crystal sword, which was so long that the end was not visible in the sky. That year almost every day, rainbows appeared over Tsi village, and the monks of the monastery across the river used to joke, "This year all the people of Tsi village are going to attain rainbow body."

While Rinpoche was in the womb, there were many occasions on which his mother entered a dark place, but she could see because of the appearance of a light, which sometimes scared her. One day a snake holding a shining object in its mouth came into the house and then disappeared into the wall in front of a couple of people.

Almost every night a za[303] kept appearing on the roof of the house. The raven without the upper part of its beak, which lives at Dodrupchen Monastery, was seen many times at this distant village. Without any seeds having been sown, a kind of flower unknown in that part of the country covered the roof of the house.

When he was born before dawn, although it was still dark, things became clearly visible because of a light. Many times the baby was found on the upper floor of the house, although he could not walk. His parents, thinking that he must be climbing the stairs, sealed them off. Still they found him on the upper floor a number of times.

Once a big maṇi stone, a stone on which prayers are carved, fell on Rinpoche. Many of his bones seemed to have been broken, but after a few hours all trace of damage had disappeared. Many people heard him reciting the siddhi mantra, the prayer mantra of Guru Rinpoche, many times.

One day, a disciple of the third Dodrupchen named Guru came to see him. When Rinpoche saw him, he instantly said, "Guru! Guru!" and blessed him by putting his hand on Guru's head and chanting, OṂ ĀḤ HŪṂ, VAJRA GURU PADMA SIDDHI HŪṂ.

The fifth Dzogchen Rinpoche Thupten Chökyi Dorje (1872–1935) gave the following prophecy for Dodrupchen Monastery to indicate where the tülku of the third Dodrupchen would be found.

> The main source of manifestation of the vajra master,
> The lord of the Buddha lineages, is the Glorious Mountain of
> Ngayab Continent.
> In the center, which is the great pure land of Sambhogakāya,
> There are four emanations: of his body, speech, mind, and virtues.
> The manifestation of his action
> Has taken birth to the south of the monastery,
> At a place among mountains with rocks and trees,
> To a skillful means [father] and a wisdom [mother] named Ka
> and Da

As an auspicious child of the Earth Hare.
There are signs that he will benefit the Dharma and beings.
At the request of devotees,
I, the fifth Dzogchen Tülku Dharmavajra,
Wrote whatever was recalled to my deluded mind.
May the dawn of virtues and goodness fill the earth.

The great Dzogchen yogī Yukhok Chatralwa also said, "In a dream I saw two sacred vases on one maṇḍala, so there will be two incarnations. If the offerings are made to the protectors, you shall find the tülkus very soon."

Then Dzogchen Rinpoche instructed them to conduct the search south of the monastery up to the valleys of Li and Tsang. When the search party from Dodrupchen Monastery visited Tsi village, before his parents knew of their arrival, Rinpoche told them, "Today guests are coming," and he sang happily. When the party who came to examine him presented him with books, rosaries, and other possessions of the previous Dodrupchen mixed with those belonging to other people, he picked up his predecessor's things without a single mistake, saying, "This is mine."

Then the list of names was presented to Dzogchen Rinpoche for his final determination. He picked the name of the present Dodrupchen Rinpoche and composed a long-life prayer for the child, and gave him the name Thupten Thrinle Palzangpo. Many other great lamas also confirmed the recognition, about which they were of one mind.

When the child was four years old, people arrived from Dodrupchen Monastery at Tsi village as the first reception party, headed by Tülku Pema Namgyal (d. 1957), a tülku of Düdjom Lingpa. On the way to the monastery the party camped for the night, and the next morning some of the horses were missing. People searched all around but were unable to find them. They asked Rinpoche where they would find those horses. He pointed his tiny finger toward a mountain, and there they found the horses.

The final reception party, led by Khenpo Könme (1859–1935), received him at Tsangchung plain, about two miles from the monastery. The old khenpo, who came riding a dzo,[304] was accompanied by about one hundred of his monk students. The students in a line after the khenpo came on foot wearing orange-colored monks' robes and holding books in shokalis (cases) as a symbol of their being students of scriptures.

Also at this place Rinpoche met with Rigdzin Tenpe Gyaltsen (1927–1961), who had also been recognized as a fourth Dodrupchen and who was being taken to the monastery to be enthroned simultaneously with him.

Buddhists believe that if you are a highly enlightened person, you can manifest yourself in the form of many beings simultaneously as your incarnations for the service of others. So there are many Dodrupchen incarnations, who are originally emanated by the first Dodrupchen.

Both Rinpoches were brought to Dodrupchen Monastery and into the assembly hall of the main temple by a great company of monks and laypeople, many weeping tears of joy and faith. There they were both enthroned simultaneously, and the occasion was celebrated with great joy.

At Dodrupchen Monastery just after the enthronement ceremonies were completed, Rinpoche stood up on the throne and, laughing, recited *The Seven-Line Prayer* and some verses from *Zheng Shik Pema,* to everybody's astonishment.

Then he visited the temple of the Dharma protectors, and from the huge volume of prayers to them, he pulled out the brief one-folio prayer to the Dharma protectors written by the first Dodrupchen and gave it to his father. He could not recognize the letters but recited the prayer by heart, missing one line. Despite the missing line, the meaning was complete.

At the suggestion of Khenpo Könme, his attendants used to give him candy and ask questions, and in response he would tell them about his visions and recollections of past lives. For example:

Q: Where do you come from?
A: From Zangdok Palri.

Q: What is Zangdok Palri like?
A: [Folding his tiny hands in the shape of a heart/mountain] It is like this.

Q: Who lives there?
A: Guru Rinpoche.

Q: Who else is there?
A: Chenrezik is there.

Q: Do you know Sin-gyal Raksha Thötreng?
A: Yes.

Q: What does he look like?
A: Many mouths, many eyes, colorful. [He laughed.]

Another time the questions and answers went as follows: "Where is your residence?" He pointed toward the forest in which the hermitage of his previous life was situated and said, "There." Trying to fool him, they said, "Nothing is there but trees." He replied, "No! no! My house is there!"

Sometimes the Rinpoches made tormas from the tsampa in their bowls and, throwing them, they would say, "May obstacles be turned away." People could see sparks coming from the tormas.

One night he was going to bed but started to recite unknown verses beginning with: "I have never been separate from the enlightenment."[305] His attendant tried to write down some of what he recalled. It was a seven-line verse with profound philosophical and meditational meaning. Later on, Kyala Khenpo wrote a commentary on those verses, interpreting them in three ways, according to Mahāyoga, Anuyoga, and Atiyoga. Now we have lost both the verses and the commentary by Khenpo.

Khenpo Könme stated, "From the evidence of the signs displayed in childhood, Rinpoche could manifest as a powerful adept with miracles comparable to Do Khyentse." After he grew up, however, except for a few instances, he never displayed any signs of miraculous attainment. In addition, when other lamas, including the other fourth Dodrupchen Rinpoche, displayed miracles or gave prophecies, he repeatedly said to them, "In this age it is not appropriate to display any miracle. It may be harmful to one's life, activities, or the Buddha Dharma. It may cause the secrets of the tantra to be dispersed."

From the age of four, when they were enthroned together, until the age of twenty, the two incarnations of the third Dodrupchen lived and received training together. From the age of five, they started to read the texts with their tutors Puchung Rang-rik and Chökor Lotsül. Monks in general, and especially tülkus, are trained to recite texts very fast, until they can recite an unseen text at sight as fast as one that has already been memorized. The Rinpoches perfected their recitation trainings in less than one year, which was an excellent achievement.

From the age of seven (1933), they began to study the scriptural texts. Their first teacher was Lushül Khenpo, Könchok Drönme (Könme, 1859–1936). They studied the *Mañjushrīstotra, Nāgārjuna's Message to a*

Friend, Bodhicharyāvatāra, and then *Yönten Dzö,* a text of complete exposition of sūtra and tantra by Jigme Lingpa. But when they got halfway through *Yönten Dzö,* Könme Khenpo died after a brief illness at the age of seventy-seven, displaying many signs of high spiritual attainment.

In their eleventh year (1937) both Rinpoches went to Gekong Monastery in Dzachukha, where they received the empowerment and the entrustment of *Nyingthig Yabzhi* and *Longchen Nyingthig* from Khenpo Künzang Chötrak (Khenpo Künpal, 1872–1943), a disciple of Paltrül Rinpoche and the third Dodrupchen. Entrusting them with the lineage, Khenpo told them, "My lineage is authentic, short, powerful, and blessed; it is more extraordinary than other lineages. Now I have handed over the property of the father into the hands of the son." And he was very happy and repeatedly asked the Rinpoches to propagate and uphold the pure golden lineage of Nyingthig, without mixing it with others. During that winter the Rinpoches returned to Dodrupchen Monastery.

At the age of fourteen (1940) Rinpoche became seriously ill. He went to see Apang Tertön, Ogyen Thrinle Lingpa (d. 1945), who was staying at the sacred Mount Drong-ri. One day Apang Tertön gave him a bowl of chang, fermented beer, to drink. But Rinpoche hesitated. For although he was not an ordained monk, he didn't have the habit of drinking, in order to uphold the discipline of his monastic tradition. But then he thought, "It must be a blessing of the lama," and he drank all of it without any further hesitation. As a result there arose a wonderful awareness, which cannot be explained by words or conceived by thoughts. He was able to answer spontaneously whatever questions the lama had for him, but he made no effort to say anything beyond the answers elicited by the questions. Later, when he went outside the house and felt the wind's touch, it brought an innate confidence that all appearances or existents are unreal like a dream, and a spontaneous revulsion from saṃsāra arose in him. With the arising of these inexplicable feelings of peace and revulsion, a spontaneous realization of innate awareness was born in him.

The next day he went to the lama to present his meditative experiences. Years later Rinpoche said of the meeting, "I felt that I was talking to the lama like a baby." The lama confirmed his realization and gave him a detailed prophecy of the events of his life till the age of twenty-five. And he also identified Dodrupchen Rinpoche as one of the doctrine holders of the ter teachings discovered by the lama himself. He advised Rinpoche to receive teachings from Yukhok Chatralwa, as Chatralwa was Rinpoche's karmic lama.

One day while Rinpoche was in retreat at So-thok Gyalwe Wenne, he suddenly told his attendant that he had to go to meet Yukhok Chatralwa. With one attendant and a mount, he went to the lama's hermitage, which is about two days' distance. On the way he met his sister, but she did not recognize him because she did not expect that he would be traveling so simply. When he reached the hermitage, the lama was seriously ill. He had not taken food for many days and could hardly move. Rinpoche had an ordinary conversation with the lama for a few hours, upon which the lama asked his attendant to bring him some food. To their surprise he ate some food and slowly recovered completely with no trace of illness. Because of old age, Chatralwa could not stand up. But saying, "I was said to be an old disciple of Dodrupchen, so I have to serve tea to Rinpoche myself," he would pick up the teapot and pour the tea into Rinpoche's cup. People thought that this was an indication of his accepting the popular belief in his identification as a tülku of Dola Jigme Kalzang, a principal disciple of the first Dodrupchen.

In the spring of his fifteenth year (1941), Rinpoche conferred the complete empowerments and Lung of *Longchen Nyingthig* on about a thousand monks and nuns at Dodrupchen Monastery.

From ten to eighteen years of age Rinpoche did most of his intellectual studies at Dodrupchen Monastery. His teachers included Chökor Khenpo Kün-ga Lodrö, Kyala Khenpo Chöchok, Shorwak Khenpo Sherap Trakpa, Kephan Khenpo Thuksung, and Garwa Tülku Dorchok. His studies included sūtric texts on the preliminary mind training (Blo sByong), Madhyamaka, Abhidharma, and Vinaya; and tantric texts such as the *Guhyagarbha-tantra,* the *Sādhanas of the Three Roots* and *Vajrakīla* of *Longchen Nyingthig,* some of *The Seven Treasures* by Longchen Rabjam, and *Yeshe Lama.*

He received training in chanting, music, and mystical gestures (mudrā), preparation of maṇḍalas and tormas, and so on—all the functions of a vajra acharya (grand master). In addition to the preliminary practice, he completed the retreat recitation trainings of *Rigdzin Düpa, Yumka Dechen Gyalmo, Palchen Düpa, Vajrakīla,* and the *Guhyagarbha-tantra.*

In the spring of his nineteenth year (1945), in accordance with the prophecy of Apang Tertön, both Dodrupchen Rinpoches went on pilgrimage to Central Tibet with a party of hundreds of people. Also following Apang Tertön's instructions, they kept their identities secret, except at Mindroling Monastery and Tsering Jong Nunnery. Everywhere else, it was stated that the treasurer of Dodrupchen was traveling to the holy places to make offerings on behalf of the two Rinpoches. They visited many pilgrimage places and monasteries, including Radreng, Lhasa; the three great monasteries, Drepung, Sera, and Ganden; Kangri Thökar; Drak Yangdzong; Dorje Trak; Mindroling; Samye; Tsering Jong; and the holy places of Yarlung.

Rinpoche did a retreat practicing the sādhana of *Yumka Dechen Gyalmo* (The Queen of Great Bliss), in the room of Jigme Lingpa at Tsering Jong Nunnery. In that retreat he repeatedly experienced for long periods the cessation of all ordinary thoughts and the prevalence of a state of ultimate luminescence (Don Gyi Od gSal) free from conceptualization. At the Kodrzö Ling, the temple of Dharma protectors of Samye Monastery, the oracle spontaneously went into a trance and became possessed by the Dharmapāla Tsiu Marpo. He ran to Rinpoche and, making obeisance, offered him the ritual instrument, the "hook," in his hand. Finally, in the autumn of his twentieth year, on the twenty-fifth day of the ninth month of the Fire Dog year (1946), they returned to Dodrupchen.

Soon after their return from pilgrimage, Tülku Jigme Phüntsok, who was the head of the administration of Dodrupchen Monastery, supported by most of the monks and lay patrons, requested Rinpoche to take charge of the administration of the monastery with its branch monasteries and parishes (Lha sDe), although many people, such as my teacher Kyala Khenpo, had strong reservations, saying, "Rinpoche should never have the burden of administration responsibilities, as his predecessor never had, because it will distract him from focusing on learning and dealing with the spiritual needs of people." While the third Dodrupchen was present, Dodrupchen Monastery became one of the most flourishing learning institutions in Eastern Tibet, but after the death of Könme Khenpo, the monastery swiftly declined and had hit the rock bottom of its history when Rinpoche was urged to take it over. Rinpoche accepted the responsibility. From that time until the age of thirty (1956), when he was forced to flee, Rinpoche discharged both the functions of the spiritual and the administrative heads of the monastery.

At about twenty-two, Rinpoche visited Joro Monastery, in the Trokyab principality of Gyarong Province. The monks of that monastery made a lance from which was suspended a painting of the Dharmapāla

Tsiu Marpo. They requested Rinpoche to give blessings and to produce a sign before everybody that the flag was possessed by the dharmapāla. Rinpoche refused their request. But the people of Gyarong are known for their persistence, and when the ceremony of the protector was taking place, one of the monks brought in the flag and stood in front of Rinpoche in the midst of about fifty monks. Rinpoche, visibly annoyed with their persistence, hit the flag with a handful of grain, whereupon the lance shook violently. Pulling the flag bearer away and circumambulating the temple once, it retired upstairs to the shrine room of the protectors.

At twenty-four (1950) he went to Yukhok Chatralwa, believed to be a manifestation of Vimalamitra, to receive teachings. The lama taught him the entire practice of Trekchö and Thögal of Dzogpa Chenpo, "like the filling of one vase from another." The lama was a great scholar, but he had stopped giving public teachings or textual explanations. He only gave instructions to students individually, according to each one's capacity, need, and experience. This teaching style is called Nyamtri or Nyongtri, instructions according to the progress of the meditator's experience. Yukhok Chatralwa had the power of knowing the minds of others. When people went to see him, they were apprehensive about the arising of their own bad thoughts.

Rinpoche built a shedra complex with a temple and a residence for the khenpo surrounded by rooms for the students. When I was studying in the shedra, there were twenty-five regular students and about the same number of auditing students. All the regular students were on scholarships granted by the monastic funds provided by Rinpoche. The main courses of study at the shedra were Pramāna (logic), Prajñāpāramitā (transcendental wisdom), Madhyamaka (middle-way philosophy), Abhidharma (Buddhist psychology and metaphysics), and Vinaya (monastic and lay disciplines) of sūtra and *Yizhin Dzö, Yönten Dzö,* and *Guhyagarbha-tantra* of tantra. However, teachings on the three-root sādhanas, and so on, and of *Dzogpa Chenpo* were given not in this facility, but in a more secluded environment for selected advanced students.

In the spring of his twenty-fifth year (1951) Rinpoche left for Dege Province to receive various lineal transmissions. From Khyentse Chökyi Lodrö (1893–1959) of Dzongsar Monastery, Rinpoche received the empowerments (dBang) and textual transmissions (Lung) of *Semde Adön Chogye, Longde Dorje Zampa, Me-ngagde,* the thirteen divisions of *Kama, Düpa Do, Gongpa Zangthal, Trölthik, Longchen Nyingthig,* and the *Sung-*

bum of Khyentse Wangpo as well as the empowerments of *Kālachakra, Guhyasamāja, Chakrasaṃvara, Hevajra,* and *Vajrabhairava.* From Kongtrül Pema Tri-me Lodrö (1901–1959?) of Zhechen Monastery, Rinpoche received the empowerments and textual transmissions of the *Changter* cycle of Rigdzin Gödem, the thirteen volumes of the *Minling* cycle, the three major traditions of *Kagye,* and the *Kagyü Ngagdzö.* From Namtrül Drodül Karkyi Dorje of Gyarong Monastery, Rinpoche received the empowerments and textual transmissions of *Rinchen Terdzö, Kagye Deshek Düpa, Lama Gongdü,* the six volumes of Jatsön, *Terchö* of Namchö, *Terchö* of Nyima Trakpa, and the nine volumes of Jigme Lingpa. He also studied poetry and *Guhyagarbha-tantra* with Khenpo Thup-nyen of Dzogchen Monastery.

In return Rinpoche gave the empowerment of *Khandro Nyingthig* to Khyentse Chökyi Lodrö[306] and many other transmissions to his teachers.

Among the teachers from whom he received scholarly instructions were Khenpo Könchok Drönme, Khenpo Kang-nam, Khenpo Chöchok, Tülku Dorchok, and Khenpo Thup-nyen. He received lineal transmission of various teachings from the fifth Dzogchen Rinpoche, Gekong Khenpo, Khyentse Chökyi Lodrö, Zhechen Kongtul, and Gyarong Namtrül. He received the inner instructions and introduction to Dzogpa Chenpo realization from Apang Tertön and Yukhok Chatralwa.

He conferred the empowerments and lung of the thirteen volumes of *Lama Gongdü,* and the thirteen texts of *Kama* on one to two thousand monks at Dodrupchen Monastery. One day, while he was distributing blessed water from the vase, the water ran out and no one was waiting to replenish it, as is normally done. Visibly irritated, he shook the vase a couple of times and then resumed the distribution of blessed water to the rest of the assembly, even though no one had refilled it.

With foreknowledge of the changing situation, he constructed a large and beautiful but solid temple out of bricks with a tile roof, which was then a new kind of structure in Golok, saying, "It might be useful if people have to abandon the monastery for a few years."

Rinpoche commissioned the carving of the wooden blocks of *Dzödün* in seven volumes by Longchen Rabjam. Soon most of Golok was filled with the copies of *Dzödün.* He built a large image of Guru Rinpoche and images of all the teachers of the lineages of *Vima Nyingthig, Khandro Nyingthig,* and *Longchen Nyingthig.* The images were made of copper gilded with gold. He collected a large library, including new editions of

Kanjur, Tenjur, Kama, and *Rinchen Terdzö* in addition to many other volumes of sūtras and tantras. Rinpoche also provided a number of endowments for ceremonies and studies to Dodrupchen and other monasteries.

At the request of devotees he visited different parts of Golok, Serta, Amdo, Rekong, Mewa, Gyarong, and Minyak, where he gave initiations and instructions to tens of thousands of people.

In the summer of the Fire Monkey year (1956), he gave the empowerment of *Rinchen Terdzö* at the Dodrupchen Monastery. He also gave instructions on the meditation of Dzogpa Chenpo to many fortunate people individually, according to the Nyongtri tradition.

Soon Rinpoche decided to leave his beloved land because of the dangers of the changing political situation in Tibet. Many decades before, the third Dodrupchen had examined his dreams about the future political dangers. One night he dreamed that someone brought a message written on a slate, saying "Khyentse Wangpo sent it to you." On the slate he saw the following lines:

> The great river will flow from power [i.e., west or red] to peace
> [i.e., east or white].
> The two insects will move through both upper lands and lower
> lands.
> Through the conforming rhythm [of the tunes] of the flute,
> The Land of Coolness [Tibet] will be plunged into darkness.
>
> At that time, when the top-knot [the lama]
> Hears that he should go north for ten, ten,
> Sixteen, and four,
> He will become scared and will go to the Noble Land [India],
> In a pleasant place, in the midst of a thick forest,
> While dwelling in a peaceful samādhi, before him,
> Many sky-dressed people[307] will assemble
> [And] will enter into the path of Mahāyāna.
> The profound and vast excellent path shall shine as the daylight.[308]

Rinpoche secretly arranged for a group of thirteen to leave, breaking them into three parties. Five of us—my tutor Kyala Khenpo, Rinpoche's mother, Rinpoche's nephews Thupten Jorgye and Rigdzin Phünstok, and I myself—left for Lhasa first, as he advised us, on the first day of the twelfth month of the Fire Monkey year (1957). Rinpoche's uncle Lama Sangye and Sönam, his nephew, planned to stay behind and come as the last group. But Rinpoche himself, along with a young attendant of Rinpoche's named Jamyang, two nephews of Rinpoche named Dechen Dorje and Künden, and the mother of the nephews, planned to leave in the second group.

While Rinpoche was on a visit to Panchen Monastery in Mar Valley, two days to the east of Dodrupchen Monastery, one night he and the people of his party secretly fled, disguised as lay pilgrims.

Taking very little money and carrying some belongings on their backs, they walked for ten days until they reached Kardze town. This was the first experience for Rinpoche and his companions not only of traveling on foot but of carrying bags on their backs, which inflicted exhaustion and sores. During most of the journey they hid in caves, woods, or hills during the day and crossed the high mountains and steep valleys at night. At Kardze, they were lucky to be able to get crammed into a Chinese truck going to Lhasa.

According to the original plan, our party was supposed to wait for Rinpoche in Drak Yangdzong, where Guru Rinpoche and many sages had meditated in the past, two days south of Lhasa. But Rinpoche took longer than we expected, and on the second day of the second month of the Fire Bird year (1957), Kyala Khenpo died, because of his age and the hardship of traveling. Worrying that Rinpoche and his party hadn't been able to escape, we set out to return to Lhasa, and just halfway, by luck, we ran into Rinpoche and his companions, and we all headed for Lhasa together.

In Lhasa, Rinpoche had many long-standing noble and ordinary devotees, but he chose not to get in touch with any of them. However, he did meet Zhechen Kongtrül Rinpoche (1901–1959?), one of his teachers, and Dilgo Khyentse Rinpoche (1910–1991). Kongtrül Rinpoche advised him to go to Kongpo because it is a pleasant and more prosperous place than Lhasa. Rinpoche responded with silence.

It is Rinpoche's nature that he hardly discloses his plans in advance, unless it is necessary. So when we left Golok, we thought we were just going to Lhasa. But after making simple offerings to the holy places in Lhasa, he said, "We are going to Zhigatse," a town in Western Tibet. After spending a few days in Zhigatse, he said, "Now we are going to India." But at the border, as we didn't have money to claim we were traders, we couldn't get a passport from the authorities to go to India. Even if we could avoid the border guards, India wouldn't let us in, as there was no recognition of refugee status for Tibetans at that time. After waiting for months, Rinpoche got a letter from Prince Palden Thöndrup Namgyal (who later became the Chögyal) of Sikkim, instructing the border guards to let him enter Sikkim, a state on the border of India and Tibet, later absorbed into India.

At the age of thirty-one, on the nineteenth day of the eighth month of the Fire Bird year (October 12, 1957), Rinpoche arrived in Gangtok, the capital of Sikkim. Once again he was adorned with the robes of a lama with recognition as the Dodrupchen. From then on he made Sikkim, the land blessed by Guru Rinpoche as one of the "hidden lands,"[309] as his permanent residence. His coming to Sikkim wasn't just an incident, but a mission that was to be fulfilled. Apang Tertön Ogyen Thrinle Lingpa (d. 1945), one of Rinpoche's teachers, had prophesied it many decades earlier, saying:

> A hidden yogī from the valley of Kongpo[310]
> Will come to the Valley of Rice [Sikkim] when the changes take place.
> And an incarnation of [Prince] Murum Tsepo and Sangye Lingpa[311]
> Will demonstrate the esoteric activities of a tantric yogī.
> People who see, hear, think of, or touch him will be liberated from the inferior realms.[312]

In 1958, Rinpoche performed a number of ceremonies for his ailing teacher Khyentse Chökyi Lodrö in Sikkim and Darjeeling. During a ceremony of "sending back the welcoming ḍākinīs," Khyentse Rinpoche had a vision[313] of lamas including Jigme Lingpa in a vast clear space. Among them there was also an unknown lama with a round face and short beard, who had wrapped his long hair around his head.

At the age of thirty-three, in the winter of 1959, Rinpoche made a pilgrimage to major Buddhist pilgrimage places in India and Nepal. The years 1959 and 1960 were most difficult, not just because of being a refugee in a country with a different culture and language, but also because first Khyentse Chökyi Lodrö, one of Rinpoche's root teachers, passed away in Sikkim, in the spring of 1959, and then Trülzhik Pawo Dorje of Minyak, another great ascetic lama and a close friend of Rinpoche's passed away in Sikkim in 1960. The fate of the whole of Tibet and of the Tibetans trapped in their own burning home country became unknown. Rinpoche wrote:

The whole world is changing before us like a magic show.
The existents are unreliable like bubbles.
The monasteries, the loved ones in Dharma, and the kin—
All have become mere memories.
Although I cannot see them, their fate is apparent.
Thinking this, I am sad.
I will exert all my efforts in earning the essence of Dharma.

Holy teachers and kind friends
Were here just now but, like gatherings at a fair,
Have disappeared, and I find myself alone, left behind.
Thinking this, I feel sad. . . .

Placing the concepts of happiness and sadness in the emptiness sphere, and
Tossing worldly chores like camphor to the air,
I embrace the unexcelled sacred swift path,
Which is the heart-essence of ḍākas and ḍākinīs, and
The crucial heart-artery of Dharmakāya, which has no reference point or basis.

The Namgyal Institute of Tibetology (later renamed the Sikkim Research Institute of Tibetology), an institute of Tibetan studies, was opened near Gangtok by the joint efforts of the governments of India and Sikkim. Since April of 1960, Rinpoche has held the position of a fellow representing the Nyingma school at this institute.

He took as his consort Khandro Pema Dechen of the Dekyi Khangsar family of Drukla of Kongpo Valley. Since the age of sixteen, Khandro had meditated for many years in caves and huts at many sacred mountains and hermitages, often with very little sustenance. In addition to many other practices, she accumulated thirteen sets of the fivefold hundred thousand ngöndro practice.

As the activities of bodhisattvas are always open and giving for the benefit of others and the Dharma, without thinking of the limitations and hardships of his own life as a new refugee, Rinpoche kept spending all that he could manage to support Dharma projects. He commissioned zinc blocks to reprint the *Longchen Dzödün,* in seven volumes, by Longchen Rabjam. After many years they were completed with the dedicated service of Lama Sangye, one of Rinpoche's devout attendants, despite his ill health and summer heat of 100 degrees Fahrenheit in Vārāṇasī.

Rinpoche also commissioned wooden blocks carved for the printing of many liturgical texts of the *Longchen Nyingthig.* As a result, these texts, which had been very difficult to obtain in exile, became easily available, and it helped those teachings to be spread in both the Eastern and Western hemispheres. Since the middle of the 1960s it has been easy and even profitable to print Tibetan texts, but in the early 1960s the printing involved great difficulty and expenditure with no commercial values.

After the *Dzödün* was printed, he presented the blocks to the late king of Bhutan, since that country had been one of the seats of Longchen Rabjam, and to this day there are a considerable number of Bhutanese who follow the Nyingthig tradition. He hoped that more editions would be produced from the blocks under the patronage of the royal government of Bhutan.

Since the first publication of the *Dzödün,* he published many more texts, including a second edition of the *Dzödün* in seven volumes, *Ngalso Korsum* in three volumes, the *Sungbum of Jigme Lingpa* in nine volumes, the *Sungbum of the Third Dodrupchen* in five volumes, and many prayers and texts that are part of the course books of the Chöten Gompa.

In 1972, Rinpoche recognized the seventh Dzogchen Rinpoche, Jigme Losal Wangpo (b. 1964) as the fifth Dzogchen Rinpoche—the lama who had recognized Rinpoche himself. The enthronement of the seventh Dzogchen Rinpoche was held in the royal temple at Gangtok on October 8, 1972, and Rinpoche officiated.

At the age of forty-seven, in the summer of 1973, Rinpoche visited the West and East coasts of the United States. He gave teachings and established a Dharma Center named Mahasiddha Nyingmapa Center in Massachusetts. Some years later the center built a temple with a stūpa and a couple of meditation cabins on a small piece of land in South Hawley in western Massachusetts. This center has remained small and simple. Rinpoche always advised the members, "We should try our best to avoid using the Dharma or the Dharma center to gain petty powers, emotional ambitions, or worthless names. Our goal is not to make the center into a famous organization, but to make it a simple, peaceful, and natural abode. Only then can the center become a source of true benefits to the minds of people, whoever is associated with it."

Since 1973, once every two years, Rinpoche visits the Mahasiddha Center and Buddhayana in the United States to teach Dharma, and he has transmitted many teachings, including *Nyingthig Yabzhi, Longchen Nyingthig,* and the teachings of ngöndro, *Rigdzin Düpa, Yumka,* and

Dzogpa Chenpo. He has also visited a number of European and South Asian countries many times to teach and to bestow empowerments.

So far as I know, Rinpoche's major transmissions of empowerments, textual transmissions and teachings have included *Longchen Nyingthig* seventeen times, the empowerment and lung of *Nyingthig Yabzhi* twelve times, the empowerments and lung of *Nyingma Kama* three times, the empowerment of *Lama Gongdü* twice, the empowerment of the six volumes of Jatsön three times, and the empowerment of *Rinchen Terdzö* three times. Also he gave the textual transmission of the *Dzödün* and the works of the third Dodrupchen Rinpoche many times.

Rinpoche is one of the great masters of Dzogpa Chenpo meditation, and he teaches it to many disciples in the tradition of *Nyongtri,* teaching according to the experiences of the individual meditators. His *Nyongtri* tradition mainly came to him from his teacher Yukhok Chatralwa, but it originally came from Longchen Rabjam and Jigme Lingpa through the lineage of the first Dodrupchen, Paltrül Rinpoche, and the third Dodrupchen.

Since 1960, Rinpoche has lived mainly at the Chöten Gompa near Gangtok in Sikkim. On May 31, 1979, Rinpoche opened a drupdra, a meditation school, at the Chöten Gompa and named it Drubde Pema Öling. Monks there are, by rotation, doing three-year and three-month meditation trainings in strict retreats. Soon he started to receive many resident students at the Chöten Gompa. Today he has about five hundred resident monks and novices at the gompa. Most of them are teenage boys who are from Bhutan, Sikkim, and Nepal, or the sons of Tibetan refugees. Rinpoche single-handedly looks after their board, lodging, education, and health care. Many of the students have completed their education and have been sent back to where they came from to propagate the Dharma.

For years, Rinpoche has frequently visited Bhutan to serve the Dharma and its followers in many places, including Yongla Gon. The Nyingthig lineage has a long-standing connection with Bhutan, since Longchen Rabjam lived and propagated Dharma there for a long time. He built the Tharpa Ling Monastery in Eastern Bhutan. His son Tülku Trakpa Özer was born to his Bhutanese consort, Kyipa. Also, one of the main disciples of Jigme Lingpa was Jigme Küntröl of Bhutan, who built the Yongla Gon Monastery in Eastern Bhutan.

Beginning in 1984, Rinpoche has visited Golok, his home valley, many times and has given the empowerments of *Longchen Nyingthig,*

Nyingthig Yabzhi, and many other transmissions and teachings at Dodrupchen Monastery, which is being rebuilt. He has also reopened the scripture college at Dodrupchen Monastery. In the summer of 1994, on his sixth return to Dodrupchen Monastery, Rinpoche gave the empowerments of *Rinchen Terdzö.* People had only a couple of weeks' notice of the *Rinchen Terdzö* transmission, but over seven thousand monks and nuns, including about three hundred tülkus and khenpos, assembled for the transmission from Golok, Serta, Amdo, Gyarong, Minyak, and other areas.

Rinpoche is always engaged in quiet activities that may be simple in nature or of great significance. He is constantly devoting his life to an unending cycle of service. The goal of all his efforts is to serve others, to make a difference, to make the Dharma accessible, without any personal expectation or interest in fame or glory. He repeats, "I am doing all that I can for the service of Dharma and beings. I am sorry if anybody is expecting me to be doing things for the sake of niceties or glamour, but I don't care enough for that." Yet he is always aware of the needs and concerns of others without regard to high or low, and he supports them with his kindness according to their needs and wishes, without concern for his own interests.

He is neither excited by good circumstances nor depressed by bad circumstances, as he accepts all with equanimity saying, "Life is too short and too precious to waste in worrying over silly things." He is careful to stay away from any source of disharmony, dispute, and secular or religious politics in order to protect the integrity and purity of the Dharma tradition. Despite the many opportunities to do so, he never acts to improve his own position but works only for the benefit of people and to serve Dharma. He maintains the integrity of not pandering to the expectations or wishes of others when these are not truly in their own best interests, but always gives to people what they really need, even if it is not what they think they want at the moment. He is most appalled by people who flatter. He says, "I feel myself burning with shame before people who come to me and say the nicest things while thinking the opposite." He is a most tolerant person who never blames others for their misdeeds or ungratefulness, saying, "All that happens is because of karma. What else can I or they do except try to improve the karma?" He is very careful at every step of his work but then is detached from the successs or failure of his projects. The most impressive quality of Rinpoche is not necessarily how he looks, what he says, or even what he does, but what he is. He is a powerful and solid person of an utmost simple, most profound, and infinite presence. Yet he doesn't want anyone to become attached or be dependent on him. And he doesn't impose his authority on others, since he is so ordinary and unassuming—a natural display of the true nature.

Of the two fourth Dodrupchen Rinpoches, Thupten Thrinle Palzang Rinpoche never talked about the dangers that were coming. But he knew, and suddenly left and escaped to India. He is dedicating his life not just to preserving the tradition but to spreading the most sublime tradition of *Longchen Nyingthig* in India and abroad. Rigdzin Tenpe Gyaltsen Rinpoche always warned us since about 1950, "A day will come when we will not have the right to have even a cup of tea to enjoy. If you can, dedicate your life to Dharma training, and spend your property for a worthy cause. At least enjoy your life and wealth while you have the freedom." He also used to tell us about the escape routes through the no-man's-land in the north, but he himself never wanted to leave. His destiny was to go to prison and die with those people who were in the greatest pain. The two Rinpoches both knew the situation and had the choice in their hands; their goals of preserving and helping others were the same, but the roles they had to play were different.

Lineage Tree

THE Longchen Nyingthig lineage came from the primordial Buddha and reached Jigme Lingpa (1730–1798), the founder of the tradition, through the following lineage:

1. Samantabhadra Dharmakāya.
2. Vajrasattva, Sambhogakāya.
3. Prahevajra (Garab Dorje), the Nirmāṇakāya, the first human master of Dzogpa Chenpo.
4. Mañjushrīmitra.
5. Shrīsiṃha.
6. Jñānasūtra.
7. Vimalamitra received the Nyingthig transmissions from both Shrīsiṃha and Jñānasūtra.
8. Guru Rinpoche, Padmasambhava, received the Nyingthig transmissions from Shrīsiṃha and Mañjushrīmitra and concealed the teachings of *Longchen Nyingthig,* the essence of Nyingthig teachings, as ter. King Trisong Detsen (790–858), who was one of the previous incarnations of Jigme Lingpa, received Nyingthig teachings from Vimalamitra and *Longchen Nyingthig* teachings from Guru Rinpoche.
9. Künkhyen Longchen Rabjam (1308–1363) received the Nyingthig transmissions from Guru Rinpoche when he was princess Pemasal. He also received Nyingthig transmissions from Rigdzin Kumārādza and Shö Gyalse.
10. Rigdzin Jigme Lingpa (1730–1798) discovered the *Longchen Nyingthig* as a mind ter and propagated it to his disciples. Thus he became the founder of the Longchen Nyingthig lineage. Jigme Lingpa was the incar-

nation of the king who received the Nyingthig transmissions from Guru Rinpoche and Vimalamitra. Jigme Lingpa also was an incarnation of Vimalamitra and received the transmission from Longchen Rabjam in pure visions.

After Jigme Lingpa, the Longchen Nyingthig lineage was propagated through different branches of lineages. The following is a list of the main masters of different stages of the Longchen Nyingthig lineage with the names of their principal disciples, who are also practitioners and/or holders of Longchen Nyingthig lineage, from Jigme Lingpa himself to the present teachers.

At many places in the lineage, you will find that a master is someone's teacher and at the same time his disciple. This is because a master could receive a rare transmission or blessing from various sources, including his own disciple. Masters could also exchange teachings in order to receive transmissions that came through different lineages. Also, in order to train in the teachings, masters could receive the same transmission many times from the same or different masters. Receiving transmissions repeatedly is not just the beginning of a training, but is also the practice itself.

FIRST STAGE

Rigdzin Jigme Lingpa (also known as Khyentse Özer, Khyentse Lha, and Pema Wangchen, 1730–1798), who revealed the *Longchen Nyingthig* teachings as a mind ter. Among his chief disciples were:[314]

1. Thekchen Lingpa Drotön Tharchin (1700–1776)*[315]
2. Trati Ngachang Thrinle Dorje (Kong-nyön, Bepe Naljor)
3. Thangdrokpa Pema Rigdzin Wangpo*
4. Seventh Chakzampa Tendzin Yeshe Lhundrup of Chuwori*
5. First Dodrupchen Jigme Thrinle Özer (1745–1821)
6. Chöje Trakphukpa of Latö*
7. Lopön Jigme Küntröl of Bhutan
8. Gyalyum Dölkar[316] of Dewa Pushü, consort of Jigme Lingpa
9. Thukse of Lhotrak*
10. Sungtrül of Lhotrak*

11. Fifth Potong Rigdzin Thrinle Lhündrup of Jortse*[317]
12. Jigme Gyalwe Nyuku (1765–1843) of Dzachukha
13. Jigme Ngotsar (Getse Lama, Sönam Tendzin) of Dzachukha
14. Ratön Ngawang Tendzin Dorje*[318]
15. Jetsün Jñānatārādīpam (Yeshe Chödron)
16. Lhading Jetsun of Gyang-ru, Tsang
17. Longchen Rolpa Tsal (Tendzin Sherap, 1768–1817)* of Nakshö
18. Ngawang Palden Chökyong,* the Trichen of Sakya
19. Ngawang Kün-ga Phende,* brother of Sakya Trichen
20. Gomchen, Ngawang Chötrak
21. Getse Gyurme Tsewang Choktrup (1764–?)* of Kathok[319]
22. Phüntsok Palbar* and Tashi Tsering Palbar* of Depa Lha Gyatri[320]
23. Depa Pushü
24. King Dega Zangpo* (1768–1790) of Dege
25. Queen Tsewang Lhamo of Dege
26. Drikung Chetsang Tendzin Pema Gyaltsen (1770–1826),* son of Trati Ngakchang[321]
27. Third Rabjam Rigdzin Paljor (1770–1809)* of Zhechen
28. Third Nyima Takpa Jigme Tenpede (1772–1817)*
29. Tsele Götsang Tülku Jigme Tenpe Gyaltsen* of Kongpo
30. Göntse Tülku* of Mön Tsona
31. Özer Thaye, nephew of Jigme Lingpa
32. Rigdzin Chenpo* of Dorje Trak
33. Eighth Chakzampa Khyenrap Thutop of Chuwori*
34. Tsogyal Tülku* of Palri
35. Drikung Chungtsang Gyalse Nyinche Özer (Chökyi Gyaltsen, 1793–?),* son of Jigme Lingpa

SECOND STAGE

1. First Dodrupchen Jigme Thrinle Özer (Changchup Dorje, Künzang Zhenphen, Sönam Chöden, and Drubwang Dzogchenpa,[322] 1745–1821), the "principal Doctrine-holder" (rTsa Ba'i Ch'os bDag) of Longchen Nyingthig. Among his disciples were:

1. Dola Jigme Kalzang (Kyewu Yeshe Dorje)
2. Arik Geshe Champa Gelek Gyaltsen (1727–1803)* of Ragya
3. Second Ponlop Pema Sangak Tendzin (1731–1805)* of Dzogchen
4. First Namtul Namkha Tsewang Choktrup[323] (Jigme Mikyö Dorje, 1744–?)* of Gyarong Gon
5. Third Dzogchen Ngeton Tendzin Zangpo[324] (1759–1792)*
6. Chögyal Ngawang Dargye (1759–1807),* a Mongolian king in the Blue Lake region[325]
7. Sokpo Ngawang Tentar (Tentar Lharampa 1759–?),* a Geluk scholar from Alaksha, Mongolia
8. First Gyaltsap Pema Sang-ngak Tendzin (1760–?)* of Zhechen[326]
9. Getse Gyurme Tsewang Choktrup (1764–?)* of Kathok
10. First Situ Chökyi Lodrö* of Kathok[327]
11. Jigme Gyalwe Nyuku (1765–1843) of Dzachukha
12. Palchen Namkha Jigme (1769–1833) of Changlung (founded Khyunglung Gonpa in Rekong, which once housed 1,900 tantrikas)
13. Third Rabjam Rigdzin Paljor (1770–1809)* of Zhechen[328]
14. Namke Nyingpo of Lhotrak
15. Chöying Topden Dorje (1786–1848) of Rekong, founder of Göde (Kohudeh) Monastery
16. Khyunglung Repa Tamtsik Dorje of Dzomo'i Ne of Golok
17. Queen-Regent Gajeza, Tsewang Lhamo of Dege
18. King Tsewang Dorje Rigdzin (1786–1847)* of Dege
19. Chakla Khenchen Gyalse Pema Thekchok (?–1849)*
20. King Tsewang Lhundrup (?–1825)* of Tsakho
21. Fourth Dzogchen Mingyur Namkhe Dorje (1793–?)
22. Do Khyentse Yeshe Dorje (1800–1866)
23. Ḍākinī Losal Dölma (1802–1861), sister of Do Khyentse
24. Gyalse Zhenphen Thaye (1800–?) of Dzogchen
25. Third Pönlop Namkha Chökyi Gyatso (1806–1821) of Dzogchen

26. Thukchok Dorje of Kyilung, Golok
27. Tertön Dechen Dorje of Rekong
28. Drubwang Jigme Namkha Gyaltsen (founded Gön Lakha of Rekong, which once housed 1,900 tantrikas)
29. Drubwang Thatral Dorje (also Gön Lakha) of Rekong, the teacher of Pema Gyatso, Shuksep Jetsun's root teacher.
30. Pema Thutop Dorje of Rekong
31. Alak Pema Rangtröl
32. Ngadak Yeshe Gyatso[329]

2. Dza Trama Lama, Jigme Gyalwe Nyuku (1765–1843), one of the greatest Longchen Nyingthig masters. Among his disciples were:

1. Fourth Dzogchen Migyur Namkhe Dorje (1793–?)
2. Gyalse Zhenphen Thaye (1800–?)
3. Paltrül Ogyen Jigme Chökyi Wangpo (1808–1887)
4. Jamyang Khyentse Wangpo (1820–1892)
5. Khamtrül Chökyi Nyima of Drukpa Kagyü
6. Second Dodrupchen Jigme Phüntsok Jung-ne (1824–1863/4)
7. Mura Tülku Pema Dechen Zangpo of Dzachukha
8. Khenchen Pema Dorje of Dzogchen

THIRD STAGE

1. Dola Jigme Kalzang (Kyewu Yeshe Dorje and Chökyi Lodrö). Among his disciples were:

1. Dza Trama Lama Jigme Gyalwe Nyuku (1765–1843)
2. Fourth Dzogchen Mingyur Namkhe Dorje (1793–?)
3. Gyalse Zhenphen Thaye (1800–?) of Dzogchen
4. Paltrül Ogyen Jigme Chökyi Wangpo (1808–1887)
5. Sokpo Chun Wang Tashi Jung-ne (?–1841),* son of King Ngawang Dargye

2. Fourth Dzogchen Mingyur Namkhe Dorje (1793–?). Among his disciples were:

1. Jigme Gyalwe Nyuku (1765–1843)
2. Do Khyentse Yeshe Dorje (1800–1866)
3. Gyalse Zhenphen Thaye (1800–?) of Dzogchen

4. Paltrül Ogyen Jigme Chökyi Wangpo (1808–1887)
5. Khenchen Sengtruk Pema Tashi of Dzogchen
6. Khenchen Pema Dorje of Dzogchen
7. Nyakla Pema Düdül (1816–1872), who attained rainbow body
8. Jamyang Khyentse Wangpo (1820–1892)
9. Nyoshul Lama Lungtok Tenpe Nyima (1829–1901)
10. Adzom Drukpa Drodül Pawo Dorje (1842–1934)
11. Kunzang Dechen Dorje, the tülku of Jigme Gyalwe Nyuku
12. Third Dodrupchen Jigme Tenpe Nyima (1865–1926)
13. First Do Rinpoche Tri-me Trakpa, a tülku of Sherap Mebar (Do Khyentse's son)[330]

3. Do Khyentse Yeshe Dorje (1800–1866), the mind tülku[331] of Jigme Lingpa. Among his disciples were:

1. Ḍākinī Losal Dölma (1802–1861), sister of Do Khyentse
2. Paltrül Ogyen Jigme Chökyi Wangpo (1808–1887)
3. Khenchen Pema Dorje of Dzogchen
4. Nyakla Pema Düdül (1816–1872)
5. King Tsewang Lhündrup of Phüntsok Dzong, Gyarong
6. King Namkha Lhündrup of Trokyab, Gyarong
7. Dorje Palzang of Alo, Trokyab
8. Second Dodrupchen Jigme Phüntsok Jung-ne (1824–1863/4)
9. Sherap Mebar (1829–1842), son of Do Khyentse and a tülku of Dodrupchen
10. Dechen Rikpe Raltri (1830–1874), son of Do Khyentse
11. First Do Rinpoche Tri-me Trakpa, the tülku of Sherap Mebar
12. Jinpa Zangpo, the teacher of Sönam Namgyal (1874–1953) of Yilhung, who attained rainbow body

4. Gyalse Zhenphen Thaye (Rikpe Dorje, 1800–?) of Dzogchen Monastery. Among his disciples were:

1. Fourth Dzogchen Mingyur Namkhe Dorje (1793–?)
2. Paltrül Ogyen Jigme Chökyi Wangpo (1808–1887)

3. Khenpo Pema Dorje of Dzogchen
4. Jamyang Khyentse Wangpo (1820–1892)
5. Lingtrül Thupten Gyaltsen of Dzogchen

5. Paltrül Rinpoche Ogyen Jigme Chökyi Wango (1808–1887), the speech tülku of Jigme Lingpa. Among his disciples were:

1. Khenpo Pema Dorje of Dzogchen
2. Nyoshül Lama Lungtok Tenpe Nyima (?–1902?)
3. Gemang Önpo Tendzin Norbu (Tenli/Ten-ga) of Dzachukha
4. First Situ Chökyi Lodrö* of Kathok
5. Alak Do-ngak Gyatso (Gyawa Do-ngak)
6. Adzom Drukpa Drodül Dorje (1842–1934)
7. Thupten Gelek Gyatso (1844–1904)* of Bamda, Dzika
8. Ju Mipham Namgyal (1846–1912)*
9. Künzang Dechen Dorje, the tülku of Gyalwe Nyuku
10. Khenpo Könchok Özer of Dzogchen
11. Khenpo Künzang Sönam (Künsö) of Minyak
12. First Do Rinpoche Tri-me Trakpa, tülku of Sherap Mebar
13. Tertön Lerap Lingpa (Sögyal, 1856–1926)* of Nyak-rong
14. Third Dodrupchen Jigme Tenpe Nyima (1856–1926)
15. Lushül Khenpo Könchok Drönme (1859–1936) of Dodrupchen
16. Fifth Dzogchen Thupten Chökyi Dorje (1872–1935)
17. Khenpo Künzang Palden (1872–1943) of Gekong, Dzachukha

6. Khenpo Pema Dorje (Pema Dorje and Pema Tamchö Özer) of Dzogchen Monastery. Among his disciples were:

1. Jamyang Khyentse Wangpo (1820–1892)
2. Dechen Rikpe Raltri, son of Do Khyentse
3. Ju Mipham Namgyal (1846–1912)*
4. Third Dodrupchen Jigme Tenpe Nyima (1865–1926)
5. Third Gyaltsap Gyurme Pema Namgyal (1871–1926)* of Zhechen
6. Fifth Dzogchen Thupten Chökyi Dorje (1872–1935)

7. Jamyang Khyentse Wangpo (1820–1892), the body tülku of Jigme Lingpa. Among his Nyingma disciples were:

1. Tertön Chogyur Lingpa (1829–1870)* of Nangchen
2. Adzom Drukpa Drodül Pawo Dorje (1842–1924)
3. Ju Mipham Namgyal (1846–1912)*
4. Tertön Lerap Lingpa (Sögyal, 1856–1926)* of Nyak-rong
5. Jetrung Champa Jungne (1856–1922)* of Kham Ri-woche[332]
6. Tertön Rang-rik Dorje* of Nyak-rong
7. Third Dodrupchen Jigme Tenpe Nyima (1865–1926)
8. Amye Khenpo Tamchö Özer of Dodrupchen
9. Third Gyaltsap Gyurme Pema Namgyal (1871–1926)* of Zhechen
10. Fifth Dzogchen Thupten Chökyi Dorje (1872–1935)
11. Khenpo Künzang Palden (1872–1943) of Gekong
12. Second Situ Chökyi Gyatso (1880–1925)* of Kathok
13. Khenpo Lhagyal (Abu Lhagong, ?–1953?) of Dzog-chen
14. Gyurme Ngeton Wangpo* of Dza Phukhung[333]

FOURTH STAGE

1. Gemang Önpo Tendzin Norbu (Tanli/Tenga) of Gemang, nephew of Gyalse Zhenphen Thaye (1800–?). Among his disciples were:

1. Khenpo Yönten Gyatso (Yon-ga) of Gemang, nephew of Gyalse Zhenphen Thaye
2. Khenpo Könchok Drönme (Könme, 1859–1936) of Dodrupchen
3. Gyakong Khenpo Zhenphen Chökyi Nangwa (1871–1927) of Dzogchen
4. Khenpo Kunzang Palden (Künpal, 1872–1943) of Gekong
5. Khenpo Lhagyal (Abu Lhagong, ?–1953?) of Dzog-chen
6. Bathul Khenpo, Thupten Chötrak (Thupga) of Changma hermitage, Dzachukha

2. Nyoshül Lama Lungtok Tenpe Nyima (1829–1901). Among his disciples were:

1. Ju Mipham Namgyal (1846–1912)*
2. Thartse Pönlop Loter Wangpo (1847–1914)* of Ngor Monastery
3. Tertön Rang-rik Dorje* of Nyak-rong
4. Tertön Lerab Lingpa (Sögyal, 1856–1926)* of Nyak-rong
5. Tertön Thutop Lingpa
6. Khenpo Ngawang Palzang (Ngachung, 1879–1941) of Kathok
7. Khenpo Gyaltsen Özer

3. Adzom Drukpa Drodül Pawo Dorje (Natsok Rangtröl, 1842–1924). Among his disciples were:

1. Togden Shākyashrī (1853–1919)
2. Tertön Lerap Lingpa (Sögyal, 1856–1926)* of Nyak-rong
3. Fifth Dzogchen Rinpoche Thupten Chökyi Dorje (1872–1935)
4. Khenpo Kunzang Palden (Künpal, 1872–1943) of Gekong
5. Yukhok Chatralwa Chöying Rangtröl (1872–1951/2)
6. Khenpo Ngawang Palzang (1879–1941) of Kathok
7. Second Situ Chökyi Gyatso (1880–1925)* of Kathok
8. First Zenkar Pema Ngödrup Rölwe Dorje (1881–1943)
9. Second Pema Norbu Künzang Tendzin (1887–1932) of Palyül
10. Second Do Rinpoche Zilnön Gyepa Dorje (1890–1939)
11. Paltrül Künzang Zhenphen Özer of Tsö, Amdo[334]
12. Nyakla Changchub Dorje (?–1978?)[335]
13. Khyentse Chökyi Lodrö (1893–1959) of Dzongsar
14. Gyalse Gyurme Dorje (1895?–1959?), son of Adzom Drukpa
15. Dilgo Khyentse Tashi Paljor (1910–1991) of Zhechen

4. Kham-nyön Dharma Senge (Ra-gang Chöpa, Sönam Phüntsok, ?–1890). Among his main disciples were:

1. Pema Gyatso (Chi-me Dorje) of Amdo[336]
2. Shuksep Jetsün Lochen Chönyi Zangmo (1865–1953)

3. Trakkar Tülku Lobzang Palden Tenzin Nyentrak (1866–1928)*[337] of Kamdze, a Geluk monastery in Trehor, Kham

FIFTH STAGE

1. Garwa Khenpo Jigme Ösal (?–1926) of Dodrupchen Monastery. Among his disciples were:

   1. Cha Lama Tingdzin Zangpo* of Wangda, Golok
   2. Chökor Khenpo Kün-ga Lodrö (Kangnam, ?–1957) of Dodrupchen
   3. Dong-nge Khenpo Gyurme Thrinle (Jigkom, ?–1959)* of Tarthang
   4. Shorwak Khenpo Sherap Trakpa (?–1959) of Dodrupchen
   5. Yakgo Önpo Samdrup Dorje* of Mar Dhida Gön
   6. Garwa Lama Nortra of Dzika Valley
   7. Garwa Tülku Dorchok of Dodrupchen

2. Amye Khenpo, Tamchö Özer (Champa Özer) of Dodrupchen Monastery. Among his disciples were:

   1. Shukchung Tülku Tsültrim Zangpo (1884–?)* of Do Valley[338]
   2. Washül Khenpo Tamlo of Tungkar Gön, Ser Valley

3. Lushül Khenpo Könchok Tenpe Drönme (Könme, 1859–1936) of Dodrupchen Monastery. Among his disciples were:

   1. Detso Khenpo Sönam Palden* of Tarthang[339]
   2. Tri Kalden* of Kharda Gon, Ngawa
   3. Yakza Khandro Zangmo of Shukchung
   4. Kyangtrül, Töndrup Dorje (1892–1959) of Wangda
   5. Lobsang Lungtok Gyatso (Drachen, ?–1959) of Lauthang, Minyak
   6. Pushül Sönam Trakpa of Wangröl
   7. Kyala Khenpo Chechok Thöndrup (1893–1957) of Dodrupchen
   8. Choktrül Thupten Chökyi Dawa (1894–1959)* of Tarthang[340]
   9. Yakshül Khenpo Lodrö of Dodrupchen

10. Akong Khenpo Lobzang Dorje* of Tarthang
11. Shatsang Khenpo Könchok Tsering of Dodrupchen
12. Khenpo Chöyak of Shukchung
13. Fourth Dodrupchen Rigdzin Tenpe Gyaltsen (1927–1961)
14. Fourth Dodrupchen Thupten Thrinle Palzang (b. 1927)

4. Third Dodrupchen Jigme Tenpe Nyima (1865–1926). Among his disciples were:

1. Tertön Lerap Lingpa (Sögyal, 1856–1926)* of Nyakrong
2. Chagmo Tülku Rolpe Dorje* of Golok
3. Diphuk Duktsa (Chöje) Tenpe Gyaltsen* of Amdo
4. Sershül Khenpo Ngawang Kün-ga of Dodrupchen
5. Garwa Khenpo Jigme Ösal (?–1926) of Dodrupchen
6. Amye Khenpo Tamchö Özer of Dodrupchen
7. Lushül Khenpo Könchok Dronme (1859–1936) of Dodrupchen
8. Gekong Khenpo Künzang Palden (1872–1943) of Dzachukha
9. Tülku Tri-me (1881–1924),* brother of the third Dodrupchen
10. Tülku Pema Dorje, brother of the third Dodrupchen
11. Tülku Tsültrim Zangpo (1884–?)* of Shukchung
12. Second Do Rinpoche Zilnön Gyepa Dorje (1890–1939)
13. Chökor Khenpo Kun-ga Lodrö (?–1957) of Dodrupchen
14. Khyentse Chökyi Lodrö (1893–1959) of Dzongsar
15. Kyala Khenpo Chechok Thöndrup (1893–1957) of Dodrupchen

5. Shuksep Jetsün Lochen Chönyi Zangmo (1865–1953) of Kang-ri Thökar. Among her disciples were:

1. Kangshar Rinpoche
2. Ogyen Chödzom
3. Dza Trülzhik Ngawang Chökyi Lodrö (b. 1924)*
4. Jigme Dorje (b. 1929?), the tülku of Sem-nyi Rinpoche

6. Gyakong Khenpo Zhenphen Chökyi Nangwa (Zhen-ga, 1871–1927) of Dzogchen, the incarnation of Gyalse Zhenphen Thaye and the author of notations on the "thirteen major scholarly texts." Among his disciples were:

1. Khenpo Lhagyal (Abu Lhagong, ?–1953?) of Dzogchen
2. Pathur Khenpo Thupten Chöphel of Changma hermitage
3. Kangkar (Kongka) Karma Chökyi Senge (1903–1956)* of Minyak, who had many Chinese disciples
4. Khenpo Thupten Nyentrak (?–1959) of Dzogchen
5. Chötrak of Rahor, Tsangtha
6. Khenpo Tsewang Rigdzin of Mewa, who rose up into the sky and vanished forever before the eyes of many people in 1959
7. Khenpo Lodrö of Trayap*
8. Chötrak of Serkha, Minyak

7. Fifth Dzogchen Thupten Chökyi Dorje (1872–1935). Among his disciples were:

1. Gyakong Khenpo Zhenphen Chökyi Nangwa (1871–1927) of Dzogchen
2. Gekong Khenpo Kunzang Palden (1872–1943) of Dzachukha
3. Khenpo Lhagyal (Abu Lhagong, ?–1953?) of Dzogchen
4. Situ Chökyi Gyatso (1880–1925)* of Kathok
5. First Zenkar Pema Ngödrup Rölwe Dorje (1881–1943) of Kyilung
6. Second Pema Norbu Künzang Tendzin (1887–1932) of Palyül
7. Namtrül Drodül Karkyi Dorje* of Gyarong Gön
8. Khandro Dechen Wangmo* of Gyarong Gön
9. Khyentse Chökyi Lodrö (1893–1959) of Dzongsar
10. Dilgo Khyentse Tashi Paljor (1910–1991) of Zhechen
11. Fourth Dodrupchen Rigdzin Tenpe Gyaltsen (1927–1961)
12. Fourth Dodrupchen Thupten Thrinle Palzang (b. 1927)

8. Gekong Khenpo Künzang Palden (Künpal and Thupten Künzang Chötrak, 1872–1943) of Dzachukha. Among his disciples were:

1. Khenpo Ngawang Palzang (1879–1941) of Kathok
2. Khyentse Chökyi Lodrö (1893–1959) of Dzongsar
3. Kongtrül Pema Thrime Lodrö (1901–1959?)* of Zhechen[341]
4. Pathur Khenpo Thupten Chöphel (Thubga) of Dzachukha
5. Khenpo Nüden of Kathok*
6. Pöpa Tülku Do-ngak Tenpe Nyima (?–1959)
7. Fourth Dodrupchen Rigdzin Tenpe Gyaltsen (1927–1961)
8. Fourth Dodrupchen Thupten Thrinle Palzang (b. 1927)

9. Yukhok Chatralwa Chöying Rangtröl (1872–1952). Among his disciples were:

1. Garwa Lama Nortra of Dzika Valley
2. Dzirong Lama Chogden of Dzika
3. Pöpa Tülku Do-ngak Tenpe Nyima (?–1959)
4. Khenpo Nüden of Kathok*
5. Tsültrim Dorje of Ngaze
6. Önpo Pema Rigdzin* of Jang-gang, Ser Valley
7. Fourth Dodrupchen Thupten Thrinle Palzang (b. 1927)

10. Kathok Khenpo Ngawang Palzang (Ngachung and Pema Ledreltsal, 1879–1941). Among his disciples were:

1. Second Pema Norbu Künzang Tendzin (1887–1932) of Palyül
2. Chaktsa Tülku of Tralak Gön
3. Khenpo Lekshe Jorden* of Kathok
4. Khenpo Nüden* of Kathok
5. Khyentse Chökyi Lodrö (1893–1959) of Dzongsar
6. Gyurme Dorje (1895?–1959?), son of Adzom Drukpa
7. Poda Khenpo Dorje (1897?–1970?)
8. Tülku Arik (?–1988)* of Tromge, Nyak-rong
9. Khenpo Munsel (1916–1994) of Wangchen Töpa, Golok
10. Chatral Sangye Dorje (b. 1913)

11. Shedrup Tenpe Nyima (1920–?), the tülku of Nyo-shül Lungtok[342]

11. Pathur Khenpo Thupten Chöphel (Thubga) of Changma hermitage of Dzachukha. Among his disciples were:

1. Dilgo Khyentse Tashi Paljor (1910–1991) of Zhechen
2. Khenpo Chökyap (d. 1997?) of Horshül, Ser Valley
3. Khenpo Dawe Özer (Dazer) of Rahor
4. Khenpo Thupten of Mewa, Amdo
5. Khenpo Jigme Phüntsok (b. 1933)* of Nizok
6. Khenpo Thupten of Rahor

12. First Alak Zenkar Pema Ngödrup Rölwe Dorje (1881–1943) of Kyilung Monastery, Geshe, Gyarong. Among his disciples were:

1. Sangye Yeshe of Tak-rang
2. Dorje Tseten of Tak-rang

13. Dzongsar Khyentse Chökyi Lodrö (1893–1959) of Dzongsar Monastery, a tülku of Jamyang Khyentse Wangpo. Among his Nyingma disciples were:

1. Kongtrül Pema Tri-me Lodrö (1901–1959?) of Zhechen
2. Dilgo Khyentse Tashi Paljor (1910–1991) of Zhechen
3. Sixth Rabjam Gyurme Tenpe Nyima (1911–1959)* of Zhechen
4. Poda Khenpo Dorje (1897?–1970?)
5. Chatral Sangye Dorje (b. 1913)
6. Tak-rong Gyurme Trakpa (?–1975) of Yilhung
7. Khandro Tsering Chödrön (b. 1925) of Aduk House
8. Third Kathok Situ
9. Fourth Dodrupchen Thupten Thrinle Palzang (b. 1927)
10. Third Chogling Pema Gyurme (1928–1974)* of Neten
11. Dungse Thinley Norbu (b. 1931)*
12. Eleventh Minling Trichen Gyurme Kunzang Wangyal (b. 1931)*
13. Trogawa Samphel Norbu (b. 1931)* of Gyangtse
14. Sixth Dzogchen Jigtral Changchup Dorje (1935–1958)
15. Sögyal Rinpoche (b. 1947) of Dzogchen/England

14. Kyala Khenpo Chechok Thöndrup (Chöchok, 1893–1957) of Dodrupchen Monastery. Among his disciples were:

1. Tülku Drachen (?–1959) of Lauthang, Minyak
2. Alak Zhiwatso of Göde, Rekong
3. Kakor Tülku of Tergar, Rekong
4. Alo Lama Tsültrim of Trokyap, Gyarong
5. Gyutse Könchok Mönlam of Trokho, Amdo
6. Alak Dzong-ngön Lodrö of Rekong

15. Gyalse Gyurme Dorje (Ah-gyur, 1895?–1959?), son of Adzom Drukpa. Among his disciples were:

1. Khyentse Chökyi Lodrö (1893–1959) of Dzongsar
2. Pema Künzang Rangtröl
3. Adzom Druktrül Rinpoche (b. 1926)

SIXTH STAGE

1. Dilgo Khyentse Tashi Paljor (Rabsal Dawa, 1910–1991) of Zhechen Monastery, a tülku of Jamyang Khyentse Wangpo. Among his disciples were:

1. Tülku Urgyen (b. 1919)* of Nargön
2. Lama Gönpo Tseten (?–1991) of Labrang, Amdo
3. Trulzhik Ngawang Chökyi Lodrö (b. 1924)* of Dza Rongphu
4. Nyoshül Lama Jamyang Dorje (b. 1926) of Dege
5. Tsetrül Nyinche Zangpo (b. 1927)* of Taklung Gön, Yardrok
6. Dakchen Jigtral of Phüntsok Photrang (b. 1929)* of Sakya/USA
7. Eighth Khamtrül Tön-gyü Nyima* (1930–1979)
8. Dungse Thinley Norbu (b. 1931)* of Pemakö/USA
9. Chagdud Karkyi Wangchuk (b. 1930)* of Nyak-rong/USA
10. Third Pema Norbu Jigme Thupten Shedrup (b. 1932) of Palyül[343]
11. H. H. the fourteenth Dalai Lama Tendzin Gyatso (b. 1935)*
12. Eleventh Trungpa Chökyi Gyatso (1939–1987)* of Zurmang[344]

13. Second Zenkar Thupten Nyima (b. 1943) of Kyilung
14. Könchok Tenzin* of France
15. Sögyal Rinpoche (b. 1947) of Dzogchen/England
16. Tsetrül Pema Wangyal (b. 1947)* of Riwoche/France
17. Third Dzongsar Khyentse Thupten Chökyi Gyatso
18. Tarthang Choktrül Jigme Lodrö Senge (b. 1961?)*
19. Sakyong Mipham Jampal Trinley Dradül (b. 1962)* of Shambhala USA/Canada
20. Tenth Sangye Nyenpa (b. 1963)*
21. Seventh Dzogchen Jigme Losal Wangpo (b. 1964)
22. Tülku Khyentse Jigme (b. 1964)* of Riwoche/France
23. Dzigar Kongtrül*
24. Seventh Rabjam Gyurme Chökyi Senge (b. 1966)* of Zhechen
25. Namkhe Nyingpo of Lhotrak*
26. Fifth Karma Kuchen Thupten Tsültrim Norbu (b. 1970)* of Palyül
27. Fourth Chokling Gyurme Dorje (b. 1973)* of Neten

2. Chatral Rinpoche Sangye Dorje (b. 1913). Among his disciples are:

1. Gyaltsap Redring Jampal Yeshe (1911–1947)*
2. Sonam Topgye Kazi (b. 1920) of Rinak, Sikkim/USA
3. Cham Nordzin Wangmo of Rinak, Sikkim
4. Lama Tharchin (b. 1936)* of Rekong/USA
5. Chögyal Wangchuk Namgyal (b. 1953)* of Sikkim
6. Jigme Thupten Namgyal

3. Nyoshül Lama Jamyang Dorje (b. 1926). Among his disciples are:

1. Chakdud Karkyi Wangchuk (b. 1930)* of Nyak-rong/USA
2. Lama Sönam Topgyal* of Riwoche/Canada
3. Tri-me Zhingkyong* of Kathok
4. Sögyal Rinpoche (b. 1947) of Dzogchen/England
5. Tsetul Pema Wangyal (b. 1947)* of Riwoche/France

4. Fourth Dodrupchen Rigdzin Tenpe Gyaltsen (1927–1961). Among his disciples were:

1. Chökor Khenpo Kang-nam (d. 1957) of Dodrupchen
2. Kyala Khenpo Chechok Thöndrup (1893–1957) of Dodrupchen

3. Lobsang Lungtok Gyatso (Drachen, ?–1959) of Lauthang
4. Pema Namgyal (?–1957), an incarnation of Dudjom Lingpa
5. Akong Khenpo Lobzang Dorje* of Tarthang
6. Tülku Jigme Phüntsok (Jiglo, d. 1959) of Dodrupchen
7. Garwa Tülku Gyalse Padlo* of Golok
8. Yangthang Dechen Ösal Dorje (b. 1929)*
9. Jigme Ösal of Dodrupchen, a tülku of Garwa Khenpo (?–1926)
10. Gyalse Thrinle Kunkhyab (Achen)* of Nangchen
11. Terton Tülku Jigme Ösal of Tertön Gar, Rekong
12. Drubwang Tülku Alak Gönpo of Gön Lakha, Rekong
13. Dzakhen Lama Rigdzin of Go-me, Rekong

5. Fourth Dodrupchen Thupten Thrinle Palzang (b. 1927). Among his disciples are:

1. Chökor Khenpo Kang-nam (?–1957) of Dodrupchen
2. Kyala Khenpo Chechök Thöndrup (1893–1957) of Dodrupchen
3. Lobsang Lungtok Gyatso (Drachen, ?–1959) of Lauthang
4. Tülku Pema Namgyal (?–1957) of Dodrupchen
5. Tülku Jigme Phüntsok (Jiglo, ?–1959) of Dodrupchen
6. Khandro Pema Dechen of Kongpo
7. Fourth Dodrupchen Tenpe Nyima (b. 1929) of Yarlung Pemakö
8. Yangthang Dechen Ösal Dorje (b. 1929)* of Domang
9. Tülku Jigme Ösal of Dodrupchen
10. Dungse Thinley Norbu (b. 1931)* of Pemakö/USA
11. Lama Pema Tumpo (Kusum Lingpa, b. 1933) of Golok
12. Khenpo Dechen Dorje (b. 1936) of Sikkim
13. Khandro Tare Lhamo (b. 1937),* daughter of Apang Tertön
14. Thekchok Pema Gyaltsen (Theklo) (b. 1937), the tülku of Pema Dorje
15. Second Zenkar Thupten Nyima (b. 1943)

16. Chögyal Wangchuk Namgyal (b. 1953)* of Sikkim
17. Lopön Thekchok Yeshe Dorje (b. 1957) of Bhutan
18. Tenth Gönchang Tülku (b. 1962)* of Gompachang/ Sikkim
19. Seventh Dzogchen Jigme Losal Wangpo (b. 1964)
20. Tülku Chökyi Nyima of Nup-ri, Nepal
21. Tülku Jigme Gawe Lodrö, a tülku of Khenpo Kangnam
22. Fifth Dodrupchen Jigme Long-yang, a tülku of Dodrupchen Rigdzin Tenpe Gyaltsen

Works Cited

BC *Klong Ch'en sNying Thig Gi brGyud 'Debs Byin rLabs Ch'ar rGyun* (folios 2), discovered by Jigme Lingpa (1730–1798). Vol. OṂ, *Longchen Nyingthig Tsapö.* Published by Jamyang [Dilgo] Khyentse, India.

BD *Biographical Dictionary of Tibet and Tibetan Buddhism* by Khetsun Zangpo (b. 1921). Vols. 1–14. Dharmasala: Library of Tibetan Works and Archives.

BDL *Biography of Do Khyentse and His Lineage* (p. 24) by Ani Dasal, a great-great-grand-daughter of Do Khyentse. Provided through the kindness of Zenkar Rinpoche, Thupten Nyima. Manuscript.

BG *sNga 'Gyur Bla Med Kyi rGyud Kyi brJod Bya gZhi Lam Gyi dKa' gNad bKrol Ba Bla Ma'i dGongs rGyan* by Lobzang (Könchok Drönme, 1859–1936) of Dodrupchen Monastery. Manuscript.

BGT *rGya Bod Tshig mDzod Ch'en Mo.* Vols. 1–3. Mirik Petrunkhang, China.

BND *Bairo Tsana'i rNam Thar 'Dra 'Bag Ch'en Mo,* edited by Kham-nyon Dharma Senge (?–1890). Woodblock print of Lhasa, Tibet.

CD *'Jam dByangs Bla Ma Ch'os Kyi Blo Gros Kyi gSung Thor Bu'i dKar Ch'ags Ch'os Tshul Mi Zad 'Dod dGu'i Bang mDzod* (f. 9) by Tashi Paljor [Dilgo Khyentse, 1910–1991]. A manuscript provided by the kindness of Ven. Könchok Tenzin, France.

CG *Khams sMyon Dharma Senge'i Nyams mGur Ch'u Zla'i Gar Phreng* (f. 224) by Dharma Senge. Reproduced by Sonam Kazi, India, 1970.

CN *Rig 'Dzin 'Jigs Med Gling Pa'i bKa' 'Bum Yongs rDzogs Kyi bZhugs Byang Ch'os Rab rNam 'Byed* (f. 13) by Kathokpa Gyurme Tsewang Chokdrup (1764–?). Vol. Cha, *Jigling Kabum.* (Dege) Reproduced by Dodrupchen Rinpoche, Sikkim, India.

CY *Chö Yang, the Voice of Tibetan Religion and Culture.* Year of Tibet Edition. Published by the Council for Religious and Cultural Affairs, Dharamsala, India.

DB *O rGyan 'Jigs Med Ch'os Kyi dBang Po'i rNam Thar Dad Pa'i gSos sMan bDud rTsi'i Bum bChud* (f. 41) by Thupten Künzang Chötrak (1872–1943). Paltrül Sungbum, Vol. 5. Published by Zenkar Rinpoche, China.

DCS *rDo rJe 'Ch'ang Gis gSung Pa mCh'od Os Rang bZhin Gyi Tshig Dus gNad Nges Pa* (f. 36, gSer Yig, Ga), Vima Nyingthig Part I, sNying Thig Ya bZhi collection, compiled by Longchen Rabjam (1308–1363) (Adzom). Reproduced by Lama Jigtrak and Tülku Pema Wangyal, Darjeeling, India.

DD *dPal gSang Ba sNying Po'i rGyud Kyi sPyi Don Nyung Ngu'i Ngag Gis gSal Bar Byed Pa Rin Po Ch'e'i mDzod Kyi sDe Mig* by Jigme Tenpe Nyima. Vol. Ka, *Dodrupchen Sungbum*. Published by Dodrupchen Rinpoche, Sikkim, India.

DGN *rDo Grub Ch'en rNam Thar.* An autobiography of the first Dodrupchen (1745–1821) from the collection of the Dodrupchen Rinpoche. Manuscript. Three pages, including the title page and the last page, are missing.

DK *sKyabs rJe Dam Pa Ch'os dBying Rang Grol Gyi rNam Par Thar Ba Dad Pa'i 'Khri Shing* (p. 35) by Sönam Nyima. Manuscript.

DKG *sNga 'Gyur rGyud 'Bum Rin Po Ch'e'i rTogs Pa brJod Pa 'Dzam Gling Tha Gru Khyab Pa'i rGyan* (f. 250) by Jigme Lingpa. Vol. Ga, *Jigling Kabum* (Dege). Reproduced by Dodrupchen Rinpoche, Sikkim, India, 1985.

DL *mDo Khams rDzogs Ch'en dGon Gyi Lo rGyus* (p. 139) by Gyalwang Chökyi Nyima (b. 1914). Sitrön Mirik Petrünkhang, China, 1992.

DN *rDo Grub Ch'en Rin Po Ch'e sKu 'Phreng Rim Byon Gyi rNam Par Thar Pa 'Dod 'Jo Nor Bu'i Phreng Ba* by Sönam Nyima of Serta, Golok. Manuscript.

DNN *Rang bZhin rDzogs Pa Ch'en Po'i Lam Gyi Ch'a Lag sDom gSum rNam Par Nges Pa* (f. 16) by Padma Wangki Gyalpo (1487–1542). Published by Khamtrül Rinpoche, India. English: *Absolute Certainty of the Three Vows,* with Commentary by Dudjom Rinpoche. Translated by Sangye Khandro. Forthcoming from Snow Lion.

DNK *Dzogchen Lineage of Nyoshül Khenpo* (b. 1926). Manuscript.

DO *Zhal Ch'en Dri Ma Med Pa'i Od* (f. 132–140) by Longchen Rabjam, Vol. HŪṂ, *Khandro Nyingthig* (Adzom). Reproduced by Lama Jiktrak and Tülku Pema Wangyal, Darjeeling, India.

DPM *Gangs Chan Bod Ch'en Pi'i rGyal Rabs 'Dus gSal Du bKod Pa sNgon Med Dvangs Shel 'Phrul Gyi Me Long* (f. 283) by Jigtral Yeshe Dorje (1904–1987).

DSC *Dakki'i gSang gTam Ch'en Mo* (f. 7), discovered by Jigme Lingpa as a ter. Vol. OṂ, *Longchen Nyingthig Tsapö.* Published by Jamyang (Dilgo) Khyentse, India.

DSC *Klong Ch'en sNying Gi Thig Le'i rTogs Pa brJod Pa Dakki'i gSang gTam Ch'en Mo* (f. 7), discovered by Jigme Lingpa. Vol. OṂ, *Longchen Nyingthig Tsapö.* Published by Jamyang (Dilgo) Khyentse.

DT *'Phags Pa Shes Rab Kyi Pha Rol Tu Phyin Pa sDud Pa Tshigs Su bChad Pa,* Vol. Ka, *Sher Phyin* section, Kanjur (Dege).

DTN *Deb Ther sNgon Po* (Vols. 1 & 2) by Golo Zhönu Pal (1392–1481). Sitrön Mirik Petrünkhang, China, 1984.

DZ *Dul Ba gZhi* (Vinayavastu). 'Dul Ba section. Vols. 1–4. Kanjur (Dege).

DZT *O rGyan 'Jigs Med Ch'os Kyi dBang Po'i rTogs brJod bDud rTsi'i Zil Thigs* (f. 18) by Jigme Tenpe Nyima. Vol. Nga, Dodrupchen Sungbum. Published by Dodrupchen Rinpoche, India.

EL *Enlightened Living: Teachings of Tibetan Buddhist Masters,* translated by Tulku Thondup and edited by Harold Talbott. Boston: Shambhala Publications, 1990.

GD *bKyed rDzogs sGom Phyogs Dris Lan* (f. 98) by Jigme Lingpa. Vol. Ta, *Jigling Kabum* (Dege). Reproduced by Dodrupchen Rinpoche, Sikkim, India.

GDG *Ye Shes mTsho rGyal Gyi mDzad Tshul rNam Par Thar Pa Gab Pa mNgon Byung rGyud Mang Dri Za'i Glu Phreng* (p. 254), discovered by Pawo Taksham Dorje (17th cent.). Sitrön Mirik Petrünkhang, China.

GK *Dam Pa'i Ch'os Rin Po Ch'e 'Phags Pa'i Yul Du Ji lTar Tar Ba'i Tshul gSal Bar sTon Pa dGos 'Dod Kun 'Byung* (p. 340) by Tāranātha (1575–1635). Mirik Petrünkhang, China, 1985.

GL *'Gro mGon Bla Ma rJe'i gSang gSum rNam Thar rGya mTsho Las Thun Mong Phyi'i mNgon rTogs rGyal Sras Lam bZang.* An autobiography of Jigme Gyalwe Nyuku, 1765–1843. A manuscript provided by the kindness of Tülku Pema Wangyal Rinpoche, France.

GN *rDzogs Pa Ch'en Po sNying Thig Gi Khrid Yig Gu Yangs sNying Gi Thig Le* (f. 136) by Guyang Lo-de (Chingkarwa Don-yö Dorje). Published by Sherap Gyaltsen Lama, Sikkim, 1976.

GNP *dPal Sa sKyong sDe dGe Ch'os Kyi rGyal Po Rim Byon Gyi rNam Thar Ge Legs Nor Bu'i Phreng Ba* (p. 135) by Champa Kun-ga Tenpe Gyaltsen. Sitrön Mitik Petrünkhang, China, 1990.

GP *The Great Perfection* by Samten Gyaltsen Karmay. New York: E. J. Brill Leidon, 1988.

GPM *rGyud Phyi Ma* (of gSang Ba 'Dus Pa). rGyud section. Vol. Cha, Kanjur (Dege).

GR *'Phags Pa rGya Ch'er Rol Ba Zhes Bya Ba Theg Pa Ch'en Po'i mDo. mDo sDe* section. Vol. Kha, Kanjur (Dege).

GRT *'Jam dByangs Ch'os Kyi Blo Gros Kyi rTogs Pa brJod Pa sGyu Ma'i Rol rTsed* (f. 22) by Chökyi Lodrö (1893–1959).

GRD *Grub mTha' Rin Po Ch'e'i mDzod* (f. 206) by Tri-me Özer (Longchen Rabjam) (Adzom). Reproduced by Dodrupchen Rinpoche, Sikkim, India.

GZ *rNying rGyud bKa' Ma'i Thob Yig brGyud lDan Zhal Lung* by the fourth Dodrupchen Rinpoche (b. 1927). Manuscript.

HTT *Hidden Teachings of Tibet* by Tulku Thondup Rinpoche, edited by Harold Talbott. London: Wisdom, 1986.

JKT *Mañjushrīdharmamitra'i* [Khyentse Wangpo] *rTogs Pa brJod Pa 'Jigs rTen Kun Tu dGa' Ba'i gTer* (f. 50) by Jigme Tenpe Nyima. Vol. Nga, *Dodrupchen Sungbum.* Published by Dodrupchen Rinpoche.

KBZ *rDzogs Pa Ch'en Po Nying Thig Gi sNgon 'Gro'i Khrid Yig Kun bZang Bla Ma'i Zhal Lung* (f. 306) by Ögyen Jigme Chökyi Wangpo (Paltrül Rinpoche, 1808–1887). Published by Pönlop Rinpoche, Rumtek, Sikkim, India. English translations: (1) *Kün-zang La-May Zhal-lung,* vols. 1 & 2, translated by Sonam T. Kazi. Diamond-Lotus Publishing, 1989. (2) *The Words of My Perfect Teacher,* translated by the Padmakara Translation Group. New York: HarperCollins, 1994.

KGT *Dam Pa'i Ch'os Kyi 'Khor Lo'i bsGyur Ba rNams Kyi Byung Ba gSal Bar Byed Pa mKhas Pa'i dGa' sTon,* vols. 1 & 2, by Pawo Tsuklak Trengwa (1454–1566). Mirik Petrünkhang, Beijing, China.

KKR *Klong Ch'en sNying Gi Thig Le'i dBang bsKur Gyi Phreng Ba bKlag Ch'og Tu bKod Pa sKal bZang Kun dGa'i Rol sTon* (f. 165) by Dilgo Khyentse Rapsal

Dawa. Vol. Nga, *Longchen Nyingthig Tsapö*. Published by Dilgo Khyentse Rinpoche, India.

KNN *Rig 'Dzin 'Jigs Med Gling Pa'i 'Khrungs Rabs rNam Thar Nyung bsDus* (f. 3). Vol. Ta, *Jigling Kabum* (Dege). Reproduced by Dodrupchen Rinpoche, Sikkim, India.

KNR *sNga 'Gyur Ch'os Kyi Byung Ba gSal Bar Byed Pa'i Legs bShad mKhas Pa dGa' Byed Ngo mTshar gTam Gyi Rol mTsho* (p. 1058) by Ngawang Lodrö (Guru Tashi, 1550–1602). Tso-ngön Mirik Petrünkhang, China.

KS *'Jigs Med Gling Pa'i 'Khrungs Rabs gSol 'Debs* (f. 1) by Khyentse Lha. Nyingthig Döncha. Published by Dodrupchen Rinpoche, Sikkim, India.

KT *bKa' Thang sDe lNga* (p. 539), discovered by Ögyen Lingpa (1323–?). Mirik Petrünkhang, China.

KZ *'Ja' Lus rDo rJe'i* (Do Khyentse) *rNam Thar mKha' 'Gro'i Zhal Lung* (f. 99). An autobiography of Do Khyentse, 1800–1866. Reproduced by Dodrupchen Rinpoche, Gangtok, India, 1974.

KZD *Kun mKhyen Zhal Lung bDud rTsi'i Thig Pa* (f. 14) by Jigme Lingpa. Vol. HŪṂ, VOL. OM, *Longchen Nyingthig Tsapö*. Published by Jamyang (Dilgo) Khyentse, India.

KZZ *Nying Thig Gi sNgon 'Gro'i Khrid Yig Kun bZang Bla Ma'i Zhal Lung Gi Zin Bris* (f. 205) by Pema Ledreltsal (1879–1941). A xylographic print.

LG *Lo rGyus rGyal Ba gYung Gis mDzad Pa* by Gyalwa Yung (1284–1365), Part II (ff. 203–211), Khandro Nyingthig, Yabzhi collection (Adzom). Reproduced by Lama Jigtrak and Tülku Pema Wangyal, Darjeeling, India.

LK *Bla Ma dGongs Pa 'Dus Pa Las Lung bsTan bKa' rGya'i sKor* (f. 213), discovered by Sangye Lingpa (1340–1396). Vol. 6 (Ch'a), *Lama Gongdü* Cycle. Published by Lama Ngödrup and Sherab Drimay, Bhutan, 1981.

LNG *sNga 'Gyur rDo rJe Theg Pa'i bsTan Pa Rin Po Ch'e Ji lTar Byung Ba'i Tshul brJod Pa Lha dBang gYul Las rGyal Ba'i rNga Bo Ch'e'i Gra dByangs* (f. 410) by Jigtral Yeshe Dorje. Published by Düdjom Tülku Rinpoche, Kalimpong, India, 1967. English: NTB.

LRB *Karmapa Mi bsKyod rDo rJe'i gNang Ba'i Dris Lan Lung Dang Rigs Pa'i 'Brug sGra* (g. 87) by Sokdokpa Lodrö Gyaltsen (1552–1624). Reproduced by Sonam T. Kazi, Gangtok, India, 1971.

LRP *mKha' 'Gro sNying Thig Gi Lo rGyus Rin Po Ch'e'i Phreng Ba* by Chatralwa Zöpa. Khandro Nyingthig, Part II (f 233a/5–254a/6) (Adzom). Reproduced by Lama Jigtrak and Tülku Pema Wangyal, Darjeeling, India.

LS *The Life of Shabkar (1781–1851): The Autobiography of a Tibetan Yogin* (p. 737). Translated by Matthieu Ricard. Albany: SUNY, 1994. Tibetan: SB.

LST *Yon Tan Rin Po Ch'e'i mDzod Kyi dKa' gNad rDo rJe'i rGya mDud 'Grol Byed Legs bShad gSer Gyi Thur Ma* by (Sokpo) Tentar Lharampa (1759–?). Published by Jamyang (Dilgo) Khyentse, India.

LY *rGya Gar Gyi gNas Ch'en Khag La bGrod Pa'i Lam Yig* (pp. 351–395) from the Collection of the Works of Gendün Chöphel (1905–1951). Mirik Petrünkhang, China.

LYN *Rang Byung rDo rJe'i rNam Par Thar Pa Legs Byas Yong 'Dus sNye Ma* (f. 251), an autobiography of Khyentse Özer [Jigme Lingpa]. Vol. Ta, *Jigling Kabum* (Dege). Reproduced by Dodrupchen Rinpoche, Sikkim, India.

MC *mKhan Rin Po Ch'e Kun dPal La bsTod Pa bKa' Drin rJes Dran Gyi Me Tog mCh'od Pa* (f. 4) by Khyentse Chökyi Lodrö.

MD *Phags Pa Yongs Su Mya Ngan Las 'Das Pa Ch'en Po'i mDo. mDo sDe* section. Vol. Ta, Kanjur (Dege).

MG *gTer sTon Rim Par Byon Pa rNam Gyi gSol 'Debs rGyas Par bKod Pa Mos Gus rGya mTsho'i rLabs 'Phreng* by Kongtrül Yönten Gyatso (1813–1899). Vol. Ka, *Terdzö*. Published by Jamyang Khyentse, India.

MNB *Ch'os 'Byung Me Tog sNying Po sBrang rTsi'i bChud* (p. 504) by Nyang Nyima Özer (1124–1192). Pöjong Mimang Petrünkhang, Tibet, 1988.

NB *Gangs Shugs Ma Ni Lo Ch'en Rig 'Dzin dBang Mo'i rNam Par Thar Pa rNam mKhyen bDe sTer* (f. 271). An autobiography of Lochen Rigdzin Wangmo, 1865–1953. Reproduced by Sonam Kazi, India.

NCC *gZhi Khregs Ch'od sKabs Kyi Zin Bris bsTan Pa'i Nyi Ma'i Zhal Lung sNyan rGyud Ch'u Bo'ai bChud 'Dus* (f. 40) by Pema Ledreltsal (Khenpo Ngachung). Manuscript.

NCG *rDzogs Ch'en Man Ngag sDe'i sNying Thig rNam bZhi'i Thob Yig dNgos Grub Ch'u rGyun* by Dodrupchen Thupten Thrinle Palzangpo. Manuscript.

ND *'Jigs Med Phrin Las Od Zer Gyi mNgon rTogs Drang Por sMos Pa* (f. 3) by Jigme Thrinle Özer. Manuscript.

NG *sNga 'Gyur sDom rGyun Gyi mKhan brGyud Kyi rNam Thar Nyung gSal sGron Me* (f. 31) by Dharmashrī (1654–1717). Vol. 3, *Writings of Minling Lochen Dharmashrī*. Reproduced by Khorchen Tülku, India.

NGR *Padma Las 'Brel rTsal Gyi rTogs brJod Ngo mTshar sGyu Ma'i Rol Gar* (f. 147). An autobiography of Pema Ledreltsal. Published by Sonam Kazi, India, 1969.

NLC *rDzogs Pa Ch'en Po Nying Thig Gi Lo rGyus Ch'en Mo* by Zhangtön Tashi Dorje (1097–1167). Vima Nyingthig Part III (Adzom). Reproduced by Lama Jigtrak and Tülku Pema Wangyal, Darjeeling, India.

NLS *Ch'os sPyod Kyi Rim Pa rNam Par Grol Ba'i Lam Gyi Shing rTa* (f. 204) by Jigtral Yeshe Dorje. Published by Düdjom Rinpoche, Kalimpong, India.

NN *Thob Yig Nyi Zla'i rNa Ch'a* (f. 13) by Jigme Lingpa. Vol. Cha, *Jigling Kabum* (Dege). Reproduced by Dodrupchen Rinpoche, Sikkim, India.

NO *sNga 'Gyur Od gSal*. Published by Ngagyur Nyingma Institute, India, 1992.

NPG *gSang sNgags gSar rNying Gi gDan Rabs mDor bsDus Ngo mTshar Padmo'i dGa' Tshal* (f. 104) by Khyentse Wangpo (1820–1892). Vol. Tsha, *Khyentse Kabum*. Reproduced by Jamyang (Dilgo) Khyentse, India.

NS *Yon Tan Rin Po Ch'e'i mDzod Las 'Bras Bu'i Theg Pa'i rGya Ch'er 'Grel rNam mKhyen Shing rTa* (f. 440) by Khyentse Lha. Vol. Kha, *Jigling Kabum* (Adzom). Reproduced by Dodrupchen Rinpoche, India.

NT *Nags Tshal Kun Tu dGa' Ba'i gTam* by Longchen Rabjam. gTam Tshogs collection (ff. 66a–72a), Sung Thorbu (Adzom).

NTB *The Nyingma School of Tibetan Buddhism: Its Fundamentals and History* (vols. 1 & 2) by Düdjom Rinpoche, Jigtral Yeshe Dorje. Translated and edited by Gyurme Dorje with Matthew Kapstein. Boston: Wisdom, 1991.

NTG *Klong Ch'en sNying Gi Thig Le Las gNad Byang Thugs Kyi sGrom Bu* (f. 5), discovered by Jigme Lingpa. Vol. OṂ, *Longchen Nyingthig Tsapö*. Published by Jamyang (Dilgo) Khyentse, India.

NTS *sNying gTam Sum Chu Pa* (ff. 54b–57b) by Longchen Rabjam. Zhaldam collection of Sung Thorbu (Adzom).

NUG *'Jam dByangs mKhyen brTse'i dBang Po'i rNam Thar mDor bsDus Ngo mTshar Utpala'i dGa'-Tshal* (f. 118) by Lodrö Thaye. Vol. Ba, *Kongtrül Kabum*. Published by Jamyang (Dilgo) Khyentse, India.

NYG *'Jam dByangs Ch'os Kyi Blo Gros Kyi rNam Thar Ngo mTshar Yongs 'Dus dGa' Tshal* (f. 207) by Khyentse Özer (Dilgo Khyentse). A photocopy provided by the kindness of Ven. Könchok Tenzin of France.

ON *rDzogs Pa Ch'en Po'i Nyams Len Gyi gNad mThar Thug Pa'i rTsa 'Grel Od gSal Gyi sNang Ch'a* (f. 11) by Paltrül Rinpoche (1808–1887). Vol. 4, *Paltrül Sungbum*. Published by Zenkar Rinpoche, Chendu, China.

PGG *Deb Ther rDzogs lDan gZhon Nu'i dGa' sTon dPyid Kyi rGyal Mo'i Glu dByangs* (p. 202) by Ngawang Lobzang Gyatso (the fifth Dalai Lama, 1617–1682). Mirik Petrünkhang, China.

PJM *'Jigs Med 'Phrin Las Od Zer Gyi rTogs bJod dPag bSam lJon Pa'i Me Tog* by Jigme Tenpe Nyima. Töpa Natsok (ff. 6a–10b), Vol. Nga, *Dodrupchen Sungbum*. Published by Dodrupchen Rinpoche.

PK *The Esoteric Biography of Gter-chen Las-rab Gling-pa* (Tertön Sogyal) (f. 363) by Shila Bhadra (Tsültrim Zangpo, 1884–?). Published by Sangye Dorje, New Delhi, 1974.

PKG *rTogs brJod 'Pag bSam 'Khri Shing Gi 'Grel Ba* (pp. 437–647) by Jampal Yeshe Tenpe Gyaltsen. Published by Tso-ngön Mirik Loptra, 1988, China.

PKD *sNga 'Gyur rDo rJe Theg Pa gTso Bor Gyur Pa'i sGrub brGyud Shing rTa brGyad Kyi Byung Ba brJod Pa'i Pad Ma dKar Po'i rDzing Bu* (f. 284) by Gyurme Pema Namgyal (Zhechen Gyaltsap, 1871–1926). Reproduced by S. W. Tashigangpa, Ladakh, India.

PM *'Jigs Med Phrin Las Od Zer La rTogs brJod Dang 'Brel Bar gSol Ba 'Debs Pa dPag bSam lJon Pa'i Me Tog* by Jigme Tenpe Nyima. Vol. Nga (ff. 6–10), *Dodrupchen Sungbum*. Published by Dodrupchen Rinpoche, India.

RB *'Jam dByangs Ch'os Kyi Blo Gros Kyi rNam Thar Rin Ch'en Bang mDzod* (f. 260) by Do Sippa Ngawang Kün-ga Wangchuk. Manuscript.

RBP *Zab Mo'i gTer Dang gTer sTon Ji lTar Byon Pa'i Lo rGyus bKod Pa Rin Ch'en Baidurya'i Phreng Ba* (f. 235) by Kongtrül Yönten Gyatso. Vol. Ka, *Terdzö*. Reproduced by Jamyang (Dilgo) Khyentse, India.

RD *Klong Ch'en sNying Gi Thig Le Las, Nang sGrub Rig 'Dzin 'Dus Pa'i Zin Bris Rig 'Dzin Zhal Lung bDe Ch'en dPal sTer* (f. 58) by Chechok Tondrup Tsal (Kyala Khenpo, 1893–1957). Published by Dodrupchen Rinpoche, India.

RT *Ch'os 'Byung Rin Po Ch'e'i gTer mDzod bsTan Pa Rab Tu gSal Bar Byed Pa'i Nyi Od* (p. 502) by Gyalse Thukchok Tsal (Longchen Rabjam?). Böjong Petrünkhang, Tibet.

SB *sKyabs mGon Zhabs dKar rDo rJe 'Ch'ang Ch'en Po'i rNam Par Thar Pab bSam 'Phel dBang Gi rGyal Po* by Zhapkar Tsoktruk Rangtrol, vols. 1 & 2. Woodblock print of Tashi Khyil, Amdo, Tibet. English: LS.

SCG *The History of Chöten Gompa of Dearali,* Gangtok (p. 6) by the fourth Dodrupchen Rinpoche. Manuscript.

SKK *Theg Pa'i sGo Kun Las bTus Pa Shes Bya Kun Khyab* (vols. 1, 2 & 3) by Kongtrül Yönten Gyatso (1813–1899). Mirik Petrünkhang, China, 1982.

SLD *gSol 'Debs Leu bDun Ma,* discovered as ter by Rigdzin Gödem (1337–1408). Manuscript.

SM *Ma Ongs Lung bsTan gSal Byed Me Long* (f. 9) by Jigme Thrinle Özer. Manuscript.

SMM *The Seven Mountains of Thomas Merton* by Michael Mott. Boston; Houghton Mifflin, 1986.

SN *bChom lDan 'Das Ma Shes Rab Kyi Pha Rol Tu Phyin Pa'i sNying Po. Sher Phyin* section. Vol. Ka, Kanjur (Dege).

SNG *mKhyen brTse Heruka'i* [Do Khyentse] *gSang Ba'i rNam Thar Grub rTags sTon Tshul 'Thor bsDus* (f. 78) by Dechen Rikpe Raltri and others. A manuscript provided by the kindness of Zenkar Rinpoche.

TCG *gSang Ba Ch'en Po Nyams sNang Gi rTogs brJod Ch'u Zla'i Gar mKhan* (f. 26), discovered by Jigme Lingpa. Vol. OṂ, *Longchen Nyingthig Tsapö.* Published by Jamyang (Dilgo) Khyentse.

TKT *bsTan rTsis Kun Las bsTus Pa* by Tseten Zhaptrung (1910–?). Tso-ngon Mirik Petrünkhang, China.

TL *Ye Shes mKha' 'Gro bDe Ch'en rGyal Mo'i Thugs Dam bsKang Ba'i Rim Pa Tshogs gNyis Lhun Po* (f. 8) by Chö-nyön Dharma Senge. Woodblock print from Tibet.

TRL *gTer 'Byung Rin Po Ch'e'i Lo rGyus* (f. 53) by Tri-me Özer (Longchen Rabjam). Part I, *Khandro Yangtig* (Adzom). Reproduced by Lama Jigtrak and Tülku Pema Wangyal.

TT *Kun mKhyen Dri Med Od Zer Gyi rNam Thar mThong Ba Don lDan* (f. 46) by Chötrak Zangpo. Vol. 4, *Vima Nyingthig* (Adzom). Reproduced by Lama Jigtrak and Tülku Pema Wangyal, Darjeeling, India.

TTR *Gangs Chan Gyi Lo Pan rNams Kyi mTshan Tho Rags Rim* (f. 238) by Khyentse Wangpo. Vol. Dza, *Khyentse Kabum.* Reproduced by Jamyang Khyentse, India.

WJ *The Wish-Fulfilling Jewel: The Practice of Guru Yoga According to the Longchen Nyingthig Tradition* by Dilgo Khyentse. Boston: Shambhala, 1988.

WO *Las 'Phro gTer brGyud Kyi rNam bShad Nyung gSal Ngo mTshar rGya mTsho* (f. 36) by Jigme Tenpe Nyima. Vol. Nga, *Dodrupchen Sungbum.* Published by Dodrupchen Rinpoche, Sikkim, India. English: HTT.

YKG *Klong Ch'en sNying Gi Thig Le Las. rDzogs Pa Ch'en Po Ye Shes Klong Gi rGyud* (f. 12) by Jigme Lingpa. Vol. HŪṂ, *Longchen Nyingthig Tsapö.* Published by Jamyang [Dilgo] Khyentse, India.

YM *Padma 'Byung gNas Kyi rNam Par Thar Pa Yid Kyi Mun Sel* (f. 128) by Sokdokpa Lodrö Gyaltsen. Reproduced by Golok Lama Jigtse, Sikkim, India.

YS *Ye Grol Sor bZhag* by Longchen Rabjam. Manuscript.

ZL *'Jigs Med bsTan Pa'i Nyi Ma'i gZim Lam sKor* (f. 5) by Tülku Pema Namgyal (d. 1957). Manuscript.

Notes

1. Although 624–544 BCE are the dates generally accepted by the Theravādin Buddhist tradition, many scholars place the Buddha's life between the fifth and fourth centuries BCE.
2. Grasping at "self" is the concept of apprehending the existence of an entity in oneself as "I" or in beings and things as "you," "this," or "that," "table" or "chair," and so on.
3. The description of the Buddha's enlightenment is based on GR 165a/1, KNR 34/19 and SKK I-308/22.
4. Lha'i Mig Las Ye Shes mThong Ba'i Rig Pa. In some sources it is the knowledge of recollecting all the past existences, seeing all the future happenings, and realizing the exhaustion of all the contaminations.
5. sNgon Gyi gNas rJes Su Dran Pa'i Ye Shes mThong Ba'i Rig Pa.
6. Zag Pa Zad Pa Shes Pa mThong Ba'i Rig Pa.
7. Traditionally, Buddhism is classified into different schools (SKK I-361/s and DNN), as follows.

   (1) The three turnings of the wheel: (a) The first turning of the wheel is the teachings on common Buddhism (Hīnayāna, or Theravāda), which are mainly based on the four noble truths. (b) The second turning of the wheel is the teachings on Mahāyāna, mainly the scriptures of Prajñapāramitā taught at Vulture's Peak. It ascertains that the ultimate nature of every phenomenon is free from characteristics of elaboration. It emphasizes the profound meaning of emptiness through "three means of liberation": the view of emptiness (sTong Pa), the path of freedom from characteristics (mTshan Ma Med Pa), and the result of no aspirations (sMon Pa Med Pa). Followers of this teaching became the school of the Middle Way (Madhyamaka) of Mahāyāna. (c) The third turning of the wheel is the teachings that elucidate the enlightened (Buddha) essence of Mahāyāna, mainly based on the *Avataṃsaka-sūtra, Laṅkāvatāra-sūtra,* and others. It teaches that all phenomena are mere imputations (Kun bTags) of the mind, that the mind and mental events are arising merely dependent (gZhan dBang) on its habits, and that suchness is thoroughly established (Yongs Grub).

   (2) The three yānas (vehicles): (a) The teachings on four noble truths, etc., are given for shrāvakas (disciples) of Hīnayāna. (b) The teachings on interdependent arising, etc., are for pratyekabuddhas (self-realized ones) of Hīnayāna. (c) The teachings on ten stages and five paths, etc., are for bodhisattvas (seekers of the

mind of enlightenment) of Mahāyāna. (d) Also sometimes, the teachings on esoteric principles of Vajrayāna (the adamantine vehicle), the tantra of Mahāyāna, are categorized as a fourth yāna.

8. GR 200a/5, DZ I-44b/1.
9. KBZ 6B/3.
10. DP 293/6.
11. DP253/7.
12. DP 311/2.
13. The six perfections are giving, moral conduct, patience, diligence, contemplation, and wisdom. DT 19b/1.
14. BG 6a/3.
15. DT 16b/2.
16. KBZ 19a/3.
17. SN 145a/5.
18. Tantra is the continuum of the ultimate nature, with its basis, path, and result. Buddha said in GPM 150a/1: "Tantra is known as the continuum."
19. SKK III-160/3, 210/13, 212/23.
20. BG 13a/3.
21. GPM 152b/4, SKK III-159/14.
22. GPM 150a/4, SKK III-211/20.
23. The age of entering into parinirvāṇa is based on MD 317b/2.
24. This date is based on DPM 18b/5, 69a/3.
25. This date is based on DPM 79b/4, 155a/3.
26. YKG 1b/1 and other tantras. According to NPG 23a/2 *Mahāsandhi* is a corrupted spelling of *Mahāsamādhi,* and it also means mNyam Pa'i Blo Ch'en Po, the Great Mind of Evenness..
27. KBZ 282a/4: Vajrapāṇi and KNR 93/8: gSang Ba 'Dzin Pa (Vajrapāṇi).
28. NTB 455/5.
29. KBZ 285b/4.
30. DKG 58b/5, LNG 42a/4.
31. GD 161a/1, NS 24a/2.
32. The Eighteen Tantras of Mahāyoga:
    The Root Text of All the Mahāyoga Tantras: (1) rDo rJe Sems dPa' sGyu 'Phrul Drva Ba rTsa Ba'i rGyud gSang Ba sNying Po.
    Five Major Tantras: (2) Tantra of Body: Sangs rGyas mNyam sByor. (3) Tantra of Speech: Zla gSang Thig Le. (4) Tantra of Mind: gSang Ba 'Dus Pa. (5) Tantra of Quality: dPal mCh'og Dang Po. (6) Tantra of Action: Kar Ma Ma Le.
    Five Tantras of Sādhana: (7) Heruka Rol Ba. (8) rTa mCh'og Rol Ba. (9) sNying rJe Rol Ba. (10) bDud rTsi Rol Ba. (11) Phur Ba bChu gNyis Pa 'Byung Ba.
    Five Tantras of Activities: (12) Ri Bo brTsegs Pa. (13) Ye Shes rNgam Glog. (14) Dam Tshig bKod Pa. (15) Ting 'Dzin rTse gChig. (16) Glang Ch'en Rab 'Bog.
    Two Tantras for Completion: (17) rNam sNang sGyu 'Phrul Drva Ba. (18) 'Phags Pa Thabs Kyi Zhags Pa.
33. LNG 48a/2.
34. DKG 64b/5.
35. SKK I-395/7.

36. Based on GZ and also on NLS 17b/5.
37. GD 161b/6, NS 24a/3.
38. Some of the tantras of Anuyoga are as follows.
    Four Root mDo: (1) Kun 'Dus Rig Pa'i mDo (sPyi mDo). (2) Sangs rGyas Thams Chad dGongs Pa 'Dus Pa. (3) Ye Shes rNgam Glog. (4) gSang Ba Dur Khrod Khu Byug Rol Ba.
    Six Branch Tantras: (1) Kun Tu bZang Po Ch'e Ba Rang La gNas Pa'i rGyud. (2) dBang bsKur rGyal Po. (3) Ting 'Dzin mCh'og. (4) sKabs sByor bDun Pa. (5) brTson Pa Don lDan. (6) Dam Tshig bKod Pa.
    Twelve Rare Tantras: (1) Zhi Ba Lha rGyud. (2) Ch'os Nyid Zhi Ba'i Lha rGyud. (3) Khro Bo'i Lha rGyud Ch'en Mo. (4) Khro Bo'i Lha rGyud rTogs Pa Ch'en Po. (5) Thugs rJe Ch'en Po'i gTor rGyud. (6) rNal 'Byor Nang Pa'i Tshogs rGyud Ch'en Po. (7) dPal 'Bar Khro Mo. (8) Rakta dMar Gyi rGyud. (9) Me Lha Zhi Bar Kyur Ba 'Bar Pa'i rGyud. (10) Khro Bo'i sByin Sreg rDo rJe'i Ngur Mo. (11) Hūṃ mDzad Ch'en Mo. (12) Zla gSang Ch'en Mo.
39. Based on GZ.
40. GD 166a/2, NS 24a/4.
41. NCC 6b/a, NS 304a/6.
42. Twenty-one major tantras of Semde are:
    Five Early Tantras Translated by Vairochana: (1) Rig Pa'i Khu Byug. (2) rTsal Ch'en sPrug Pa. (3) Khyung Ch'en lDing Ba. (4) rDo La gSer Zhun. (5) Mi Nub Pa'i rGyal mTshan Nam mKha' Ch'e.
    Thirteen Later Tantras Translated by Vimalamitra: (6) rTse Mo Byung rGyal. (7) Nam mKha'i rGyal Po. (8) bDe Ba 'Phrul bKod. (9) rDzogs Pa sPyi Ch'ings. (10) Byang Ch'ub Sems Tig. (11) bDe Ba Rab 'Byams. (12) Srog Gi 'Khor Lo. (13) Thig Le Drug Pa. (14) rDzogs Pa sPyi sPyod. (15) Yid bZhin Nor Bu. (16) Kun 'Dus Rig Pa. (17) rJe bTsan Dam Pa. (18) sGom Pa Don Grub.
    Three Other Major Tantras: (19) Kun Byed rGyal Po. (20) rMad Byung. (21) The Thirteen Sūtras (mDo) of Semde.
43. NCC 7a/6.
44. Some of the major tantras of Longde: (1) Klong Ch'en Rab 'Byams rGyal Po. (2) Kun Tu bZang Po Nam mKha' Ch'e. (3) Rin Ch'en gDams Ngag sNa Tshogs 'Khor Lo. (4) rDo rJe Sems dPa' Nam mKha'i mTha' Dang mNyam Pa. (5) Ye Shes gSang Ba'i sGron Ma. (6) Rin Ch'en 'Khor Lo. (7) rDzogs Pa Ch'en Po Byang Ch'ub Kyi Sems Kun La 'Jug Pa.
45. NCC 7b/5, KZZ 8a/6.
46. The Major Tantras of Me-ngagde, NCC 8b/4:
    The Seventeen Tantras: (1) rDzogs Pa Rang Byung Ch'en Po. (2) Yi Ge Med Pa. (3) Rig Pa Rang Shar Ch'en Po. (4) Rig Pa Rang Grol Ch'en Po. (5) Rin Ch'en sPungs Ba. (6) sKu Dung 'Bar Ba Ch'en Po. (7) sGra Thal 'Gyur Ch'en Po. (8) bKra Shis mDzes lDan Ch'en Po. (9) rDo rJe Sems dPa' sNying Gi Me Long. (10) Kun Tu bZang Po Thugs Kyi Me Long. (11) Ngo sProd Rin Po Ch'es sPras Pa. (12) Mu Tig Phreng Ba. (13) Klong Drug Pa'i rGyud. (14) sGron Ma 'Bar Ba. (15) Nyi Zla Kha sByor. (16) Seng Ge rTsal rDzogs Ch'en Po. (17) Nor Bu 'Phra bKod.

Two Supplementary Texts: (18) Ekajaṭī Khros Ma'i rGyud. (19) Klong gSal 'Bar Ma.

47. For ter tradition, read HTT.
48. Based on NLC, DKG 48b/6 & 88a/1, NCG.
49. Based on LRP, DKG 57b/5, NCG.
50. KZD 12b/6.
51. RD6 6b/2.
52. KBZ 288b/5.
53. NTG 1b/1, RD 6b/6.
54. PKD 124/5, LNG 310b/2.
55. See NCC 9b/1, KZZ 9a/1, NGR 65b/5.
56. Some of the main texts or commentaries on *Longchen Nyingthig* written by the disciples of Jigme Lingpa and later masters are as follows.

    On Ngöndro, the Preliminary Practice:

    (a) rNam mKhyen Lam bZang, Ngöndro text (f. 13), by Jigme Thrinle Özer
    (b) Kun bZang Bla Ma'i Zhal Lung (f. 306) by Paltrül Rinpoche.
    (c) sNgon 'Gro'i dMigs Rim bsDus Pa (f. 11) by Paltrül Rinpoche.
    (d) sNgon 'Gro'i Ngag 'Don rNam mKhyen Lam bZang gSal Byed (f. 25) by Khyentse Wangpo
    (e) sNgon 'Gro'i dMigs Rim Zab Don bDud rTsi'i Nying Khu (f. 12) by Khyentse Wangpo.
    (f) sNgon 'Gro'i Khrid Yig Thar Lam gSal Byed sGron Me (f. 247) by Adzom Drukpa, Drudul Pawo Dorje.
    (g) Bla rNam La Nye Bar mKho Ba'i Yi Ge Padma Od Du bGrod Pa'i Them sKas (f. 13) by Dodrupchen, Jigme Tenpe Nyima.
    (h) Kun bZang Bla Ma'i Zhal Lung Gi Zin Bris (f. 205) by Khenpo Ngawang Palzang of Kathok.
    (i) sNgon 'Gro Kun Las bTus Pa (p. 110) by Yukhok Chatralwa.
    (j) sNgon 'Gro'i Zin Bris Blo dMan Yid Kyi Mun Sel (f. 131) by Nubpa Thrinle Chöphel of Tsang.
    (k) sNgon 'Gro'i 'Brul 'Grel rNam mKhyen Thar Gling bGrod Pa'i Them sKas by Gonpo Tseten of Amdo.
    (l) sNgon 'Gro'i rNam bShad mTshungs Med Bla Ma'i Byin rLabs Ch'ar rGyun (104) by Thekchok Yeshe Dorje of Bhutan.
    (m) lKong Ch'en sNying Thig Gi sNgon 'Gro'i Ngag 'Don Gyi 'Bru 'Grel Nyung Ngu Khro Med Bla Ma Ch'ung Ch'ung (f. 31) by Subhashita (Horlu Lama Legshed) of Nyag-rong, Kham.
    (n) Klong Ch'en sNying Thig Gi sNgon 'Gro'i Ngag 'Don Gyi 'Bru 'Grel rNam mKhyen Lam sGron (f. 82) by Chokyi Tragpa, Kham.

    On Rigdzin Düpa (Rig 'Dzin 'Dus Pa, The Assemblage of Vidhyādharas):

    (a) Rig 'Dzin 'Dus Pa'i Phyag Len mThong gSal Me Long (f. 5) by Paltrül Rinpoche.
    (b) Rig 'Dzin 'Dus Pa'i Zin Bris Rig 'Dzin Zhal Lung bDe Ch'en dPal sTer (f. 58) by Chechok Tontrup Tsal (Kyala Khenpo, Chöchok) of Dodrupchen.

    On Yumka Dechen Gyalmo (Yum Ka bDe Ch'en rGyal Mo, The Queen of Great Bliss):

(a) Yum Ka bDe Ch'en rGyal Mo'i sGrub gZhung Gi 'Grel Ba rGyud Don sNang Ba (f. 107) by Raton Ngawang Tendzin Dorje, a disciple of Jigme Lingpa.
(b) Yum Ka bDe Ch'en rGyal Mo'i sGrub gZhung Gi Zin Bris bDe Ch'en Lam bZang gSal Ba'i sGron Me (f. 22) by Dodrupchen, Jigme Tenpe Nyima.
(c) Yum Ka bDe Ch'en rGyal Mo'i rTsa sNgags Kyi 'Grel bShad rNam mKhyen bGrod Pa'i Them sKas (f. 6) by Jigme Tenpe Nyima.
(d) Yum Ka'i rTsa sGrub Kyi Ch'o Ga'i bsDus 'Grel (f. 14) by Lingtul of Wangda, Golok, a disciple of Alak Do-ngak Gyatso.
(e) Yum Ka'i Zin Bris Kha bsKong Rig 'Dzin Zhal Lung (f. 34) by Konchok Donme (Konme Khenpo) of Dodrupchen.
(f) Yum Ka bDe Ch'en rGyal Mo'i sGrub gZhung Gi Zin Bris rMong Pa'i Mun Sel (f. 19) by Sangye Özer of Gyarong, a disciple of Kyala Khenpo.
(g) Yum Ka bDe Ch'en rGyal Mo'i rTsa Ba'i sGrub Pa bDe Ch'en dPal Phreng Gi Tshig 'Grel (f. 63) by Gonpo Tseten of Amdo.

On Palchen Düpa (dPal Ch'en 'Dus Pa, The Assemblage of Great Glorious Deities):
(a) dPal Ch'en 'Dus Pa'i Las Byang Gi dGongs Don Chung Zad bShad Pa Zab Don gSal Byed Rin Ch'en sNang Ba (f. 103) by Khyentse Özer (Dilgo Khyentse).
(b) dPal Ch'en 'Dus Pa'i Zin Bris (f. 4) by Mati (Kyala Khenpo) of Dodrupchen.
(c) dPal Ch'en 'Dus Pa'i Ch'o Ga'i dMigs Rim Zhal Lung bDud rTsi'i Thig Pa (f. 39) by Garwa Khenpo Özang of Dodrupchen.
(d) dPal 'Dus sMan sGrub brTags Thabs Mar Me sMon Lam sTong Thun bChas (f. 6) by Khenpo Pema Badzar of Dzogchen.
(e) sGrub Khog Chung Zad gSal Du Byas Pa Rin Po Ch'ei Za Ma Tog (f. 14) by Dodrupchen Jikme Tenpe Nyima.

On Phurba (Phur Pa, Vajrakila):
(a) Phur Ba bDud dPung Zil gNon Gyi Zin Bris Phur Thogs mGrin Pa'i rGyan (f. 9) by Dodrupchen, Jikme Tenpe Gyaltsen [Nyima].
(b) Phur Ba'i Zin Bris bsDus Pa (f. 4) by Mati (Kyala Khenpo).

On Thukje Chenpo (Thugs rJe Ch'en Po, Avalokiteshvara):
(a) sDug bsNgal Rang Grol bsNyen Yig Grub gNyis Nor Bu'i Gan mDzod (f. 15) by Khenpo Peme Badzar of Dzogchen.
(b) sDug bsNgal Rang Grol bsNyen Yig Rig Pa 'Dzin Pa'i dGongs rGyan (f. 12) by Khenpo Pema Badzar of Dzogchen.
(c) sDug bsNgal Rang Grol Gyi sGrub Pa'i Khog dBub Rin Po Che'i Za Ma Tog (f. 22) Khenpo Ngawang Palzang of Kathok.

On Takhyung Barwa (rTa Khyung 'Bar Ba, Wrathful Guru Rinpoche):
(a) rTa Khyung 'Bar Ba'i bsNyel Tho Rin Ch'en sGon Me (f. 9) by Dodrupchen, Jigme Tenpe Nyima.

On Ladrup Thigle Gyachen (Bla sGrub Thig Le'i rGya Chan, Longchen Rabjam):
(a) Bla sGrub Thig Le'i rGya Chan Gyi bsNyen Yig Grub gNyis Shing rTa (f. 6) by Jamyang Khyentse Wangpo.

On Chod Khadö Ke-gyang (gChod mKha' 'Gro'i Gad rGyangs):

(a) mKha' 'Gro'i Gad rGyangs Kyi dMigs gNad 'Dril Ba gSal Byed sNye Ma (f. 17) by Dodrupchen, Jigme Thrinle Özer.
(b) gChod Yul mKha' 'Gro'i Gad rGyangs Kyi Man Ngag Zab Mo (f. 9) by Paltrül Rinpoche.
(c) mKha' 'Gro'i Gad rGyang Gi 'Grel Ba mKa' 'Gro'i gSang mDzod bDud rTsi'i Bum bZang (f. 31) by Rigdzin Nangdze Dorje, a disciple of Zhabkar.

On Kongshak (sKong bShags, Purification and Fulfillment Prayers):
(a) Skong bShags rDo rJe Thol Glu'i Tshig 'Grel bDus Pa (f. 47) by Pema Kunzang Rangtrol, a disciple of Adzom Gyalse Gyurme Dorje.

On Ngomon (bsNgo sMon, Dedication and Aspiration Prayers):
(a) Zangs mDog dPal Ri'i sMon Lam Gyi rNam bShad Phun Tshogs sTong lDan (f. 28) by Viryadhara.
(b) gZhi Lam 'Brs Bu'i sMon Lam Gyi 'Grel Ba (f. 5) by Khenpo Yönten Gyatso.

On Thaplam (Thabs Lam), the Path of Skillful Means:
(a) Klong Ch'en sNying Gi Thig Le Las Thabs Lam sBas Don Gyi 'Bru 'Grel Gab Don mNgon gSal (f. 24) by (Trupwang Jigme) Namkha Gyatso.
(b) bDe sTong rLung Gi rDzogs Rim sNyan rGyud Yid bZhin Nor Bu'i Shog Dril (f. 30) by Namkha Gyatso (?).
(c) Klong Ch'en sNying Gi Thig Le Las Rig 'Dzin 'Khrul 'Khor dPeu Ris (p. 24) by Namkha Gyatso (?).

On Dzogpa Chenpo
(a) Ch'os Kyi rGyal Po Lung rTogs bsTan Pa'i Nyi Ma La sPrul sKu sKu gSum Gling Pa'i Dris Lan Ka Lhun Zung 'Jug Gi gDams Pa (f. 32) by Nyoshul Lungtog.
(b) Ye Shes Bla Ma'i sPyi Don Kun bZang Thugs Kyi Tikka (f. 271) by Pema Ledreltsal (Ngawang Palzang) of Kathok.
(c) gNas Lugs rDo rJe'i Tshig rKang Gi 'Grel Ba (p. 14) by Yukhok Chatralwa.

Commentaries on Jigme Lingpa's Yon Tan Rinpoche'i mDzod and its autocommentary:
(a) rGya mTsho'i Ch'u Thig (short version) by the first Dodrupchen.
(b) rGya mTsho'i Ch'u Thig (detailed version) by the first Dodrupchen.
(c) gSer Gyi Thur Ma by Tentar Lharampa of Mongolia. LST
(d) Yon Tan Rin Po Ch'e'i mDzod Kyi dKa' 'Grel Nyin Byed sNang Ba (f. 70) (and various Sa bChad) by Paltrül Rinpoche.
(e) Zla Ba'i sGron Me and Nyi Ma'i Od Zer (vols. 1 & 2) by Khenpo Yönten Gyatso of Dzogchen.
(f) Yon Tan mDzod Kyi mCh'an 'Grel by Longchen Rolpa Tsal (Kagyur Rinpoche). Manuscript.

On 'Don 'Grigs (Rituals), dByangs Rol (Music) and gTor Ma (Offering Cakes):
(a) sNying Thig rTsa gSum gSol Kha'i 'Don 'Grigs Blo gSar Yid Kyi dGa' sTon (f. 53) by Golok Khenpo Tsondrü.
(b) Klong Ch'en sNying Gi Thig Le Las Rig 'Dzin 'Jigs Med Gling Pa'i bKa' gTer Gyi Ch'o Ga'i rNga Tshig sKal bZang dGa' bsKyed (f. 9) by (Dodrupchen) Jigme Thrinle Özer.
(c) gSang sNgags Kyi Ch'o Ga'i dByangs Rol Dang gTor Ma Sogs Kyi Lo rGyus Phan Yon mDor bsDus rGyu mTshan Shes Pa'i Gleng gZhi (f. 5) by Khyentse Özer [Dilgo Khyentse].

(d) sNying Thig Gi gTor Ma'i bCha' Yig (f. 12) by Khyentul [Do Khyentse].
(e) Klong Ch'en sNying Thig Gi gTor Ma'i dPeu Ris (p. 5) by Dilgo Khyentse (?).

Writings on or Translations of Longchen Nyingthig Teachings in English:
(a) *The Way of Power. A Practical Guide to the Tantric Mysticism of Tibet* by John Blofeld (London: George Allen & Unwin, 1970). See chap. 2, "The Preliminaries" (pp. 147–168).
(b) English introduction to *The Autobiographical Reminiscences of Ngag-dbang-dpal-bzang, Late Abbot of Kah-Thog Monastery* by Gene Smith (Gangtok: Sonam T. Kazi, 1969).
(c) *The Short Preliminary Practice of Longchen Nyingthig* by Kunkhyen Jigme Lingpa. Restructured by the fourth Dodrupchen Rinpoche (Mahasiddha Nyingmapa Center).
(d) *Tantric Practice in Nyingma* by Khetsun Sangpo Rinbochay, tr. and ed. by Jeffrey Hopkins and Anne Klein (Snow Lion, 1982).
(e) *A Wondrous Ocean of Advice for the Practice of Retreatments in Solitude* (Ri Ch'ö Zhal gDams), tr. David Christensen. (London: Rigpa, 1987).
(f) *The Wish-Fulfilling Jewel: The Practice of Guru Yoga According to the Longchen Nyingthig Tradition* (p. 108) by Dilgo Khyentse. Tr. by Könchog Tenzin (Boston: Shambhala Publications, 1988).
(g) *The Dzogchen Innermost Essence Preliminary Practice* by Jigme Lingpa. Tr. with commentary by Tulku Thondup (Library of Tibetan Works and Archives, 1989).
(h) *Kun-zang La-may Zhal-lung, The Preliminary Practices.* Vol. I & II. Tr. by Sonam T. Kazi. (Diamond-Lotus Publishing, 1989)
(i) EL. See chap. 8, *"Entering into the Path* (sPyod Yul Lam Khyer)."
(j) *The Assemblage of Vidyādharas* (Rig 'Dzin 'Dus Pa) of Long-Chen Nying-Thig, tr. Tulku Thondup (Dodrupchen Rinpoche, 1991).
(k) *The Queen of Great Bliss* (Yum-Ka bDe Ch'en rGyal Mo) of Long-Chen Nying-Thig, tr. Tulku Thondup (Dodrupchen Rinpoche, 1991).
(l) *Tibetan Buddhism: Reason and Revelation,* ed. Steven D. Goodman and Ronald M. Davidson (SUNY, Albany, 1992). See chap. 8, "Rig-'dzin'Jigs-med gling-pa and the kLong-Chen sNying-Thig," pp. 133–146.
(m) NTB. See [Life of] *Jigme Lingpa,* vol. 1, pp. 835–840.
(n) *The Words of My Perfect Teacher (Kunzang Lama'i Shelung)* by Paltrül Rinpoche, tr. Padmakara Translation Group (HarperCollins, 1994).
(o) *Meeting the Great Bliss Queen* by Anne Klein (Boston: Beacon, 1994).
(p) *Enlightened Journey: Buddhist Practice as Daily Life* by Tulku Thondop, ed. Harold Talbott (Boston: Shambhala Publications, 1995). See chaps. 10 & 12, "The Meditation of Ngöndro" and "Receiving the Four Empowerments of Ngöndro Meditation."
(q) *Dancing Moon, Ḍākinī Talk: The Secret Autobiography of Jigme Lingpa* by Janet Gyatso (forthcoming from Princeton Univ. Press).
(r) *Fearless Vision* by Steven D. Goodman (forthcoming from Rangjung Yeshe).

57. KR 126a/1, NGR 35b/3.
58. DP 5b/1.

59. BC 1a/1.
60. According to LRP 238a/1 & 243a/3, KKZ 283a/4–285b/3 and others, Mañjushrīmitra was Shrīsiṃha's main Nyingthig teacher. But Shrīsiṃha also received *Khandro Nyingthig* and other teachings from Garab Dorje and transmitted them directly to Guru Rinpoche. So Longchen Nyingthig, being the essence of both early Nyingthigs, is transmitted by Garab Dorje to Shrīsiṃha as well as coming through the lineage of Garab Dorje, Mañjushrīmitra, Shrīsiṃha, and so on.
61. "Lord" is King Trisong Detsen. "Subjects" are Guru Rinpoche's 24 (or 25) chief disciples. "Support" is Guru Rinpoche's consort, Yeshe Tsogyal.
62. sTon 'Khor dGongs Pa gChig Pa.
63. sTon 'Khor dGongs Pa dByer Med Tu Gyur Pa.
64. Summarized from TDD 235b/4.
65. This life is based on NLC 45a/6 and also on PKD 17a/4, TRL 7a/4, KGT I 565/20, DKG 4 8b/6, LNG 60a/4.
66. I have restored Sanskrit terms for many Tibetan words, following modern translators. However, some may be inaccurate, as there are many possible Sanskrit terms.
67. KBZ 283a/2: Me Tog gSal (Luminous Flower), which could be her name before she was ordained. Also BND 21a/5 gives Varani (or Barani), KNR 112/3 Prarani, and SKK I 390/2 Praharani.
68. BND 21a/4, KNR 112/3: Dha he na ta lo, which could be his name, as Uparāja is a title. DKG 48b/6: Uparāja or Dharmāshoka. SKK I 390/2: Dharma Ashoka.
69. SKK I 390/2.
70. According to BND 21b/2, KBZ 283a/5, KNR 112/11, SKK I 390/3, the nun had wonderful dreams and went to a lake to bathe. There an incarnation of Vajrapāṇi in the form of a goose, with four other geese, landed by her and touched his beak three times to the heart of the nun, and she saw a HŪṂ letter of light merge into her. When Garab Dorje was born to her amid miracles, and holding Dzogpa Chenpo tantras in his memory, men and gods celebrated with praise and joy. These sources do not mention his being abandoned by his mother.
71. According to PKD 18a/1, DKG 49b/1, SKK I 390/9, 394/6, LNG 62a/6 and others, Prahevajra received the transmissions from Vajrasattva, and according to LRP 237a/6, BND 22a/1, and KBZ 283b/6, he received them from Vajrapāṇi. There is a bodhisattva named Vajrapāṇi, but this is the Buddha Vajrapāṇi (De bZhin gShegs Pa Phyag Na rDo rJe), who is also known as the Lord (Source) of Secret Heart (gSang Ba'i bDag Po).
72. Generally, Dur Khrod (charnel or cremation ground) is a sacred place, mainly a place where bodies are cremated, buried, or disposed of. But that is not why these particular grounds are important. The charnel ground is full of significance. It is the place of the termination of ego and the end of attachment to and craving for body and life. It is a place of transforming so-called negative phenomena as natural and letting go of fear and aversion. If you read Nyingthig histories NLC, LRP, TRL, and LG, you will see that these places have natural and spiritual power and energy. They are frightening, full of roaming spirits and hunting ghosts, old and new bodies, rivers of blood, poisonous waterfalls, and life-threatening wild beasts. But they are also enjoyable places of peaceful solitude, delightful groves, blossoming flowers, abundant fruit, flocks of singing birds, tame lions and tigers, vast open

sky, as high as among the sun, moon, and stars, with no systems or norms to be shaped by, free from distractions or restrictions. It is a place where oceans of ḍākas and ḍākinīs celebrate with ceremonial "feasts." The roar of Dharma discourses is sounding everywhere, and lights from inner joy of bliss and openness are radiating. Thus, these charnel grounds are places of energy, power, and spirit both positive and negative, which it is important for an esoteric trainee to transform into esoteric power and energy of enlightenment.

73. LRP 238a/1 & 243a/3, KBZ 285b/3.
74. TRL 9b/3, LRP 238a/1.
75. DCS 16b/1 19b/2.
76. This life is based on NLC 52a/4, and also on LNG 62b/5, KBZ 284a/2, PKD 12a/2, 18b/1, DKG 49b/2, KGT 567/3 and KNR 113/21.
77. KBZ 284a/2, his father's name: bDe sKyong and mother's name: Kuhana, and he met Garab Dorje in Oḍḍiyāṇa. PKD 12a/2: His father's name: Sādhuṣhastrī. KNR 113/22: father's name: dPal lDan sKyong and mother's name: Kuhana, and he met Garab Dorje in Oḍḍiyāṇa.
78. BND 24a/4, KBZ 285a/3.
79. It is difficult to know what kind of years are meant. There are two points. (a) There was a tradition of counting every six months as a year, based on a "march" (bGrod Pa, Skt. ayana) of the sun. When the sun moves from south to north, it is on its northern march; when it moves from north to south, it is on its southern march. (b) Also, many of the ancient masters attained longevity and lived for centuries, many in light bodies and some even in their mortal bodies.
80. DCS 19b/2–23b/6.
81. LNG 65a/6.
82. This life is based on NLC 55b/1, and also on PKD 19a/5, LNG 65b/1, TRL 9b/1, KBZ 285b/1, and KGT 569-I.
83. KBZ 285b/1 and TRL 9b/2: Hastibhala. LNG 65b/1: the name of the city is Sho Khyam and the teacher's name, Haribhala. KNR 117/15: city, Zho Sha; father, King Gru Khyer, and mother, Nan Ka.
84. PKD 19b/1, LNG 65b/5, KNR 117/21, TRL 9b/5: Bhelakīrti. NLC 56/5: Bi-lekiti.
85. LRP 238a/1 & 243a/3, KBZ 285b/3.
86. TRL 9b/3, LRP 238a/1, BND 55a/1–66b/4.
87. DCS 23b/6–47a/4.
88. This life is based on NLC 60a/2, and also on PKD 20a/2, LGN 66b/5, DKG 51a/2, KGT 568/12 and KNR 118/25.
89. KNR 119/1: Father's name, Apardajana, and mother's name, rGya mTsho Ma.
90. Some think that Li was in Nepal, but most scholars consider that it is Khotan, now Xinjiang in China. However, KNR 162/24, says it is 'Jang, which is in Yunnan province of China.
91. KGT 570/1: Ba Sing.
92. DCS 27b/4–30a/3. (See also BM 70/14.)
93. This life is based on NLC 60a/1, 68a/6 and also on LGN 66b/4, 68a/2, 107b/6, DKG 52a/1, KNR 119/8, 200/20, KGT 568/11, 570/2, 572/3, and PKD 20a/2, 96b/3.

94. DKG 52a/4. KGT 570/2: light emerged.
95. LNG 68a/4: sNang Byed. NLC 63/6: Srod Byed.
96. LNG 68b/4: Bhirya. NLC 70b/5: Bi rGyal.
97. PKD 97a/1: Vimalamitra conferred the teachings of Innermost Esoteric Nyingthig upon five disciples: King Trisong Detsen, Prince Mu-ne Tsepo, Nyang Tingdzin Zangpo, Kawa Paltsek, and Chok-ro Lü'i Gyaltsen.
98. This life is based on LNG 46a/6, 78a/6, YM 19, LRP 238b/1, RBP 6b/4–34b/4, KNR 22b/10–140b/3, 150–178, GRL 10b/2, LG, KGT I-596/18–60223, and others.
99. YM 81a/4.
100. Ancient Indian traditions, including Buddhism, accept four ways of taking birth: by womb, moisture, egg, and immaculate birth, which is an instantaneous birth, such as being born from a lotus.
101. In Buddhist tantric histories there are many King Indrabhūtis. It could be a popular name for royalty, or else it is the name of a royal lineage. However, according to YM 19a/6, he is the second Indrabhūti of Oḍḍiyāṇa.
102. TRL 18a/2.
103. The four knowledge-holders are based on DD 58a/4.
104. However, according to NG 9a/1 and LY 375/15, Sahor is somewhere near Bangalpur city in Bengal and Bihar states of India.
105. NFH II-36 (488): It is the cave of Haileshi, near the town of Rumjitar in Sagarmatha District, Nepal.
106. Both the "knowledge-holder with residues" and the "knowledge-holder with control over life" are equal in terms of success. It is not necessary to attain all the states one after another. If you are a less capable person, you will achieve the first one, and then you go to the third knowledge-holder. If you are a more capable person, you can achieve the second one and move to the third. But remember that Guru Rinpoche is "manifesting" as a devotee on this path.
107. YM 24a/1, PKG 602/26. KGT I-87/14: "dBang-Po'i sDe" or "Grags-Pa." See GK 42/3 for Grags Pa'i rGyal mTsan.
108. LG 204b/3, LRP 243a/3.
109. See LNG 50b/4, NFH II-37 (n. 494), and also GP 203/21.
110. Date is based on DPM 96b/2.
111. KD 232/10.
112. WO (English: HTT).
113. TRL 44b/3.
114. RBP 17a/4, LNG 84a/2.
115. Date is based on DPM 163b/1.
116. SLD 52a/4.
117. YM 112a/2.
118. GDG 173/8.
119. However, a few biographies of Guru Rinpoche that I have read do not mention when or where he manifested the attainment of the fourth knowledge-holdership, apart from saying that he is in the knowledge-holdership of spontaneous accomplishment in Zangdok Palri (RBP 14b/2). Also to be noted, Dodrupchen writes

(DD p. 60a/1) that one can enter into Buddhahood directly after the state of the third knowledge-holder or even after any earlier attainments..

120. RT 356/11.
121. These lives are based on RBP 31b/1.
122. These lives are based on KNR 146/2, 165/19 and RBP 15a/4.
123. Dates are based on DPM 18b/5 and DPM 69a/3.
124. Their number, names, and seniority are based on DPM 154b/1, KNR 164/5, and LNG 84a/2.
125. YM 70a/3, 77a/5, PGG 67/14, DPM and RBP 17a/6.
126. These lives are based on RBP 18a/2, LNG 146a/4 and YM 68a/6.
127. This life is based on RBP 23a/3, DKG 54a/1 and LNG 93b/4.
128. LRB 5a/6.
129. This life is based on TT and also on DKG 95a/6 108a/3, LNG 119b/3 138a/2, and TRL 48b/2.
130. Or Sangphu Nethok. It was the most important center of learning in Longchen Rabjam's time. It was founded by Ngok Lekpe Sherap, a student of the great master Atīsha of India, in 1073. Ngok Lo Loden Sherap (1059–1109) and Chapa Chöseng (1109–1169) taught there. It produced many great minds of Tibet.
131. According to *Truptha Dzö,* they are the *gSer Yig Chan, gYu Yig Chan, Tung Yig Chan,* and *Zangs Yig Chan.*
132. NLC 13a/5 and DKG 98b/4.
133. NT 69b/2.
134. NTS 57a/3.
135. YS 4a/6.
136. DO 132b/5.
137. LG 136b/6.
138. Following are the names and brief descriptions of Longchen Rabjam's major works as given in *Ngo mTshar gTam Gyi Gling Bu* by the second Zhechen Rabjam Gyurme Künzang Namgyal (1713–1769):

    A. *Dzödün* (Seven Treasures) consists of seven major texts:

    1. *Yizhin Rinpoche Dzö* (Wish-Fulfilling Treasure) is in twenty-two chapters. It is a summary of the whole range of Buddhism, and it teaches the way of studying, analyzing, and meditating upon Mahāyāna Buddhism. It is accompanied by *Pema Karpo,* a detailed autocommentary, and *Zabdön Dorje Nyingpo,* an instructional writing on how to practice it.
    2. *Men-ngak Rinpoche Dzö* (Treasure of Instructions) is a treatise using different series of six constituents to summarize the Buddhist sūtras and tantras in their entirety, and to teach the essence of the path and result of Dzogpa Chenpo.
    3. *Chöying Rinpoche Dzö* (Treasure of the Ultimate Sphere) is in thirteen chapters with its autocommentary, *Lungki Terdzö.* It is an exposition of the deep and vast teachings on ground, path, and result of Semde, Longde, and Mengagde (or mainly of Longde) of Dzogpa Chenpo.
    4. *Truptha Rinpoche Dzö* (Treasure of Doctrinal Views) is in eight chapters. It is an exposition of the various philosophical standpoints of all the yānas of sūtra and four tantras of Buddhism.

5. *Thekchok Rinpoche Dzö* (Treasure of the Supreme Yāna) is in twenty-five chapters. It elucidates the meaning of the seventeen tantras and the one hundred and nineteen instructional treatises of the Me-ngagde cycle of Dzogpa Chenpo. It expounds a wide range of Buddhist doctrine, from the way in which the absolute teacher manifests as the three Buddha bodies to the achievement of the spontaneously accomplished final result of the path of Dzogpa Chenpo.
6. *Tsikton Rinpoche Dzö* (Treasure of Words and Meaning) is in eleven chapters. It is a summary of *Thekchok Rinpoche Dzö* explaining the crucial points of practice. It begins with a description of the ground and concludes with the result, the state of ultimate liberation.
7. *Neluk Rinpoche Dzö* (Treasure of the Ultimate Nature) is in five chapters. With its autocommentary, it explains the ultimate meaning of the three categories of Dzogpa Chenpo.

B. *Ngalso Korsum* (Three Cycles on Relaxing in the Ultimate Nature) consists of fifteen treatises: the three root texts, three summaries called garlands, three autocommentaries called chariots, and three instructions on practice:
1. *Semnyi Ngalso* (Relaxation in the Ultimate Nature of the Mind), the root text in thirteen chapters, explains all aspects of the path, beginning, middle, and end of the sūtric and tantric teachings. It is accompanied by *Ngedön Shingta Chenmo,* an autocommentary on the root text, in two volumes; *Künde Trengwa,* a summary (lost); *Pema Karpö Trengwa,* a summary of the autocommentary; and *Changchup Lamzang,* an instructional treatise on practice.
2. *Gyuma Ngalso* (Relaxation in the Illusory Nature), in eight chapters, is an instruction on cutting the ties of attachment through the method of the eight examples of illusory apparitions. It is accompanied by *Mandare Trengwa,* a summary, *Shingta Zangpo,* the autocommentary, and *Yizhin Norbu,* the instructional treatise on practice.
3. *Samten Ngalso* (Relaxation in the Absorption), in three chapters, explains the profound path of samādhi, the self-existent natural wisdom. It is accompanied by *Puṇḍarīke Trengwa,* a summary, *Shingta Namdak,* an autocommentary, and *Nyingpo Chüdü,* the instructional treatise on practice. In addition, there are *Lekshe Gyatso,* an outline of the *Ngalso Korsum,* and *Pema Tongden,* a catalogue of contents.

C. *Rangtröl Korsum* (Three Cycles on Natural Liberation) texts are the "meaning commentary" on the instruction of Semde, and each has three chapters explaining the basis, path, and result:
1. *Semnyi Rangtröl* with *Lamrim Nyingpo,* the meaning instruction.
2. *Chönyi Rangtröl* with *Yizhin Nyingpo,* the meaning instruction.
3. *Nyam-nyi Rangtröl* with *Rinchen Nyingpo,* the meaning instruction.

D. *Yangtig Namsum* (Three Treatises on the Inner Essence) contains the crucial points of the esoteric teachings of Me-ngagde, the Nyingthig cycle of Dzogpa Chenpo:
1. *Lama Yangtig* (or *Yangzap Yizhin Norbu*) contains thirty-five treatises. It condenses and interprets the vast teachings of the four volumes (*Seryigchen, Yu-*

yigchen, Tung-yigchen, and *Zang-yigchen* with *Trayigchen*) of *Vima Nyingthig* and the one hundred nineteen treatises of instructions.

2. *Khandro Yangtig* containing fifty-five treatises. These are revealed by Longchen Rabjam as the supplements and commentaries on *Khandro Nyingthig,* discovered by his previous incarnation.
3. *Zabmo Yangtig* is a detailed commentary on both *Vima Nyingthig* and *Khandro Nyingthig.*

139. This life is based on LYN, and also on DSC, TCG, NTG, KNR 635/16, LNG 310b/2, PKD 124b/5, RD 6b/6, RBP 219a/3, NN, and KKR 40b/2.
140. LK 101a/1.
141. LYN 7a/1 and others recognize Khyentse Wangpo, an incarnation of Jigme Lingpa, as the thirteenth one.
142. KS. See KNN.
143. LYN 9a/3.
144. See KNR 582/20 for his life.
145. KNR 638/15. LNG 311a/4: Thang 'Brog dBon Padma mCh'og Grub.
146. Copying scriptures, making offerings, giving charity, listening to teachings, memorizing them, reciting scriptures, teaching Dharma, saying prayers, and pondering the meaning of the Dharma and meditating upon it.
147. Pacifying, causing prosperity, controlling, and exorcism.
148. LYN 42a/4.
149. LYN 44a/6.
150. LYN 45a/2.
151. LYN 46b/1.
152. NYR 68b/5.
153. NYR 69b/2.
154. KZ 38b/1, KNR 724/17: he is also known as Trati Ngakchang.
155. KNR 638/2.
156. LYN 209b/2.
157. LYN 82b/5.
158. A *khal* is twenty *tres* and a *tre* is about two pints.
159. LYN 118b/4.
160. That is DKG.
161. LYN 164a/5.
162. GL 21a/1, LYN 168b/5.
163. According to GNP 93/4.
164. LYN 191b/2, DGN 70b/5, GL 65b/5.
165. KZ 33a/1 & 39a/2, KNR 641/24, 725/7.
166. Date is based on TKT 273/3.
167. Dates are based on SB, TKT, and LS. For Zhapkar's (Shabkar's) life, read LS.
168. LYN 220a/2.
169. KNR 725/1, KZ 38b/1, NPG 9a/5.
170. LYN 240b/6.
171. DB 6b/4.
172. NGR 57b/1.
173. NTG 3b/6.

174. KKR 42b/1.
175. KNR 724/19, KZ 38b/1, LYN 80b/5.
176. KNR 644/8.
177. LYN 203a/6.
178. LYN 204a/3, NTG 4a/5, KGT-I, 350/19. She reigned 1790–1798. Her husband was King Sawang Zangpo (or Kun-'Grub bDe dGa' bZang Po), r. 1768–1790. Her son was King Tsewang Dorje Rigdzin (aka Byams Pa Kun dGa' Sangs rGyas bsTan Pa'i rGyal mTshan).
179. LYN 105a/6.
180. LYN 202a/1.
181. LYN 171b/1. Three ringsels were kept in the gau of the third Dzogchen Rinpoche.
182. This life is based on DGN. I have also relied on KNR 644/14 646/23, KZ, RBP 223a/6–225b/3, PKD 127a/3–127b/5, PJM, DN, CN, PM, DZT, and DB.
183. LK 125b/2.
184. Tsampa is flour of roasted barley, which is the main staple food in Tibet.
185. These thoughts are not in the autobiography but were told orally.
186. According to Kyala Khenpo of Dodrupchen Monastery.
187. RBP 224a/2.
188. LYN 164a–164b.
189. LYN 165b/5–166a/4.
190. GL 29a/5.
191. NTG 3b/6.
192. DD 7b/5: "dGe rTse bSod Nams bsTan 'Dzin Nam 'Jigs Med Ngo mTshar."
193. LYN 191a/3.
194. PM 8a/2.
195. GD 72a/4.
196. DGN 74a/6.
197. DGN 74b/5.
198. DGN 75b/1, footnote in KNR 641, RBP 224a/6, PJM 11/14.
199. LYN 204a/4.
200. LYN 204a/2, 205a/2, KNR 644/6, GL 93a/4. Later, Getse Lama Sönam (Puṇya) Tendzin (aka Jigme Ngotsar) lived here.
201. LYN 222a/6.
202. SB 28b/6, 455a/3: Zhapkar Tsoktruk Rangtröl received *Longchen Nyingthig* transmissions from Lakha Drupchen.
203. See LST 270a/3.
204. DGN 100b/5.
205. LYN 220b/1.
206. SB 28b/6 and TKT 272/12, 19: Lakha Drupchen and Zhapkar Tsoktruk Rangtröl were ordained together by Arik Geshe in 1801.
207. According to Khenpo Chöyak of Shukchung Monastery.
208. DZT 5b/5, DB a/12.
209. The last two are listed in PM 9a/4.
210. PJM 14b/4.
211. Introduction to NGR 12 by E. Gene Smith and NTB, note 1153, vol. 2.

212. CN 7a/2.
213. Today Yarlung Monastery is being rebuilt under the guidance of Yarlung Tülku Tenpe Nyima, an incarnation of the Third Dodrupchen.
214. Dodrupchen ends his autobiography in 1813.
215. TTR 149b/6.
216. GL 124a/1.
217. KZ 90a/5.
218. KZ 93b/1.
219. KZ 107a/4. According to RBP he died at midnight on the 13th.
220. LST 270a/3.
221. KZ 107a/6.
222. SM 1b/2.
223. DZT 5a/5, DB 12a/1.
224. NGR 13b/2.
225. LK 125b/5.
226. MG 15a.
227. NGR 57a/4.
228. LS 558/3: Lo-de was also known as Chingkarwa Tön-yö Dorje, a teacher and disciple of Zhabkar. His incarnation was Trülzhik Künzang Thongtröl of Do-ngak Ling, the previous incarnation of the present Trülzhik Rinpoche, Ngawang Chökyi Lodrö (b. 1924), who now resides in Nepal.
229. GN 44b/2.
230. TL 3a/3.
231. Sherap Mebar's incarnation (see DZT 17b/3) was Do Rinpoche Tri-me Trakpa, whose incarnation was Do Rinpoche Zilnön Gyepa Dorje (1890–1939), a son of Rikpe Raltri, Do Khyentse's son.
232. This life is mainly based on GL and also on NGR, DNK and DGN.
233. GL 9a/1, 113b/1, KNR 889/17, 900/2.
234. NGR 61a/3, GL 63b/1. NGR says that this event took place in Tsāri, but GL says it happened in the hermitage of Ogyen Ling.
235. GL 65a/1.
236. NGR 62a/2.
237. ON.
238. It is KBZ.
239. There is no written biography to rely on. Mostly oral history based on what was heard from Kyala Khenpo, otherwise indicated.
240. GL 112b/4.
241. GL 138b/1.
242. This life is based on TTR 145a/5–156a/3, DL 98-122, PDK 209b/2–210a/4, KNR 819, RB 208–213 and oral traditions mainly from Kyala Khenpo.
243. This life is based on KZ, and also on SNG, BDL, DGN, and GL.
244. LNY 176a/5.
245. I heard about this event from Kyala Khenpo, who saw the marks.
246. I heard these two stories from Kyala Khenpo.
247. I used to have a piece of this whip.
248. KZ 194b/3, TTR 1167a/4.

249. PKD 127b/4 and some oral traditions.
250. DZT 5a/5, DB 12a/1.
251. I couldn't find any biography of Khenchen Pema Dorje.
252. This life is based on DZT and DB.
253. NGR 15b/1.
254. This life is based on DN and PJM. As not much has been written about his life, for some information I have mainly relied on oral tradition.
255. GL 167b/4.
256. KZ 137b/4.
257. *Zas* are mysterious but quite popular phenomenon in Tibet and also in Golok. It sounds similar to the "flying saucer" phenomena of the West. There is no account of their having crafts, but they are described as mysterious beings of or with bright light. Tibetans believe that *Zas* are one of the infinite classes of beings in the universe. Among them there are both holy ones and harmful ones..
258. This life is based on NUG, JKT, RBP 185a/4–195a/1, LNG 320b/1–328b/1, and PKD 248a/2–260b/4.
259. DB 6b/4.
260. WJ 92/22.
261. According to DNK, he died at seventy-two, and according to NRG, he was at Ari forest in the 1850s and died the year before a Tiger year. Sometime after Lungtok's death, Ngawang Palzang became twenty-nine in 1907, so Lungtok's dates must be 1830–1901.
262. This life is based on NGR 12a/4 and also on DNK.
263. This life is based on DB and also NGR.
264. This life is based on DNK 4.18–4.22 and NGR 98b/6–99b/4.
265. This life is based on oral materials from Kyala Khenpo, Khenpo Chöyak, and others.
266. *Pramāṇavārttika, Vinayasūtra, Abhidharmakosha, Abhisamayālaṃkāra,* and *Madhyamakāvatāra.*
267. EL 114/28.
268. This account was prepared by his students and reflects what they remember of the event.
269. This life is based on the oral accounts of Kyala Khenpo and on DN, DJN 11–18, and ZL.
270. Sarma means New Tantra or the followers of the New Tantric teachings. Nyingma follows Old Tantras, and all the other schools of Tibet are followers of New Tantra.
271. PK 242b/2.
272. NYG 152b/6.
273. GRT 9a/4.
274. Janet Gyatso, *In the Mirror of Memory* (Albany: SUNY, 1992). For a discussion on a few points of this text, see pp. 173–213.
275. *Kindness, Clarity, and Insight* by the fourteenth Dalai Lama. (Snow Lion 1984). For a discourse based on this and other texts of Dodrupchen, see "Union of the Old and New Translation School," pp. 200–224.
276. For translation and commentary, see HTT.
277. For a translation, see EL (pp. 117–129); for commentaries, see *Transforming Problems*

into Happiness by Lama Thubten Zöpa Rinpoche (Boston: Wisdom, 1993) and *Healing Power of Mind* by Tulku Thondup (forthcoming).

278. Although the date of his text on "memory" is later than his *Outline of Guhyagarbha,* the text on memory was written much earlier.
279. This life is based on NB.
280. According to BD IV 528–530, she was born in 1841 (Iron Ox) and died in 1940, and according to CY 130/2, she was born in the "Wood Ox year, 1852" (but the Wood Ox is 1865, not 1852, which is the year of the Water Mouse). According to LS 571, her dates are 1852–1953. According to the preface to NB, she was born in either 1853 (Water Ox) or 1865 (Wood Ox). However, she herself mentions (NB 11a/4) that she was conceived in the Water Rat year (1852) but then clearly states (NB 11b/3) that she was born in the Wood Ox year (1865), and according to Cham Wangmola of Lukhang House, a close disciple of Jestsun, she died at the end of the Water Dragon year (1953).
281. NB 38b/2. When Pema Gyatso was forty-nine, Jetsun became thirteen.
282. NB 46b/4.
283. NB 43a/3.
284. NB 106a/5, on the seventeenth of the second month of the Iron Tiger year.
285. This life is based on DL 125–128.
286. This date is based on MC. However, according to DB 40b/6, he was born in 1862, and according to NTB II-86/48 and LS XXV/40, his dates are 1870–1940.
287. This life is based on MC.
288. This life is based on DK 1–35, oral traditions, and personal witness. See BM 140)144.
289. This life is based on NGR.
290. NGR 58a/5.
291. This life is based on interviews with the first Alak Zenkar's disciples kindly arranged by the second Zenkar Rinpoche.
292. This life is based on GRT 9a/3, NYG, CD, and RB 238–257.
293. Although GRT 9a/3 says Earth Monkey year, NYG 51a/5 has Iron Monkey, 28.
294. Although GRT 10a/3 and NYG 52b/4 says Water Ox, NYG 52a/4 also gives the age of thirty-three, so, it must be Wood Ox year, as it fits the time.
295. This life is based on BD IV 703–712 and NO 129–141.
296. According to other sources, 10 and 14.
297. This life is based on oral sources and events witnessed by the author.
298. SMM 552/7.
299. This life is based on DN, oral sources, and events witnessed by the author.
300. Some believed that the fifth Jamyang Zhepa was an incarnation of Dodrupchen.
301. He was one of the only two tülkus in the whole Golok region to whom the authorities extended their recognition as a tülku in 1993. The other one is the tülku of Shangza (the tülku of Je Tsongkhapa's mother) at Arik Ragya Gön, a Gelukpa monastery.
302. This life is based on DJN 48–64, DN, SCG, oral sources, and events witnessed by the author.
303. See note 257.
304. A cross between an ox and a dri, a female yak.

305. bDag Ni Byang Ch'ub Mi Phyed Pa. . . .
306. NYG 51b/3.
307. It is difficult to have any certainty of what the actual meaning of these lines is, but they could be indicating: First line—about the coming of the revolutionary forces to the monastery from the south. Second line—about the construction of two new roads that run towards Lhasa: one along the northern highlands of Eastern Tibet, the other along its southern gorges. The third line—about the changing tunes of political propaganda. The last ten lines—about the Fourth Dodrupchen's taking residence in Sikkim, India.

    Generally "sky-dressed" means either dressed in blue clothing or naked. Here the term may refer to Drukpa (Bhutanese). *Druk* means "dragon," which in Oriental tradition is a mystical creature who lives among clouds in the sky and so is "sky-dressed," and Rinpoche has hundreds of Bhutanese disciples at his monastery in Sikkim.
308. ZL 2a/3 and other sources.
309. More than a thousand years before, Guru Rinpoche prophesied the dangers that Tibetans have faced in recent decades and advised them to go to certain places, "the hidden lands," to escape. Sikkim (Dremo Jong, the Valley of Rice) is one of the major places that he named in those prophecies.
310. Kyabje Düdjom Rinpoche (1903–1987) came from Kongpo to Sikkim and gave many teachings. Kyabje Trülzhik Pawo Dorje of Minyak came from Kongpo and spent many years, and died in Sikkim in 1960. So it could refer to either of them.
311. Dodrupchens are the incarnations of prince Murum Tsepo and Sangye Lingpa.
312. From a manuscript hand-copied by Tak-rong Gyurme Trakpa (?–1975).
313. NYG 181a/3.
314. Names of the teachers and their disciples in the lineage tree are in sequence according to their age. However, for many I can only guess their age.
315. Asterisks after names indicate that the teacher is a recipient and even could be a transmitter of the *Longchen Nyingthig* teachings, but *Longchen Nyingthig* may not be the *main* practice or teaching of that master.
316. KNR 725/7, KZ 33a/1, 39a/2.
317. LYN 80b/5, 91a/3, KNR 726/18.
318. He wrote a commentary on *Yumka Dechen Gyalmo* in 1801.
319. LYN 173b/5, 204a/6.
320. LYN 126b/1, DGN 68a/6, SB 223a/3.
321. KNR 724/19, KZ 38b/1.
322. SB 10b/3, 411a/6.
323. KZ 81b/6.
324. DGN 65b/4, DL 70/6, KNR 801/21.
325. He was the root teacher of Zhabkar Tsoktruk Rangtröl (1781–1851).
326. PKD 219b/1, KNR 919/18.
327. KZ 34b/3.
328. PKD 214b/2, KZ 34b/3, KNR 921/7.
329. CG 169b/4. He was the root teacher of Kham-nyön Dharma Senge (Ra-gang Chöpa, ?–1890).
330. DZT 17b/3, DB 37b/5.

331. According to DB 6b/4.
332. He was one of the root teachers of Kyabje Düdjom Jigdral Yeshe Dorje (1904–1987) and of Kanjur Rinpoche Longchen Yeshe Dorje (1888–1975).
333. He was one of the root teachers of Kyabje Düdjom Jigdral Yeshe Dorje (1904–1987).
334. He was the root teacher of Lama Gönpo Tseten (?–1991) of Labrang, Amdo.
335. He was the root teacher of Professor Namkhai Norbu (b. 1938) of Dege/Italy.
336. He was a disciple of Alak Pema Rangtrol and the root teacher of Shuksep Jetsun (1865–1953).
337. One of the Kanjur transmissions of Kyabje Düdjom Rinpoche came from Trakkar through Tülku Ngetön Gyatso (?–1959) of Tungkar, Ser Valley.
338. He was the root teacher of Tertrül Chi-me Rigdzin (b. 1922) of Khordong.
339. He was a principal teacher of Tarthang Choktrül Thupten Chökyi Dawa (1894–1959) and a teacher of Khenpo Ngawang Palzang.
340. His main teachers were the second Kathok Situ (1880–1925) and the second Pema Norbu (1887–1932).
341. His root teacher was the third Zhechen Gyaltsap Gyurme Pema Namgyal (1871–1926).
342. He was the root teacher of Nyoshül Lama Jamyang Dorje (b. 1926)
343. His root teacher was Choktrül Thupten Chökyi Dawa (1894–1959) of Tarthang.
344. His root teacher was Kongtrül Pema Trime Lodrö (1901–1959?) of Zhechen.

Index

PLACES, PERSONS, TEXTS, AND TERMS

Abhidharma, 7, 205, 232, 239, 271, 279, 293, 320, 322, 375
Abhisamayālaṃkāra, 205, 210, 233, 234, 244, 271, 279, 375
Akṣhobhya, 24
Amitābha, 24, 75, 77, 139, 159, 205, 210, 217, 220, 254
Anuttaratantra, 15, 41, 216
Anuyoga, 14, 16, 22, 28, 29, 100, 102, 110, 125, 318, 361
Ashoka, 81, 366
Atiyoga, 14, 16, 20, 21, 22, 29, 100, 102, 110, 125, 318
Avalokiteshvara, 19, 62, 119, 123, 170, 200, 304, 305, 363

Bairö Nyingthig, 17
Bhutan, 12, 86, 89, 95, 96, 103, 113, 132–134, 221, 251, 282, 292, 294, 295, 297, 328, 329, 334, 349, 354, 362, 375, 376
Bön, 82, 83, 101, 107, 371
Buddha Land, 23, 312

Central Asia, 12, 85, 100
Chakrasaṃvara, 142, 231, 233, 323
Charyāyoga, 15, 16
Chechok Thöndrup, Kyala Khenpo (1893–1957), 283, 342, 343, 346, 348, 349
Chetsün Nyingthig, 17, 33, 217, 261
Chetsün Senge Wangchuk, 35, 72, 217
China, 12, 34, 62, 63, 65, 68, 85, 96, 98, 104, 108, 149, 151, 160, 174, 198, 351, 352–354, 356, 357, 367
Chö Dzinpa Rangtröl, 195
Chönyi Zangmo, Shuksep Lochen (1865–1953), 251, 253, 341, 343
cutting through (Khregs Ch'od), 16, 33, 82

Ḍākinī, 25, 44, 47, 55–57, 60, 63, 66, 67, 69, 70, 78, 79, 81, 87, 92, 94–96, 99, 101, 123, 148, 156, 158, 159, 170, 171, 180, 182, 185, 191, 193, 195, 213, 216, 272, 326, 327, 336, 338, 365, 366
Dalai Lama, 97, 150, 176, 249, 294, 347, 356, 374
Dechen Gyalmo, 45, 153, 171, 195, 205, 235, 269, 272, 320, 321, 362, 376
Dege, 129, 130, 134, 137, 138, 142, 144, 149, 150, 154–157, 168, 169, 174, 175, 177, 182, 184, 186, 188, 189, 191, 192, 215, 216, 218, 257, 275, 292, 296, 322, 335, 336, 347, 351–355, 357, 376
development stage, 10, 11, 23, 24, 28, 41, 42, 121, 233, 269
Dharmapāla, 70, 177, 181, 186, 212, 303, 305, 321, 322
Dilgo Khyentse Tashi Paljor of Zhechen (1910–1991), 218, 221, 292, 325, 341, 344, 346, 347, 351, 353, 356, 357, 363, 364, 365

direct approach (Thod rGal), 17, 33, 82, 112
Dodrupchen Rinpoche: First, *see* Jigme Thrinle Özer; Second, *see* Jigme Phüntsok Jungne; Third, *see* Jigme Tenpe Nyima; Fourth, *see* Rigdzin Tenpe Gyaltsen *and* Thupten Thrinle Palzangpo
Do Khyentse Yeshe Dorje (1800–1866), 161, 179, 238, 245, 336, 337, 338
Domsum (Three Vows), 205, 226, 273, 279
Dorje Trolö, 86, 96
Dorsem Nyingthig, 17, 33, 175
Dug-ngal Rangtröl, 45, 123
Dzödün (*Seven Treasures*), 143, 154, 182, 272, 273, 284, 323, 327–329, 369
Dzökyi Demik, 243, 248, 261
Dzongsar Khyentse Chökyi Lodrö (1893–1959), 32, 278, 346

Ekajatī, 63, 216, 231, 362

father tantra, 15
Four Methods, 33, 67, 69
four stages of absorption, 5

Garab Dorje, 30, 31, 34, 36, 54, 55, 288, 333, 365–367
Garuda, 81, 145
Geluk, 14, 85, 150–152, 158, 204, 221, 229, 231, 233, 244, 248, 249, 273, 280, 293, 298, 305, 336, 341, 375
Gölo Zhönu Pal, 32, 352
Golok, 136, 153–155, 161, 173, 179, 180, 183, 191, 195, 203–205, 223, 230, 233, 234, 237, 243, 247, 248, 273, 279, 280, 283, 298, 301, 304, 306, 313, 314, 323–325, 329, 330, 336, 342–345, 347, 349, 352, 357, 363, 364, 374, 375
great perfection (rDzogs-Ch'en), 23, 116, 120, 125, 353
Guhyagarbha, 71, 79, 107, 160, 187, 198, 203, 205, 210, 226, 233, 235, 240–243, 245, 248, 249, 262, 271, 276, 284, 293, 294, 320, 322, 323, 374
Guru Rinpoche, 13, 16, 17, 22, 24–26, 30, 33, 34, 36, 43, 44, 46, 74–103 (passim), 105–109, 111, 112, 113, 118, 120, 122, 123, 133, 136, 145, 146, 153, 161, 165, 175, 180, 181, 183–187, 190, 206, 207, 216, 218, 239, 243, 250, 254, 264, 274, 291, 297, 300, 302, 315, 317, 323, 325, 326, 333, 334, 363, 365, 366, 368, 378. *See also* Padmasambhava

Hayagrīva, 24, 25, 101, 119, 159, 313
Hūṃkara, 24–26, 29, 79, 95, 101, 122

India, 4, 5, 7, 9, 11–13, 15, 22, 25, 34, 59, 61, 62, 65, 68–71, 74, 80–85, 94–98, 100, 101, 103, 104, 106, 108, 119, 221, 236, 244, 251, 255, 257, 267, 282, 292, 297, 324–327, 331, 351–357, 368, 369
Indrabhuti, 24–26, 29, 70, 368
inner tantra, 14, 16, 18, 22, 23, 62, 235

Ja, King, 1, 22–26, 28, 29
Jamyang Khyentse Chökyi Lodrö, 28
Jamyang Khyentse Wangpo (1890–1892), 27, 32, 36, 37, 133, 215, 216, 337, 338, 339, 340, 346, 347, 363
Jigme Gyalwe Nyuku (Pema Kunzang, 1765–1843), 130, 134, 143, 146, 155, 156, 161, 163, 174, 198, 200, 202, 212, 217, 218, 335–338, 353
Jigme Lingpa, Rigdzin (1730–1798), 17, 27, 36, 37, 41, 43, 44, 46, 47, 89, 97, 118–121, 123, 124, 126–131, 133, 134, 142–149, 152, 154–156, 161, 162, 165–168, 171–173, 175, 179–184, 186–188, 201, 215, 216, 222, 229, 241, 262, 269, 288, 293, 301, 302, 319, 321, 323, 326, 328, 329, 333–335, 338, 339, 351, 352, 354–357, 362, 365, 371
Jigme Phüntsok Jungne, Second Dodrupchen (1824–1863), 162, 195, 211, 214

Jigme Tenpe Nyima, Third Dodrupchen (1865–1926), 35–37, 214, 237, 279, 338–340, 343, 352, 353, 356, 357, 362, 363
Jigme Thrinle Özer, First Dodrupchen (1745–1821), 27, 36, 37, 98, 130, 133, 134, 136, 143, 147, 158, 161, 162, 173, 334, 335, 355, 357, 362, 364
Jñānasūtra, 30, 34, 46, 47, 63–69, 74, 333
Jonang, 151, 204

Kagyü, 14, 110, 119, 131, 215, 220, 228, 229, 281, 293, 323, 337, 364
Kālasiddhi, 93, 95
kama, 24, 25, 28, 65, 78, 85, 107, 143, 147, 187, 199, 225, 294, 297, 322, 323, 329
Karma Nyingthig, 17, 33
Karmapa, 17, 101, 110, 134, 139, 220, 253, 254, 354
Kathok Situ Chökyi Gyatso (1880–1925), 28, 32, 233, 244, 254, 258, 273, 276, 278, 285
Kham, 83, 86, 106–108, 130, 134, 136, 142–144, 149, 151, 154, 161, 164, 165, 168–170, 173, 183, 186, 188, 194, 217, 218, 220, 229, 247, 256, 258, 274, 277, 279, 296, 337, 340, 341, 347, 351, 352, 376
Khandro Nyingthig, 17, 33–36, 44, 46, 57, 63, 79, 82, 88, 89, 93, 98, 99, 109, 111, 112, 117, 139, 271, 323, 352, 354, 365, 370, 371
Khandro Yangtig, 34, 35, 150, 189, 195, 272, 273, 280, 357, 370
Könchok Drönme, Lushül Khenpo (1859–1936), 230, 232, 245, 247, 299, 318, 323, 339, 340, 343, 351
Kumārādza, Rigdzin (1243–1343), 35, 110, 111, 113, 272, 333
Künzang Lame Zhalung, 22, 172, 202, 229, 252

La-me Gonggyen, 235
Ladrup Thigle Gyachen, 45, 245, 273, 279
Lama Yangtin, 34, 113, 117, 126, 229, 273, 279, 370
Lhacham Pemasal, 36, 46, 272
Longchen Nyingthig, 17, 33, 34, 41–46, 89, 118, 122, 123, 128, 131, 133, 134, 136, 142–145, 148, 150, 151, 154, 162, 163, 172–174, 182, 184, 187, 191, 194, 195, 200, 202, 204–206, 210, 212, 217, 218, 220, 222, 229, 240, 245, 246, 252–254, 258, 259, 261, 266, 268, 269, 271–274, 278–281, 284, 292–294, 296, 297, 299, 309, 314, 319, 320, 322, 323, 327–329, 331, 333–335, 337, 351–354, 356, 357, 362, 364, 365, 372, 376
Longchen Rabjam, Künkhyen (1308–1363), 17, 34–36, 41, 43, 46, 47, 89, 99, 109–117, 119–121, 124, 126, 128, 134, 155, 156, 189, 209, 222, 223, 229, 233, 241, 245, 254, 266, 268, 271, 272, 274, 293, 299, 302, 320, 323, 327–329, 333, 334, 351–353, 355–357, 363, 369, 370
Longde, 16, 30, 31, 60, 71, 103, 105, 111, 322, 361, 369
Lungtok Tenpe Nyima of Nyoshül (1829–1902), 222, 338, 339, 340

Madhyamakāvatāra, 205, 207, 272, 279, 284, 375
mahāmudra, 81, 95, 121, 196
Mahāyoga, 14, 16, 22–26, 29, 41, 71, 97, 100, 102, 110, 248, 318, 360
maṇḍala, 10, 19, 23, 28, 41, 49, 79, 81, 85, 89, 93, 97, 99, 101, 102, 103, 161, 184, 185, 239, 268, 301, 307, 312, 313, 316, 320
Mandāravā, 80, 94, 95
Mañjushrīmitra, 11, 24, 25, 30, 31, 34, 46, 47, 57–63, 74, 79, 103, 122, 216, 333, 365, 366
Me-ngagde, 16, 30, 32–34, 41, 60, 63, 71, 79, 89, 111, 322, 361, 369, 370
Mingyur Namkhe Dorje, Fourth Dzogchen Rinpoche (1793–?), 35, 36, 37, 161, 175, 238, 336–338
Minling Lochen Dharmashrī (1654–1717), 27, 32, 105, 355

Minling Terchen Gyurme Dorje (1646–1714), 27, 32, 35, 37
Mön, 12, 131, 150, 151, 158, 168, 174, 336, 364
Mongolia, 12, 131, 150, 151, 158, 168, 174, 336, 364
mother tantra, 15
Mu-ne Tsepo, 34, 89, 98, 368

Ngawang Palzang, Kathok Khenpo (1879–1941), 224, 225, 259, 266, 280, 296, 341, 344, 345, 362–364, 375, 380
Nepal, 4, 12, 29, 80, 81, 83, 85, 93, 94, 100, 105, 106, 123, 130, 145, 146, 221, 282, 292, 294, 297, 326, 329, 349, 367, 368, 373
Ngotsar Gyume Rölgar, 266
nondual tantra, 15
Nupchen Sangye Yeshe, 15, 26, 29, 31, 99, 281
Nyingma, 14–18, 22–24, 44, 48, 74, 79, 85, 100, 110, 126, 128, 129, 133, 134, 145, 150, 151, 154, 155, 174, 177, 187, 188, 198–201, 210, 215, 218, 220, 229, 231, 233, 240–242, 244, 247–249, 256, 272, 273, 281, 292–294, 309, 327, 328, 329, 339, 346, 355, 365, 374
Nyingthig: Early, 17, 34; Later, 17
Nyingthig Yabzhi, 35, 142, 176, 182, 183, 202, 229, 259, 261, 273, 274, 278, 293, 299, 309, 319, 328, 329

Oḍḍiyāṇa, 10, 55, 70, 74, 77, 80, 81, 90, 112, 264, 367, 368
Ösal Dorje Sangdzo, 229
outer tantra, 16, 23

Padmasambhava, 13, 33, 36, 47, 61, 74, 77, 78, 83, 90, 91, 96, 97, 123, 206, 298, 333. *See also* Guru Rinpoche
Palchen Düpa, 45, 280, 291, 294, 320, 363
Paltrül Rinpoche (Ogyen Jigme Chökyi Wangpo, 1808–1887), 22, 133, 154, 155, 160, 161, 172, 174, 195, 198–202, 204, 212, 213, 222–227, 229, 230, 231, 237, 238, 239, 253, 256, 258, 268, 269, 270, 284, 319, 329, 339, 353, 356, 362–365
Pema Lingpa, 99
Pema Ngödrup Rolwe Dorje, First Alak Zenkar (1881–1943), 197, 275, 341, 344, 346
Phagme Nyingthig, 218
pure land (buddha fields), 19, 23, 25, 48, 49, 51, 52, 53, 57, 69, 84, 89–93, 96, 102, 105, 112, 118, 139, 156, 157, 158, 179, 180, 185, 190, 193, 198, 205, 206, 207, 210, 212, 231, 239, 244, 251, 254, 261, 272, 274, 286, 310, 313, 315
pure vision, 22, 24, 30, 33, 41, 43, 46, 59, 62, 70, 79, 86, 88, 93, 99, 101, 103, 110, 111, 112, 120, 124, 126, 127, 147, 159, 172, 179, 216, 217, 218, 219, 231, 240, 334

rainbow body, 17, 69, 72, 82, 92, 104, 108, 206, 229, 239, 315, 338
Ratna Lingpa, 108, 142, 273, 274
relics, 82, 97, 117
Rigdzin Düpa, 41, 45, 165, 212, 244, 245, 269, 279, 291, 320, 328, 362
Rigdzin Tenpe Gyaltsen (Rigdzin Jalu Dorje), Fourth Dodrupchen (1927–1961), 290, 298, 317, 331, 342, 344, 345, 348, 350

Sakya, 14, 110, 119, 129–131, 139, 154, 182, 188, 209, 211, 215, 218, 220, 241, 244, 271, 279, 281, 293, 335, 347
Samantabhadra, 25, 28, 30, 31, 34, 36, 47–49, 52, 77, 119, 123, 128, 158, 202, 210, 268, 302, 333
Samye, 34, 35, 43, 44, 71, 72, 83–85, 88, 89, 96, 97, 103–107, 110, 112, 114, 116, 120, 124, 130, 138, 139, 143, 145–148, 163–165, 182–186, 218, 321
Sattvavajra, 20, 21

Semde, 16, 30, 31, 57, 60, 71, 100, 102–105, 111, 322, 361, 369, 370
Senge Dongchen, 45
Seven Treasures, 121, 124, 320, 369. *See also* Dzödün
Shākyadevī, 81, 94, 95
Shāntarakṣhita, 13, 78, 83–85, 96, 97, 101, 103, 107, 222, 271, 284
Shrīsiṃha, 16, 30, 31, 34, 36, 46, 47, 57, 60–63, 65, 66, 68, 74, 79, 82, 100, 103, 177, 199, 205, 256, 271, 333, 365, 366
Sikkim, 95, 255, 282, 326, 327, 329, 348, 349, 351–355, 357, 376
Songtsen Gampo, King (617–698), 13, 119, 305
Sūtra, 7, 11, 12, 14, 15, 65, 85, 102, 103, 104, 106, 110, 120, 154, 199, 200, 203, 209, 210, 234, 235, 244, 248, 258, 262, 263, 271, 319, 322, 323, 359, 361, 369, 375

Takhyung Barwa, 45, 280, 363
Tamchö Dechen Lamchok, 159
Tantra, 10–19, 21–25, 28, 29, 30, 33, 41, 43, 44, 52, 55, 56, 60, 63, 71, 72, 79, 81, 82, 85, 86, 88, 89, 98, 99, 100, 102, 103, 104, 106, 107, 110, 111, 112, 117, 120, 126, 129, 134, 160, 174, 187, 198, 199, 200, 203, 204, 209, 210, 218, 219, 226, 231–235, 239, 241–244, 248, 249, 258, 262, 263, 268, 271, 276, 279, 280, 281, 284, 285, 292, 293, 306, 318, 319, 320, 322, 323, 360, 361, 366, 369, 375, 383, 384
Taphak Yizhin Norbu, 253
terma, 24, 25, 28, 88, 143, 147, 187
three states of awareness, 5, 6
Three Words That Penetrate the Essence, 57, 60, 210, 291
Thupten Thrinle Palzangpo, Fourth Dodrupchen (b. 1927), 28, 32, 35, 37, 316, 355
Trisong Detsen, King (790–858), 13, 36, 44, 46, 70, 76, 83, 85, 88–90, 93, 96, 98, 103, 105, 109, 118, 123, 124, 134, 144, 145, 215, 333, 366, 368
Trölthik Gongpa Rangtröl, 121
Tsasum Ösal Nyingthig, 17
Tsokye Nyingthig, 218

Vairochana, 17, 24, 30, 31, 33, 44, 46, 57, 63, 71, 85, 89, 97, 102–106, 131, 185, 361
Vajradhara, 19, 188, 270
Vajrakīla, 24, 25, 43, 81, 93, 96, 98, 102, 105, 106, 133, 142, 154, 159, 173, 216, 266, 267, 272, 274, 280, 291, 312, 320, 363
Vajrapāṇi, 19, 22, 23, 24, 28, 53, 54, 156, 305, 360, 366
Vajrasattva, 20, 21, 23–25, 29–31, 34, 36, 47, 51, 53–55, 65, 68, 111, 185, 220, 333, 366
Vima Nyingthig, 17, 33–35, 44, 71, 73, 88, 110, 111, 113, 117, 126, 156, 323, 351, 355, 357, 370, 371
Vinaya, 7, 14, 15, 110, 199, 239, 259, 280, 320, 322, 352, 375

Yangsang Khadrö Thukthik, 195
Yarlung, 92, 102, 134, 139, 142, 155–157, 160, 170, 176, 183, 184, 186, 188, 191, 195, 198, 203, 211–213, 217, 238, 288, 321, 349, 372
Yeshe Lama, 45, 133, 154, 184, 189, 194, 229, 261, 270, 271, 273, 274, 279, 284, 294, 309, 320
Yeshe Tsogyal, 36, 44, 86, 88–93, 95, 96, 99, 102, 106, 122, 216, 274, 366
Yogatantra, 15, 16, 79
Yönten Dzö, 133, 142, 143, 150, 159, 165, 184, 204, 205, 223, 226, 231, 235, 254, 271, 279, 281, 284, 293, 294, 319, 322

Zabmo Yangtig, 34, 371
Zhangtön Tashi Dorje, 35, 73, 355

Credits

THE line drawings on pages 48–68 and 215 from *Nyingme Chöjung* by Kyabje Dudjom Rinpoche are reproduced by permission of H. E. Zhenphen Rinpoche. Most of the other line drawings are provided by the lamas of Chorten Gompa, Sikkim, India.

The photograph credits are as follows:

Page 74: Jonathan and Joan Miller
Page 251: Collection of Tsewang Namdrol
Pages 256 and 267: Collection of Rigpa
Page 279: Chögyal of Sikkim
Pages 292 and 314: Ven. Matthieu Ricard